BRITAIN

FOR LEARNERS OF ENGLISH

OXFORD
UNIVERSITY PRESS

Great Clarendon Street, Oxford OX2 6DP

Oxford University Press is a department of the University of Oxford.
It furthers the University's objective of excellence in research, scholarship,
and education by publishing worldwide in

Oxford New York

Auckland Cape Town Dar es Salaam Hong Kong Karachi
Kuala Lumpur Madrid Melbourne Mexico City Nairobi
New Delhi Shanghai Taipei Toronto

With offices in

Argentina Austria Brazil Chile Czech Republic France Greece
Guatemala Hungary Italy Japan Poland Portugal Singapore
South Korea Switzerland Thailand Turkey Ukraine Vietnam

OXFORD and OXFORD ENGLISH are registered trade marks of
Oxford University Press in the UK and in certain other countries

ACKNOWLEDGEMENTS

*The authors and publisher are grateful to those who have given permission to reproduce
the following extracts and adaptations of copyright material:* pp31 & 116 Extract
from *Notes from a Small Island* by Bill Bryson published by Black Swan in 1996.
Reproduced by permission of Random House Group Ltd. p44 Extract from
'Mad about Plaid' by A. A. Gill, *The Sunday Times*, 23 January 1994 © Times
Newspapers Ltd 1994. Reproduced by permission of N I Syndication Ltd.
p44 Extract from 'Who gives a Caber Toss' by Harry Ritchie, *The Sunday Times*,
23 January 1994 © Times Newspapers Ltd 1994. Reproduced by permission
of NI Syndication Ltd. p55 Extract from 'Events: Cross-Border weekend event
2007' from http://www.schoolsacrossborders.org. Schools Across Borders is a
registered charity in Ireland. Reproduced by permission. p132 Extract from
'A sad lesson' by Paul Sims from *The Daily Mail*, 26 October 2007 © Daily Mail.
Reproduced by permission. p191 Extract from 'A saboteur in the shrubs takes
rival's hanging baskets' by Paul Sims from http://www.dailymail.co.uk/new/
article 28 July 2007 © Daily Mail 2007. Reproduced by permission. pp69, 87
& 154 Extracts from *Yes, Prime Minister* by Anthony Jay and Jonathan Lynn
© Anthony Jay & Jonathan Lynn published by BBC Books. Reproduced by
permission of Random House Group Ltd and the Copyright agent: Alan Brodie
Representation Ltd, 6th floor, Fairgate House, 78 New Oxford Street, London
WE1A 1HB, info@alanbrodie.com.

Sources: p45 www.timesonline.co.uk/tol/comment/columnists/minette_
marrin/article2702726; p141 *How to be inimitable* by George Mikes, Penguin
Books 1966, first published by André Deutsch © George Mikes 1960. p60
Writing home by Alan Bennett, Faber and Faber 1994. p62 Extract from an
article by John Peel, *The Radio Times* 2–8 December 2000. p115 Extract from
http://www.dailymail.co.uk/news/article-481129/Victory-Britains-metric-
martyrs-Eur. p00 Extract from http://ec.europa.eu/unitedkingdom/press/
euromyths/myths21_en.htm; p173 Extract from *The English* by Jeremy
Paxman, Penguin 1999. p183 Extract from *How to be an alien* by George Mikes.
p134 Extract from 'Liberal Summerhill tries discipline' by Stan Griffiths and
Maurice Chittenden, *The Sunday Times*, 4 June 2006.

*The publisher would like to thank the following for their kind permission to reproduce
copyright material:* Cover image courtesy Stockbyte/Getty Images. Alamy pp20
(Neil Holmes/Holmes Garden Photos), 22 (*Charles the King walked for the last time
through the streets of London* 1649/The Print Collector), 25 (Julie Woodhouse/
Chatsworth), 39 (Tim Gainey), 45 (Lordprice Collection), 85 (Anne-Marie Palmer),
105 (Jim Wileman), 111 (Jack Sullivan), 119 (The Photolibrary Wales), 124 (Jeff
Morgan), 129 (John Bond/Chapel), 129 (Robert Estall/Mosque), 130 (Gregory
Wrona), 139 (Brinkstock/Manchester University), 129 (Geophotos/Colchester
University), 129 (JMS/Keele University), 147 (Lifestyle), 149 (*Tesco Generation
Banksy, Essex Road, London/Simon Woodcock*), 156 (Allan Gallery), 162 (Alan
Francis), 164 (PhotoMax), 177 (David Lyons), 178 (David Askham), 181 (Mark
Hughes Photography), 183 (Adam James), 191 (Nigel Tingle), 206 (Jon Arnold
Images Ltd), 209 Chris Howes/Wild Places Photography/rock), 210
(nagelestock.com), 214 (Tim Hill), 215 (Mary Evans Picture Library); BBC ©
pp51 (Frost Report), 102 (swingometer), 107 (Dixon of Dock Green), 122 (*The
Vicar of Dibley*); Bridgeman Art Library pp21 (*Queen Elizabeth I in Coronation Robes*
English School/National Portrait Gallery), p116 (*The Ark Raleigh* English
School/Private Collection), 209 (*Skegness is So Bracing* John Hassall/National
Railway Museum York); Corbis pp8 (Peter Adams/Zefa), 99 (Owen Franken),
125 (Image 100), 129 (Michael Nicholson/Synagogue), 129 (Philippa Lewis/
Edifice/Sikh Temple), 189 (Peter Aprahamian); Mary Evans Picture Library
p10 (Britannia and John Bull); Getty Images pp12 (Southern Rock/harp), 12
(Richard Elliott/bag pipes), 13 (Dale Durfee), 17 (Charles Ernest Butler/The
Bridgeman Art Library), 19 (Hulton Archive/Handout), 26 (Portrait of Queen
Victoria 1859 after Franz Xavier Winterhalter/Bridgeman Art Library), 38
(Peter King/Hulton Archive), 52 (Photo and Co/Stone), 61 (Windsor & Wienhahn/
The Image Bank), 63 (Miki Duisterhof/Stock Food Creative), 68 (Sean Hunter/
Dorling Kindersley RF), 72 (Michael Betts), 78 (Peter Macdiarmid), 80 (Adrian
Dennis/AFP), 82 (Keystone/Stringer/Hulton Archive), 83 (Ian Waldie), 98 (Leon
Neal/AFP/entry to hosue of Lords), 128 (Jeff J Mitchell), 141 (Christopher
Furlong), 143 (Anthony Marsland), 146 (Dominic Burke), 180 (Matt Cardy),
184 (Gallo Images), 187 (STasker/Photonica), 193 (Ian Waldie), 195 (David
Rogers), 197 (Carl de Souza/ AFP), 207 (Karen Bleier/AFP), 213 (Jonathan
Knowles/St Patrick's Day), 213 (Siegfried Layda/The Image Bank/Halloween);
Impact Photos pp23 (Carolyn Clarke/Spectrum Colour Library); iStockphoto
pp110 (Anthony Baggett), 208 (StarFishDesign); National Portrait Gallery
pp21 (*Henry VIII* Hans Holbein the Younger NPG 157); National Trust Photo
Library p64 (David Noton); OUP pp14 (Eyewire), 15 (Digital Stock), 16
(Photodisc), 25 (Chris King/Nelson's Column), 30 (Eyewire), 36 (Photodisc),
37 (Photodisc), 41 (Digital Vision), 47 (Mike Chinery), 48(Stockbyte). 58 (Jan
Tadeusz), 59 (Photodisc), 87 (Corel), 107 (Alamy/Police chase), 109 (Photodisc),
133 (Chris King), 139(Digital Vision/Oxford), 163 (Corel), 173 (Alchemy
Mindworks Inc), 176 (Alchemy Mindworks Inc), 188 (Picturesbyrob), 199
(Photodisc), 212 (Photodisc), 213 (Corel/New Year's Day), 213 (Photodisc/Fire),
213 (Corbis/Digital Stock/Remembrance Day), 213 (Purestock/Christmas Day);
Press Association pp55 (Niall Carson/PA Wire/Empics), 92 (PA Wire), 93
(PA Archive), 98 (Empics/Black Rod), 120 (John Giles/Empics/Free Derry), 192
(Gareth Copley/PA Archive); Rex Features pp44 (Con Tanasiuk/Design Pics Inc),
77, 102 (Peter Snow), 120 (Action Press/UFF), 142 (J K Press); Robert Harding
Picture Library p92 (Adam Woolfitt), Transport for London p166.

Logos by kind permission: The AA www.theaa.com, ASDA, Barclays plc, The
Conservative Party, The Daily Express (Northern & Shell Network), The Daily
Mail, Daily Mirror (c/o Mirrorpix), The Daily Star (Northern & Shell Network)
The Daily Telegraph, The Guardian c/o The Guardian News and Media Ltd 2008,
HSBC, The Independent, The Labour Party, The Liberal Democrats, Lloyds plc,
Marks & Spencer (http://corporate.marksandspencer.com/), Morrisons, NHS
Department of Health www.dh.gov.uk, The National Trust, The RAC, RBS The
Royal Bank of Scotland, J Sainsbury plc, The Sun (c/o www.nisyndication.com),
The Times (c/o www.nisyndication.com), Waitrose Ltd www.waitrose.com.

Illustrations by: Tabitha Macbeth p11; Peter Bull pp9, 28, 33, 34, 89, 91, 113,
207; Mark McLaughlin pp174 and 175.

James O'Driscoll

BRITAIN
FOR LEARNERS OF ENGLISH

Understand the country and its people

second edition

OXFORD

4

Contents

Introduction

Who this book is for

This book is for learners of English who need to know more about Britain. It is for all people who recognize that a knowledge of British life is necessary to improve their understanding of the English language. It will be especially useful for students on British Studies courses and those who are studying British culture as part of their general English course.

How many times have you not fully understood a phrase in a British text and found that the dictionary does not help? How many times have you understood every word that a British person has said but not understood what he or she meant? In any society, writers and speakers often leave some things unsaid or unexplained because they assume that their readers or listeners have the same background knowledge that they have. You may have reached a high level of proficiency in English, but find British people hard to understand because you lack this background knowledge. This book aims to fill the gap so that, when you encounter British writers and speakers, you will be in the same position as an averagely educated British person.

Of course, it is impossible for you to put yourself in exactly the same position as natives of Britain. They have been sharing distinctly British experiences and influences ever since they were born. Therefore, this book also looks behind the details which every British person knows, so that you can get an insight into the British approach to life in general. In this respect, you have an advantage over many British people. You have knowledge and experience of another culture which you can compare with British culture and make your understanding of it sharper.

What this book is about

This book contains all the basic information you need about British institutions and everyday life. But it has more than that. Throughout this book, particular attention is paid to the attitudes of British people. Knowledge of these is very important because they are what 'colour' the language used by British people. For example, to understand the word 'Catholic' as used in Britain, it is not enough to know its dictionary meaning; you also have to know something about the general place of religion in British people's minds, the different religious groups in the country, their reputations, and senses of identity (see chapter 13). Because these matters are so important, there are two chapters devoted entirely to them: one about how British people feel about themselves (chapter 4) and one about their attitudes to certain aspects of life in general (chapter 5).

After a short introductory chapter, there are five long chapters (2–6) which set the historical, geographical, attitudinal, and political scene. Then there are five short chapters (7–11) on the various political and legal institutions, followed by a chapter (12) on the British relationship with the rest of the world. The remaining chapters (13–23) describe all the other areas of British life, moving gradually from more 'collective' aspects, such as education and the economy, to more individual ones such as housing and food. But in all of these, attention is paid both to public structures and individual experience and habits.

All the pieces of information in this book are included for one or both of two possible reasons. Some of them, for example the mention of the Union Jack (see page 14), are there because they form part of a British person's general knowledge. But others, for example the description of the pairing system in Parliament (see page 74), are not so well-known. They are there to serve as an illustration of a more general point.

This book is not an encyclopaedia. Britain shares many characteristics with other countries. This book concentrates on what makes Britain different, with the emphasis on common knowledge rather than specialist knowledge; that is, on the things that most British people 'know'. These are the things that you need to know if you want to understand them.

Using this book

In each chapter, there is a main text plus extra material in the margins and elsewhere, which is presented in various forms (tables, pictures, texts, etc.). You will sometimes find an invitation to refer to this extra material in the main text, indicated by the following style of text: Why is Britain 'great'?

As you read, remember that there are different kinds of information. For example, when you read (on page 11) that St. Andrew is the patron saint of Scotland, you are getting a definite fact. However, some of the most important aspects of a place cannot be described in terms of fact. For example, this book often refers to the importance of privacy in Britain. This is not a fact; it is only an interpretation of the facts. Of course, such comments have not been made lightly – and in most cases, other commentators on Britain have made the same ones. But it is always possible that another commentator, looking at the same set of facts, might arrive at a different conclusion.

At the end of each chapter there is a Questions section, intended to stimulate further thought and discussion, and usually a few Suggestions for further reading and other activities. But if you would like to spend more time studying and considering the aspects of British life described in each chapter, you will find the Workbook which accompanies this book very helpful. As well as exercises to help you consolidate your learning of British life and vocabulary, the workbook has extra texts for you to work with, so that you can widen your knowledge at the same time.

A note on terminology

In this book, you will encounter the words 'state', 'country' and 'nation'. These are similar in meaning but are not used interchangeably. The word 'state' has a political meaning. It is used when referring to a unit of governmental authority. The word 'nation' is used when referring to English, Scottish, Welsh or Irish people and when the focus is on the sense of identity which these people feel. The word 'country' is used more generally, to refer to either Britain or one of its nations without specific allusion to either government or people.

01 Country and people

This is a book about Britain. But what exactly is Britain? And who are the British? The table below illustrates the problem. You might think that, in international sport, the situation would be simple – one country, one team. But you can see that this is definitely not the case with Britain. For each of the four sports or sporting events listed in the table, there are a different number of national teams which might be described as 'British'. This chapter describes how this situation has come about and explains the many names that are used when people talk about Britain.

Geographically speaking

Lying off the north-west coast of Europe, there are two large islands and hundreds of much smaller ones. The largest island is called Great Britain. The other large one is called Ireland (Great Britain and Ireland). There is no agreement about what to call all of them together (Looking for a name).

Politically speaking

In this geographical area there are two states. One of these governs most of the island of Ireland. This state is usually called The Republic of Ireland. It is also called 'Eire' (its Irish language name). Informally, it is referred to as just 'Ireland' or 'the Republic'.

The other state has authority over the rest of the area (the whole of Great Britain, the north-eastern area of Ireland and most of the smaller islands). This is the country that is the main subject of this book. Its official name is The United Kingdom of Great Britain and Northern Ireland, but this is too long for practical purposes, so it is usually known by a shorter name. At the Eurovision Song Contest, at the United Nations and in the European parliament, for instance, it is referred to as 'the United Kingdom'. In everyday speech, this is often

Why is Britain 'Great'?

The origin of the adjective 'great' in the name Great Britain was not a piece of advertising (although modern politicians sometimes try to use it that way!). It was first used to distinguish it from the smaller area in France which is called 'Brittany' in modern English.

National teams in selected sports

	England	Wales	Scotland	Northern Ireland	Republic of Ireland
Olympics	Great Britain				Ireland
Cricket	England and Wales		Scotland	Ireland	
Rugby union	England	Wales	Scotland	Ireland	
Football	England	Wales	Scotland	Northern Ireland	Republic of Ireland

shortened to 'the UK' and in internet and email addresses it is '.uk'. In other contexts, it is referred to as 'Great Britain'. This, for example, is the name you hear when a medal winner steps onto the rostrum at the Olympic Games. The abbreviation 'GBP' (Great Britain Pounds) in international bank drafts is another example of the use of this name. In writing and speaking that is not especially formal or informal, the name 'Britain' is used. The normal everyday adjective, when talking about something to do with the UK, is 'British' (Why is Britain 'Great'?).

Great Britain and Ireland

SCOTLAND

Edinburgh

NORTHERN
IRELAND • Belfast

Isle of
Man

REPUBLIC
OF IRELAND Dublin
(EIRE)

UNITED KINGDOM
OF GREAT BRITAIN AND
NORTHERN IRELAND

WALES   ENGLAND

Cardiff

London

Channel
Islands

0   100   200km
0   100 miles

Looking for a name

It's not easy to keep geography and politics apart. Geographically speaking, it is clear that Great Britain, Ireland and all those smaller islands belong together. So you would think there would be a (single) name for them. During the nineteenth and twentieth centuries, they were generally called 'The British Isles'. But most people in Ireland and some people in Britain regard this name as outdated because it calls to mind the time when Ireland was politically dominated by Britain.

So what can we call these islands? Among the names which have been used are 'The north-east Atlantic archipelago', 'The north-west European archipelago', 'IONA' (Islands of the North Atlantic) and simply 'The Isles'. But none of these has become widely accepted.

The most common term at present is 'Great Britain and Ireland'. But even this is not strictly correct. It is not correct geographically because it ignores all the smaller islands. And it is not correct politically because there are two small parts of the area on the maps which have special political arrangements. These are the Channel Islands and the Isle of Man, which are 'crown dependencies' and not officially part of the UK. Each has complete internal self-government, including its own parliament and its own tax system. Both are 'ruled' by a Lieutenant Governor appointed by the British government.

The four nations

People often refer to Britain by another name. They call it 'England'. But this is not correct, and its use can make some people angry. England is only one of 'the four nations' in this part of the world. The others are Scotland, Wales, and Ireland. Their political unification was a gradual process that took several hundred years (see chapter 2). It was completed in 1800 when the Irish parliament was joined with the parliament for England, Scotland, and Wales in Westminster, so that the whole area became a single state – the United Kingdom of Great Britain and Ireland. However, in 1922, most of Ireland became a separate state (see chapter 12).

At one time, culture and lifestyle varied enormously across the four nations. The dominant culture of people in Ireland, Wales and Highland Scotland was Celtic; that of people in England and Lowland Scotland was Germanic. This difference was reflected in the languages they spoke. People in the Celtic areas spoke Celtic languages; people in the Germanic areas spoke Germanic dialects (including the one which has developed into modern English). The nations also tended to have different economic, social, and legal systems, and they were independent of each other.

Some historical and poetic names

Albion is a word used by poets and songwriters to refer, in different contexts, to England or to Scotland or to Great Britain as a whole. It comes from a Celtic word and was an early Greek and Roman name for Great Britain. The Romans associated Great Britain with the Latin word 'albus', meaning white. The white chalk cliffs around Dover on the English south coast are the first land formations one sights when crossing the sea from the European mainland.

Britannia is the name that the Romans gave to their southern British province (which covered, approximately, the area of present-day England and Wales). It is also the name given to the female embodiment of Britain, always shown wearing a helmet and holding a trident (the symbol of power over the sea), hence the patriotic song which begins 'Rule Britannia, Britannia rule the waves'. The figure of Britannia has been on the reverse side of many British coins for more than 300 years.

Other signs of national identity

Briton is a word used in official contexts and in writing to describe a citizen of the United Kingdom. 'Ancient Britons' is the name given to the people who lived in southern Britain before and during the Roman occupation (AD 43–410). Their heirs are thought to be the Welsh and their language has developed into the modern Welsh language.

Caledonia, **Cambria** and **Hibernia** were the Roman names for Scotland, Wales and Ireland respectively. The words are commonly used today in scholarly classifications (for example, the type of English used in Ireland is sometimes called 'Hiberno-English' and there is a division of geological time known as 'the Cambrian period') and for the names of organizations (for example, 'Glasgow Caledonian' University).

Erin is a poetic name for Ireland. **The Emerald Isle** is another way of referring to Ireland, evoking the lush greenery of its countryside.

John Bull (see below) is a fictional character who is supposed to personify Englishness and certain English virtues. (He can be compared to Uncle Sam in the USA.) He appears in hundreds of nineteenth century cartoons. Today, somebody dressed as him often appears at football or rugby matches when England are playing. His appearance is typical of an eighteenth century country gentleman, evoking an idyllic rural past (see chapter 5).

Today, these differences have become blurred, but they have not completely disappeared. Although there is only one government for the whole of Britain, and everybody gets the same passport regardless of where in Britain they live, many aspects of government are organized separately (and sometimes differently) in the four parts of the United Kingdom. Moreover, Welsh, Scottish and Irish people feel their identity very strongly. That is why they have separate teams in many kinds of international sport.

Other tokens of national identity

The following are also associated by British people with one or more of the four nations.

Surnames
The prefix 'Mac' or 'Mc' (such as McCall, MacCarthy, MacDonald) is Scottish or Irish. The prefix 'O' (as in O'Brien, O'Connor) is Irish. A large number of surnames (for example, Evans, Jones, Morgan, Price, Williams) suggest Welsh origin. The most common surname in both England and Scotland is 'Smith'.

First names for men
The Scottish of 'John' is 'Ian' and its Irish form is 'Sean', although all three names are common throughout Britain. Outside their own countries, there are also nicknames for Irish, Scottish and Welsh men. For instance, Scottish men are sometimes known and addressed as 'Jock', Irishmen are called 'Paddy' or 'Mick' and Welshmen as 'Dai' or 'Taffy'. If the person using one of these names is not a friend, and especially if it is used in the plural (e.g. 'Micks'), it can sound insulting.

Clothes
The kilt, a skirt with a tartan pattern worn by men, is a very well-known symbol of Scottishness (though it is hardly ever worn in everyday life).

Identifying symbols of the four nations

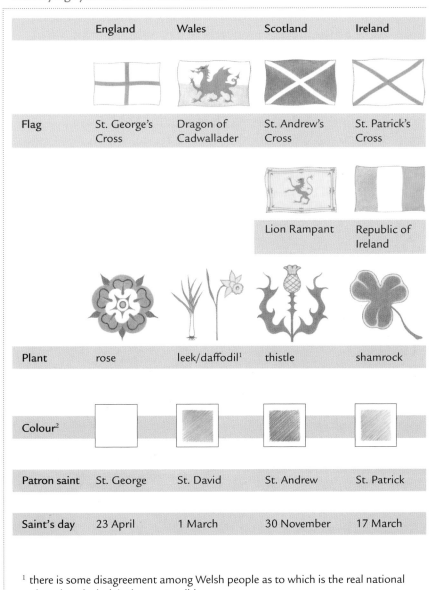

	England	Wales	Scotland	Ireland
Flag	St. George's Cross	Dragon of Cadwallader	St. Andrew's Cross	St. Patrick's Cross
			Lion Rampant	Republic of Ireland
Plant	rose	leek/daffodil[1]	thistle	shamrock
Colour[2]				
Patron saint	St. George	St. David	St. Andrew	St. Patrick
Saint's day	23 April	1 March	30 November	17 March

[1] there is some disagreement among Welsh people as to which is the real national plant, but the leek is the most well-known

[2] as typically worn by sports teams of the different nations

Characteristics

There are certain stereotypes of national character which are well known in Britain. For instance, the Irish are supposed to be great talkers, the Scots have a reputation for being careful with money and the Welsh are renowned for their singing ability. These are, of course, only caricatures and not reliable descriptions of individual people from these countries. Nevertheless, they indicate some slight differences in the value attached to certain kinds of behaviour in these countries.

Populations in 2006

Northern Ireland
1.7

Scotland
5.1

50.8

3.0
Wales

England

(figures in millions)

UK Total	60.6

These figures are estimates provided by the Office for National Statistics (England and Wales), the General Register Office for Scotland and the Northern Ireland Statistics and Research Agency. In the twenty-first century, the total population of Britain has risen by about a quarter of a million each year.

The dominance of England

There is, perhaps, an excuse for the people who use the word 'England' when they mean 'Britain'. It cannot be denied that the dominant culture of Britain today is specifically English. The system of politics that is used in all four nations today is of English origin, and English is the main language of all four nations. Many aspects of everyday life are organized according to English custom and practice. But the political unification of Britain was not achieved by mutual agreement. On the contrary, it happened because England was able to assert her economic and military power over the other three nations (see chapter 2).

Today, English domination can be detected in the way in which various aspects of British public life are described. For example, the supply of money in Britain is controlled by the Bank of England (there is no such thing as a 'Bank of Britain'). Another example is the name of the present monarch. She is universally known as 'Elizabeth II', even though Scotland and Northern Ireland have never had an 'Elizabeth I'. (Elizabeth I of England and Wales ruled from 1553 to 1603). The common use of the term 'Anglo' is a further indication. (The Angles were a Germanic tribe who settled in England in the fifth century. The word 'England' is derived from their name.) When newspapers and the television news talk about 'Anglo-American relations', they are talking about relations between the governments of Britain and the USA (and not just England and the USA).

In addition, there is a tendency in the names of publications and organizations to portray England as the norm and other parts of Britain as special cases. Thus there is a specialist newspaper called

Musical instruments

The harp is an emblem of both Wales and Ireland. Bagpipes are regarded as distinctively Scottish, although a smaller type is also used in traditional Irish music.

(Right) A harp.
(Far right) A Scottish bagpipe.

the *Times Educational Supplement*, but also a version of it called the *Times Educational Supplement (Scotland)*. Similarly, the umbrella organization for employees is called the 'Trades Union Congress', but there is also a 'Scottish Trades Union Congress'. When something pertains to England, this fact is often not specified in its name; when it pertains to Wales, Scotland or Northern Ireland, it always is. In this way, these parts of Britain are presented as something 'other'.

National loyalties

The dominance of England can also be detected in the way that many English people don't bother to distinguish between 'Britain' and 'England'. They write 'English' next to 'nationality' on forms when they are abroad and talk about places like Edinburgh as if it was part of England.

Nevertheless, when you are talking to people from Britain, it is safest to use 'Britain' when talking about where they live and 'British' as the adjective to describe their nationality. This way you will be less likely to offend anyone. It is, of course, not wrong to talk about 'people in England' if that is what you mean – people who live within the geographical boundaries of England. After all, most British people live there (Populations in 2006). But it should always be remembered that England does not make up the whole of the UK (Careful with that address!).

Careful with that address!

When you are addressing a letter to somewhere in Britain, do not write anything like 'Edinburgh, England' or 'Cardiff, England'. You should write 'Edinburgh, Scotland' and 'Cardiff, Wales' – or (if you feel 'Scotland' and 'Wales' are not recognizable enough) write 'Great Britain' or 'United Kingdom' instead.

The people of Britain

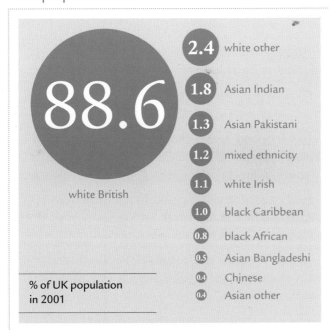

% of UK population in 2001	
88.6	white British
2.4	white other
1.8	Asian Indian
1.3	Asian Pakistani
1.2	mixed ethnicity
1.1	white Irish
1.0	black Caribbean
0.8	black African
0.5	Asian Bangladeshi
0.4	Chinese
0.4	Asian other

One of the questions in the 2001 census of the UK was 'What is your ethnic group?' and the categories above were offered as choices. Here are some of the results, listed in order of size.

As you can see, about one in nine people identified themselves as something other than 'white British'. The largest category was 'white other', but these people were from a variety of places and many were only temporarily resident in Britain. As a result, they do not form a single identifiable community. (For these and other reasons, the same is largely true of those in the white Irish and black African categories.) By far the largest recognizable ethnic grouping was formed by people whose ethnic roots are in the Indian subcontinent (Indian, Pakistani and Bangladeshi in the chart); together they made up more than two million people. The other established, recognizable ethnic group in Britain were black Caribbeans (a little over half a million people).

What this chart does not show are all the people who came to Britain from eastern Europe (especially Poland) in the years 2004–2007. Their numbers, estimated between three quarters of a million and one million, represent the largest single wave of immigration to Britain in more than 300 years. However, it is not clear at this time how many will set up home in Britain.

Another point about the people of Britain is worth noting. Since the 1980s, more people immigrate to Britain than emigrate from it every year. A quarter of all babies born in Britain are born to at least one foreign-born parent. At the same time, emigration is also very high. The people of Britain are changing.

There has been a long history of migration from Scotland, Wales and Ireland to England. As a result, there are millions of people who live in England but who would never describe themselves as English (or at least not as only English). They may have lived in England all their lives, but as far as they are concerned they are Scottish or Welsh or Irish – even if, in the last case, they are citizens of Britain and not of Eire. These people support the country of their parents or grandparents rather than England in sporting contests. They would also, given the chance, play for that country rather than England.

The same often holds true for the further millions of British citizens whose family origins lie outside Britain or Ireland. People of Caribbean or south Asian descent, for instance, do not mind being described as 'British' (many are proud of it), but many of them would not like to be called 'English' (or, again, not only English). And whenever the West Indian, Indian, Pakistani or Bangladeshi cricket team plays against England, it is usually not England that they support!

There is, in fact, a complicated division of loyalties among many people in Britain, and especially in England. A black person whose family are from the Caribbean will passionately support the West Indies when they play cricket against England. But the same person is quite happy to support England just as passionately in a sport such as football, which the West Indies do not play. A person whose family are from Ireland but who has always lived in England would want Ireland to beat England at football but would want England to beat (for example) Italy just as much.

This crossover of loyalties can work the other way as well. English people do not regard the Scottish, the Welsh or the Irish as 'foreigners' (or, at least, not as the same kind of foreigner as other foreigners!). An English commentator of a sporting event in which a Scottish, Irish or Welsh team is playing against a team from elsewhere in the world tends to identify with that team as if it were English.

QUESTIONS

1 Which of the names suggested in this chapter for the group of islands off the north-west coast of Europe do you think would be the best? Can you think of any others?

2 Is there the same kind of confusion of and disagreement about names in your country as there is in Britain and Ireland? How does this happen?

3 Think of the well-known symbols and tokens of nationality in your country. Are they the same types of real-life objects (e.g. plants and clothes) that are used in Britain?

4 In the British government, there are ministers with special responsibility for Scotland, Wales and Northern Ireland, but there is no minister for England. Why do you think this is?

Flag

The Union flag, often known as the 'Union Jack', is the national flag of the UK. It is a combination of the cross of St. George, the cross of St. Andrew and the cross of St. Patrick.

02 History

Prehistory

Two thousand years ago there was an Iron Age Celtic culture throughout the north-west European islands. It seems that the Celts had intermingled with the peoples who were there already; we know that religious sites that had been built long before their arrival continued to be used in Celtic times.

For people in Britain today, the chief significance of the prehistoric period is its sense of mystery. This sense finds its focus most easily in the astonishing monumental architecture of this period, the remains of which exist throughout the country. Wiltshire, in south-western England, has two spectacular examples: Silbury Hill, the largest burial mound in Europe, and Stonehenge (Stonehenge). Such places have a special importance for some people with inclinations towards mysticism and esoteric religion. For example, we know that Celtic society had a priestly caste called the Druids. Their name survives today in the Order of Bards, Ovates, and Druids.

Stonehenge

Stonehenge was built on Salisbury Plain some time between 5,000 and 4,300 years ago. It is one of the most famous and mysterious archaeological sites in the world. One of its mysteries is how it was ever built at all with the technology of the time (some of the stones come from over 200 miles away in Wales). Another is its purpose. It appears to function as a kind of astronomical clock and we know it was used by the Druids for ceremonies marking the passing of the seasons. It has always exerted a fascination on the British imagination, and appears in a number of novels, such as Thomas Hardy's *Tess of the D'Urbervilles*.

These days, it is not only of interest to tourists but is also held in special esteem by certain minority groups. It is now fenced off to protect it from damage.

The Roman period (43–410)

The Roman province of Britannia covered most of present-day England and Wales, where the Romans imposed their own way of life and culture, making use of the existing Celtic aristocracy to govern and encouraging them to adopt Roman dress and the Latin language. They never went to Ireland and exerted an influence, without actually governing there, over only the southern part of Scotland. It was during this time that a Celtic tribe called the Scots migrated from Ireland to Scotland, where, along with another tribe, the Picts, they became opponents of the Romans. This division of the Celts into those who experienced Roman rule (the Britons in England and Wales) and those who did not (the Gaels in Ireland and Scotland) may help to explain the emergence of two distinct branches of the Celtic group of languages.

The remarkable thing about the Romans is that, despite their long occupation of Britain, they left very little behind. To many other parts of Europe they bequeathed a system of law and administration which forms the basis of the modern system and a language which developed into the modern Romance family of languages. In Britain, they left neither. Moreover, most of their villas, baths and temples, their impressive network of roads, and the cities they founded, including Londinium (London), were soon destroyed or fell into disrepair. Almost the only lasting reminders of their presence are place names like Chester, Lancaster and Gloucester, which include variants of the Latin word *castra* (a military camp).

The Germanic invasions (410–1066)

The Roman occupation had been a matter of colonial control rather than large-scale settlement. But during the fifth century, a number of tribes from the European mainland invaded and settled in large numbers. Two of these tribes were the Angles and the Saxons. These Anglo-Saxons soon had the south-east of the country in their grasp. In the west, their advance was temporarily halted by an army of (Celtic) Britons under the command of the legendary King Arthur (King Arthur). Nevertheless, by the end of the sixth century, they and their

Hadrian's Wall

Hadrian's Wall was built by the Romans in the second century across the northern border of their province of Britannia (which is nearly the same as the present English-Scottish border) in order to protect it from attacks by the Scots and the Picts.

Some important dates in British history

55 BC[*] The Roman general Julius Caesar lands in Britain with an expeditionary force, wins a battle and leaves. The first 'date' in popular British history.

AD 43 The Romans come to stay.

61 Queen Boudicca (or Boadicea) of the Iceni tribe leads a bloody revolt against the Roman occupation. It is suppressed. There is a statue of Boadicea, made in the nineteenth century, outside the Houses of Parliament, which has helped to keep her memory alive.

410 The Romans leave Britain

432 St. Patrick converts Ireland to Christianity.

597 St. Augustine arrives in Britain and establishes his headquarters at Canterbury.

way of life predominated in nearly all of present-day England. Celtic culture and language survived only in present-day Scotland, Wales and Cornwall.

The Anglo-Saxons had little use for towns and cities. But they had a great effect on the countryside, where they introduced new farming methods and founded the thousands of self-sufficient villages which formed the basis of English society for the next thousand or so years.

When they came to Britain, the Anglo-Saxons were pagan. During the sixth and seventh centuries, Christianity spread throughout Britain from two different directions. By the time it was introduced into the south of England by the Roman missionary St. Augustine, it had already been introduced into Scotland and northern England from Ireland, which had become Christian more than 150 years earlier. Although Roman Christianity eventually took over everywhere, the Celtic model persisted in Scotland and Ireland for several hundred years. It was less centrally organized and had less need for a strong monarchy to support it. This partly explains why both secular and religious power in these two countries continued to be both more locally based and less secure throughout the medieval period.

Britain experienced another wave of Germanic invasions in the eighth century. These invaders, known as Vikings, Norsemen or Danes, came from Scandinavia. In the ninth century they conquered and settled the islands around Scotland and some coastal regions of Ireland. Their conquest of England was halted when they were defeated by King Alfred of the Saxon kingdom of Wessex (King Alfred). As a result, their settlement was confined mostly to the north and east of the country.

However, the cultural differences between Anglo-Saxons and Danes were comparatively small. They led roughly the same way of life and spoke different varieties of the same Germanic tongue. Moreover, the Danes soon converted to Christianity. These similarities made political unification easier, and by the end of the tenth century, England was a united kingdom with a Germanic culture throughout. Most of Scotland was also united by this time, at least in name, in a (Celtic) Gaelic kingdom.

King Arthur

King Arthur is a wonderful example of the distortions of popular history. In folklore and myth (and on film), he is a great English hero, and he and his Knights of the Round Table are regarded as the perfect example of medieval nobility and chivalry. In fact, he lived long before medieval times and was a Romanized Celt trying to hold back the advances of the Anglo-Saxons – the very people who became 'the English'!

793 The great monastery of Lindisfarne on the east coast of Britain is destroyed by Vikings and its monks killed.

878 The Peace of Edington partitions the Germanic terrtories between King Alfred's Saxons and the Danes.

973 Edgar, a grandson of Alfred, becomes king of nearly all of present-day England and for the first time the name 'England' is used.

* BC means 'before Christ'. All the other dates are AD (in Latin *anno domini*), which signifies 'year of Our Lord'. Some modern historians use the notation BCE ('Before Common Era') and CE ('Common Era') instead.

King Alfred

King Alfred was not only an able warrior but also a dedicated scholar (the only English monarch for a long time afterwards who was able to read and write) and a wise ruler. He is known as 'Alfred the Great' – the only monarch in English history to be given this title. He is also popularly known for the story of the burning of the cakes.

While he was wandering around his country organizing resistance to the Danish invaders, Alfred travelled in disguise. On one occasion, he stopped at a woman's house. The woman asked him to watch some cakes that were cooking to see that they did not burn, while she went off to get food. Alfred became lost in thought and the cakes burned. When the woman returned, she shouted angrily at Alfred and sent him away. Alfred never told her that he was her king.

1066

This is the most famous date in English history. On 14 October of that year, an invading army from Normandy defeated the English at the Battle of Hastings. The battle was close and extremely bloody. At the end of it, most of the best warriors in England were dead, including their leader, King Harold. On Christmas day that year, the Norman leader, Duke William of Normandy, was crowned king of England. He is known in popular history as 'William the Conqueror' and the date is remembered as the last time that England was successfully invaded.

The medieval period (1066–1458)

The successful Norman invasion of England (1066) brought Britain into the mainstream of western European culture. Previously, most links had been with Scandinavia. Only in Scotland did this link survive, the western isles (until the 13th century) and the northern islands (until the fifteenth century) remaining under the control of Scandinavian kings. Throughout this period, the English kings also owned land on the continent and were often at war with the French kings.

Unlike the Germanic invasions, the Norman invasion was small-scale. There was no such thing as a Norman area of settlement. Instead, the Norman soldiers who had invaded were given the ownership of land – and of the people living on it. A strict feudal system was imposed. Great nobles, or barons, were responsible directly to the king; lesser lords, each owning a village, were directly responsible to a baron. Under them were the peasants, tied by a strict system of mutual duties and obligations to the local lord, and forbidden to travel without his permission. The peasants were the English-speaking Saxons. The lords and the barons were the French-speaking Normans. This was the start of the English class system (Language and social class).

The system of strong government which the Normans introduced made the Anglo-Norman kingdom the most powerful political force in Britain and Ireland. Not surprisingly therefore, the authority of the English monarch gradually extended to other parts of these islands in the next 250 years. By the end of the thirteenth century, a large part of eastern Ireland was controlled by Anglo-Norman lords in the name of their king and the whole of Wales was under his direct rule (at which time, the custom of naming the monarch's eldest son the 'Prince of Wales' began). Scotland managed to remain politically independent in the medieval period, but was obliged to fight occasional wars to do so.

The cultural story of this period is different. In the 250 years after the Norman Conquest, it was a Germanic language, Middle English, and not the Norman (French) language, which had become the dominant one in all classes of society in England. Furthermore, it was the Anglo-Saxon concept of common law, and not Roman law, which formed the basis of the legal system.

1066 The Battle of Hastings.

1086 King William's officials complete the Domesday Book, a very detailed, village-by-village record of the people and their possessions throughout his kingdom.

1170 The murder of Thomas Becket, the Archbishop of Canterbury, by soldiers of King Henry II. Becket becomes a popular martyr and his grave is visited by pilgrims for hundreds of years. *The Canterbury Tales*, written by Geoffrey Chaucer in the fourteenth century, recounts the stories told by a fictional group of pilgrims on their way to Canterbury.

1171 The Norman baron known as Strongbow and his followers settle in Ireland.

Despite English rule, northern and central Wales was never settled in great numbers by Saxons or Normans. As a result, the (Celtic) Welsh language and culture remained strong. Eisteddfods, national festivals of Welsh song and poetry, continued throughout the medieval period and still continue today. The Anglo-Norman lords of Ireland remained loyal to the English king but, despite laws to the contrary, mostly adopted the Gaelic language and customs.

The political independence of Scotland did not prevent a gradual switch to English language and customs in the lowland (southern) part of the country. Many Anglo-Saxon aristocrats had fled there after the Norman conquest. In addition, the Celtic kings saw that the adoption of an Anglo-Norman style of government would strengthen royal power. By the end of this period, a cultural split had developed between the lowlands, where the way of life and language was similar to that in England, and the highlands, where Gaelic culture and language prevailed – and where, due to the mountainous terrain, the authority of the Scottish king was hard to enforce.

It was in this period that Parliament began its gradual evolution into the democratic body which it is today. The word 'parliament', which comes from the French word *parler* (to speak), was first used in England in the thirteenth century to describe an assembly of nobles called together by the king.

Robin Hood

Robin Hood is a legendary folk hero. King Richard I (1189–99) spent most of his reign fighting in the 'crusades' (the wars between Christians and Muslims in the Middle East). Meanwhile, England was governed by his brother John, who was unpopular because of all the taxes he imposed. According to legend, Robin Hood lived with his band of 'merry men' in Sherwood Forest outside Nottingham, stealing from the rich and giving to the poor. He was constantly hunted by the local sheriff (the royal representative) but was never captured.

Language and social class

As an example of the class distinctions introduced into society after the Norman invasion, people often point to the fact that modern English has two words for the larger farm animals: one for the living animal (cow, pig, sheep) and another for the animal you eat (beef, pork, mutton). The former set come from Anglo-Saxon, the latter from the French that the Normans brought to England. Only the Normans normally ate meat; the poor Anglo-Saxon peasants did not!

1215 An alliance of aristocracy, church and merchants force King John to agree to the Magna Carta (Latin meaning 'Great Charter'), a document in which the king agrees to follow certain rules of government. In fact, neither John nor his successors entirely followed them, but the Magna Carta is remembered as the first time a monarch agreed in writing to abide by formal procedures.

1275 Llewellyn, a Welsh prince, refuses to submit to the authority of the English monarch.

1284 The Statute of Wales puts the whole of that country under the control of the English monarch.

1295 The Model Parliament sets the pattern for the future by including elected representatives from urban and rural areas.

1328 After several years of war between the Scottish and English kingdoms, Scotland is recognized as an independent kingdom.

The sixteenth century

In its first outbreak in the middle of the fourteenth century, bubonic plague (known in England as the Black Death) killed about a third of the population of Great Britain. It periodically reappeared for another 300 years. The shortage of labour which it caused, and the increasing importance of trade and towns, weakened the traditional ties between lord and peasant. At a higher level of feudal structure, the power of the great barons was greatly weakened by in-fighting (The Wars of the Roses).

Both these developments allowed English monarchs to increase their power. The Tudor dynasty (1485–1603) established a system of government departments staffed by professionals who depended for their position on the monarch. The feudal aristocracy was no longer needed for implementing government policy. It was needed less for *making* it too. Of the traditional two 'Houses' of Parliament, the Lords and the Commons, it was now more important for monarchs to get the agreement of the Commons for their policies because that was where the newly powerful merchants and landowners were represented.

Unlike in much of the rest of Europe, the immediate cause of the rise of Protestantism in England was political and personal rather than doctrinal. The King (Henry VIII) wanted a divorce, which the Pope would not give him. Also, by making himself head of the 'Church of England', independent of Rome, all church lands came under his control and gave him a large new source of income.

This rejection of the Roman Church also accorded with a new spirit of patriotic confidence in England. The country had finally lost any realistic claim to lands in France, thus becoming more consciously a distinct 'island nation'. At the same time, increasing European exploration of the Americas meant that England was closer to the geographical centre of western civilization instead of being, as previously, on the edge of it. It was in the last quarter of this adventurous and optimistic century that Shakespeare began writing his famous plays, giving voice to the modern form of English.

It was therefore patriotism as much as religious conviction that had caused Protestantism to become the majority religion in England by the end of the century. It took a form known as Anglicanism, not so very different from Catholicism in its organization and ritual. But in

The Wars of the Roses

During the fifteenth century, the power of the greatest nobles, who had their own private armies, meant that constant challenges to the position of the monarch were possible. These power struggles came to a head in the Wars of the Roses, in which the nobles were divided into two groups, one supporting the House of Lancaster, whose symbol was a red rose, the other the House of York, whose symbol was a white rose. Three decades of almost continual war ended in 1485, when Henry Tudor (Lancastrian) defeated and killed Richard III (Yorkist) at the Battle of Bosworth Field.

Off with his head!

Being an important person in the sixteenth century was not a safe position. The Tudor monarchs were disloyal to their officials and merciless to any nobles who opposed them. More than half of the most famous names of the period finished their lives by being executed. Few people who were taken through Traitor's Gate (see below) in the Tower of London came out again alive.

1534 The Act of Supremacy declares Henry VIII to be the supreme head of the church in England.

1536 The administration of government and law in Wales is reformed so that it is exactly the same as it is in England.

1538 An English language version of the Bible replaces Latin bibles in every church in the land.

1560 The Scottish parliament abolishes the authority of the Pope and forbids the Latin mass.

1580 Sir Francis Drake completes the first voyage round the world by an Englishman.

the lowlands of Scotland, it took a more idealistic form. Calvinism, with its strict insistence on simplicity and its dislike of ritual and celebration became the dominant religion. It is from this date that the stereotype image of the dour, thrifty Scottish developed. However, the highlands remained Catholic and so further widened the gulf between the two parts of the nation. Ireland also remained Catholic. There, Protestantism was identified with the English, who at that time were making further attempts to control the whole of the country.

Henry VIII

Henry VIII is one of the most well-known monarchs in English history, chiefly because he took six wives during his life. He has the popular image of a *bon viveur*. There is much truth in this reputation. He was a natural leader but not really interested in the day-to-day running of government and this encouraged the beginnings of a professional bureaucracy. It was during his reign that the reformation took place. In the 1530s, Henry used Parliament to pass laws which swept away the power of the Roman Church in England. However, his quarrel with Rome was nothing to do with doctrine. It was because he wanted to be free to marry again and to appoint who he wished as leaders of the church in England. Earlier in the same decade, he had had a law passed which demanded complete adherence to Catholic belief and practice. He had also previously written a polemic against Protestantism, for which the pope gave him the title *Fidei Defensor* (defender of the faith). The initials F.D. still appear on British coins today.

Elizabeth I

Elizabeth I, daughter of Henry VIII, was the first of three long-reigning queens in British history (the other two are Queen Victoria and Queen Elizabeth II). During her long reign she established, by skilful diplomacy, a reasonable degree of internal stability in a firmly Protestant England, allowing the growth of a spirit of patriotism and general confidence. She never married, but used its possibility as a diplomatic tool. She became known as 'the virgin queen'. The area which later became the state of Virginia in the USA was named after her by one of the many English explorers of the time (Sir Walter Raleigh).

1588 The Spanish Armada. A fleet of ships sent by the Catholic King Philip of Spain to help invade England, is defeated by the English navy (with the help of a violent storm!).

1603 James VI of Scotland becomes James I of England as well.

1605 The Gunpowder Plot. A group of Catholics fail in their attempt to blow up the king in Parliament (see chapter 23).

The seventeenth century

When James I became the first English king of the Stuart dynasty, he was already James VI of Scotland, so that the crowns of these two countries were united. Although their governments continued to be separate, their linguistic differences were lessened in this century. The kind of Middle English spoken in lowland Scotland had developed into a written language known as 'Scots'. However, the Scottish Protestant church adopted English rather than Scots bibles. This and the glamour of the English court where the king now sat caused modern English to become the written standard in Scotland as well. (Scots gradually became just 'a dialect'.)

In the seventeenth century, the link between religion and politics became intense. At the start of the century, some people tried to kill the king because he wasn't Catholic enough. By the end of the century, another king had been killed, partly because he seemed too Catholic, and yet another had been forced into exile for the same reason.

This was the context in which, during the century, Parliament established its supremacy over the monarchy. Anger grew in the country at the way the Stuart monarchs raised money without, as tradition prescribed, getting the agreement of the House of Commons first. In addition, ideological Protestantism, especially Puritanism, had grown in England. Puritans regarded the luxurious lifestyle of the king and his followers as immoral. They were also anti-Catholic and suspicious of the apparent sympathy towards Catholicism of the Stuart monarchs.

This conflict led to the Civil War (The Civil War), which ended with complete victory for the parliamentary forces. James's son, Charles I, became the first monarch in Europe to be executed after a formal trial for crimes against his people. The leader of the parliamentary army, Oliver Cromwell, became 'Lord Protector' of a republic with a military government which, after he had brutally crushed resistance in Ireland, effectively encompassed all of Britain and Ireland.

But by the time Cromwell died, he, his system of government, and the puritan ethics that went with it (theatres and other forms of amusement had been banned) had become so unpopular that the executed king's son was asked to return and become King Charles II.

The Civil War

This is remembered as a contest between aristocratic, royalist 'Cavaliers' and puritanical parliamentarian 'Roundheads' (because of the style of their hair-cuts). The Roundheads were victorious by 1645, although the war periodically continued until 1649.

1642 The Civil War begins.

1649 Charles I is executed. For the first and only time, Britain briefly becomes a republic and is called 'the Commonwealth'.

1660 The Restoration of the monarchy and the Anglican religion.

However, the conflict between monarch and Parliament soon re-emerged in the reign of Charles II's brother, James II. Again, religion was its focus. James tried to give full rights to Catholics, and to promote them in his government. The 'Glorious Revolution' ('glorious' because it was bloodless) followed, in which Prince William of Orange, ruler of the Netherlands, and his Stuart wife Mary accepted Parliament's invitation to become king and queen. Parliament immediately drew up a Bill of Rights, which limited some of the monarch's powers. It also allowed Dissenters (those Protestants who did not agree with the practices of Anglicanism) to practise their religion freely. This meant that the Presbyterian Church, to which the majority of the lowland Scottish belonged, was guaranteed its legality. However, Dissenters were not allowed to hold government posts or become Members of Parliament (MPs).

St. Paul's Cathedral

Ring-a-ring-a-roses

Ring-a-ring-a-roses,
a pocket full of posies.
Atishoo! Atishoo!
We all fall down.

This is a well-known children's nursery rhyme today. It is believed to come from the time of the Great Plague of 1665, which was the last outbreak of bubonic plague in Britain. The ring of roses refers to the pattern of red spots on a sufferer's body. The posies, a bag of herbs, were thought to give protection from the disease. 'Atishoo' represents the sound of sneezing, one of the signs of the disease, after which a person could sometimes 'fall down' dead in a few hours.

The Battle of the Boyne

After he was deposed from the English and Scottish thrones, James II fled to Ireland. But the Catholic Irish army he gathered there was defeated at the Battle of the Boyne in 1690 and laws were then passed forbidding Catholics to vote or even own land. In Ulster, in the north of the country, large numbers of fiercely anti-Catholic Scottish Presbyterians settled (in possession of all the land). The descendants of these people are still known today as Orangemen (after their patron William of Orange). They form one half of the tragic split in society in modern Northern Ireland, the other half being the 'native' Irish Catholic (see page 29 The creation of Northern Ireland).

1666 The Great Fire of London destroys most of the city's old wooden buildings. It also destroys bubonic plague, which never reappears. Most of the city's finest churches, including St. Paul's Cathedral, date from the period of rebuilding which followed.

1688 The Glorious Revolution.

1690 The Presbyterian Church becomes the official 'Church of Scotland'.

The eighteenth century

In 1707, the Act of Union was passed. Under this agreement, the Scottish parliament was dissolved and some of its members joined the English and Welsh parliament in London and the former two kingdoms became one 'United Kingdom of Great Britain'. However, Scotland retained its own system of law, more similar to continental European systems than that of England's. It does so to this day.

Politically, the eighteenth century was stable. Monarch and Parliament got on quite well together. One reason for this was that the monarch's favourite politicians, through the royal power of patronage (the ability to give people jobs), were able to control the election and voting habits of a large number of MPs in the House of Commons.

Within Parliament, the bitter divisions of the previous century were echoed in the formation of two vaguely opposed, loose collections of allies. One group, the Whigs, were the political 'descendants' of the parliamentarians. They supported the Protestant values of hard work and thrift, were sympathetic to dissenters and believed in government by monarch and aristocracy together. The other group, the Tories, had a greater respect for the idea of the monarchy and the importance of the Anglican Church (and sometimes even a little sympathy for Catholics and the Stuarts). This was the beginning of the party system in Britain.

The only part of Britain to change radically as a result of political forces in this century was the highlands of Scotland. This area twice supported failed attempts to put a (Catholic) Stuart monarch back on the throne. After the second attempt, many inhabitants of the highlands were killed or sent away from Britain and the wearing of highland dress (the tartan kilt) was banned. The Celtic way of life was effectively destroyed.

It was cultural change that was most marked in this century. Britain gradually acquired an empire in the Americas, along the west African coast and in India. The greatly increased trade that this allowed was one factor which led to the Industrial Revolution. Other factors were the many technical innovations in manufacture and transport.

The origins of modern government

The monarchs of the eighteenth century were Hanoverian Germans with interests on the European continent. The first of them, George I, could not even speak English. Perhaps this situation encouraged the habit whereby the monarch appointed one principal, or 'prime', minister from the ranks of Parliament to head his government. It was also during this century that the system of an annual budget drawn up by the monarch's Treasury officials for the approval of Parliament was established.

1707 The Act of Union is passed.

1708 The last occasion on which a British monarch refuses to accept a bill passed by Parliament.

1746 At the battle of Culloden, a government army of English and lowland Scots defeat the highland army of Charles Edward, who, as grandson of the last Stuart king, claimed the British throne. Although he made no attempt to protect his supporters from revenge attacks afterwards, he is still a popular romantic legend in the highlands, and is known as 'Bonnie Prince Charlie'.

1763 The English writer Samuel Johnson coins the famous phrase, 'When a man is tired of London, he is tired of life'.

1771 For the first time, Parliament allows written records of its debates to be published freely.

1782 James Watt invents the first steam engine.

In England, the growth of the industrial mode of production, together with advances in agriculture, caused the greatest upheaval in the pattern of everyday life since the Germanic invasions. Areas of common land, which had been used by everybody in a village for the grazing of animals, disappeared as landowners incorporated them into their increasingly large and more efficient farms. (There remain some pieces of common land in Britain today, used mainly as parks. They are often called 'the common'.) Millions moved from rural areas into new towns and cities. Most of these were in the north of England, where the raw materials for industry were available. In this way, the north, which had previously been economically backward, became the industrial heartland of the country. The right conditions also existed in lowland Scotland and south Wales, which further accentuated the differences between these parts of those countries and their other regions. In the south of England, London came to dominate, not as an industrial centre, but as a business and trading centre.

Nelson's Column

Chatsworth House: a country seat

Despite all the urban development of the eighteenth century, social power and prestige rested on the possession of land in the countryside. The outward sign of this prestige was the ownership of a 'country seat' – a gracious country mansion with land attached. More than a thousand such mansions were built in this century.

1783 After a war, Britain loses the southern half of its North American colonies (giving birth to the USA).

1788 The first British settlers (convicts and soldiers) arrive in Australia.

1800 The separate Irish parliament is closed and the United Kingdom of Great Britain and Ireland is formed.

1805 A British fleet under the command of Admiral Horatio Nelson defeats Napoleon's French fleet at the Battle of Trafalgar. Nelson's Column in Trafalgar Square in London commemorates this national hero, who died during the battle.

1829 Robert Peel, a government minister, organizes the first modern police force. The police are still sometimes known today as 'bobbies' ('Bobby' is a short form of the name 'Robert').

Catholics and non-Anglican Protestants are given the right to hold government posts and become MPs.

The nineteenth century

Not long before this century began, Britain lost its most important colonies (north American ones) in a war of independence. At the start of the century, it was locked in a war with France, during which an invasion of the country was a real possibility. Soon after the end of the century, it controlled the biggest empire the world had ever seen.

One section of this empire was Ireland. During this century, it was in fact part of the UK itself, and it was during this century that British culture and way of life came to predominate in Ireland. In the 1840s, the potato crop failed two years in a row and there was a terrible famine. Millions of peasants, those with Gaelic language and customs, either died or emigrated. By the end of the century, almost the whole of the remaining population had switched to English as their first language.

Another part of the empire was made up of Canada, Australia, and New Zealand, where British settlers had become the majority population. Another was India, an enormous country with a culture more ancient than Britain's. Tens of thousands of British civil servants and troops were used to govern it. At the head of this administration was a viceroy (governor) whose position within the country was similar to the monarch's in Britain itself. Because India was so far away, and the journey from Britain took so long, these British officials spent most of their working lives there and so developed a distinct way of life. The majority, however, remained self-consciously 'British' as they imposed British institutions and methods of government on the country. Large parts of Africa also belonged to the empire. Except for South Africa, where there was some British settlement, most of Britain's African colonies started as trading bases on the coast, and were only incorporated into the empire at the end of the century. As well as these areas, the empire included numerous smaller areas and islands. Some, such as those in the Caribbean, were the result of earlier British settlement, but most were included because of their strategic position along trading routes.

The growth of the empire was encouraged by a change in attitude during the century. Previously, colonization had been a matter of settlement, commerce, or military strategy. The aim was simply to

Queen Victoria

Queen Victoria reigned from 1837–1901. During her reign, although the modern powerlessness of the monarch was confirmed (she was sometimes forced to accept as Prime Minister people whom she personally disliked), she herself became an increasingly popular symbol of Britain's success in the world. As a hard-working, religious mother of ten children, devoted to her husband, Prince Albert, she was regarded as the personification of contemporary morals. The idea that the monarch should set an example to the people in such matters was unknown before this time and has created problems for the monarchy since then (see chapter 7).

1833 The first law regulating factory working conditions limits the number of hours that children are allowed to work.

Slavery is made illegal throughout the British Empire.

1868 The TUC (Trades Union Congress) is formed.

1886 After much debate, an atheist is allowed to sit in the House of Commons.

1893 The first socialist, Keir Hardie, is elected to Parliament. He enters the House of Commons for the first time wearing a cloth cap (which remained a symbol of the British working man until the 1960s).

possess territory, but not necessarily to govern it. By the end of the century, colonization was seen as a matter of destiny. During the century, Britain became the world's foremost economic power. This, together with long years of political stability unequalled anywhere else in Europe, gave the British a sense of supreme confidence, even arrogance, about their culture and civilization. The British came to see themselves as having a duty to spread this culture and civilization around the world. Being the rulers of an empire was therefore a matter of moral obligation (The White Man's Burden).

There were great changes in social structure. Most people now lived in towns and cities. They no longer depended on country landowners for their living but rather on the owners of industries. These owners and the growing middle class of tradespeople and professionals held the real power in the country. Along with their power went a set of values which emphasized hard work, thrift, religious observance, the family, an awareness of one's duty, absolute honesty in public life, and extreme respectability in sexual matters. This is the set of values which are now called Victorian.

Middle-class religious conviction, together with a belief that reform was better than revolution, allowed reforms in public life. These included not only political reforms, but also reforms which recognized some human rights (as we now call them). Slavery and the laws against people on the basis of religion were abolished, and laws were made to protect workers from some of the worst excesses of the industrial mode of production. Public services such as the post and the police were begun.

Despite reform, the nature of the new industrial society forced many people to live and work in very unpleasant surroundings. Writers and intellectuals of this period either protested against the horrors of this new style of life (for example, Dickens) or simply ignored it. Many, especially the Romantic poets, praised the beauties of the countryside and the virtues of country life. This was a new development. In previous centuries, the countryside wasn't something to be discussed or admired. But from this time on, most British people developed a sentimental attachment to the idea of the countryside (see chapter 5).

The White Man's Burden

Here are some lines from the poem of this title by Rudyard Kipling (1865–1936), who is sometimes referred to (perhaps unfairly) as 'the poet of imperialism'.

Take up the White Man's burden —
  Send forth the best ye breed —
Go, bind your sons to exile
  To serve tour captives' need;
To wait in heavy harness
  On fluttered folk and wild —
Your new-caught, sullen peoples,
  Half-devil and half-child.

Other races, the poem says, are 'wild' and have a 'need' to be civilized. The white man's noble duty is to 'serve' in this role. This is not a quest for mere power. The duty is bestowed by God, whom Kipling invokes in another poem (*Recessional*) in a reference to the British empire in tropical lands:

God of our fathers, known of old,
  Lord of our far-flung battle-line,
Beneath whose awful hand we hold
  Dominion over palm and pine.

1902 Nationwide selective secondary education is introduced.

1908 The first old-age pensions are introduced.

1911 The power of the House of Lords is severely reduced and sick pay for most workers is introduced.

1914 Great Britain declares war on Germany. Until the 1940s, the First World War was known in Britain as 'The Great War'.

1916 The 'Easter Rising' in Ireland.

The British empire at its peak (1919)

1918 The right to vote is extended to women (see chapter 10).

1920 Partition of Ireland.

1921 Treaty between Britain and the Irish parliament in Dublin.

1926 General Strike.

1928 The right to vote is extended again. All adults can now vote.

1939 Britain declares war on Germany.

1942 The Beveridge report is published, which leads to the eventual creation of the NHS (see chapter 18).

1944 Free compulsory education (up to the age of 15) is established.

1946 The National Health Service is established (see chapter 18).

Coal mines and railways are nationalized. Other industries follow (see chapter 15).

1949 Ireland becomes a republic.

The twentieth century

Around the beginning of the twentieth century, Britain ceased to be the world's richest country. Perhaps this caused a failure of the Victorian confidence in gradual reform. Whatever the reason, the first 20 years of the century were a period of extremism in Britain. The Suffragettes, women demanding the right to vote, were prepared to damage property and even die for their beliefs; some sections of the army appeared ready to disobey the government over its policies concerning Ulster in Ireland; and the government's introduction of new taxation was opposed so absolutely by the House of Lords that even Parliament, the foundation of the political system, seemed to have an uncertain future. But by the 1920s, these issues had been resolved (although only temporarily in the case of Ulster) and the rather un-British climate of extremism died out.

The British empire reached its greatest extent in 1919. By this time, however, it was already becoming less of an empire and more of a confederation. At the same international conference at which Britain acquired new possessions under the Treaty of Versailles, Australia, Canada, New Zealand and South Africa were all represented separately from Britain. A couple of years later, Britain lost most of its oldest colony (The creation of Northern Ireland).

The real dismantling of the empire took place in the 25 years following the Second World War. In the same period, it gradually became clear that Britain was no longer a 'superpower' in the world and its forces were no longer able to act unilaterally. In 1956, for instance, British and French military action to stop the Egyptian government taking over the Suez canal failed because it did not receive American support. During the 1950s, it had been generally understood that a conference of the world's great powers involved the USA, the Soviet Union and Britain. But in 1962, the Cuban missile crisis, one of the greatest threats to global peace in the twentieth century, was resolved without reference to Britain. And when, in 1974, the island of Cyprus, a former British colony, was invaded by Turkey, British military activity was restricted to airlifting the personnel of its military base

The creation of Northern Ireland

By the beginning of the twentieth century, most people in Ireland wanted either internal self-government (which was known as 'home rule') or complete independence from Britain. Liberal governments in Britain had attempted at various times to make this idea a reality. However, the one million Protestants in the province of Ulster in the north of the country were violently opposed to it. They did not want to belong to a country dominated by Catholics. They formed less than a quarter of the total Irish population, but in six of the nine counties of Ulster they were in a 65% majority.

In 1920, the British government partitioned the country between the (Catholic) south and the (Protestant) six counties, giving each part some control of its internal affairs. But this was no longer enough for the south. There, support for complete independence had grown as a result of the British government's savage repression of the 'Easter Rising' in 1916. War followed. The eventual result was that in 1922, the south became independent from Britain.

The six counties, however, remained within the United Kingdom. They became the British province of 'Northern Ireland' (see chapter 12).

1953 Coronation of Elizabeth II.

1958 The Clean Air Act is the first law of widespread application to attempt to control pollution.

Life Peerage Act (see chapter 9).

1959 The first motorway is opened.

1963 The school leaving age is raised to 16.

1968 The 'age of majority' (the age at which somebody legally becomes an adult) is reduced from 21 to 18.

1969 British troops are sent to Northern Ireland (see chapter 12).

Capital punishment is abolished.

1971 Decimal currency is introduced (see chapter 15).

1973 Britain joins the European Economic Community.

1982 The Falklands/Malvinas War (see chapter 12).

there to safety – even though it was one of the guarantors of Cypriot independence. At the end of the century, in 1997, Britain handed Hong Kong back to China, thus losing its last imperial possession of any significant size.

It was from the start of the twentieth century that the urban working class (the majority of the population) finally began to make its voice heard. In Parliament, the Labour party gradually replaced the Liberals (the 'descendants' of the Whigs) as the main opposition to the Conservatives (the 'descendants' of the Tories). In addition, trade unions managed to organize themselves. In 1926, they were powerful enough to hold a General Strike, and from the 1930s until the 1980s the Trades Union Congress (see chapter 15) was probably the single most powerful political force outside the institutions of government and Parliament.

Since then, the working class has faded as a political force. They say history moves in cycles. At the start of the twenty-first century, a historian pointed out that Britain in some ways had more in common with the start of the twentieth century than with its middle. In 1900, a general sense of prosperity was combined with a rather high long-term unemployment rate and concerns about an 'underclass'. This is exactly where Britain stood in 2000, but clearly different from 1950, when a sense of austerity was combined with a very low rate of unemployment. In 1900, domestic servants comprised a full 10% of the workforce. In 1950 this figure was

Britain (re)joins 'Europe'

When the European Coal and Steel Community was formed in 1951, the British government thought it was an excellent idea – but nothing to do with Britain! Long years of an empire based on sea power meant that the traditional attitude to mainland Europe had been to encourage stability there, to discourage any expansionist powers there, but otherwise to leave it well alone.

But as the empire disappeared, and the role of 'the world's policeman' was taken over by the USA, the British government decided to ask for membership of the newly-formed European Communities. There was opposition to the idea from those (both inside and outside the country) who argued that Britain was an 'island nation' and thus essentially different in outlook from nations in mainland Europe. Finally, ten years after its first application, Britain joined in 1973.

1984 British Telecom is privatized. This is the first time that shares in a nationalized company are sold directly to the public (see chapter 15).

1990 First Gulf War (see chapter 12).

1994 The channel tunnel opens (see chapter 17).

1999 The hereditary element in the House of Lords is severely restricted (see chapter 9).

2003 Second Gulf War (see chapter 12).

2007 British troops leave Northern Ireland (see chapter 12).

down to 3% and still falling. But by 2000, with so many professional women with no time to look after the house or the children, it was back up to 8% and increasing every year. Even the average speed of traffic through London was the same in 1900 and 2000, while in 1950 it was much faster!

QUESTIONS

1 In Britain, as in most countries, history and popular myth are mixed up together. How many cases can you find in this chapter of stories which are of doubtful historical truth?

2 At present there is discussion in Britain about the idea of establishing a 'national day' (which Britain has never had). National days usually commemorate some important event in a country's history. Which event in British history do you think is most worthy of such commemoration?

3 How would you describe the changing relations between religion and politics in British history? Are the changes that have taken place similar to those in your country?

4 Britain is unusual among European countries in that, for more than 300 years now, there has not been a single revolution or civil war. Why do you think this is?

SUGGESTIONS

Understanding Britain by John Randle (Blackwell, Oxford) is a readable history of Britain, written with the student in mind.

The Story of English was a BBC series of programmes which is now available on DVD. Episodes two to four are largely historical in content and very interesting. The series was also made into a book.

There is a strong tradition of historical novels in English (set at various times in British history). The writings of Georgette Heyer, Norah Lofts, Jean Plaidy, Rosemary Sutcliffe, and Henry and Geoffrey Treece are good examples.

For the real history enthusiast, you cannot do better than read *The Isles* by Norman Davies (Papermac). It's 1,000 pages long and very scholarly. But it's also very readable.

A Passage to India by E. M. Forster is set in India at the height of the British Empire and is an examination of colonial attitudes. (There is also a film of the book.) *The Raj Quartet* by Paul Scott is also set in India, this time in the final years of British rule there.

What happened in the twentieth century?

There are many opinions about whether the events of the twentieth century and Britain's role in it were good or bad. Here is one view:

What an enigma Britain will seem to historians when they look back on the second half of the twentieth century. Here is a country that fought and won a noble war, dismantled a mighty empire in a generally benign and enlightened way, created a far-seeing welfare state – in short, did nearly everything right – and then spent the rest of the century looking on itself as a chronic failure.

Bill Bryson, *Notes from a Small Island*

03 Geography

It has been claimed that the British love of compromise is the result of the country's physical geography. This may or may not be true, but it is certainly true that the land and climate in Britain have a notable lack of extremes. Britain has mountains, but none of them are very high; it also has flat land, but you cannot travel far without encountering hills; it has no really big rivers; it doesn't usually get very cold in the winter or very hot in the summer; it has no active volcanoes, and an earth tremor which does no more than rattle teacups in a few houses is reported in the national news media.

Climate

The climate in Britain is more or less the same as that of the north-western part of the European mainland. The popular belief that it rains all the time in Britain is simply not true. The image of a wet, foggy land was created two thousand years ago by the invading Romans and was perpetuated in the twentieth century by Hollywood. In fact, London gets no more rain in a year than most other major European cities, and less than some (How wet is Britain?).

The amount of rain that falls on a town in Britain depends on where it is. Generally speaking, the further west you go, the more rain you get. The mild winters mean that snow is a regular feature of the higher areas only. Occasionally, a whole winter goes by in lower-lying parts without any snow at all. The winters are in general slightly colder in the east of the country than they are in the west, while in summer the south is warmer and sunnier than the north.

How wet is Britain?

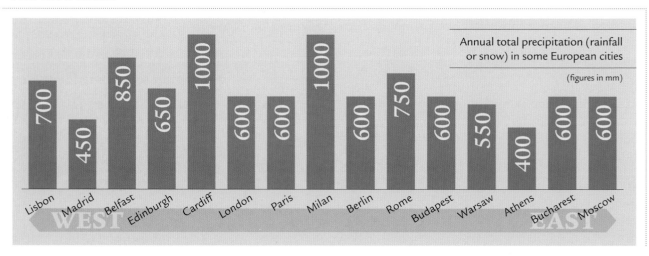

Annual total precipitation (rainfall or snow) in some European cities

(figures in mm)

Lisbon	Madrid	Belfast	Edinburgh	Cardiff	London	Paris	Milan	Berlin	Rome	Budapest	Warsaw	Athens	Bucharest	Moscow
700	450	850	650	1000	600	600	1000	600	750	600	550	400	600	600

WEST ← → EAST

The British landscape

Britain and Ireland: where people live

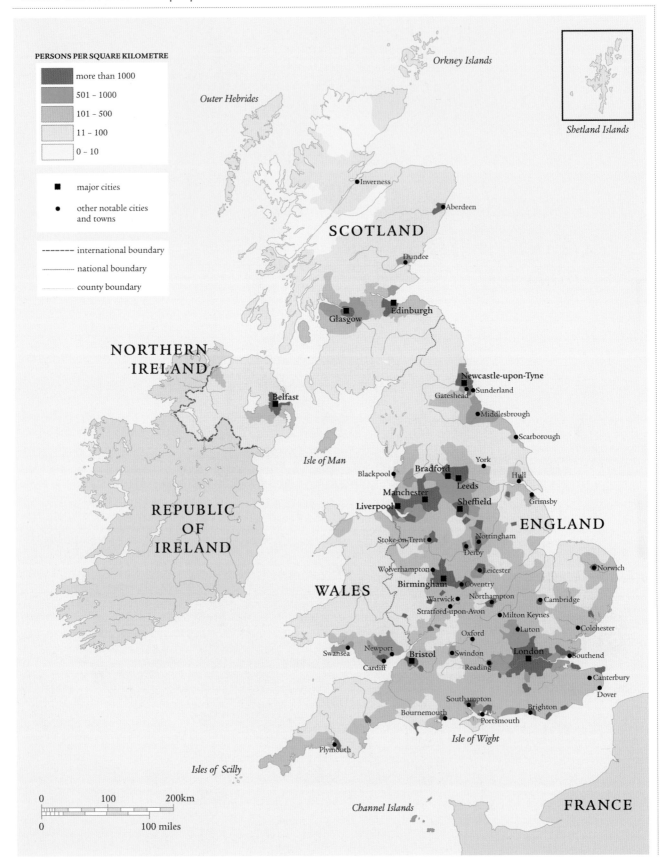

PERSONS PER SQUARE KILOMETRE

- more than 1000
- 501 – 1000
- 101 – 500
- 11 – 100
- 0 – 10

- ■ major cities
- ● other notable cities and towns

- ------- international boundary
- ·········· national boundary
- ———— county boundary

Orkney Islands

Outer Hebrides

Shetland Islands

Inverness

Aberdeen

SCOTLAND

Dundee

Glasgow   Edinburgh

NORTHERN
IRELAND

Newcastle-upon-Tyne

Gateshead ● Sunderland

Belfast

● Middlesbrough

● Scarborough

Isle of Man

REPUBLIC
OF
IRELAND

York

Blackpool   Bradford

Hull

Manchester   Leeds

Liverpool   Sheffield

Grimsby

ENGLAND

Stoke-on-Trent

Nottingham

Derby

WALES

Wolverhampton

Leicester

Norwich

Birmingham   Coventry

Warwick   Northampton

Cambridge

Stratford-upon-Avon

Milton Keynes

Colchester

Oxford   Luton

Swansea   Newport

Bristol   Swindon

London   Southend

Cardiff   Reading

Canterbury

Dover

Southampton

Brighton

Bournemouth   Portsmouth

Isle of Wight

Plymouth

Isles of Scilly

0   100   200km

0   100 miles

Channel Islands

FRANCE

Why has Britain's climate got such a bad reputation? Perhaps it is for the same reason that British people always seem to be talking about the weather. This is its changeability. There is a saying that Britain doesn't have a climate, it only has weather. It may not rain very much altogether, but you can never be sure of a dry day; there can be cool (even cold) days in July and some quite warm days in January.

The lack of extremes is the reason why, on the few occasions when it gets genuinely hot or freezing cold, the country seems to be totally unprepared for it. A bit of snow or a few days of frost and the trains stop working and the roads are blocked; if the thermometer goes above 80°F (27°C) (How hot or cold is Britain?), people behave as if they were in the Sahara and the temperature makes front-page headlines. These things happen so rarely that it is not worth organizing life to be ready for them.

Land and settlement

Britain has neither towering mountain ranges nor impressively large rivers, plains or forests. But this does not mean that its landscape is boring. What it lacks in grandeur it makes up for in variety. The scenery changes noticeably over quite short distances. It has often been remarked that a journey of 100 miles (160 kilometres) can, as a result, seem twice as far. Overall, the south and east of the country are comparatively low-lying, consisting of either flat plains or gently rolling hills. Mountainous areas are found only in the north and west, although these regions also have flat areas (The British Landscape).

Human influence has been extensive. The forests that once covered the land have largely disappeared. Britain has a greater proportion

How hot or cold is Britain?

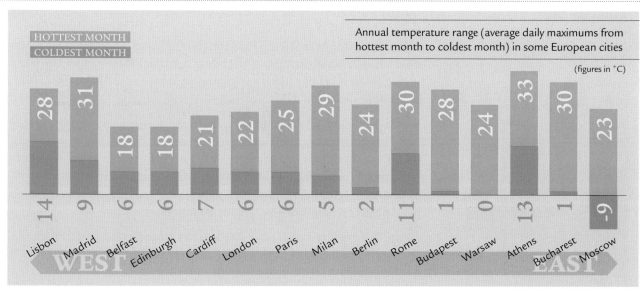

Many people in Britain are more comfortable with the Fahrenheit scale of measurement (F). To them, a temperature 'in the upper twenties' means that it is freezing and one 'in the low seventies' will not kill you – it is just pleasantly warm.

of grassland than any other country in Europe except Ireland. One distinctive human influence, especially common in southern England, is the enclosure of fields with hedgerows. This feature increases the impression of variety. Although many hedgerows disappeared in the second half of the twentieth century (farmers dug them up to increase the size of their fields and become more efficient), there are still enough of them to support a variety of bird life.

Much of the land is used for human habitation. This is not just because Britain is densely populated in most areas (Britain and Ireland: where people live). Partly because of their habitual concern for privacy and their love of the countryside (see chapter 5), the English and the Welsh don't like living in blocks of flats in city centres and the proportion of people who do so is lower than in continental European countries. As a result, cities in England and Wales have, wherever possible, been built outwards rather than upwards (although this is not so much the case with Scottish cities). For example, the London area has about three times the population of the Athens area but it occupies about ten times the amount of land.

However, because most people (almost 80%) live in towns or cities rather than in villages or in the countryside, this habit of building outwards does not mean that you see buildings wherever you go in Britain. There are areas of completely open countryside everywhere and some of the mountainous areas remain virtually untouched.

The environment and pollution

It was in Britain that the word 'smog' (a mixture of smoke and fog) was first used. As the world's first industrialized country, its cities were the first to suffer this atmospheric condition. In the nineteenth century, London's 'pea-soupers' (thick fogs) became famous through descriptions of them in the works of Charles Dickens and in the Sherlock Holmes stories. The situation in London reached its worst point in 1952. At the end of that year a particularly bad smog, which lasted for several days, was estimated to have caused between 4,000 and 8,000 deaths.

Water pollution was also a problem. In the nineteenth century it was once suggested that the Houses of Parliament should be wrapped in enormous wet sheets to protect those inside from the awful smell of the River Thames. Until the 1960s, the first thing that happened to people who fell into the Thames in London was that they were rushed to hospital to have their stomachs pumped!

Then, during the 1960s and 1970s, laws were passed which forbade the heating of homes with open coal fires and which stopped much of the pollution from factories. At one time, a scene of fog in a Hollywood film was all that was necessary to symbolize London. This image is now out of date, and by the end of the 1970s it was said to be possible to catch fish in the Thames outside Parliament.

Climate change

On 10 August 2003, a momentous event occurred at Heathrow airport just outside London. There, a temperature of 37.9°C was recorded. This may not look an especially significant figure to you, but to the British it had great psychological impact. This is because many of them still think in the old Fahrenheit scale – and 37.9°C is 100.2°F. It was the first time in British history that the temperature had passed the 100°F mark.

Since that day, temperatures of more than 100°F have been recorded several times in several different places in Britain. People have become generally aware of climate change. In Britain, there seem to be three trends: (1) like the rest of Europe, temperatures are generally rising; (2) the difference between the warmer, drier south-east and the cooler, wetter north-west is becoming more pronounced; (3) extreme weather conditions are becoming more frequent – so perhaps the British will start to be more prepared for them!

A wind farm

However, as in the rest of Europe, the great increase in the use of the motor car in the last quarter of the twentieth century caused an increase in a different kind of air pollution. This problem is serious enough for weather forecasts to have an 'air quality' section and on some occasions for official advice to be given that certain people (such as asthma sufferers) should not even leave their houses, and that nobody should take any vigorous exercise.

Now that the reduction of greenhouse gases has become a pressing global need, how to provide for Britain's energy needs and/ or reduce its energy consumption has become a national issue, especially as the country's oil reserves in the North Sea will not last much longer. There is a possibility that new nuclear power stations will be built because they do not emit greenhouse gases. But they are politically unpopular and there is doubt about their environmental friendliness (they *do* cause some greenhouse gases to be emitted, both in their construction and in the disposal of the waste they create). Various attempts at using 'green' energy sources are being made. One of these is solar power, but for obvious reasons there is a limit to its possibilities in Britain. Others are tidal power and even wave power. The one which has really developed is wind power. Wind farms are now quite a common feature of the British landscape. But they are not universally popular either. Some local people and nature lovers feel strongly that they ruin the countryside – and so local tourist boards are often opposed to them too. One way around this problem is to construct them offshore in the sea, and this too has been done.

Britain under attack

Some people worry that Britain's political sovereignty is in danger from the European Union and from Scottish and Welsh independence movements (see chapter 12). This may or may not be true. But what is certainly true is that Britain itself – the island – is in very real danger from the sea. For one thing, global warming means rising sea levels everywhere, so that low-lying coastal areas are threatened. For another, the Atlantic waves which hit Britain's north, west and south coasts are getting taller. This means they have more energy than before – energy with which to strip sand from beaches, undermine cliffs and damage coastal defences. Finally, the east coast, although safe from those Atlantic waves, is actually sinking anyway (as the south-east corner of Britain tilts downwards). Every year, little bits of it vanish into the North Sea. Sometimes the land slips away slowly. But at other times it slips away very dramatically (as when in 1992 the guests of the Holbeck hotel, built on a clifftop near Scarborough, had to leave their rooms in a hurry; the cliff was collapsing into the sea – and so was their hotel).

London is in special danger because it is also vulnerable to flooding through tidal surges along the River Thames. One flood in the seventeenth century left the Westminster area under nearly two metres of water. In 1953 a tidal surge killed 300 people in the Thames Estuary to the east of London. Realization of the scale of the disaster that would have been caused if this surge had reached London provoked the construction of the Thames Barrier, completed in 1983. Since then, it has been used to protect London from flooding an average of three times every year. It is widely thought that the Barrier will soon be inadequate. New defences are being considered.

London

London (the largest city in western Europe) dominates Britain. It is home to the headquarters of all government departments, the country's parliament, its major legal institutions, and the monarch. It is the country's business and banking centre and the centre of its transport network. It contains the headquarters of the national television networks and all the national newspapers. It is about seven times larger than any other city in the country. About a fifth of the total population of the UK lives in the wider London area.

The original walled city of London was quite small. (It is known colloquially today as 'the square mile'.) It did not contain Parliament or the royal court, since this would have interfered with the autonomy of the merchants and traders who lived and worked there. It was in Westminster, another 'city' outside London's walls, that these national institutions met. Today, both 'cities' are just two areas of central London. The square mile (also known simply as 'the City') is home to the country's main financial organizations. During the daytime, more than a quarter of a million people work there, but fewer than 10,000 people actually live there.

Two other well-known areas of London are the West End and the East End. The former is known for its many theatres, cinemas and expensive shops. The latter is known as the poorer residential area of central London. It is the traditional home of the Cockney (see chapter 4) and for centuries it has been home to successive waves of immigrant groups.

There are many other parts of central London, some of them quite distinctive in character, and central London itself makes up only a very small part of Greater London. In common with many other European cities, the population in the central area decreased in the second half of the twentieth century. The majority of 'Londoners' live in its suburbs, millions of them travelling into the centre each day to work. These suburbs cover a vast area of land stretching in all directions. The most recent trend has been an expansion of London to the east, down towards the Thames Estuary.

Like many large cities, London is in some ways untypical of the rest of the country in that it is so cosmopolitan. Although all of Britain's cities have some degree of cultural and racial variety, the variety is by far the greatest in London. More than 300 languages are spoken there; its restaurants offer cuisine from more then 70 different countries. In fact, nearly a third of the people in London were born outside Britain.

The variety does not stop there. London has most of both the richest and the poorest areas in Britain. Despite this, you have less chance of being the victim of a crime there than you have in many other British cities. In late 2007, it was voted the most popular city in the world in an on-line poll of international tourists. It is also the most frequent choice for Chinese companies expanding into Europe. This popularity is probably the result of its combination of apparently infinite cultural variety and a long history which has left intact many visible signs of its richness and drama.

The better side of town

In the industrial age, the air in Britain's towns and cities used to be very polluted. And the prevailing winds throughout Britain are from the west. For these two reasons, the more desirable areas of the average British town or city were to the west of its centre. This probably explains why, even now, when industrial pollution is no longer a problem, it is the western suburbs of most towns and cities in Britain which are the richest.

Southern England

The area surrounding the outer suburbs of London has the reputation of being 'commuter land'. This is the most densely populated area in the UK which does not include a large city, and millions of its inhabitants travel into London to work every day.

Further out from London the region has more of its own distinctive character. The county of Kent, which you pass through when travelling from Dover or the channel tunnel to London, is known as 'the garden of England' because of the many kinds of fruit and vegetables grown there. The Downs, a series of hills in a horseshoe shape to the south of London, are used for sheep farming (though not as intensively as they used to be). The southern side of the Downs reaches the sea in many places and form the white cliffs of the south coast. Many retired people live along this coast. Employment in the south-east of England has always been mainly in trade, the provision of services and light manufacturing. There was never much heavy industry. It therefore did not suffer the slow economic decline that many other parts of England experienced during the twentieth century.

The region known as 'the West Country' has an attractive image of rural beauty in British people's minds – notice the use of the word 'country' in its name. There is some industry and one large city (Bristol was once Britain's most important port after London), but farming is more widespread than it is in most other regions. Some parts of the West Country are well-known for their dairy produce, such as Devonshire cream, and fruit. The south-west peninsula, with its rocky coast, numerous small bays (once noted for smuggling activities) and wild moorlands such as Exmoor and Dartmoor, is the most popular holiday area in Britain. The winters are so mild in some low-lying parts of Cornwall that it is even possible to grow palm trees, and the tourist industry has coined the phrase 'the Cornish Riviera'.

East Anglia, to the north-east of London, is also comparatively rural. It is the only region in Britain where there are large expanses of uniformly flat land. This flatness, together with the comparatively dry climate, has made it the main area in the country for the growing of wheat and other arable crops. Part of this region, the area known as the Fens, has been reclaimed from the sea, and much of it still has a very watery, misty feeling to it. Further east, the Norfolk Broads are criss-crossed by hundreds of waterways, but there are no towns here, so it is a popular area for boating holidays.

The Midlands of England

Birmingham is Britain's second largest city. During the Industrial Revolution (see chapter 2), Birmingham and the area to its north and west (sometimes known as the Black Country) developed into the country's major engineering centre. Despite the decline of heavy industry in the twentieth century, factories in the Birmingham area still convert iron and steel into a vast variety of goods.

The great wildlife invasion

In the last 50 years, a combination of the British preference for building outwards and intensive farming in the countryside has had a curious effect. In the eighteenth and nineteenth centuries, millions of people migrated to Britain's towns and cities. The British changed into a nation of urban dwellers. More recently, British animals have been doing the same thing! And for much the same reason. It's all about where you can make a living. In the countryside, decades of intensive farming and monoculture (the cultivation of a single crop over a large area) have led to food shortages for many species. But all those back gardens, lanes and parks in Britain's towns and suburbs are not farmed this way. There, a wide and tempting variety of flora and fauna is to be found. For all those starving rural animals, it's too good an opportunity to miss.

The pioneers were the foxes. They started in the 1950s and have become mainly urban animals. Many other species have followed. Shrews, squirrels, roe deer and brown hares have all been spotted in cities and many more have colonized suburban back gardens. As more species take this route, more 'employment' becomes available for other species there. It's a mass migration. Some wildlife experts believe suburban gardens are now so important to wildlife they should be classified as a special type of habitat.

The north-south divide

In 1854, a novel called *North and South* appeared. It tells the story of a woman from the south of England who finds herself living in the horrors of the grim north of England. Since around that time, the 'north-south divide' has been part of English folklore. It denotes a supposed big difference between the poor north and the rich south (although there is no recognized geographical boundary between the two). Historically, there is much truth in this generalization. The south has almost always had lower rates of unemployment and more expensive houses. This is especially true of the south-eastern area surrounding London. (This area is sometimes referred to as 'the Home Counties', an indication, perhaps, of London's domination of public life.)

So well-known are these stereotypes that statisticians and economists sometimes attempt to draw the boundary between north and south based purely on wealth, so that a relatively poor place is designated 'north' (and vice versa) because of this fact alone.

In the last quarter of the twentieth century, the decline of heavy industry, which was mostly confined to the north, caused large-scale migration of well-qualified workers from north to south, so that the north-south divide seemed to be getting even wider.

However, the picture now is not that simple. Net migration in this century has been the other way around – towards the north – and some of the poorest areas in the country are actually in London. Indeed, one well-known (northern) journalist has claimed that if the same kind of novel were written today the big divide would be between London and the rest of England – and London would be the awful half!

There are other industrial areas in the Midlands, notably the towns between the Black Country and Manchester known as The Potteries (famous for producing china such as that made at the factories of Wedgwood, Spode and Minton) and several towns further east such as Derby, Leicester, and Nottingham. On the east coast, Grimsby, once one of the world's greatest fishing ports, has become the country's major fish processing centre.

Although the Midlands do not have many positive associations in the minds of British people, tourism has flourished in 'Shakespeare country' (centred on Stratford-upon-Avon, Shakespeare's birthplace), and Nottingham has successfully capitalized on the legend of Robin Hood (see chapter 2).

Northern England

The Pennine mountains run up the middle of northern England like a spine. On either side, the large deposits of coal (used to provide power) and iron ore (used to make machinery) enabled these areas to lead the Industrial Revolution. On the western side, the Manchester area (connected to the port of Liverpool by canal) became, in the nineteenth century, the world's leading producer of cotton goods; on the eastern side, towns such as Bradford and Leeds became the world's leading producers of woollen goods. Many other towns sprang up on both sides of the Pennines at this time, concentrating on certain auxiliary industries or on coal mining. Further south, Sheffield became a centre for the production of steel goods. Further north, around Newcastle, shipbuilding was the major industry.

In the minds of British people, the prototype of the noisy, dirty factories that symbolize the Industrial Revolution is found in the once-industrial north of England. But the achievements of these new industrial towns also induced a feeling of civic pride in their inhabitants and an energetic realism, epitomized by the clichéd saying 'where there's muck there's brass' (wherever there is dirt, there is money to be made). The decline in heavy industry in Europe in the second half of the twentieth century hit the industrial north of England hard. For a long time, the region as a whole had a level of unemployment significantly above the national average.

The towns on either side of the Pennines are flanked by steep slopes on which it is difficult to build and are surrounded by land, most of which is unsuitable for any agriculture other than sheep farming. Therefore, the pattern of settlement in the north of England is often different from that in the south. Open and uninhabited countryside is never far away from its cities and towns. The typically industrial landscape and the very rural landscape interlock. The wild, windswept moors which are the setting for Emily Brontë's famous nineteenth century novel *Wuthering Heights* seem a world away from the smoke and grime of urban life – in fact, they are just up the road (about 15 kilometres) from Bradford!

Further away from the main industrial areas, the north of England is sparsely populated. In the north-western corner of the country is the Lake District. The Romantic poets Wordsworth, Coleridge and Southey (the 'Lake Poets') lived here and wrote about its beauty. It is the favourite destination of people who enjoy walking holidays and the whole area is classified as a National Park (the largest in England).

Scotland

Scotland has three fairly clearly marked regions. Just north of the border with England are the southern uplands, which consists of small towns, quite far apart from each other, whose economy depends to a large extent on sheep farming. Further north, there is the central plain. Finally, there are the highlands, consisting of mountains and deep valleys and including numerous small islands off the west coast. An area of spectacular natural beauty, it occupies the same land area as southern England but fewer than a million people live there. Tourism is important in the local economy, and so is the production of whisky.

It is in the central plain and the strip of east coast extending northwards from it that more than 80% of the population of Scotland lives. In the late twentieth century, this region had many of the same difficulties as the industrial north of England, although the North sea oil industry helped to keep unemployment down.

Scotland's two major cities have very different reputations. Glasgow, the larger of the two, is associated with heavy industry and some of the worst housing conditions in Britain (the district called the Gorbals, although now rebuilt, was famous in this respect). However, this image is one-sided. Glasgow has a strong artistic heritage. At the turn of the last century the work of the Glasgow School (led by Charles Rennie Mackintosh) put the city at the forefront of European design and architecture. In 1990, it was the European City of Culture. Over the centuries, Glasgow has received many immigrants from Ireland and in it there is an echo of the same divisions in the community that exist in Northern Ireland (see chapter 4). For example, of its two famous rival football teams, one is Catholic (Celtic) and the other is Protestant (Rangers).

Edinburgh, which is smaller than Glasgow, has a comparatively middle-class image (although class differences between the two cities are not really very great). It is the capital of Scotland and the seat of its parliament. It is associated with scholarship, the law, and administration. This reputation, together with its many fine historic buildings, and also perhaps its topography (a rock in the middle of the city on which stands the castle) has led to its being called 'the Athens of the north'. The annual Edinburgh Festival of the Arts is internationally famous (see chapter 22).

Wales

As in Scotland, most people in Wales live in one small part of it. In the Welsh case, it is the south-east of the country that is most heavily populated. As we have seen, coal has been mined in many parts of Britain, but just as British people would locate the prototype factory of

The Lake District

A view overlooking Thirlmere Valley in the Lake District, Cumbria.

SAD

Aberdeen, on the east coast of Scotland, has done well out of North Sea oil. But its people have a problem in the winter. They are nearly 60 degrees north and on top of that, almost the whole city is built in granite, a grey stone which just soaks up the little light available. And it is this lack of light (not the cold wind) which researchers blame for depression in the city. They estimate that as many as 20% of the people there suffer from a condition known as SAD (Seasonal Affective Disorder), some of them so seriously that they become suicidal.

In fact, SAD has increased all over Britain in the past two decades. Changed living and working patterns mean that people spend far less time outdoors than they used to, and so experience less daylight than they used to.

the industrial revolution in the north of England, so they would locate its prototype coal mine in south Wales. Despite its industry, no really large cities have emerged in this area (Cardiff, the capital of Wales, has a population of about a third of a million). It is the only part of Britain with a high proportion of industrial *villages*. Coal mining in south Wales has now almost entirely ceased and, as elsewhere, the transition to other forms of employment has been slow and painful.

Most of the rest of Wales is mountainous. Because of this, travel between south and north is very difficult. As a result, each part of Wales has closer contact with its neighbouring part of England than it does with other parts of Wales: the north with Liverpool, and mid-Wales with the English West Midlands. The area around Mount Snowdon in the north-west of the country is very beautiful and is the largest National Park in Britain.

Northern Ireland

With the exception of Belfast, which is famous for the manufacture of linen (and is still a shipbuilding city), this region is, like the rest of Ireland, largely agricultural. It has several areas of spectacular natural beauty. One of these is the Giant's Causeway on its north coast, so-called because the rocks in the area look like enormous stepping stones.

QUESTIONS

1 How is the pattern of human settlement in your country different from that in Britain?

2 Does the capital city of your country stand in the same relation to the rest of the country as London does to Britain?

3 Are the different stereotype reputations of north and south in England similar to those in your own country?

SUGGESTIONS

The ongoing BBC series *Coast* has lots of fascinating information. You can see parts of it on the internet and there are DVDs.

If you enjoy travel writing, there are several books which offer accounts of journeys through or around Britain. *The Kingdom by the Sea* by the respected novelist Paul Theroux is an example. An amusing and informative journey through northern England is *Pies and Prejudice: In Search of the North* by Stuart Maconie. It says a lot about how northerners feel about themselves – and about the south.

Some novels evoke a sense of place. Nineteenth century examples are the works of Thomas Hardy, who set his stories in the south–west of England (in an area which he called Wessex – see chapter 2), and *Wuthering Heights* by Emily Brontë, set in the Yorkshire moors. More recently, Graham Swift's novel *Waterland* takes account of the effect of the landscape of the Fens on the actions of the people who live there.

Ugly Bug Ball

One small indication of the generally benign nature of British geography is the fact that even the mosquitoes are relatively harmless – almost nobody bothers to take precautions against their bites.

There is, however, a notable exception in one part of Britain – the Scottish Highlands. This is the territory of a cousin of the mosquito, the midgie (some people say 'midge'). Midgies are much, much smaller than mosquitoes. But they are fiercer and there are many, many more of them, usually in 'clouds' around your head!

Midgies make picnics in the highlands a gamble, camping uncomfortable and outdoor cocktails impossible. You know the image of the British always moaning about the weather. Well, Highlanders are always moaning about the midgies. Recently, one group of Highlanders decided to abandon the struggle and celebrate instead. They held the world's first midgie festival, including an Ugly Bug Ball, a 'midge-summer night's party' featuring a mardi-gras style procession with midgie masks. The organizers claimed that, in their tenacious single-mindedness (when they go after you, they get you), midgies were 'a brilliant symbol for our country [Scotland]'.

04 Identity

How do British people identify themselves? Who do they feel they are? Everybody has an image of themselves, but the things that make up this image can vary. For example, in some parts of the world, it is very important that you are a member of a particular family; in other parts of the world, it might be more important that you come from a particular place; in others, that you belong to a certain social class, or are a member of a certain profession, or work for a certain company; in still others, that you belong to a certain religious group or that you always vote for a certain political party. This chapter explores the loyalties and senses of identity most typically felt by British people.

Ethnic identity: the four nations

National ('ethnic') loyalties can be strong among the people in Britain whose ancestors were not English (see chapter 1). For many people living in England who call themselves Scottish, Welsh or Irish, this loyalty is little more than a matter of emotional attachment. But for others, it goes a bit further and they may even join one of the sporting and social clubs for 'exiles' from one of these nations. These clubs promote national folk music, organize parties on special national days and foster a consciousness of doing things differently from the English.

For people living in Scotland, there are constant reminders of their distinctiveness. First, several important aspects of public life, such as education and the legal and welfare systems, are organized separately, and differently, from the rest of Britain. Scotland even prints its own banknotes (although these are the same currency as the rest of Britain). Second, the Scottish way of speaking English is very distinctive. A modern form of the dialect known as Scots (see chapter 2) is spoken in everyday life by most of the working classes in the lowlands. It has many features which are different from other forms of English and cannot usually be understood by English or Welsh people. Third, there are many symbols of Scottishness which are well-known throughout Britain (see chapter 1).

However, the feeling of being Scottish is not that simple (What does it mean to be Scottish?). This is partly because of the historical cultural split between highland and lowland Scotland. A specifically Scottish Gaelic sense of cultural identity is, in modern times, felt only by a few tens of thousands of people in some of the Western Isles of Scotland and the adjoining mainland. These people speak Scottish Gaelic (which they call 'Gallic') as a first language.

What does it mean to be Scottish?

On 25 January every year, many Scottish people attend 'Burns suppers'. At these parties, they read from the work of the eighteenth-century poet Robert Burns (regarded as Scotland's national poet), wear kilts, sing traditional songs, dance traditional dances (called 'reels'), and eat haggis (made from sheep's heart, lungs, and liver).

Here are two opposing views of this way of celebrating Scottishness.

The sentimental nationalist

That national pride that ties knots in your stomach when you see your country's flag somewhere unexpected is particularly strong among the Scots. On Burns night, people all over the world fight their way through haggis and Tam O'Shanter[1], *not really liking either. They do it because they feel allegiance to a small, wet, under-populated, bullied country stuck on the edge of Europe.*

Many Scottish Scots hate the romantic, sentimental view of their country: the kilts, the pipes, the haggis, Bonnie Prince Charlie. The sight of a man in a skirt, or a Dundee cake[2], makes them furious. To them, this is a tourist view of Scotland invented by the English. But I adore the fierce romantic, tartan, sentimental Scotland. The dour McStalinists are missing the point – and the fun.

In the eighteenth century, the English practically destroyed Highland Scotland. The normalising of relations between the two countries was accomplished by a novelist, Sir Walter Scott, whose stories and legends intrigued and excited the English. Under his direction, the whole country reinvented itself. Everyone who could get hold of a bit of tartan wore a kilt, ancient ceremonies were invented. In a few months, a wasteland of dangerous beggarly savages became a nation of noble, brave, exotic warriors. Scott did the best public relations job in history.

The realpolitik[3] Scot doesn't see it like that. He only relates to heavy industry, 1966 trade unionism, and a supposed class system that puts Englishmen at the top of the heap and Scottish workers at the bottom. His heart is in the Gorbals, not the Highlands. But I feel moved by the pipes, the old songs, the poems, the romantic stories, and just the tearful, sentimental nationalism of it all.

A. A. Gill, *The Sunday Times* 23 January 1994 (adapted)

[1] the title of a poem by Burns, and also the name for the traditional cap of highland dress
[2] a rich fruit cake, supposedly originating from the town of Dundee
[3] an approach to politics based on realities and material needs, not on morals or ideals

The realist

When I assure English acquaintances that I would rather sing a chorus of Land Of Hope And Glory *than attend a Burns supper, their eyebrows rise. Who could possibly object to such a fun night out?*

In fact, only a few Scots are prepared to suffer the boredom of these occasions. The people who are really keen on them aren't Scottish at all. They think they are, especially on January 25 or Saint Andrew's Day or at internationals at Murrayfield[1], when they all make a great business of wearing kilts, dancing reels, reciting their Tam O'Shanters, *and trying to say 'loch'[2] properly without coughing up phlegm. But these pseudo-Scots have English accents because they went to posh public schools. They are Scottish only in the sense that their families have, for generations, owned large parts of Scotland – while living in London.*

This use of Scottish symbols by pseudo-Scots makes it very awkward for the rest of us Scots. It means that we can't be sure which bits of our heritage are pure. Tartan? Dunno[3]. Gay Gordons?[4] Don't care. Whisky? No way, that's ours. Kilts worn with frilly shirts? Pseudo-Scottish. Lions rampant? Ours, as any Hampden[5] crowd will prove. And Burns suppers? The Farquhar-Seaton-Bethune-Buccleuchs[6] can keep them. And I hope they all choke on their haggis.

Harry Ritchie, *The Sunday Times* 23 January 1994 (adapted)

[1] the Scottish national rugby stadium
[2] 'loch' is Scottish Gaelic for 'lake'
[3] I don't know
[4] the name of a particular reel
[5] the Scottish national football stadium
[6] see What's in a name?

The people of Wales do not have as many reminders of their Welshness in everyday life. The organization of public life is similar to that of England and there are not so many well-known symbols of Welshness. In addition, a large minority of the people in Wales probably do not consider themselves to be especially Welsh at all. In the nineteenth century, large numbers of Scottish, Irish and English people went to find work there, and today many English people still make their homes in Wales or have holiday houses there. As a result, a feeling of loyalty to Wales is often similar in nature to the fairly weak loyalties to particular geographical areas found throughout England (see below) – it is regional rather than nationalistic.

However, there is one single highly important symbol of Welsh identity – the Welsh language. Everybody in Wales can speak English, but it is not everybody's first language. For about 20% of the population (that's more than half a million people), the mother tongue is Welsh. For these people, Welsh identity obviously means more than just living in the region known as Wales. Moreover, in comparison to the other small minority languages of Europe, Welsh is in a strong position. Thanks to successive campaigns, the language receives a lot of public support. All children in Wales learn it at school, there are many local newspapers in Welsh and a Welsh television channel, and all public notices and signs are written in both Welsh and English.

The question of identity in Northern Ireland is a much more complex issue and is dealt with at the end of this chapter.

And what about English identity? For the last 200 years, most people who describe themselves as English have made little distinction in their minds between 'English' and 'British'. This confusion can still be found in the press (The bulldog spirit) and in public life. For example, at international football or rugby matches when the players stand to

The bulldog spirit

Here is an example of a point of view where England and Britain seem to be the same thing.

'The bulldog spirit' is a phrase evoking courage, determination and refusal to surrender. It is often brought to life as 'the British bulldog' (although this typically calls to mind an Englishman!). It was this spirit which thrilled a columnist for *The Sunday Times* newspaper when she watched a rugby world cup match in 2007. She writes that although she is not usually interested in spectator sports, she found herself gripped by the semi-final between France and England. In her opinion, England won the match as a result of:

> *... dogged, unyielding courage [which] we think of as a great national virtue ... and I realised I was extremely proud of [the players] and proud of England ... it reawakened a sense of national solidarity in me [and] presumably that is what it was doing for every other Englishman and woman.*

(Minette Martin, *The Sunday Times* 21 October 2007)

However, she concludes her article by commenting that this spirit of patriotism 'is not something you can teach in Britishness lessons'. And the title of her article was 'To understand Britishness, watch rugby'!

A national hero for the Welsh

Compared to the Scottish and the Irish, the Welsh have few national icons or heroes. So the prominence recently accorded to the memory of Owain Glyndwr (Owen Glendower in English) is a sign of the times (The rise in ethnic and national profiles). In the first years of the fifteenth century, Glyndwr captured all the castles which the English had built to help them rule in Wales, and established an independent Wales with its own parliament. No other Welshman has matched this achievement. It lasted for only five years. Inevitably, Glyndwr was defeated. However, he never actually surrendered and there is no reliable record of his death – two points which have added to his legendary status in Welsh folklore.

In the year 2000, the Welsh national assembly helped to organize countrywide celebrations to mark the six hundredth anniversary of Glyndwr's revolt. Stamps were issued with his likeness, and streets, parks, and public squares were named after him throughout Wales. In 2007, a statue of him was installed in the square of the town of Corwen in his heartland, and the Welsh band Manic Street Preachers wrote and issued a song about him. There is a campaign to make 16 September, the date Glyndwr started his revolt, a national holiday in Wales.

The rise in ethnic and national profiles

In the twenty-first century, indigenous ethnic and national identities have become more public. The most obvious sign of this is the Scottish parliament and the Welsh assembly (see chapter 12). Here are some others:

1) The ten-yearly census, and other official forms, has always had a question on ethnic origin. Now it also has a question on national identity, in which people choose as many as they like from British, English, Scottish, Welsh, Irish and 'Other'.

2) Of the many islands off the west coast of Scotland, the best known is Skye. Its name was made famous by a song about the escaping Bonnie Prince Charlie after the battle of Culloden (see chapter 2). But in 2007, it was officially renamed. It is now called by its Gaelic name, Eilean a' Cheo, which means 'the misty isle'.

3) The Cornish language is a relative of Welsh. Its last few native speakers died more than a century ago. But local scholars have attempted to revive it and it is estimated that about 3,000 people in Cornwall, who have learnt the language in evening classes, can speak it with some proficiency. There has even been a full-length feature film in Cornish. And in 2002, in response to a campaign, the British government recognised Cornish as an official minority language. This means it now has legal protection under European law. It also means that when visitors to Cornwall arrive there, they see signs announcing that they have entered *Kernow*.

attention to hear the anthems of the two teams, the Scottish, Irish, and Welsh have their own songs, while the English one is just *God Save the Queen* – the same as the *British* national anthem. However, as part of the growing profile of ethnic identity generally (The rise in ethnic and national profiles), the 'English' part, distinct from 'British', is becoming clearer. Not so long ago, English supporters at those football and rugby matches used to wave the Union Jack flag; now they wave the cross of St. George. And at the Commonwealth Games (see chapter 12), where England and the other parts of Britain compete separately, England has even found its own anthem (*Land of Hope and Glory*). In 2004, a poll asked teenagers in England and their teachers whether they thought of themselves first and foremost as English, British or European. A clear majority chose 'British', but there was a sharp difference between the teachers and the pupils. Only 12% of the teachers chose 'English', but 25% of the pupils did so. (Very, very few chose 'European'.) Nevertheless, exactly what makes 'English' and 'British' distinct from each other is not at all clear (What does it mean to be English?).

Other ethnic identities

The peoples of the four nations have been in contact for centuries. As a result, there is a limit to their significant differences. With minor variations and exceptions, they look the same, eat the same food, have the same religious heritage (Christianity), learn the same language first (English) and have the same attitudes to the roles of men and women. The same is largely true (with wider variations and exceptions) for those whose family origins lie in continental Europe, for example the hundreds of thousands who have Italian or Polish heritage (as a result of immigration in the decade following the Second World War).

The situation for the several million people in Britain whose family roots lie elsewhere in the world is different. For one thing, most of them look different, which means they cannot *choose* when to advertise their ethnic heritage and when not to. There are hundreds of different ethnicities represented in Britain. From the point of view of numbers and length of time in Britain, two major groupings may be identified.

The longest-established of these groups are black Caribbeans. Most members of this community were born in Britain. The great wave of immigration from the Caribbean began in 1948, when about 500 Jamaicans and Trinidadians, most of whom had fought for Britain in the Second World War, arrived on the steamship *Empire Windrush*. In the next 14 years, many more arrived, where they took mostly low-paid jobs. Many worked on London's buses and trains. (For a decade, London Transport actually recruited directly from the island of Barbados.) After 1962, immigration from the Caribbean slowed down, but remained significant until the mid 1970s.

Of the major minority ethnic groups, the cultural practices of black Caribbeans are nearest to those of the white majority. For example, among them can be found the same proportion of Christian and non-religious people (though they often retain their own churches, which tend to be evangelical in style – see chapter 13) and their distinctive language variety, known as creole or patwa, stands in the same relation to English as Scots does (see above). Several forms of Caribbean music, such as calypso, reggae and ska, have taken root in Britain and have had an influence beyond the Caribbean community. The most popular, well-attended annual street festival in the whole of Europe, the Notting Hill Carnival, was started by Caribbean immigrants.

Black Caribbeans today often take pride in their cultural roots. Like the children and grandchildren of Irish, Scottish and Welsh immigrants to England before them, this pride seems to be increasing as their cultural practices, their everyday habits and attitudes, gradually become less distinctive.

The other major grouping consists of those whose cultural roots lie in and around the Indian subcontinent. In Britain, they are known collectively as 'Asians'. The first wave of Asian immigration to Britain took place at about the same time as that from the Caribbean. The second took place in the late 1960s and early 1970s, when large numbers of people of Asian origin arrived from east African countries. The following decades saw continued Asian immigration, though at a slower rate.

Members of these communities stuck closely together when they first came to Britain and now usually marry among themselves (more so than in the black Caribbean community) so that they have retained, in varying degrees, their languages (chiefly the closely related ones of Hindi, Urdu, Bengali, Punjabi, and Gujarati), their (non-Christian) religions, their music, and their dress and food preferences. In their culture, parents often expect to have more control over their children than most white or black parents expect to have, a fact which can make life difficult for young Asians who have been born and brought up in Britain and subscribe to the values of mainstream British culture.

The term 'Asian', however, masks some significant cultural differences. For example, while average levels of education among people of Indian origin are above the British average, and many fill professional roles in society, those of people whose family roots lie in Pakistan or Bangladesh are below the national average. For many of the latter, their ethnic identity is less important than their religious one (Islam). In recent decades, some young British Muslims have reacted against their immigrant parents' attempts to assimilate to British culture. They have made a conscious attempt to adhere more strictly to Islamic practices, some interpretations of which can alienate them from mainstream British values. On the other hand, most people of Indian origin (who are largely Hindus or Sikhs) and many of Pakistani and Bangladeshi origin, have been able to forge a distinct hybrid identity as British Asians with which they feel comfortable and which has found a voice in the mainstream media (Goodness Gracious Me) and in the musical form of bhangra.

What does it mean to be English?

In 2005, the (British) government decided it was time to put English identity on the map. It launched a website called Icons Online, in which the public were asked to give their ideas for English symbols.

In order to get things started, a panel of advisers drew up a first list. It included structures such as Stonehenge (see chapter 2) and the Angel of the North (see chapter 22), vehicles such as the Routemaster London bus (see chapter 17) and the SS Empire Windrush, small objects such as a cup of tea (see chapter 20) and the FA Cup (see chapter 21), and 'cultural' products such as the King James Bible (see chapter 13) and a portrait of Henry VIII (see chapter 2) by Hans Holbein.

But even in this starter list, you can see that finding distinctively English icons is difficult. Stonehenge was not built by the English, but by the ancestors of the modern Welsh; a cup of tea comes from India; King James was Scottish; Henry VIII was arguably as Welsh as he was English – and his portrait painter was, of course, German.

The Angel of the North, a steel sculpture by English artist Antony Gormley

The family

With regard to family life, Britain is overall a fairly typical northern European country. That is, in comparison with most other places in the world, family identity is rather weak and the notion of family has a generally low profile. Significant family events such as weddings, births and funerals are not automatically accompanied by large gatherings of people. It is still common to appoint people to certain roles on such occasions, such as best man at a wedding or godmother and godfather when a child is born. But for most people these appointments are of sentimental significance only. They do not imply lifelong responsibility. In fact, family gatherings of any kind beyond the household unit are rare. For most people, they are confined to the Christmas period.

Goodness Gracious Me

In the early years of mass migration to Britain from southern Asia and the Caribbean, characters from these places appeared on British TV and film only as objects of interest, and sometimes of fun. By the start of this century, they had taken control of the microphone and were able to define themselves and explore their situation as black British or British Asians. The following is one example.

In the 1960 film *The Millionairess*, the famous (white) comic actor Peter Sellers played an Indian doctor. Obviously out of place in a sophisticated European world, his character kept uttering the expression of surprise 'goodness, gracious me', in a parody of a supposedly typical Indian accent.

Four decades later, this same phrase became the title of a TV comedy sketch show. But this time it was uttered (at the start of each show) in a Yorkshire accent, and the show itself was written and performed by British Indians. Some of the sketches poked fun at British attitudes to Indians and some explored and poked fun at the attitudes and aspirations of British Indians themselves.

The show was hugely popular, not only with the Asian audience but with the majority white audience as well. Its creators, Sanjeev Bhaskar and Meera Syall, went on to make the even more popular mock interview show called *The Kumars at No. 42*. Other acclaimed examples of British Asian creativity are the films *My Beautiful Launderette*, *My Son the Fanatic* and *Bend it Like Beckham*.

Is there a generation gap any more?

The 'teenager' was invented in the 1950s. The concept was encouraged by advertisers who spied a new market. Awareness of it was then heightened during the social revolution of the 1960s. By the end of that decade, the phrase 'generation gap' had become a staple of the English language. It alluded to the sharply divergent attitudes of parents and their teenage children – and the conflict between them which was the expected norm. This idea of teenagers as a sort of separate species, endlessly rowing with their parents, is now part of British folklore.

However, a 2002 study in Britain indicated that this stereotype may be outdated. The study found that four out of five British teenagers living at home said they were happy with family life and that they got on well with their parents; a third had not had a single argument with them in the past year (and in any case most arguments were about mundane things like 'tidying up'); only 10% said they definitely did not get on with their parents. In the long term, therefore, the rebellious teenager may turn out to have been a short-lived phenomenon of a few decades in the twentieth century.

And here is another indication of these improved relations. In the late twentieth century, young people in Britain used to fly the family nest and set up house by themselves at a much earlier age than in most other countries. The average age at which they leave home these days, although still lower than the European average at the time of writing, is rising fast. This trend may also be the result of the high cost of housing, so they just can't afford to live away from the family home. But part of the reason must be that they just like living there.

Of course, the family unit is still the basic living arrangement for most people. But in Britain this definitely means the nuclear family. There is little sense of extended family identity, except among some ethnic minorities. This is reflected in the size and composition of households. It is unusual for adults of different generations within the family to live together. The average number of people living in each household in Britain is lower than the European average; the proportion of people living alone is higher.

Even the stereotypical nuclear family of a married father and mother and their children became much less common in the last quarter of the twentieth century. The proportion of children born outside marriage has risen dramatically and now accounts for more than 40% of births. However, these trends do not necessarily mean that the nuclear family is breaking down. There is much talk in Britain of 'single-parent families' as a social problem, but in fact 85% of children are born to parents who, married or not, are living together, and about half the children in Britain live with the same two parents for the whole of their childhood. It is just that many people have less respect for the formalities of marriage than they used to. Indeed, many adults now routinely refer to their regular sexual partners as their 'partner', rather than 'husband', 'wife', 'boyfriend' or 'girlfriend', thus avoiding any indication of whether they are married or not.

Geographical identity

A sense of identity based on place of birth is, like family identity, not very common or strong in most parts of Britain – and perhaps for the same reason. People are just too mobile and very few live in the same place all their lives.

There *is* quite a lot of local pride, but it arises because people are happy to live in what they consider to be a nice place and often when they are fighting to preserve it. It does not usually mean that the people of a locality feel strongly that they *belong* to that place (Crap Towns).

There is somewhat more of a sense of identity with a larger geographical area. In some cases, there is quite a strong sense of identification with a city. One notable example is Liverpool, whose people, known as Liverpudlians or Scousers, are very conscious of the distinct identity of their city, the result of a long history as an international port and consequent cultural and ethnic mix (with a strong Irish component). The same is true of the people of Newcastle, (known as Geordies) partly because of the position of their city in the far north of England, far away from most other centres of population. In addition, Mancunians (from Manchester), Glaswegians (from Glasgow), and Londoners are each often proud to be identified in this way (What is a Cockney?). In other cases, identity is associated with a county. These are the most ancient divisions of England. Although they often have little administrative significance these days (see chapter 8), they still claim the allegiance of some

What's in a name?

In England, the notion of the honour of the family name is almost non-existent (though it exists to some degree in the upper classes, in the other three British nations and among ethnic minorities). In fact, it is very easy to change your family name – and you can choose anything you like. In the 1980s, one person changed his surname to Oddsocks McWeirdo El Tutti Frutti Hello Hippopotamus Bum. There was no rule to stop him doing this. All he needed was £5 and a lawyer to witness the change.

There are also no laws in Britain about what surname a wife or child must have. Because of this freedom, names can be useful pointers to social trends. The case of double-barrelled names is an example. These are surnames with two parts separated by a hyphen: for example, Barclay-Finch. For centuries, they have been a symbol of upper-class status (originating in the desire to preserve an aristocratic name when there was no male heir). Until recently, most people in Britain have avoided giving themselves double-barrelled names – they would have been laughed at for their pretensions. In 1962, only one in every 300 surnames was double-barrelled.

By the start of the twenty-first century, however, one person in 50 had such a name. Why the change? Are lots of people pretending to be upper-class? No, the motivations for the new trend are different. One of them is feminism. Although an increasing number of women now keep their maiden name when they marry, it is still normal to take the husband's name. Independent-minded women are now finding a compromise by doing both at the same time – and then passing this new double-barrelled name onto their children. Another motive is the desire of parents from different cultural backgrounds for their children to have a sense of both of their heritages.

people. Yorkshire, in the north of England, is a notable example. Another is Cornwall, in the south-western corner of England. Even today, some Cornish people still talk about 'going to England' when they cross the county border – a testament to its ethnic Celtic history.

At the larger regional level, there is one well-known sense of identity. Many people in the north of England are very conscious that they are 'northerners' – and proud of it. Stereotypically, they see themselves as tougher, more honest and warmer-hearted than the soft, hypocritical and unfriendly 'southerners'. This feeling was stronger in the industrial past (see chapter 3), so that northerners saw the rich southerners as living off the sweat of their labour. But a strong sense of difference remains. Take the example of the popular TV chef Jamie Oliver, with his informal, vibrant Cockney personality, and Sainsbury's. In 1999, Jamie Oliver's success persuaded the supermarket chain, Sainsbury's, to hire him for an advertising campaign. This was a great success – Sainsbury's food sales rocketed. But only in the south of England. There, Oliver's 'cheeky-chappy' Cockney-ness went down very well. But up in the north of England, it left the viewers cold. There, many people claimed they couldn't understand him and Sainsbury's sales actually *decreased* for a while.

Class

Historians say that the class system has survived in Britain because of its flexibility. It has always been possible to buy, marry or work your way up, so that your children will belong to a higher social class than you do. As a result, the class system has never been swept away by a revolution and an awareness of class forms a major part of most people's sense of identity.

People in Britain regard it as difficult to become friends with somebody from a different 'background'. This feeling has little to do with conscious loyalty, and nothing to do with a positive belief in the class system itself – most people say they do not approve of clear class differences. It results from the fact that the different classes have different sets of attitudes and daily habits. Typically, they eat different food at different times of day (and call the meals by different names – see chapter 20), they talk about different topics using different styles and accents of English, they enjoy different pastimes and sports (see chapter 21), they have different values about what things in life are most important, and different ideas about the correct way to behave.

An interesting feature of the class structure in Britain is that it is not just, or even mainly, relative wealth or the appearance of it, which determines someone's class. Of course, wealth is part of it. But it is not possible to guess a person's class just by looking at his or her clothes, car or bank balance. The most obvious sign comes when a person opens his or her mouth, giving the listener clues to the speaker's attitudes and interests.

Crap Towns

British people rarely feel a sense of loyalty to the place where they live. At Christmas 2003, there was an unexpected bestseller in the bookshops. It was called *Crap Towns: the 50 worst places to live in the UK*. It consisted, simply, of 50 essays, each saying horrible, insulting things about a particular town somewhere in Britain.

Now, since this list of shame included many large towns, the book was nasty about the homes of a sizeable chunk of the British population. So you might think that a lot of people in the country would have taken offence. Well, some did. But in fact, the book sold especially well in the towns that featured in it. One bookshop in Oxford (ranked the thirty-first worst) picked a particularly vicious quote from the essay on this town, blew it up and stuck it in the window. And when the editors turned up there to sign copies, rather than being booed and driven out of town with pitchforks, they were cheered and feted. It was the same all over the country. One of the very few negative reactions was from the people of Slough (between London and Oxford), renowned in Britain as an especially unglamorous place. They seemed insulted by their town's ranking as only the forty-first worst. Why, they wanted to know, wasn't it number one?

But even more indicative than *what* the speaker says is the *way* that he or she says it. The English grammar and vocabulary used in public speaking, radio and television news broadcasts, books, and newspapers (and also – unless the lessons are run by Americans – as a model for learners of English) is known as 'standard British English'. Most working-class people, however, use lots of words and grammatical forms in their everyday speech which are regarded as 'non-standard'.

Nevertheless, nearly everybody in the country is capable of using standard English (or something very close to it) when the situation demands it. They are taught to do so at school. Therefore, the clearest indication of a person's class is often his or her accent, which most people do not change to suit the situation. The most prestigious accent in Britain is known by linguists (though not by the general population) as 'Received Pronunciation' (RP). It is the combination of standard English spoken with an RP accent that is usually meant when people talk about 'BBC English' or 'the Queen's English'.

RP is not associated with any particular part of the country. The vast majority of people, however, speak with an accent which is geographically limited. In England and Wales, anyone who speaks with a strong regional accent is automatically assumed to be working class. Conversely, anyone with a 'pure' RP accent is assumed to be upper or upper-middle class. (In Scotland and Northern Ireland, the situation is slightly different; in these places, some forms of regional accent are almost as prestigious as RP.)

During the last quarter of the twentieth century, the way that people identify themselves with regard to class changed. In Britain, as in many other places, a certain amount of 'social climbing' goes on; that is, people try to appear as if they belong to as high a class as possible. These days, however, the opposite is more common. By the conventional criterion of occupation, there are more middle class adults in Britain today than working class ones. And yet surveys consistently show that more people describe themselves as working class! This is one manifestation of a well-known phenomenon known as 'inverted snobbery', whereby middle-class people try to adopt working-class values and habits. They do this in the belief that the working classes are in some way 'better' (for example, more honest). Nobody wants to be thought of as snobbish. The word 'posh' illustrates this opposite tendency. It is used by people from all classes to mean 'of a class higher than the one I (the speaker) belong to' and it is normally used with negative connotations. To accuse someone of being posh is to accuse them of being distant and/or pretentious.

In this climate, the unofficial segregation of the classes in Britain has become less rigid than it was. A person with a working-class accent is no longer prohibited from most high-status jobs by that reason alone. Nobody takes elocution lessons any more in order to sound more upper class. It is now acceptable for radio and television presenters to speak with 'an accent' (i.e. not to use strict RP). It is also notable that, at the time of writing, only one of the last seven British Prime Ministers went to a school for upper-class children – while almost every previous Prime Minister in history did.

What is a Cockney?

Traditionally, a true Cockney is anybody born within the sound of Bow bells (the bells of the church of St. Mary-le-Bow in the city of London). In fact, the term is commonly used to denote people who come from a wider area of the innermost eastern suburbs of London and also an adjoining area south of the Thames.

'Cockney' is also used to describe a strong London accent and, like any such local accent, is associated with working-class origins.

A notable feature of Cockney speech is rhyming slang, by which, for example, 'wife' is referred to as 'trouble and strife', and 'stairs' as 'apples and pears' (usually shortened to 'apples'). Some rhyming slang has passed into general informal British usage: examples are 'use your loaf' meaning 'think' (from 'loaf of bread' meaning 'head') and 'have a butcher's' meaning 'have a look' (from 'butcher's hook' meaning 'look').

The three classes

A stereotype view of the upper, middle and working classes (left to right), as seen in a satirical television programme of the 1970s. This view is now quite a long way from the reality, but still lives on in people's minds.

Women's football

In most areas of public life, in theory if not always in practice, women in Britain have gained parity with men. But there is one area that has been lagging behind: sport. Take a look at the sports pages of any British newspaper and you will find approximately ten per cent of the space devoted to sport played by women; watch TV sports coverage and you will see that women only appear in individual sports such as athletics or tennis.

But women's team sports are now catching up. At the turn of the century, football overtook netball as the most popular sport for British women. In 1993, there were only 500 female football teams in the whole country; by 2007 there were more than 7,000. A few of them are semi-professional and are beginning to get media coverage. (This increased coverage has been assisted by the fact that in recent years the England women's team has been more successful in international competitions than the England men's team.)

This new development is partly the result of women wanting to play sports that give them more exercise than 'gentler' sports formerly thought more suitable. But it is also the result of the rise of male football stars such as David Beckham whose images are far less aggressively masculine than they were in the past. These changed attitudes mean that women football players are no longer vulnerable to the stigma of being 'un-feminine'.

In general, the different classes mix more readily and easily with each other than they used to. There has been a great increase in the number of people from working-class origins who are home owners (see chapter 19) and who do traditionally middle-class jobs (see chapter 15). The lower and middle classes have drawn closer to each other in their attitudes. And the relation between wealth and perceived social class seems to be even looser than it used to be. One survey in 2006 concluded that a large minority (more than three million) of the wealthiest 20% of people in the country regard themselves as working class, while almost as high a proportion (almost two million) of the poorest 20% regard themselves as middle class.

Men and women

Generally speaking, British people invest about the same amount of their identity in their gender as people in other parts of northern Europe do. On the one hand, society no longer overtly endorses differences in the public and social roles of men and women, and it is illegal to discriminate on the basis of sex. On the other hand, people still (often unconsciously) expect a fairly large number of differences in everyday behaviour and roles.

In terms of everyday habits and mannerisms, British society probably expects a sharper difference between the sexes than most other European societies do. For example, it is still far more acceptable for a man to look untidy and scruffy than it is for a woman; and it is still far more acceptable for a woman to display emotions and everyday affection than it is for a man. But the number of these differences is being reduced. For example, it is no longer considered effeminate for men to get professional grooming services such as manicures. Conversely, large numbers of British women now regard getting drunk occasionally just as much a part of everyday life as most British men.

As far as domestic roles are concerned, differentiation between the sexes has decreased sharply in the past few decades. Although they would still normally complement the woman, not the man, on a beautifully decorated or well-kept house, most people assume that a family's financial situation is not just the responsibility of the man. And although everyday care of the children is still generally seen as mainly the woman's responsibility (this is probably why nearly half of the jobs done by women are part-time – for men, the figure is 10%), it is generally expected that men should play their full part in chores such as changing babies' nappies, putting the children to bed, dressing them, feeding them and helping them with homework. Indeed, in a 2003 study of attitudes towards these matters across Europe, British men scored an 'egalitarianism rating' of 94 – second only to Danish men, and higher than the men of countries traditionally regarded as strong on gender equality such as the Netherlands and Norway.

As for public roles, a large number of occupations have ceased to be associated with either men or women. But there are some notable exceptions, even among young people (Men, women, and work). Look at the table below. With regard to positions of power and influence, there are contradictions. Britain was one of the first European countries to have a woman Prime Minister and a woman chairperson of debate in its parliament. However, at the time of writing only one in five MPs is a woman, only one in nine university heads is a woman, and of the executive directors in Britain's top 100 companies, fewer than five per cent are women. In 2007, there were slightly more female medical students than male ones; and yet only 12% of the professors at Britain's medical schools were women.

Men, women, and work

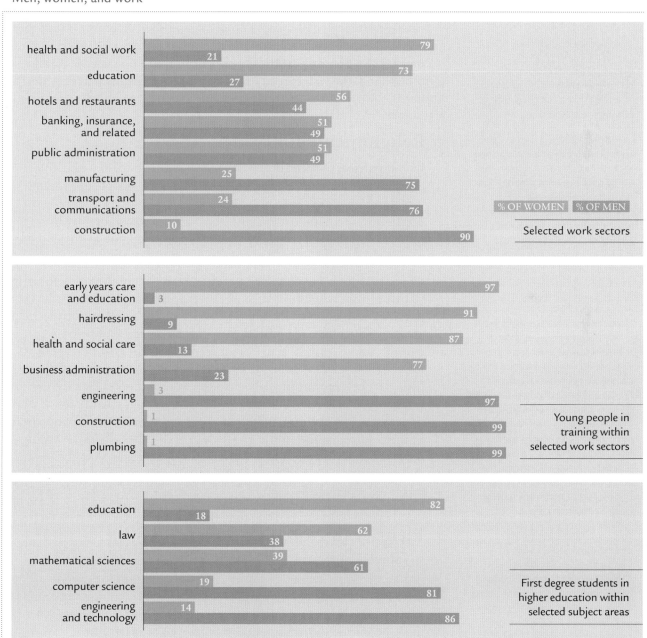

% OF WOMEN % OF MEN

Selected work sectors

	% of women	% of men
health and social work	79	21
education	73	27
hotels and restaurants	56	44
banking, insurance, and related	51	49
public administration	51	49
manufacturing	25	75
transport and communications	24	76
construction	10	90

Young people in training within selected work sectors

	% of women	% of men
early years care and education	97	3
hairdressing	91	9
health and social care	87	13
business administration	77	23
engineering	3	97
construction	1	99
plumbing	1	99

First degree students in higher education within selected subject areas

	% of women	% of men
education	82	18
law	62	38
mathematical sciences	39	61
computer science	19	81
engineering and technology	14	86

Source: Equal Opportunities Commission 2006

The sign of the cross

Britain, like any EU state, is a country where freedom of religion is a right, that is, unless you're playing football in Glasgow.

In February 2006, Glasgow Celtic were playing a match against their arch rivals Glasgow Rangers. The Celtic goalkeeper on that day was Artur Boruc. Like most Polish people, he is a Catholic. And so, just as many of his fellow Catholic continental footballers would do, when a particularly critical moment arrived in the match, he made the sign of the cross. Now he has a criminal record.

How can this be? To understand it, you need to know that the rivalry between Celtic and Rangers is based on religion and that the enmity between their respective fans is similar to that between the two communities in Northern Ireland. (One Scottish comedian once described Glasgow as 'Belfast Lite'.) At local derbies, Celtic fans sing rousing choruses of IRA anthems, while Rangers fans sing of being up to their ears in Fenian (Irish Republican) blood.

To counter this outpouring of sectarian hatred – which frequently leads to violence at Celtic-Rangers matches, Scotland had introduced a law criminalizing behaviour which could aggravate religious prejudice. And in this context, even crossing yourself was deemed such behaviour.

Social and everyday contacts

British people give a relatively high importance to the everyday personal contacts that they make. Some writers on Britain have talked about the British desire to 'belong', and it is certainly true that the pub, or the working man's club, or the numerous other clubs devoted to various sports and pastimes play an important part in many people's lives. In these places, people forge contacts with other people who share some of the same interests and attitudes. For many people, these contacts are an important part of their social identity. Another factor is work, which is how many people make their social contacts. Partly as a result of this, some people's profession or skill is also an important aspect of their sense of identity.

However, since British people do not spend their free time out of the house any more than they do in most other European countries, these means of self-identification should not be overemphasized. On the other hand, the widespread use of the internet means that they don't need to (Making contact and finding your roots).

Religion and politics

In comparison to some other European countries, and with the exception of Northern Ireland (see below), some people in Scotland (The sign of the cross) and in the Islamic community, neither religion nor politics is an important part of a person's social identity in modern Britain. This is partly because the two do not, as they do in some other countries, go together in any significant way.

Of course, there are many people who regard themselves as belonging to this or that religion, church or party. Some people among the minority who are actively religious and the very small minority who are active members of political parties feel this sense of belonging strongly and deeply. It may form a very important part of their own idea of themselves as individuals. But even for these people it plays little part in determining other aspects of their lives such as where they work, which trade union they belong to, who their friends are or who they would like their neighbours to be. For the vast majority of parents in the country (some ethnic groups excepted), the religion or voting habits of their future son-in-law's or daughter-in-law's family are of only passing interest and rarely the major cause of objection to the proposed marriage.

Identity in Northern Ireland

In this part of the UK, the pattern of identity outlined above does not apply. Here, ethnicity, family, politics, and religion are all inter-related, and social class has a comparatively minor role in establishing identity. Northern Ireland is a polarized society where most people are born into, and stay in, one or other of the two communities for the whole of their lives.

On one side of the divide are people whose ancestors came from lowland Scotland or England. They are self-consciously Protestant and want Northern Ireland to remain part of the UK. On the other side are people whose ancestors were native Irish. They are self-consciously Catholic and would like Northern Ireland to become part of the Irish Republic.

Although the two communities live side by side, their lives are segregated. They live in different housing estates, listen to different radio and television programmes, register with different doctors, take prescriptions to different chemists, march to commemorate different anniversaries and read different newspapers. Their children go to different schools, so that those who go on to university often find themselves mixing with people from the 'other' community for the first time in their lives. For the majority who do not go to university, merely talking to somebody from the other community is a rare event (Crossing the borders).

The extremes of these hard-line attitudes are gradually softening. It should also be noted that they apply to a lesser extent among the middle-classes. It is indicative that while in football, a mainly working-class sport, Northern Ireland and the Republic have separate teams, in rugby union, a more middle-class sport, there is only one team for the whole of Ireland, in which Protestants from the north play alongside Catholics from the south with no sign of disharmony whatsoever.

Being British

The largest possible sense of identity that a British person could feel is that they are British. How important is this to British people? Do they feel they 'belong' to Britain?

The short answers to these questions seem to be 'not very' and 'not really'. The 2001 census asked a 'national identity' question, in which people could tick as many boxes as they liked out of British, English, Irish, Scottish, Welsh or 'other'. Only 46% altogether ticked the 'British' box (fewer than the 51% who ticked the 'English' box) and only a third ticked it as their only choice (as compared to the half who ticked one of the four nation boxes as their only choice). Likewise, a poll of English teenagers in 2002 found that less than half felt the national flag was important to them. Half of the respondents to an opinion poll in 2007 even said they would emigrate if they could.

On the other hand, 75% of those same respondents agreed that they felt 'proud to be British'. How can we make sense of this apparent contradiction? The answer is that British people are not normally *actively* patriotic. They often feel uncomfortable if, in conversation with somebody from another country, that person refers to 'you' where 'you' means Britain or the British government. They do not like to feel that they are personally representing their country.

A divided community

This is the 'peace wall', built in 1984, which separates the Catholic Falls Road and the Protestant Shankill Road – a vivid sign of segregation in Belfast. Although the troubles in Northern Ireland are at an end (see chapter 12), the wall remains. In fact, there is now an economic reason for keeping it there – it is a favourite of visitors to Belfast who want 'Troubles Tourism'.

Crossing the borders

Schools Across Borders is an educational project based in Ireland which encourages secondary school pupils from divided or different communities to communicate with each other. In May 2007, it organized a Cross-Border Weekend, in which a small number of students from both communities in Northern Ireland and also some from Dublin participated. Here is an edited extract from a report of the weekend's activities:

Walking together as a group through the Springfield and Falls areas, our Belfast Protestant friends felt uneasy, but safe with the group! Then it was the turn of the Belfast Catholic and Dublin friends to sense similar levels of quaking in their boots, as we were brought through the Shankill by our Protestant friends! This was the first time any of the Belfast students had actually walked through these streets 'on the other side'. Everyone admitted that there was no real risk of intimidation, but it still felt intimidating! The exercise focused minds on what is needed to make progress: more walking, more friends, more reasons to visit these areas!

We will continue to carry the message that these students have started: to cross borders and to celebrate the role that all young people have in opening up the city to each other ... We encourage all young people in Belfast to do the same: keep crossing the borders. Get out there, make it go around!

Source: www.schoolsacrossborders.org/ cross_border.html

Notwithstanding this low-key approach to being British, the turn of the millennium saw the subject of 'Britishness' become a topic of great public concern in the country. There are several possible reasons for this explosion of interest. Perhaps it reflects the need to find common values in a multicultural society (see chapter 5). Perhaps it is the realization that the UK by itself now has far less influence on the rest of the world than it used to have, or perhaps it is the fear that the UK might actually break up (for both of these, see chapter 12).

However, it is not clear how much this concern for Britishness is felt by individual British people. Some feel that it is merely something encouraged in official circles and that the concern itself is actually very un-British! When in 2006, the government suggested there should be a British national day, many people scoffed at the idea; the fact that Britain does *not* have such a day is, they said, a perfect sign of Britishness – only younger, less stable nations have to bother with all that flag-waving rubbish! (There is actually a lot of support for the idea, but this is just because people would like another public holiday, which is something that Britain has very few of – see chapter 23).

The only time that public opinion really becomes patriotic is when it is felt that British identity – whatever that may be – is threatened from the outside, for instance through the activities of the European Union (see chapter 12). This is perhaps why the British cling so obstinately to certain distinctive ways of doing things (see chapter 5).

Personal identity: a sense of humour

Finally, how do British people think of themselves as individuals? What sort of a person does he or she like to think of himself or herself as? It is difficult to generalize. But if there is one personal quality which most British people cling to above all others, it is a sense of humour. Of course, most people in Britain, like most people in the world, would not like to be thought of as dishonest, cowardly, unkind, ugly, stupid, or just generally insignificant. But perhaps the worst shame of all for them would be to be regarded as a person with no sense of humour.

In Britain, you do not have to tell the best jokes to be humorous. Nor is there a proper time and place for humour. A mildly funny remark is appreciated in all but the most formal situations. It does not have to be especially clever. It is just an everyday way of talking. People expect it. Raising a smile or getting a laugh is a good enough reason for saying anything, even if it is something you don't mean. (It is for this reason that some people see the British as hypocritical.) And if the 'joke' is at your own expense, so much the better. The ability to laugh at yourself and to 'take a joke' is highly prized. The imperative to present yourself as having this quality is amazingly strong. A doctor was once asked how patients reacted to being told they had cancer. He said that, after the initial shock, their most common reaction was to make a joke out of it!

You may notice in the above comments two other personal qualities which are generally highly prized in Britain: bravery in the face of misfortune (sometimes known as the 'stiff upper lip') and modesty. The quality which connects these two is the sense of humour.

QUESTIONS

1 This chapter considers several factors that go towards creating a person's sense of identity. Some of these are more important in Britain and some not so important. Are the same factors the important ones in your country?

2 In the early years of the twentieth century, the playwright and social commentator George Bernard Shaw remarked that an Englishman only had to open his mouth to make another Englishman despise him. What was he talking about? Would he say the same thing today?

3 Do the social classes in your country define themselves in the same way as they do in Britain? Do language, accent, clothes, money, habits, and attitudes play the same roles in your country?

4 If you had been born and brought up in Britain, what ethnic identity would you prefer to have?

SUGGESTIONS

If you are interested in the different types of English spoken in Britain, *English Accents and Dialects* by Hughes and Trudgill (Edward Arnold) is an academic but accessible book with long example texts, which are available on recordings.

Pies and Prejudice: In Search of the North is an amusing book which says a lot about how (different kinds of) northern English people feel about themselves - and about the South.

Many comedy TV programmes depend for their humour on senses of identity and/or habits and values indicative of a certain identity. For British Asians, watch on TV or find DVDs of *Goodness Gracious Me* and *The Kumars at No. 42*. For social class in England, *Only Fools and Horses* portrays Cockney values and *Keeping Up Appearances* makes fun of the pretensions of some middle-class people. For professional identities, there is *The Office* and *The IT Crowd*.

A very readable study of how English people identify themselves by the way they behave is *Watching the English* by the anthropologist Kate Fox (Hodder & Stoughton). Also very readable is *Native Land* by another anthropologist, Nigel Barley (Penguin).

Making contact and finding your roots

Britain is a geographically mobile society. People's lives take them in such different directions that they meet and talk to thousands of people in their lives. Some of them become friends, but often only temporarily, as they then move on again. And, because extended family gatherings are rare, even family members can lose touch.

Doesn't this make British people lonely? Perhaps it does, if we are to believe evidence from the internet. In the year 2000, in the spare room of their north London house, Julie and Steve Pankhurst set up a website called *Friends Reunited*. They only did it because Julie was pregnant and wanted to trace any old school friends who had already had babies. But they had tapped into something big. The website took off like a rocket. Five years later, it had 12 million registered users and the Pankursts set up *Genes Reunited*, which rapidly became the country's largest ancestry site.

Websites of this kind have become enormously popular in Britain. In particular, tracing family roots is a booming activity. From being an arcane pastime for a few amateur historians, genealogy has entered the mainstream. It is so popular that when, in 2001, the complete data for the 1901 British census went online, the huge number of visitors made the site crash!

05 Attitudes

The British, like the people of every country, tend to be attributed with certain characteristics which are supposedly typical. However, it is best to be cautious about accepting such characterizations too easily. In the case of Britain, there are three reasons for this. The first three sections of this chapter deal with them in turn, and at the same time explore some images and characteristics of the British.

Stereotypes and change

Societies change over time while their reputations lag behind. Many things which are often regarded as typically British derive from books, songs or plays which were written a long time ago and which are no longer representative of modern life.

One example of this is the popular belief that Britain is a 'land of tradition'. This is what most tourist brochures claim. It is a reputation based on what can be seen in public life, on centuries of political continuity and on its attendant ceremonies. And at this level – the level of public life – it is true. The annual ceremony of the state opening of Parliament, for instance, carefully follows customs which are centuries old (see chapter 9). So does the military ceremony of 'trooping the colour'. Likewise, the changing of the guard outside Buckingham Palace never changes.

However, in their private everyday lives, the British are probably less inclined to follow tradition than the people of most other countries. There are very few age-old customs that are followed by the majority of families on certain special occasions. The country has fewer local parades or processions with genuine folk roots than most other countries. The English language has fewer sayings or proverbs in common everyday use than many other languages. The British are too individualistic for these things.

There are many examples of supposedly typical British habits which are simply not typical any more. For example, the stereotyped image of the London 'city gent' includes the wearing of a bowler hat. In fact, this type of hat has not been commonly worn for a long time.

Food and drink provide other examples. The traditional 'British' (or 'English') breakfast is a large 'fry-up' (see chapter 20) plus cereal with milk and also toast, butter and marmalade, all washed down with tea. In fact, very few people in Britain actually have this sort of breakfast. Most just have the cereal, tea and toast, or even less. What the vast majority of British people have in the mornings is therefore much closer to what

Land of tradition

In the early 1990s, London's famous red buses were privatized – that is, they stopped being state-owned and became privately owned. The different bus companies wanted to paint their buses in their own company colours. But many people, fond of the familiar red bus, were against this change and the government ruled that all buses had to stay red, both because this is what the people of London wanted and also because it believed this would be better for the tourist trade. For the same reason, when the iconic version of the London red bus, the famous Routemaster (see chapter 17), was taken out of regular service, it became a bus for tourist trips.

they call a 'continental' (i.e. mainland European) breakfast than it is to a British one. The image of the British as a nation of tea-drinkers is also somewhat outdated (see chapter 20). And the tradition of afternoon tea with biscuits, scones, sandwiches, or cake has always been a minority activity, confined to retired people and the leisured upper-middle class (although preserved in tea shops in tourist resorts).

Even when a British habit conforms to the stereotype, the wrong conclusions can sometimes be drawn from it. The British love of queueing is an example. Yes, British people do form queues when they wait for something, but this does not mean that they enjoy it. In 2007, supermarkets reported that no less than 65% of shoppers in Britain had personally witnessed, or even been victims of, 'queue rage'; that is people being abusive or violent about a delay or a perceived unfairness in a queue (because, for example, the person in front is not ready to pay when the cashier has finished, or has left goods on the conveyor belt while looking for more items). Research suggests that eight minutes is the 'tipping point'. It would therefore seem wrong to conclude that their habit of queuing shows that the British are a patient people.

English versus British

Because English culture dominates the cultures of the other three nations (see chapter 1), everyday habits, attitudes, and values among the peoples of the four nations are very similar. However, they are not identical, so that sometimes it is hard to know whether one is describing the British as a whole or just the English. The reason why people queue so much is one example (Why the British (or English?) queue). Another example is notable because it is so unusual – anti-intellectualism.

Among many people in Britain, there exists a suspicion of education and 'high culture'. This is manifested in a number of ways. For example, teachers and academic staff, although respected, do not have as high a status in society as they do in most other countries. Nobody normally proclaims their academic qualifications or title to the world at large. No professor would expect, or want, to be addressed as 'professor' on any but the most formal occasion.

Traditionally, large sections of both the upper and working class in Britain were not interested in their children getting to university (see chapter 14). This strange lack of enthusiasm for education has certainly decreased. Nevertheless, it is still unusual for parents to arrange extra private tuition for their children, even if they can easily afford it. And among the upper classes, too much intelligence and academic prowess in a person is still viewed with suspicion because it suggests this person might not be a 'team player'; among the working class, such attributes in a man are still sometimes regarded as effeminate (which is probably why girls generally do better than boys at school in England).

Why the British (or English?) queue

The Hungarian humourist George Mikes once wrote that 'An Englishman, even if he is alone, forms an orderly queue of one'. This implies a love of queuing for its own sake. But the British journalist A. A. Gill believes there is a more practical reason: 'The English queue because they have to. If they didn't, they'd kill each other'. In a book published in 2005, Gill argues that the English care about (un)fairness more than anything else and that therefore they are always angry about something. It is this anger, he says, which motivated so many great English engineers, inventors and social reformers in the past few centuries. And rather than let this anger turn to useless violence, he says, the English have developed 'heroic self-control'. Queueing is just one small example.

Gill's book brings up the English/British confusion again. Like many people who live in England, Gill considers himself to be not English but Scottish – and it is specifically the English that he is writing about. But in fact, many of those great engineers, inventors and reformers he mentions were Scottish! Even the title of Gill's book shows the confusion. It's supposed to be about the English but it's called *The Angry Island*. As you know, England is not an island.

English anti-intellectualism:
vocabulary

The slang word 'swot' was first used in English public schools (see chapter 14). It denoted someone who worked hard and did well academically. It was a term of abuse. Swots were not popular.

School life can still be tough for an academically minded pupil in England. If a student shows a desire to learn, they may be reviled as a 'teacher's pet'; if he or she is successful in the attempt, they may be reminded that 'nobody likes a smartarse'.

And it doesn't get much better in adult life. The word 'clever' often has negative connotations. It suggests a person who cannot quite be trusted (as in the expression, 'too clever by half'). And to refer to a person as somebody who 'gets all their ideas from books' is to speak of them negatively. It raises the suspicion that they are lacking in 'common sense', which is something the English value very highly.

Even the word 'intellectual' itself is subject to negative connotations. Here is a short extract from a diary written by a renowned (English) author and social observer (and therefore intellectual).

Colin Haycraft and I are chatting on the pavement when a man comes past wheeling a basket of shopping.

'Out of the way, you so-called intellectuals', he snarls, 'blocking the way.'

It's curious that it's the intellectual that annoys, though it must never be admitted to be the genuine article but always 'pseudo' or 'so-called'. It is, of course, only in England that 'intellectual' is an insult anyway.

Alan Bennett, *Writing Home*

Such attitudes are held consciously only by a small proportion of the population. And it isn't that people in Britain don't like to know things. They are, for example, passionate about quizzes, which are among the most popular of all TV programmes. Almost every pub and social club in the country holds regular 'quiz nights'. Factual knowledge is something to be proud of. But abstract thinking and scholarship is not. Many everyday words and expressions in the English language (English anti-intellectualism: vocabulary) testify to this anti-intellectual tendency.

Anti-intellectual attitudes can be found in all four nations of the Isles. However, they are probably better seen as a specifically English characteristic, and not a British one. The Scottish have always placed a high value on education for all classes. The Irish of all classes place a high value on being quick, ready, and able with words. The Welsh have long exported teachers to other parts of Britain and beyond.

A multicultural society

The third reason for caution about generalizations relates to the large-scale immigration to Britain from places beyond the four nations since the Second World War (see chapter 4). In its cities at least, Britain is a multicultural society. There are areas of London, for example, in which a distinctively Indian way of life predominates, with Indian shops, Indian clothes, and Indian languages.

These 'new British' people have brought widely differing sets of attitudes with them which sometimes diverge greatly from more traditional British ones. In some cases, clashes of values become apparent (Attitudes to multiculturalism). However, there is a limit to these divergences in comparison with those in the USA. There, the numbers in ethnic communities are larger and the physical spaces between them and other communities greater, so that it is possible for people to live their whole lives in such communities without ever really learning English. This hardly ever happens in Britain.

It is therefore still possible to talk about British characteristics in general (as the rest of this chapter does). In fact, the new British have made their own contribution to British life and attitudes. They have, for example, probably helped to make people more informal in their behaviour (see below) and they have changed the nature of the 'corner shop' (see chapters 4 and 15).

Conservatism

The British have rather few living folk traditions and are too individualistic to have many of the same everyday habits as each other. However, this does not mean that they like change. They don't. They may not behave in traditional ways, but they like symbols of tradition. For example, there are some very untraditional attitudes and habits with regard to the family in modern Britain (see chapter 4).

Nevertheless, politicians often cite their enthusiasm for 'traditional family values' (both parents married and living together, parents as the main source of authority for children, etc.) as a way of getting support.

In general, the British value continuity over modernity for its own sake. They do not consider it especially smart to live in a new house (in fact, there is prestige in living in an obviously old one – see chapter 19). They have a general sentimental attachment to older, supposedly safer times. A survey conducted in 2005 found that they believed pollution was worse than it had been 50 years before (when there were killer smogs – see chapter 3) and that they worked longer hours than 50 years before (when Saturday morning work was the norm for everybody). They did not even seem aware that they were far wealthier than people in the 1950s (when an average unemployed person could survive for just one month before running out of money – now the period is seven months). The British like their Christmas cards to depict scenes from past centuries (see chapter 23); they like their pubs to look old (see chapter 20); they complained bitterly when their system of currency was changed.

Being different

The British can be stubbornly conservative about anything which is perceived as a token of Britishness. In these matters, their conservatism can combine with their individualism – they are rather proud of being different. It is, for example, very difficult to imagine that they will ever change from driving on the left-hand side of the

Big Brother is watching you

It is a curious fact that, for a people who value privacy, the British have allowed themselves to become one of the most spied-upon nations in the world. In 2007, there were around four and a half million closed-circuit TV (CCTV) cameras in Britain. That's one for every 14 people in the country. One estimate claims that Britain now has more of them than the rest of Europe combined. In London, the average person is caught on one of these cameras about 300 times a day.

Attitudes to multiculturalism

In the twenty-first century, Britain is experiencing record levels of both immigration and emigration (see chapter 1). This means that the cultural backgrounds of people living in Britain are changing fast and becoming increasingly varied. This is one reason why 'multiculturalism' is a hot topic of debate in Britain these days.

In fact, people are often unclear about what is meant when this word is used. Does it suggest a 'salad bowl', in which the different ingredients, although mixed together and making an appetizing whole, are still distinct? Or does it suggest a 'melting pot', in which the ingredients all blend together, each making their contribution to a single overall taste?

The dominant perception seems to be that it is the 'salad-bowl' model that has been applied in Britain and there is a growing perception that it has gone too far. In 2004, Trevor Phillips, the chairman of the official Commission for Racial Equality, himself a black Caribbean, suggested that policies designed to recognize and respect different cultural groups may tend to keep these groups separate (so that they are not even in the same bowl). And of course separation leads to lack of understanding, which can lead to hostility. (Although overt racism is less common than it used to be, and probably less common than in many other parts of Europe, there are still thousands of racially or ethnically motivated attacks on people each year.)

Some members of mainstream British culture interpret 'multiculturalism' in yet another way. They seem to think it means their own cultural ingredients are simply excluded from the bowl or pot. Around Christmas time, for example, the press is full of horror stories of the cancellation of school nativity plays and the banning of appearances of Father Christmas or of 'Merry Christmas' signs in town centres. These things happen because some people in positions of authority believe that public celebration of a Christian festival would offend non-Christians, and would also perhaps be against the law.

In most cases, both beliefs are wrong. But in response to fears of this kind – and more general concerns about the nature of 'Britishness', the government has changed the procedure for becoming a British citizen. Previously, applicants simply had to be resident for five years and have a record of good behaviour, at which point they received a naturalization certificate through the post. Now they have to study an official book called Life in the UK and then pass a 'citizenship test' based on it. After that, they attend a formal ceremony at which their citizenship is conferred upon them. (Interestingly, when Life in the UK was first published, it emerged that most British born-and-bred people could not achieve the required 75% pass mark!)

Suspicion of the metric system

Suspicion of metric measures is an undercurrent that runs through British society. Here is a very short extract from an article in the *Radio Times* (see chapter 16) commenting on a BBC documentary programme about Hadrian's Wall (see chapter 2).

> *[We were informed that]* '*stretching from Newcastle to Carlisle for 118 kilometres, Hadrian's Wall was four metres high and three metres wide'. Are we being fed kilometres and metres by the back door? The nation deserves to know.*

John Peel in *The Radio Times* 2–8 December 2000.

The writer is not trying to make a serious point here. It is just a remark in an article which is generally humorous in tone. (The statement 'the nation deserves to know' is an ironic echo of the pompous demands of politicians.) But the fact the writer considered it worth drawing attention to the measurements quoted is indicative. He knew it would resonate with his readers.

The prestige of the countryside

Most people like their cars to look clean and smart. But a surprisingly large number of car owners in Britain now spend time making them look dirty. Deliberately! These people are owners of 4x4s, those big spacious vehicles with a lot of ground clearance. They are expensive and a status symbol but when all they are used for is the school run and trips to the supermarket, other people sneer at the owners.

Many 4x4 owners have found an answer. Spray-on mud! They buy this amazing product (which has a secret ingredient to make it stick but no stones so it doesn't scratch paintwork) on the internet. This way, they can give their vehicles that just-back-from-the-country look.

road to driving on the right. It doesn't matter that nobody can think of any intrinsic advantage of driving on the left. Why should they change just to be like everyone else? Britain has so far resisted pressure from business people to adopt Central European Time, remaining stubbornly one hour behind; and it continues to start its financial year not, as other countries do, at the beginning of the calendar year but rather at the beginning of April.

Systems of measurement are another example. For decades now, British authorities have been promoting the scales that are used nearly everywhere else in the world (which in Britain are known collectively as the 'metric system'). But they have had only partial success. It is only in the twenty-first century that people in Britain have become accustomed to buying petrol for their cars in litres or have started to understand the TV weather forecasters when they mention a temperature on the Celsius scale (and many still have to 'translate' it into Fahrenheit – see chapter 3). British people continue to measure distances and themselves using scales of measurement that are not used anywhere else in Europe. (How tall? How far? How heavy?). British manufacturers are obliged to give the weight of their packaged goods in kilos and grams, but many also give the equivalent in pounds and ounces because they know that the latter are more likely to mean something to people (see chapter 15).

In fact, this last aspect of measurement has become a celebrated public issue in Britain. In 2001, two greengrocers in the north-east of England were prosecuted by their local government authority for selling their fruit and vegetables by the pound. The case attracted huge national publicity. They became know as the 'metric martyrs'. A Metric Martyrs Fund was set up and received so many donations that it was able to hire the country's best lawyers. Since then, the fund has supported many other traders who have fallen foul of the law regarding weights and measures. But the issue at stake for the fund is not just pounds and ounces. In 2002, it defended a restaurant which was threatened with prosecution for the opposite reason – not for refusing metric measures but for using them! British law stipulates that draught beer must be sold in pints or parts thereof, but this was an Austrian themed restaurant and so the beer was sold in one litre mugs. In 2006, the fund supported a brewing company over the same matter. What drives the Metric Martyrs Fund and its supporters, then, is not principally a love of British habits of measurement or a hatred of EU regulations in particular; it is a (characteristically British) hatred of conformist regulations in general.

Love of nature

Britain was the first country in the world to appoint a government-sponsored conservation body (the Nature Conservancy, in 1949) and it was in Britain that the first large green pressure group was founded (the World Wildlife Fund in 1961, now the Worldwide Fund for Nature). This is not a coincidence. Ever since they became a nation of city dwellers, the British have had a reverence for nature and an idealized vision of the countryside. To the British, the countryside has almost none of the negative associations which it has in some countries, such as poor facilities, lack of educational opportunities, unemployment and poverty. To them, the countryside means peace and quiet, beauty, health, and no crime. Indeed, having a house 'in the country' carries prestige – see The prestige of the countryside. Most of them would live in a country village if they thought they could find a way of earning a living there. Ideally, this village would consist of thatched cottages (see chapter 19) built around an area known as the 'village green'. Nearby there would be a pond with ducks on it. Nowadays, such a village is not actually very common, but it is a stereotypical picture that is well-known to the British.

Some history connected with the building of high-speed rail links through the channel tunnel (see chapter 17) is indicative of the British attitude. On the continental side of the tunnel, communities battled with each other to get the new line built through their town. It would be good for local business. But on the English side, the opposite occurred. Nobody wanted the rail link near them! Communities battled with each other to get the new line built somewhere else. Never mind business – they wanted to preserve their peace and quiet. (That is one reason why the high-speed link on the British side was completed so much later.)

Perhaps this love of the countryside is another aspect of British conservatism. The countryside represents stability. Those who live in towns and cities take an active interest in country matters and they regard it as both a right and a privilege to be able to go 'into the country' when they want. Large areas of the country are official 'national parks' where almost no building is allowed. There is an organization called the Ramblers' Association to which more than a hundred thousand enthusiastic country walkers belong. It is in constant battle with landowners to keep open the public 'rights of way' across their lands. Maps can be bought which mark the routes of all the public footpaths in the country. Walkers often stay the night at a youth hostel. The Youth Hostels Association is a charity whose aim is 'to help all, especially young people of limited means, to a greater knowledge, love and care of the countryside'.

When they cannot get into the countryside, many British people still spend a lot of their time with 'nature'. They grow plants. Gardening is one the most popular hobbies in the country, and gardening programmes on radio and TV are also very popular. When in 2002, a well-known TV gardener called Alan Titchmarsh had his own series, sales of basic gardening tools such as rakes rose by 50%. Indeed, all he had to do was advise the use of a particular implement and within days they had sold out across Britain. The Garden Industry Manufacturers' Association had to ask the BBC for advance warning about what would be mentioned in the following week's show! Even those people who do not have a garden can participate. Each local authority owns several areas of land which it rents very cheaply to these people in small parcels. On these 'allotments', people grow mainly vegetables.

How tall?

If a British person asks you how tall you are, it would probably not help for you to say something like 'one, sixty-three'. He or she is not likely to understand. Instead, you would have to say 'five foot four'. This means 5 feet and 4 inches.

1 inch = 2.53 cm

12 inches = 1 foot = 30.48 cm

How far?

If you see a road sign saying 'Oxford 50', this does not mean that Oxford is 50 kilometres away – it is 50 miles away. All road signs in Britain are shown in miles. Similarly, for shorter distances, most people talk about yards rather than metres.

1 yard = 0.92 m

1760 yards = 1 mile = 1.6 km

How heavy?

Similarly, it would not help a British person to hear that you weigh 67 kilos. It will be more informative if you say you are 'ten stone seven' or 'ten-and-a-half stone' – that is, 10 stone and 7 pounds.

1 lb = 0.456 kg

14 lbs = 1 stone = 6.38 kg

Along with love of nature comes a strong dislike of anything that seems 'unnatural'. In the early years of this century, it was government policy to make Britain 'the European hub' of genetically modified (GM) plant technology. But opposition to GM was so strong that all GM companies withdrew their application to grow GM crops in Britain. Similarly, at the time of writing, most people are against the government's proposal to build a new generation of nuclear power stations.

Love of animals

Rossendale Memorial Gardens in Lancashire is just one of more than a hundred animal cemeteries in Britain. It was started by a local farmer who ran over his dog with a tractor. He was so upset that he put up a headstone in its memory. Now, Rossendale has thousands of graves and plots for caskets of ashes, with facilities for every kind of animal, from a budgie to a lioness. As in America, many people are prepared to pay quite large sums of money to give their pets a decent burial. The British tend to have a sentimental attitude to animals. Half of the households in Britain keep at least one domestic pet. Most of them do not bother with such grand arrangements when it dies, but there are millions of informal graves in people's back gardens. Moreover, the status of pets is taken seriously. It is, for example, illegal to run over a dog in your car and then keep on driving. You have to stop and inform the owner.

But the love of animals goes beyond sentimental attachment to domestic pets. Wildlife programmes are by far the most popular kind of television documentary. Millions of families have 'bird tables' in their gardens. These are raised platforms on which birds can feed, safe from local cats, during the winter months. There is even a special teaching hospital (called Tiggywinkles) which treats injured wild animals.

Perhaps this overall concern for animals is part of the British love of nature. Studies indicating that some wild species is decreasing in numbers become prominent articles in the national press. In 2000, for example, *The Independent* offered a prize of £5,000 for the first scientific paper which established the reason for the decline of the sparrow. Thousands of people are enthusiastic bird-watchers. This peculiarly British pastime often involves spending hours lying in wet and cold undergrowth trying to get a glimpse of a rare species.

Public-spiritedness and amateurism

In public life, Britain has traditionally followed what might be called 'the cult of the talented amateur', in which being too professionally dedicated is looked at with suspicion. 'Only doing your job' has never been accepted as a justification for actions. The assumption behind many of the features of public life in Britain is that society is best served by everybody 'chipping in' – that is, by lots of people giving a little of their free time to help in a variety of matters. This can be seen in the structure of the civil service (see chapter 8), in the circumstances under which MPs do their work (see chapter 9), in the use of unpaid

The National Trust

A notable indication of the British reverence for both the countryside and the past is the strength of the National Trust. This is an officially recognized charity whose aim is to preserve as much of Britain's countryside and as many of its historic buildings as possible by acquiring them 'for the nation'. With more than three million members, it is the largest conservation charity in Europe. It is actually the third largest landowner in Britain (after the Crown and the Forestry Commission). Included in its property is more than 600 miles of the coastline. The importance of its work has been supported by several laws, among which is one which does not allow even the government to take over any of its land without the approval of Parliament.

❀ National Trust

non-lawyers to run much of the legal system (see chapter 11) and in some aspects of the education system (see chapter 14).

This characteristic, however, is on the decline. In all the areas mentioned above, 'professionalism' has turned from having a negative connotation to having a positive one. Nevertheless, some new areas of amateur participation in public life have developed in the last decade, such as the increase in Neighbourhood Watch schemes (see chapter 11). Moreover, tens of thousands of 'amateurs' are still actively involved in charity work (see chapter 18). Indeed, such work is the basis of many people's social life. As well as giving direct help to those in need, they raise money by organizing jumble sales, fêtes and flag days (on which they stand in the street asking for money in return for small stickers which people can put onto their clothes). This voluntary activity is a basic part of British life. It has often been so effective that whole countrywide networks have been set up without government help (Self-help). It is no accident that many of the world's largest and

The RSPCA

The general desire for animal welfare has official recognition. Cruelty to animals of any kind is a criminal offence, and offences are investigated by a well-known charity, the Royal Society for the Prevention of Cruelty to Animals (RSPCA). It may be a typical quirk of British life for this organization to have royal patronage, while the equivalent charity for children – the National Society for the Prevention of Cruelty to Children (the NSPCC) – does not.

The great foxhunting debate

Throughout the twentieth century, foxhunting was the occasional pastime of a tiny minority of the British population (no more than a few tens of thousands). Traditionally, 'hunting' (as the foxhunters call it) works like this: A group of people on horses, dressed up in special riding clothes (some of them in eighteenth-century red jackets), ride around the countryside with a pack of hounds. When these dogs pick up the scent of a fox, a horn is blown, somebody shouts 'Tally ho!' and then dogs, horses and riders all chase the fox. Often the fox gets away. But if it does not, the dogs get to it first and tear it to pieces.

As you might guess, in a country of animal lovers, where most people live in towns and cities, foxhunting is generally regarded with disgust. In fact, in 2004 Parliament voted to make it illegal.

But that is not the end of the story. In the year leading up to the ban on foxhunting, there were demonstrations in London involving hundreds of thousands of people. Blood was spilt as demonstrators fought with both anti-hunt groups and with the police. Some pro-hunt demonstrators even staged a brief 'invasion' of Parliament.

And since the ban? Well, the debate continues. At the time of writing, it is the policy of the main opposition party to lift the ban. Meanwhile, hunting

groups (known as 'hunts') have continued their activities and claim that their memberships have increased. Officially, they have turned to 'trail hunting', in which the dogs follow a scent rather than a live fox, and which therefore is not illegal. But in practice it is difficult to control dogs if they pick up the scent of a live fox and there are allegations that the spirit (if not the letter) of the law is being routinely broken.

How can all this have happened? How can such a basically trivial matter, with direct relevance to so few people, have excited such passions among so many people? And how can it be that some people are apparently willing and able to break the law? The answer is that this single issue draws together many features which are dear to British people's hearts.

Love of animals To many people, foxhunting is nothing more than barbaric cruelty to animals which has no place in a civilized twenty-first century society – and the fact that it is such a noisy and public celebration of barbarism only makes it worse. But foxhunters argue that fox numbers have to be controlled and that other methods of killing them are crueller.

Social class Foxhunting is associated with the upper class and the rich and there is anger that such people are still appaerently able to indulge in organized

violence against an animal. Many feel that it proves the old saying about there being 'one law for the rich and one for the poor'. On the other hand, foxhunters argue that such a 'class-war' view is an urban-dweller's misunderstanding of the fabric of rural life, both socially and economically.

Reverence for the countryside This debate pits country people against 'townies'. Many of the former see the ban as a symbol of discrimination against them by the urban majority. And because of their romanticized idea of the countryside, some of the latter are willing to accept that they do not understand 'country ways', and so perhaps they do not have the right to oppose foxhunting, and a few have even come to view it as a symbol of an ideal, rural England.

Individualism and conservatism The British always feel a bit uncomfortable about banning anything when it does not directly hurt other people, especially if, like foxhunting, it is a centuries-old tradition. There is also a long tradition of disobedience to 'unjust' laws. Even some of those who regard foxhunting as cruel suspect this might be one of those cases and have doubts about the ban.

At the time of writing it is not clear how the situation will develop.

most well-known charities (e.g. Oxfam, Amnesty International, and Save the Children) began in Britain. Note also that, each year, the country's blood transfusion service collects over two million donations from unpaid volunteers.

Formality and informality

The tourist view of Britain involves lots of formal ceremonies. Encouraged by this, some people have drawn the conclusion that the British are rather formal in their general behaviour. This is not true. There is a difference between observing formalities and being formal in everyday life. Attitudes towards clothes are a good indication of this difference. It all depends on whether a person is playing a public role or a private role. When people are 'on duty', they have to obey some quite rigid rules on this matter. A male bank employee, for example, is expected to wear a suit and tie, even if he cannot afford a very smart one.

On the other hand, when people are not playing a public role – when they are just being themselves – there seem to be no rules at all. The British are probably more tolerant of 'strange' clothing than people in most other countries (The scruffy British). What you wear is considered to be your own business. You may find, for example, the same bank employee, on his lunch break in hot weather, walking through the streets with his tie round his waist and his collar unbuttoned. He is no longer 'at work', so he can look how he likes – and for his employers to criticize him for his appearance would be seen as a gross breach of privacy.

This difference between formalities and formality is the key to what people from other countries sometimes experience as a coldness among the British. The key is this: being friendly in Britain often involves showing that you are not bothering with the formalities. This means *not* addressing someone by his or her title (Mr, Mrs, Professor, etc.), *not* dressing smartly when entertaining guests, *not* shaking hands when meeting and *not* saying 'please' when making a request. When they avoid doing these things with you, the British are not being unfriendly or disrespectful – they are implying that you are in the category 'friend', and so all the rules can be ignored. To address someone by their title or to say 'please' is to observe formalities and therefore distancing. The same is true of shaking hands. Although this sometimes has the reputation of being a very British thing to do, it is actually rather rare. Most people would do it only when being introduced to a stranger or when meeting an acquaintance (but not a close friend) after a long time.

Similarly, most British people do not feel welcomed if, on being invited to somebody's house, they find the host in smart clothes and a grand table set for them. They do not feel flattered by this – they feel intimidated. It makes them feel they can't relax. Buffet-type meals, in which people do not sit down at table to eat, are a common form of hospitality. If you are in a British person's house and are told to 'help yourself' to something, your host is not being rude or suggesting that you are of no importance – he or she is showing that you are completely accepted like 'one of the family'.

The British, especially the English, have a reputation for being reserved in their dealings with other people, for being polite rather than openly friendly or hostile (A hundred ways to say 'sorry'). This reputation is probably still justified. For example, an opinion poll at the end of 2007 found that the single aspect of everyday life which worried British people more than anything else (more than immigration, terrorism, or personal debt) was 'anti-social behaviour'; that is, other people being rude or inconsiderate. The only emotion habitually displayed in public is laughter. However, there are signs that this traditional habit of reserve is breaking down. Although it is still not the dominant convention, more and more people now kiss when meeting a friend (both women and women, and men and women do this, but still only rarely men and men). Perhaps the sight of all kinds of extreme emotions on reality TV shows has made British people more comfortable with the public display of emotions. And certainly, they shocked themselves by their very public outpouring of grief following the sudden death of Princess Diana in 1997. It is possible, in fact, that the everyday behaviour of the British is returning to the more emotional tenor which it had in the centuries before the Victorian 'stiff upper lip' became dominant.

Privacy and sex

The idea of privacy underlies many aspects of British life. It is not just a matter of privacy in your own home (see chapter 19). Just as important is the individual's right to keep personal information private. Despite the increase in informality, it is still seen as rude to ask somebody what are called 'personal' questions (for example, about how much money they earn and about their family or sex life) unless you know them very well.

The modern British attitude to sex is an example of how, while moral attitudes have changed, the habit of privacy is still deeply ingrained. British (like American) public life has a reputation for demanding puritanical standards of behaviour. Revelations about extra-marital affairs or other deviations from what is considered normal in private life have, in the past, been the ruin of many public figures. This would seem to indicate a lack of respect for privacy – that the British do not allow their politicians a private life. However, appearances in this matter can be misleading. In all such cases, the disgrace of the politician concerned has not been because of his sexual activity. It has happened because this activity was mixed up with a matter of national security, or involved breaking the law, or the abuse of his position. The scandal was that in these cases, the politician has not kept his private life and public role separate enough. When no such connections are involved, there are no negative consequences for the politician. In 2004, there were no calls for a top government minister to resign when it was

A hundred ways to say 'sorry'

People from other countries often comment on how polite the English (or do they mean the British?) are. And it is true that they say 'thank you' more often than the people of other countries. They also say 'sorry' a lot. But 'sorry' can mean an awful lot of different things. Here is a list (adapted) from A. A. Gill.

I apologize.
I don't apologize.
You can take this as an apology but we both know it isn't one.
Excuse me.
I am sad for you.
I can't hear you.
I don't understand you.
You don't understand me.
I don't believe it.
I don't believe you.
I'm interrupting you.
Will you (please) shut up!
I am angry.
I am very angry.

It all depends on the way you say it. But why are there so many ways? Gill comments:

Being able to apologize without meaning it – and so without losing face – but at the same time allowing the other person, having got their apology, to back down is a masterfully delicate piece of verbal engineering.

The scruffy British

Although the British are much more interested in clothes than they used to be, they are still, by the standards of other western European countries, not very good at wearing them. If you are somewhere in a Mediterranean holiday area, it is usually possible to spot the British tourist from other European tourists – he or she is the one who looks badly dressed! And although they spend more money on clothes than they used to, many people get some of their clothes from second-hand charity shops – and are not at all embarrassed to admit this.

Supporting the underdog

Some customs of road use illustrate the British tendency to be on the side of 'the underdog' (i.e. the weaker side in any competition). On the roads, the underdog is the pedestrian. The law states that if a person has just one foot on a zebra crossing, then vehicles must stop. And they usually do. Conversely, British pedestrians interpret the colour of the human figure at traffic lights as advice, not as instruction. If the figure is red but no cars are approaching, they feel perfectly entitled to cross the road immediately. In Britain, jaywalking (crossing the road by dodging in between cars) has never been illegal.

Lovely weather we're having

The well-known stereotype that the British are always talking about the weather can be explained in the combination of the demands of both privacy and informality. Unlike many others, this stereotype is actually true to life. But constant remarks about the weather at chance meetings are not the result of polite conventions. They are not obligatory. Rather, they are the result of the fact that, on the one hand, personal questions would be rude while, at the same time, silence would also be rude. The weather is a very convenient topic with which to 'fill the gap'.

revealed he was having an affair with a married woman. But after it was revealed that he had used his position to secure this woman certain advantages, there were, and eventually he was forced to do so.

At the public level, Britain seems to have dispensed with sexual puritanism almost completely. Until quite recently, references to sex in popular entertainment were clothed in innuendo and clumsy double entendre. These days they are explicit. However, at the personal level, it seems that sex is still treated as an absolutely private matter. Sex may no longer be 'bad' but it is still embarrassing. In 2002, a survey found that only a minority of the children who phone a child-support line are seeking help because of bullying or physical abuse (which was why such lines were set up); almost half were from children seeking the most basic advice about sex and pregnancy. It also found that only one in three teenagers said they felt able to talk to their parents about sex. Sex education in schools remains only partial, largely because teachers are too embarrassed to deal with it. The Victorian undercurrent remains, and this may explain why Britain has the highest rate of unwanted teenage pregnancies in Europe.

The same mixture of tolerance and embarrassment can be seen in the official attitude to prostitution in Britain. It is not illegal to be a prostitute in Britain, but it is illegal to publicly behave like one. It is against the law to 'solicit' – that is, to do anything in public to find customers.

QUESTIONS

1 Frequent reference is made in this chapter and the previous one to British individualism. How many examples can you find? Can you think of any others?

2 In what sense is the Metric Martyrs Fund in Britain misleadingly named? Can you think of any similar organization in your country?

3 Is privacy a value which is respected in your country as much as it is respected in Britain? And in the same way?

4 Which, if any, of the British characteristics described in this chapter would you regard as also characteristic of people in your country?

SUGGESTIONS

George Mikes' humorous books about the English, such as *How to be an Alien, How to be Inimitable,* and *How to be Decadent* (Penguin) are easy and fun to read. As they span 30 years, they offer insights into how attitudes in Britain changed in the final decades of the twentieth century.

Read *Notes from a Small Island* by Bill Bryson, a humorous and perceptive tour around Britain by an 'outsider' who has lived there for many years.

Try *The Angry Island* by A. A. Gill and see what you think.

06 Political life

Look at the extract from a fictional diary below. It is taken from the book of *Yes, Prime Minister*, a popular radio and television comedy from the 1980s. Like all political satire, this programme could only have been popular because people believe that it is, at least partly, a true reflection of reality. It can therefore serve to illustrate the British attitude to politicians and politics.

The killer instinct

In this extract, from *Yes, Prime Minister*, the Prime Minister has just resigned. There are two candidates to be the new Prime Minister, Eric Jeffries and Duncan Short, both of them ministers in the present government. Another minister, Jim Hacker, also wants the job. He has recently learnt some scandalous information about events in the pasts of the other two candidates, so now he has the opportunity to make them withdraw. This is an extract from his diary.

I told Duncan that some information had come my way. Serious information. To do with his personal financial operations. I referred to the collapse of Continental and General. He argued that there was nothing improper about that. I replied that technically there wasn't, but if you looked at it in conjunction with a similar case at Offshore Securities ... I indicated that, if he stayed in the running for PM[1], I would be obliged to share my knowledge with senior members of the party, the Fraud Squad, and so forth. The Americans would also have to know. And Her Majesty ...

He panicked. 'Hang on! Financial matters can be misinterpreted.'

I sipped my drink and waited. It didn't take long. He said that he didn't really want Number Ten[2] at all. He felt that the Foreign Office was a much better job in many ways. 'But I won't support Eric!' he insisted hotly.

'How would it be if you transferred all your support to someone else?' I suggested.

Duncan looked blank. 'Who?'

'Someone who recognised your qualities. Someone who'd want you to stay on as Foreign Secretary. Someone who would be discreet about Continental and General. Someone you trust.'

Gradually, I saw it dawning upon him. 'Do you mean – you?' he asked.

I pretended surprise. 'Me? I have absolutely no ambitions in that direction.'

'You do mean you,' he observed quietly. He knows the code.

I told Eric what I knew. He went pale. 'But you said you were going to help me get elected Prime Minister.'

I pointed out that my offer to help him was before my knowledge of the shady lady from Argentina. And others. 'Look, Eric, as party Chairman I have my duty. It would be a disaster for the party if you were PM and it came out. I mean, I wouldn't care to explain your private life to Her Majesty, would you?'

'I'll withdraw,' he muttered.

I told him reassuringly that I would say no more about it. To anyone.

He thanked me nastily and snarled that he supposed that bloody Duncan would now get Number Ten.

'Not if I can help it,' I told him.

'Who then?'

I raised my glass to him, smiled and said, 'Cheers.'

The penny dropped[3]. So did his lower jaw. 'You don't mean – you?'

Again I put on my surprised face. 'Me?' I said innocently. 'Our children are approaching the age when Annie and I are thinking of spending much more time with each other.'

He understood perfectly. 'You do mean you.'

Adapted from *Yes, Prime Minister* by Antony Jay & Jonathan Lynn

[1] PM is short for 'Prime Minister'
[2] Number Ten Downing Street is where the Prime Minister lives
[3] Eric finally understood (that Hacker intended to be PM)

The public attitude to politics

Politicians do not have a good reputation with the British people. To describe someone as 'a politician' is to criticize him or her, suggesting a lack of trustworthiness. It is not that people hate their politicians. They just regard them with suspicion. They do not expect them to use their position to amass personal wealth – and any stories of them 'fiddling' their expenses always makes the headlines. But they do expect them to be frequently dishonest. People are not really shocked when the government is caught lying. On the other hand, they would be very shocked indeed if it was discovered that the government was doing anything definitely illegal.

At an earlier point in the 'diary', Jim Hacker is wondering why the Prime Minister has resigned. He does not believe the rumour that there are one million pounds' worth of diamonds in the Prime Minister's house. This is partly because he does not think the Prime Minister could be so corrupt but also because 'it's never been officially denied ... The first rule of politics is Never Believe Anything Until It's Been Officially Denied'. This is the basis of the joke in the extract. Duncan and Eric are only sure that Jim wants to be Prime Minister when he implies that he doesn't!

The lack of enthusiasm for politicians is reflected in the general ignorance of who they are. Less than half of the adults in Britain know the name of their local Member of Parliament (MP), even though there is just one of these for each area. Many do not even know the names of the important government ministers or leaders of the major political parties. Another indication is the comparative lack of generosity with regard to politician's expenses (Freeloaders!).

The British were not always so unenthusiastic. In centuries past, it was a maxim that nobody should mention politics or religion in polite conversation. If anybody did, there was a danger that the conversation would become too heated and that people would become violent. However, there has been no real possibility of a revolution or even of a radical change in the style of government for almost two centuries now. This stability is taken for granted. Most people rarely become passionate about politics and nobody regards it as a 'dangerous' topic of conversation. They are more likely to regard it as a boring topic of conversation. Over the years, this lack of enthusiasm has increased. But it has not turned to complete disenchantment. A general feeling of confidence in the stability and workability of the system remains.

Yes, Prime Minister is just one of many programmes and publications devoted to political satire. All of them are consistently and bitingly critical. Moreover, their criticism is typically not about particular policies but about the attitudes of politicians, their alleged dishonesty and disloyalty, and the general style of political life. Given this, you might think that people would be angry, that there would be demands for a 'clean-up', even public demonstrations. Not at all! The last demonstrations about such matters took place 160 years ago.

Freeloaders!

A freeloader is somebody who arranges to get food, drink, and other benefits without having to pay or work for them. The British media is fond of suggesting that this is what government ministers and MPs are. It often has stories about the 'scandalous' amounts of money they spend in the course of their official duties. Fingers are pointed at individuals who, for example, take a special flight across the Atlantic rather than an ordinary one, or stay at five-star hotels rather than cheaper ones. Figures are often published showing the total value of the 'perks' of government ministers – their rent-free residences, the cars and drivers at their disposal, and so on.

But really, this is a peculiarly British preoccupation. British politicians generally live poorly when compared to their counterparts in other European countries. British public life is habitually mean with expenses. As one British minister said in 1999, 'When you go abroad, the hospitality exceeds ours. The food and wine on offer has to be sampled to be believed'. On the other hand, 'the wine served at our receptions would be rejected from the Oddbins bargain basement. It is filth'. (Oddbins is a chain of drinks shops.)

Other countries regard the eating, travelling and entertaining standards of their government representatives as a matter of national prestige. But not the British. More important to them is that their politicians don't get too many big ideas about themselves.

You might also think that the politicians themselves would be worried about the negative picture that these satires paint of them. Apparently not! On the back cover of the 1989 edition of *Yes, Prime Minister*, for instance, there was a tribute from Margaret Thatcher, the real Prime Minister of Britain at the time. In it, she refers to the book's 'closely observed portrayal of what goes on in the corridors of power' (suggesting it is accurate) and how this portrayal 'has given me hours of pure joy'.

In Britain, it is generally accepted that politics is a dirty business, a necessary evil. Therefore, politicians make sure that they do not appear too keen to do the job. They present themselves as being politicians out of a sense of public duty. That is why, in the extract, Jim Hacker does not suggest that he actually wants to be Prime Minister. To admit this openly would make him seem dangerously keen on power for its own sake.

The style of democracy

Although they may not have much respect for the present institutions of the law (see chapter 11), the British have a deep respect for the principle of law. Of course, lots of crimes are committed, as in any other country, but there is little systematic lawbreaking by large sections of the population. For example, tax evasion is not the national pastime that it is said to be in some countries.

However, while 'the law' as a concept is respected, the British are comparatively unenthusiastic about making new laws. The traditional feeling is that, while you have to have laws sometimes, wherever possible it is best to do without them. In many aspects of life, the country has comparatively few rules and regulations. This lack of regulation works both ways. Just as there are comparatively few rules telling the individual what he or she must or must not do, so there are comparatively few rules telling the government what it can or cannot do. Two unique aspects of British life will make this clear.

First, Britain is one of the very few European countries whose citizens do not have identity cards. Before the 1970s, when tourism to foreign countries became popular (and so passports became more common), most people in the country went through life without ever owning a document whose main purpose was to identify them. British people are not obliged to carry identification with them. You do not even have to have your driving licence with you in your car. (If the police ask to see it, you have 24 hours to take it to them.)

Second, it was not until this century that a law was passed which entitles people to demand information held by public bodies. Moreover, this Freedom of Information Act is not quite as free as its name suggests. People usually have to pay to get the information they want. In addition, many requests for information are refused on the grounds that disclosure is 'not in the public interest' and the Act does not apply to the increasing number of private companies

Official Secrets

In 1992, the existence of MI6, the British Secret Service, was publicly admitted by government for the first time. Nobody was surprised. Everybody already knew that there was a secret service, and that its name was MI6. But the admission itself was a surprise. British governments do not like public revelations of their activities, even if these are no longer secret. (In this case, the reason for the new openness was that, with the cold war over, it was considered necessary to admit the existence of MI6, so that it could justify why it needed money from taxpayers.)

During the 1980s, for instance, the government tried to prevent the publication of the book *Spycatcher* (the memoirs of an MI6 agent), even after it had already been published in several other countries and could therefore not contain any genuine secrets.

Despite greater general openness, the British government still sometimes charges people with breaking the Official Secrets Act. In 2007 it successfully prosecuted a government official and a political researcher, who were sent to prison for six months and three months respectively, for telling the press about what the American president said at a meeting with the British Prime Minister. It even tried to prevent the press from reporting this same case, but was eventually unsuccessful.

The headquates of MI6 on the bank of the Thames at Vauxhall, London.

engaged in public work. Finally, and ironically, the '30-year rule', which restricts access to government papers for 30 years, is still in place. Indeed, the traditional habit of 'discretion' in public life is still there. There is also a law (the Official Secrets Act) which obliges many government employees not to tell anyone about the details of their work. It seems that in Britain, both your own identity and also the information which the government has about your identity are regarded as private matters.

These two aspects are characteristic of the relationship in Britain between the individual and the state. To a large degree, the traditional assumption is that both should leave each other alone as much as possible. The duties of the individual towards the state are confined to not breaking the law and paying taxes. There is no national service (military or otherwise), people are not obliged to vote at elections if they can't be bothered, and people do not have to register a change of address with a government authority.

Similarly, the government in Britain has a comparatively free hand. It would be correct to call the country 'a democracy' in the generally accepted sense of this word. But in Britain, this democracy does not involve much participation in governing and lawmaking. There is no concept of these things being done 'by the people'. If the government wants to make an important change in the way that the country is run – to change, for example, the electoral system or the powers of the Prime Minister – it does not have to ask the people. It does not even have to have a special vote in Parliament in which an especially high proportion of MPs must agree.

In many countries, an important change of this nature – a constitutional change – cannot be made without a referendum, in which everybody in the country has the chance to vote 'yes' or 'no'. In other countries, such as the USA, people often have the chance to vote on particular proposals for changing laws that directly affect their everyday life, such as smoking in public places or the location of a new hospital. Nothing like this happens in Britain. There has only been one countrywide referendum in history (in 1975, on whether the country should stay in the European Community). In Britain, democracy has never meant that the people have a hand in the running of the country; rather it means that they choose who is to govern the country, and then let them get on with it.

The constitution

Britain is a constitutional monarchy. That is, it is a country governed by a king or queen who accepts the advice of a parliament. It is also a parliamentary democracy. That is, it is a country whose government is controlled by a parliament elected by the people. In other words, the basic system is not so different from anywhere else in Europe. The highest positions in the government are filled by members of the directly elected parliament. In Britain, as in many European countries, the official head of state, whether a monarch (e.g. Belgium, the Netherlands, Denmark) or a president (e.g. Germany, Greece, Italy) has little real power.

However, there are features of the British system of government which make it different from other countries and which are not 'modern' at all. Most notably, Britain is almost alone among modern states in that it does not have 'a constitution'. Of course, there are rules, regulations, principles and procedures for the running of the country – all the things that political scientists and legal experts study and which are known collectively as 'the constitution'. But there is no single written document which can be appealed to as the highest law of the land. Nobody can refer to 'article 6' or 'the first amendment' or anything like that, because nothing like that exists.

Instead, the principles and procedures by which the country is governed and from which people's rights are derived come from a number of different sources. They have been built up, bit by bit, over the centuries. Some of them are written down in laws agreed by Parliament, some have been spoken and then written down (judgements made in a court) and some have never been written down at all. For example, there is no written law in Britain that says anything about who can be the Prime Minister or what the powers of the Prime Minister are – even though that person is probably the most powerful person in the country. Instead, these things have been established, and are constantly being modified, by custom and practice. Similarly, there is no single written document which asserts people's rights. Some rights which are commonly accepted in modern democracies (for example, the rights not to be discriminated against on the basis of sex or race) have been formally agreed by Parliament in certain laws; but others (for example, the rights not to be discriminated against on the basis of religion or political views) have not. Nevertheless, it is understood that these latter rights are also part of the constitution.

The style of politics

Despite modern innovations such as the televising of Parliament, political life in Britain is still influenced by the traditional respect for privacy and love of secrecy. It is also comparatively informal. In both Parliament and government, there is a tendency for important decisions to be taken not at official public meetings, or even at prearranged private meetings, but at lunch, or over drinks, or in chance encounters in the corridors of power. It used to be said that the House of Commons was 'the most exclusive club in London'. And indeed, there are many features of Parliament which cause its members (MPs) to feel a special sense of belonging, even when they have radically opposed political philosophies. First, constitutional theory says that Parliament has absolute control over its own affairs and is, in fact, the highest power in the land. Second, there are the ancient traditions of procedure. Many of these serve to remind MPs of a time when the main division in politics was not between this

Skeletons in the cupboard

In modern Britain, the 1950s are often spoken of as a golden age of innocence. But innocence can go hand in hand with ignorance – ignorance of what your government is doing to you. In the early years of this century, it became clear that British governments in the fifties were prepared to use people as guinea pigs in their military experiments. One spectacular example is the 1952 flood in the village of Lynmouth, widely believed to have been caused by experiments in affecting the weather.

Another is the terrible effects of radiation among the British servicemen who were involved in atomic weapons testing. A third of them died of bone cancer or leukaemia contracted as a direct result of their role in the tests. Worse, many veterans of the tests have incurred genetic disorders that have been passed on to their children. Worse still, evidence suggests that many were deliberately ordered into dangerous positions in order to test the effects of nuclear fallout.

As evidence of this kind emerges, it is perhaps not surprising that British people no longer have the blind trust in the activities of government that they used to.

The pairing system

The pairing system is an excellent example of the habit of cooperation among political parties in Britain. Under this system, an MP of one party is 'paired' with an MP of another party. When there is going to be a vote in the House of Commons, and the two MPs know that they would vote on opposite sides, neither of them bother to turn up for the vote. In this way, the difference in numbers between one side and the other is maintained, while the MPs are free to get on with other work. The system works very well. There is never any 'cheating'.

The millions who break the law every weekend

The lack of any constitution or unified legal code in Britain results in some curious anomalies Although British people generally take laws and regulations very seriously, there are a few laws which people routinely break, *en masse*. Did you know, for example, that millions of English people flout the law every weekend when they play or watch football? Back in medieval times, the king was worried that his soldiers weren't getting enough archery practice, so he made football illegal. This law has never been repealed. Nobody has ever seen the need to bother.

Similarly, generations of Jewish people have quite happily, and without problems, lived in the English city of Leicester – even though until the year 2000 they were breaking the law by doing so. A thirteenth-century city charter stated that 'no Jew or Jewess ... to the end of the world, shall inhabit or remain in Leicester'. Clearly this contravened every decent person's understanding of what is acceptable in a modern democracy. But it was only in 2000 that the city council, mindful of the city's multicultural image, got round to renouncing the charter.

party and that party but rather between Parliament itself and the monarch. Even the architecture of the Palace of Westminster (the home of Parliament) contributes to this feeling. It is so confusing and apparently unplanned that only 'insiders' can find their way around in it.

These features, together with long years of political stability, have led to a habit of genuine cooperation among politicians of different parties. When you hear politicians arguing in the House of Commons or in a television studio, you might think they hate each other. This is rarely the case. Often they are good friends. And even when it is the case, both normally see the practical advantage of cooperation. The advantage is that very little time is wasted fighting about how political business is to be conducted fairly. For example, the order of business in Parliament is arranged by representatives of the parties beforehand. Another example is television advertising. By agreement, political parties are not allowed to buy time on television. Instead, each party is given a strict amount of time. A very notable example is the system of 'pairing' of MPs (The pairing system).

The party system

Britain is often said to have a 'two-party system'. This is because members of just two parties normally occupy more than 85% of all of the seats in the House of Commons and one of them, by itself, controls the government. One reason for the existence of this situation is the electoral system (see chapter 10). The other is the origin of British political parties. Unlike in most other countries, they were first formed inside Parliament and only later extended to the public. During the eighteenth century, MPs tended to divide into two camps, those who usually supported the government of the time and those who usually did not. During the nineteenth century, it became the habit that the party which did not control the government presented itself as an alternative government. This idea of an alternative government has received legal recognition. The leader of the second biggest party in Parliament receives the title 'Leader of Her Majesty's Opposition', and even gets an extra salary for this role. He or she chooses a 'shadow cabinet', thereby presenting the image of a team ready to fill the shoes of the government at a moment's notice.

As a result of these origins, neither party existed solely to look after the interests of one particular group in society. Furthermore, although they differed broadly in their general outlooks, the two parties did not exist to promote single, coherent political philosophies. The main reason for their existence was to gain power by forming an effective coalition of groups and opinions. It is true that the Labour party – one of the present two big parties – was formed outside Parliament, and, as its name implies, did exist to promote the interests of a particular group (the working class).

A guide to British political parties

Conservative party

History
Developed from the group of MPs known as the Tories in the early nineteenth century (see chapter 2) and still often known informally by that name (especially in newspapers, because it takes up less space).

Traditional Outlook
Right of centre; stands for hierarchical authority and minimal government interference in the economy; likes to reduce income tax; gives high priority to national defence and internal law and order.

Since 1979
In government until 1997, aggressive reform of education, welfare, housing and many public services designed to increase consumer-choice and/or to introduce 'market economics' into their operation.

Organization
Leader has relatively great degree of freedom to direct policy.

Traditional voters
The richer sections of society, plus a large minority of the working classes.

Money
Mostly donations from business people.

Labour party

History
Formed at the beginning of the twentieth century from an alliance of trade unionists and intellectuals. First government in 1923.

Traditional Outlook
Left of centre; stands for equality, for the weaker people in society and more government involvement in the economy; more concerned to provide full social services than to keep income tax low.

Since 1979
Originally, opposition to Conservative reforms, but then acceptance; in government since 1997, emphasis on community ethics and equality of opportunity rather than equal distribution of wealth; has loosened ties to trade unions (see chapter 15).

Organization
In theory, policies have to be approved by annual conference; in practice, leader has more power than this implies.

Traditional voters
Working class, plus a small middle-class intelligentsia.

Money
Formerly most from trade unions, now mostly from business people.

Liberal Democratic party

History
Formed in the late 1980s from a union of the Liberals (who developed from the Whigs in the early nineteenth century) and the Social Democrats (a breakaway group of Labour politicians).

Policies
Regarded as centre or slightly left of centre; in favour of greater unification with the EU; more emphasis on the environment than other parties; believes in giving greater powers to local government and reform of the electoral system (see chapter 10).

Traditional voters
From all classes, but more from middle class.

Money
Much poorer than the big two.

Nationalist parties

Both Plaid Cymru ('party of Wales' in the Welsh language) and the SNP (Scottish National Party) stand ultimately for independence from the UK, although their supporters often include those who just want greater internal self-government.

Both parties have usually had a few MPs at Westminster in the last 50 years, but well under half of the MPs representing their respective countries.

Parties in Northern Ireland

The four main parties here represent either the Protestant or the Catholic communities (see chapter 4). The Protestant ones are the Democratic Unionists and the Ulster Unionists and the Catholic ones are Sinn Fein and the Social Democratic and Labour Party. Between them they normally win all the Irish seats in Westminster and the vast majority of seats in the Northern Ireland Assembly. The Alliance Party, which asks for support from both communities, has a handful of seats in the assembly, and in 2010 won its first seat in Westminster.

Other parties

There are numerous very small parties. The three largest in recent years have been (1) The Green party, which is supported by environmentalists, (2) The British National Party (BNP), which campaigns against immigration and (3) The United Kingdom Independence Party (UKIP), which wants Britain to leave the European Union. Partly because of the electoral system (see chapter 10), it is hard for these parties to win a seat in Parliament. So far, only the Greens have done so (one seat in 2010). But they do better in local elections. The first two have a handful of seats on local councils, and all three have won seats in the European parliament.

However, as soon as it replaced the Liberal party as one of the big two (in the first decades of the twentieth century), it fitted into the established framework. It is very difficult for smaller parties to challenge the dominance of the bigger ones. If any of them seem to have some good ideas, these are adopted by one of the big parties, who try to appeal to as large a section of the population as possible.

The fact that the party system originated inside Parliament has other consequences. Parties do not, as they do in many other countries, extend into every area of public life in the country. Universities, for example, each have their political party clubs, but when there is an election for officers of the student union, it is not normally fought along national party divisions. The same is true of elections within trade unions (see chapter 15).

Another consequence is that it is usually a party's MPs who have most control over party policy. This does not mean the parties are undemocratic. Their members who are not MPs can have an effect on policy in a number of ways. First, they elect the party leader. Second, they can make their views known at the annual party conference. Third, the local party has the power to decide who is going to be the party's candidate for MP in its area at the next election. However, these powers are limited by one important consideration – the appearance of unity. Party policies are always presented as potential government policies, and a party's leading MPs as potential ministers. If you want to look like a realistic potential government, you don't want to show the public your disagreements. Party conferences are always televised. As a result they tend to be showcases whose main purpose is not genuine debate but rather to boost the spirits of party members and show the public a dynamic, unified party. Similarly, if a local party decides not to re-select the present MP as their candidate in an election, or rejects the recommendation of the national party, it betrays disagreement and argument.

The modern situation

During the last half century, the traditional confidence in the British political system has weakened. At first sight, this phenomenon seems paradoxical. After all, the general direction of public policy has been the same since 1979, suggesting stability and a high level of public confidence. Two developments may help to explain it.

The first concerns the perceived style of politics. Top politicians have always had various personal advisers to help them with matters of policy and presentation (for instance by writing their speeches). But in recent years it is their public relations advisers, whose job is to make them look good in the media, who have become their closest (and therefore most powerful) advisers. To characterize this role and the importance attached to it, the word 'spin doctor' has entered the British vocabulary. This emphasis on presentation above all else, on style over substance, was most noticeable in Tony Blair's Labour government (1997–2007). But it appears to have been adopted by all the main parties to some degree (World's first face transplant).

The second is a more serious matter. It concerns the style of democracy and it has constitutional significance. There are signs that the traditional right of the individual to freedom from interference by the state is being eroded. The proliferation of CCTV cameras (see chapter 5) is one example. Another is the national DNA database. In 2007, about 5% of the population had their DNA stored on police databases. This proportion is growing rapidly because, at the time of writing, the police have the right to take – and keep – a DNA sample from anybody they arrest, even if that person is not subsequently charged with an offence. A further example is the increased powers the authorities have to search people and their homes and to detain them without charging them. Under the present anti-terrorist laws, a suspect can be kept in police custody for 42 days without charge (the government originally suggested 90 days) and more than a hundred thousand people have been searched.

These changes have not taken place without protest. But it seems that fear of crime, illegal immigration and terrorism have been enough to allow them through. There is one other change which British governments have been promoting since the early 1990s – identity cards. But at the time of writing, they have still not been introduced. There remains a general feeling that there would be something very un-British about them and some people are very strongly opposed to them. For the British, it seems, it is the absence of ID cards which symbolizes their traditional dedication to the rights of the individual more than anything else.

World's first face transplant

Private Eye is a well-established satirical magazine. Its cover always shows a photo of a well-known person or event, with satirical captions and speech bubbles added to it. The cover below reflects the feeling in modern Britain that politicians are interested in appearances above all else. It also reflects the feeling that, if you look below the surface, they are all the same. The 'before' photo is of Tony Blair, the Labour Prime Minister of Britain from 1997 to 2007. The 'after' photo is of David Cameron, who had recently become leader of the Conservative party. (At that time, 2005, the Conservatives had had three bad election results and four different leaders in eight years. Many people felt that the choice of Cameron was intended to copy Labour.)

Interestingly, when Gordon Brown took over as Prime Minister in 2007, his advisers were careful to present him as a very down-to-earth person, someone who was not interested in image.

In the early years of this century several incidents occurred in which the right to free speech and public protest also seemed to be under threat. In such cases, the authorities again appealed to the threat of terrorism as a justification for their actions. Such incidents draw attention to Britain's lack of a written constitution, which means that principles such as free speech have little legal definition. It also means there is no reliable way of deciding when, if at all, this right does not apply. Free speech is understood to be a basic principle. However, it can sometimes appear to clash with another principle, such as the right not to be discriminated against. For example, several people have found that, in exercising their right to freely air their opinion, they may be breaking laws against discrimination on the basis of sexual orientation, leading one public figure in 2006 to complain that people were now afraid to say what they think even in the local pub. (Taking extreme care not to say anything offensive is known as 'political correctness', or 'PC' for short, and the over-zealous application by authorities of anti-discrimination laws is referred to by critics as 'political correctness gone mad'.) (Free speech?) Britain, almost uniquely in the world, is a country which has been politically stable for centuries. In addition, basic civil rights were also established (in principle if not always in practice) generations ago. As a result, its people tend to take these rights for granted and so perhaps have become lazy about defending them.

Free speech?

Annual party conferences in Britain have nothing to do with genuine debate and everything to do with morale-boosting. TV cameras are there, and the last thing a party wants is to be seen having furious internal arguments. At the same time, it is still expected that speakers addressing the conference will occasionally have to face the odd bit of heckling. Heckling, the shouted interruption of a public speaker, is a time-honoured practice in British politics. It livens up boring speeches and part of the measure of a politician's worth is his or her ability to deal with it. But not at the 2005 Labour party conference. When Walter Wolfgang, an 82-year-old party veteran, shouted 'nonsense' during a speech in which the Foreign Secretary was explaining why British troops were in Iraq, he was astonished to find two large men appear in front of him and then drag him out of the hall. He was arrested under the Prevention of Terrorism Act. 'New Labour' always had a reputation for 'control freakery'. But nobody thought it had gone so far.

Of course, Labour leaders recognized this incident as a public relations disaster and apologized profusely and publicly to Mr Wolfgang. But they were not so ready with their apologies to the 500 other people outside the conference who were also detained as suspected terrorists, including several for wearing T-shirts with uncomplimentary words about the Prime Minister emblazoned on them. (One of them was a local resident out walking his dog!) Instead, they joined police in attempting to justify this behaviour on the grounds that it 'sends a clear message to would-be terrorists'.

But what was the message it sent to everybody else?

In modern Britain, it is not only the authorities with which the principle of free speech can sometimes conflict. It can also conflict with the values of a certain section of society. The best example of the latter remains the Salman Rushdie case (The Rushdie affair). As long as everybody in a country shares the same attitudes about what is most important in political life and about people's rights and obligations, there is no real need to worry about inconsistencies or ambiguities in the law. Laws can just be interpreted in changing ways to match the change in prevailing opinion. This is what used to happen in Britain. But, in Britain today, different sections of society can sometimes have radically different priorities. The Rushdie case was the first notable example of what can happen as a result. In these circumstances, the traditional laissez-faire attitude to the law can become dangerous, and it may be necessary to frame something like a written constitution as a way of establishing certain basic principles.

QUESTIONS

1 How does the general attitude to politics and politicians in Britain compare to that in your country?

2 Do you think the 'pairing system' as described in this chapter is a good practice?

3 How does the role of political parties in Britain differ from their role in your country?

4 How does the balance between government power and people power in your country compare with the present situation in Britain?

SUGGESTIONS

Try to watch some of the *Yes, Prime Minister* programmes. They are available on DVD. The book of the same name (the supposed 'diaries') is published by BBC books. More recent TV satires are *Bremner, Bird and Fortune* (which presents topical sketches) and *The Thick of It* (which was made in a fly-on-the-wall 'documentary' style and portrayed modern spin doctoring).

The book *The English* by Jeremy Paxman is a general discussion of British country and people. But because Paxman has spent all his life presenting current affairs and interviewing politicians on TV, it has a political focus.

The Rushdie affair

In 1989, *The Satanic Verses* was published. It was the work of the respected author Salman Rushdie, a British citizen from a Muslim background. Many Muslims in Britain were extremely angry about the book's publication. They regarded it as a terrible insult to Islam. They therefore demanded that the book be banned and that its author be taken to court for blasphemy (using language to insult God).

However, to do either of these things would have been directly against the long-established tradition of free speech and freedom of religious views. In any case, there was nothing in British law to justify doing either. There were (and still are) censorship laws, but they related only to obscenity and national security. There was (and still is) a law against blasphemy, but it referred only to the Christian religion. Moreover, the tendency in the second half of the twentieth century had been to apply both types of law as little as possible and to give priority to the principle of free speech.

Whatever one's views on this matter, it cannot be denied that the law, as it is, appears both to discriminate against religions other than Christianity and to be inconsistent. It appears to be discriminatory because it is only illegal to blaspheme against Christ; it appears inconsistent because to have any blasphemy law at all is a contradiction of the principle of freedom of religious views.

07 The monarchy

The appearance

The position of the monarch in Britain illustrates the contradictory nature of the constitution. From the evidence of written law only, the Queen has almost absolute power, and it all seems very undemocratic. The American constitution talks about 'government for the people by the people'. There is nothing in Britain like that. In fact, there is no legal concept of 'the people' at all.

Every autumn, at the state opening of Parliament, Queen Elizabeth II makes a speech. In it, she says what 'my government' intends to do in the coming year. And it is her government, not the people's. As far as the law is concerned, she can choose anybody she likes to run the government for her. There are no restrictions on who she picks as her Prime Minister. The same is true for her choices of people to fill some hundred or so other ministerial positions. And if she gets fed up with her ministers, she can just dismiss them. Officially speaking, they are all 'servants of the Crown' (not of 'the country' or 'the people'). She also appears to have great power over Parliament. It is she who summons a parliament, and she who dissolves it (i.e. tells it that it no longer exists). In addition, nothing that Parliament has decided can become a law until she has given it the royal assent.

Similarly, it is the Queen who embodies the law in the courts. In the USA, when someone is accused of a crime, the court records will show that 'the people' have accused this person. In other countries, it might be 'the state' that makes the accusation. But in Britain, it is 'the Crown' – a reference to the legal authority of the monarch. And when an accused person is found guilty, he or she is sent to one of 'Her Majesty's' prisons.

The reality

In practice, of course, the reality is very different. In fact, the Queen cannot just choose anyone to be Prime Minister. She has to choose someone who will command majority support in the House of Commons. This is because the law says that 'her' government can only collect taxes with the agreement of the Commons, so if she did not choose such a person, the government would stop functioning. In practice, the person she chooses is the leader of the strongest party in the Commons. Similarly, it is really the Prime Minister who decides who the other government ministers are going to be (although officially the Prime Minister simply 'advises' the monarch who to choose).

It is the same story with Parliament. Again, the Prime Minister will talk about 'requesting' a dissolution of Parliament when he or she wants to hold an election, but it would normally be impossible for the monarch to refuse this 'request'. Similarly, while in theory the Queen could refuse the royal assent to a bill passed by Parliament, no monarch has actually done so since the year 1708. Indeed, the royal assent is so automatic that the Queen doesn't even bother to give it in person. Somebody else signs the documents for her.

In reality, the Queen has almost no power at all. When she opens Parliament each year, the speech she makes has been written for her. She makes no secret of this fact. She very obviously reads out the script that has been prepared for her, word for word. If she strongly disagrees with one of the policies of the government, she might ask the government ministers to change the wording in the speech a little beforehand, but that is all. She cannot actually stop the government going ahead with any of its policies.

The royal family

Queen Elizabeth, the Queen Mother This was the official title of the mother of Queen Elizabeth II. She died at the age of 101 in 2002. Her tours of bombed areas of London during the Second World War with her husband, King George VI, made her popular with the British people and she remained popular until her death.

Queen Elizabeth II was born in 1926 and became Queen in 1952. At the time of writing, she is the second longest-reigning monarch in British history. She is widely respected for the way in which she performs her duties and is generally popular.

Prince Philip Mountbatten married Queen Elizabeth II in 1947. His outspoken opinions on certain matters have sometimes been embarrassing to the royal family.

Prince Charles, the Prince of Wales, was born in 1948. As the eldest son of Queen Elizabeth II and Prince Philip, he is heir to the throne. He is concerned about the environment and living conditions in Britain's cities. He sometimes makes speeches which are critical of aspects of modern life.

Princess Diana married Prince Charles in 1981. The couple separated in 1992 and later divorced. Diana died in a car accident in 1997. During her lifetime, she was a glamorous figure and the public loved her. They felt able to identify with her in a way that they could not with other 'royals'. (She was, in fact, the first Englishwoman ever to marry an heir to the throne.)

Camilla, Duchess of Cornwall married Prince Charles in 2005. Her long relationship with Charles is widely believed to have been a major cause of his separation from Diana. For this reason, she is not very popular with the public. On the other hand, people are generally sympathetic to those involved in long-lasting love affairs, so it is likely that she will become more popular (or at least less unpopular) as time passes.

Princess Anne is the Queen's daughter (also known as the Princess Royal), and was born in 1950. She separated from her husband after they had one son and one daughter. She married again in 1992. She is widely respected for her charity work.

Prince Andrew, the Duke of York was born in 1960 and is the Queen's second son. He is separated from his wife, Sarah Ferguson (known to the popular press as 'Fergie'). They have two daughters.

Prince Edward the Queen's youngest son, was born in 1964. He married Sophie Rhys Jones in 1999. He and his wife are the Earl and Countess of Wessex.

Prince William (born 1982) is the eldest son of Charles and Diana and therefore the next in line to the throne after his father. He and his brother **Prince Henry** (born 1984), like Charles and Andrew before them, have both embarked on military careers.

Honours

Twice a year, an Honours List is published. The people whose names appear on the list are then summoned to Buckingham Palace, where the Queen presents them with a token which entitles them to write (and be formally addressed with) KG, or KCB, or MBE, or many other possible combinations of letters, after their names. The letters stand for titles such as 'Knight of the Order of the Garter', 'Knight Commander of the Order of the Bath', 'Member of the British Empire', and so on.

Traditionally, it was by giving people titles such as these that the monarch 'honoured' a person as a reward for some service. These days, the decision about who gets which honour is usually taken by the Prime Minister (see chapter 8). And, as you can see, the names of the titles don't seem to make much sense in modern times. But that does not stop people finding it a real honour to be given a title by the monarch herself! A high proportion of honours are given to politicians and civil servants, but they are also given to business people, sports stars, rock musicians and other entertainers.

The Beatles with their MBEs in 1965, the first pop musicians to receive such an honour.

The role of the monarch

What, then, is the monarch's role? Many opinions are offered by political and legal experts. Three roles are often mentioned. First, the monarch is the personal embodiment of the government of the country. This means that people can be as nasty as they like about the real government, and can argue that it should be thrown out, without being accused of being unpatriotic. Because of the clear separation between the symbol of government (the Queen) and the actual government, changing the government does not threaten the stability of the country. Other countries without a monarch have to use something else as the symbol of the country. In the USA, for example, one of these is its flag, and to damage a copy of the flag is actually a criminal offence.

Second, it is argued that the monarch is a possible final check on a government that is becoming dictatorial. Just supposing the government managed to pass a bill through Parliament which was obviously terribly bad as well as being unpopular, the monarch could refuse the royal assent. Similarly, it is possible that if a Prime Minister who had been defeated at a general election were to ask immediately for another dissolution of Parliament (so that another election could take place), the monarch could refuse the request and dismiss the Prime Minister.

Third, the monarch has a very practical role to play. By being a figurehead and representative of the country, Queen Elizabeth II can perform the ceremonial duties which heads of state often have to spend their time on. This way, the real government has more time to get on with the actual job of running the country.

The value of the monarchy

However, all these advantages are hypothetical. It cannot be proved that only a monarch can provide them. Other modern democracies manage perfectly well without one. The real importance of the British monarchy is probably less to do with the system of government and more to do with social psychology and economics (The economic argument). The monarchy gives British people a symbol of continuity, and a harmless outlet for expressions of national pride. It provides a focus of reverence for those people who have a tendency to hero-worship. Even in very hard times, Britain has never looked like turning to a dictator to get it out of its troubles, and the grandeur of its monarchy may have been one reason for this.

Occasions such as the state opening of Parliament, the Queen's official birthday and royal weddings, as well as everyday ceremonial events such as the changing of the guard, help to make up for the lack of pageantry in people's lives. (There is no countrywide tradition of local parades in Britain.) In addition, the glamorous lives of 'the royals' provide a source of entertainment that often takes on the characteristics of a soap opera. The separation of Prince Charles and Princess Diana in 1992, for example, was accompanied by vast amounts of discussion far beyond the possible political implications, even in the more 'serious' newspapers. Since the Princes 'Wills' and 'Harry' grew up, most of the press has been more interested in their love lives than in the implications of their military roles in Iraq and Afghanistan.

The future of the monarchy

The British monarchy as an institution has not been a burning issue in British politics for several hundred years. There is almost no public debate about the existence of the monarchy itself. Very few people in Britain would use 'monarchist' or 'republican/anti-monarchist' as a defining feature of their political beliefs, not even the minority who would like a republic. Most people are either vaguely in favour, or they just don't care one way or the other.

There is, however, much debate about what kind of monarchy Britain should have. During the last two decades of the twentieth century, there was a general cooling of enthusiasm. The Queen herself remained popular. But various marital problems in her family lowered the prestige of royalty in many people's eyes. The problem was that, since Queen Victoria's reign, the public had been encouraged to look up to the royal family as a model of Christian family life. When it became obvious that the current royal family, as a whole, was no such thing, the result was to give royalty a bad name.

The change in attitude can be seen by comparing Elizabeth's twenty-fifth anniversary as Queen with her fiftieth anniversary (her 'Golden Jubilee'). In 1977, there were neighbourhood street parties throughout the country, most of them spontaneously and voluntarily organized. But in 2002, nothing like this took place. The BBC broadcast a live service of thanksgiving but the occasion got no mention on the front pages of most national newspapers. In 2008, a government minister suggested that school children should be encouraged to swear an oath of allegiance to the Queen (in the same way that American children swear allegiance to the flag). The public showed little enthusiasm for this idea.

But there is nothing personal about this cooling of enthusiasm. The Queen herself is widely admired. And, as she lives through her eighties, this respect and affection for her will grow. She has seen eleven Prime Ministers, invited more than a million people to her garden parties and paid official visits to well over a hundred countries.

The one aspect of the monarchy about which most people feel consistently negative is how much it costs. In 1992, a fire damaged Windsor Castle, one of the Queen's favourite homes. There was public sympathy for the Queen, but when the government announced that public money was going to pay for the repairs, the sympathy quickly turned to anger. The Queen had recently been reported as the richest woman in the world, so people didn't see why she shouldn't pay for

The economic argument

Tourist brochures for Britain usually give great prominence to the monarchy. It is impossible to estimate exactly how much the British royal family and the events and buildings associated with the monarchy help the tourist industry, or exactly how much money they help to bring into the country, but most people working in tourism think it is an awful lot.

Edward and Mrs Simpson

For the last two centuries, the public have wanted their monarch to show high moral standards. In 1936, Edward VIII, the uncle of the present queen, was forced to abdicate (give up the throne) because he wanted to marry a woman who had divorced two husbands. (On top of that, she was not even an aristocrat – she was an American!) The government and the major churches in the country insisted that Edward could not marry her and remain king. He chose to marry her. The couple then went to live abroad. In spite of the constitutional crisis that he caused, the Duke of Windsor (as Edward later became) and his wife were popular celebrities in Britain all their lives, and in popular history the king's abdication is an example of the power of romance.

One's bum year

The Sun is Britain's most popular daily newspaper (see chapter 16). This was its front page headline after the Queen had spoken of 1992 as an *annus horribilis* (Latin for 'a horrible year'). As well as the separation of Charles and Diana, it included the fire at Windsor Castle and the news that Australia was intending to become a republic.

The headline uses the word 'bum' (which, in colloquial British English, means 'horrible'). It also mimics the supposed frequent use by the Queen of the pronoun 'one' to mean 'I' or 'me'. The headline thus mixes the very formal-sounding 'one' with the very colloquial 'bum'. It is impossible to imagine that such a disrespectful (and unsympathetic) headline could have appeared in earlier decades.

Two kingdoms?

Since 1999, Scotland has had its own parliament, and many people in that country want complete independence from the UK. However, it is testimony to the enduring popularity of the British monarchy that most of them do not want a republic. The Scottish National Party, whose policy is complete independence, says it wants to keep Elizabeth II and her successors as the Scottish head of state. If that happened, the situation would revert to that of the seventeenth century in Britain, when the monarch ruled two separate kingdoms.

The royal family is aware of this possibility. After 1999, there was talk that Princess Anne, who already has many special ties with Scotland, would make Holyroodhouse in Edinburgh her permanent home and become the Queen's representative in Scotland. However, this has not yet occurred.

them herself! In the same decade, public opinion forced her to decide that she would start paying taxes on her private income and some members of the royal family were dropped from the Civil List. (This is the money which the Queen and some of her relatives get from Parliament each year so that they can carry out various public duties.)

People continue to believe that the royal family gets too much money. Nevertheless, the monarchy remains broadly popular. They appear unconvinced by republican arguments that it is an outdated institution which prevents British people from living in a true democracy or that it hinders genuine equality among them. This is despite the fact that they realize the monarchy is an anachronism. Opinion polls show that, although the vast majority are in favour of the monarchy, they believe that Britain will not have one 100 years from now.

The Queen herself is aware of the public perception. After the fire at Windsor Castle, parts of Buckingham Palace (her official London residence) were opened to public visitors for the first time. The intention was to use the money raised to pay for the repairs. But in fact, the palace, and some other royal residences, have remained open to the paying public ever since. Since that time, the queen has also cooperated in the making of several TV documentaries about her everyday life. These changes are perhaps an indication of the future royal style – a little less grand, a little less distant.

QUESTIONS

1 Why does the British Prime Minister continue to 'advise' the Queen when everybody knows he or she is really just telling her what to do?

2 The attitude of the British people towards their royal family has changed over the last thirty years or so. Why do you think this has happened?

3 Would you advise the British people to get rid of their monarchy?

4 Is there a monarch in your country, or somebody who plays a similar role? If so, how does their position compare with that of the British monarch?

SUGGESTIONS

The Queen and I by Sue Townsend (Mandarin) is a fantasy in which the Queen has a dream about her country becoming a republic. It includes humorous characterizations of some main members of the royal family.

Books about the monarchy abound. Among them are: *The Prince of Wales: A biography* by Jonathan Dimbleby (Little, Brown and Company), *The Queen* by Kenneth Harris (Orion), *Elizabeth R: The Role of the Monarchy Today* by Antony Jay (BBC Books), *Diana, Her True Story* and *Diana, Her New Life*, both by Andrew Morton (Michael O'Mara Books Limited).

08 The government

When the media talk about 'the government', they usually mean one of two things. In one meaning, it refers to all the politicians who run government departments (there are several politicians in each department) or have other special responsibilities, such as managing the activities of Parliament. There are normally about a hundred members of 'the government' in this sense. Although there are various ranks, each with their own titles (Ministers and departments), members of the government are usually known as 'ministers'. Unlike in the USA and some other countries in Europe, it is rare for a person from outside Parliament to become a minister.

The other meaning of the term 'the government' is more limited. It refers only to the most powerful of these politicians, namely, the Prime Minister and the other members of the cabinet. There are usually about twenty people in the cabinet (though there are no rules about this). Most of them are the heads of the government departments.

Partly as a result of the electoral system (see chapter 10), Britain, unlike much of western Europe, normally has 'single-party government'. That is, all members of the government belong to the same political party. Coalition government (which involves several parties) has traditionally been regarded as a bad idea. In the twentieth century, Britain had a total of only 21 years of coalition governments (1915–1922 and 1931–1945). Even when, briefly in the 1970s, no single party had a majority of seats in Parliament, no coalition was formed. There was a 'minority government' instead. The coalition government which was formed in 2010 (see chapter 10) is seen as an experiment.

The habit of single-party government has helped to establish the tradition known as collective responsibility. That is, every member of the government, however junior, shares in responsibility for every policy of the government – even if he or she did not take any part in making it. Of course, individual government members hold different opinions but they are expected to keep these private. By convention, no member of the government can criticize government policy in public. Any member who does so must resign.

The cabinet

Obviously, no government wants an important member of its party to start criticizing it. This would lead to divisions in the party. Therefore, the leading politicians in the governing party usually become members of the cabinet, where they are tied to government policy by the convention of collective responsibility.

Ministers and departments

Most heads of government departments have the title 'Secretary of State' (as in, for example, 'Secretary of State for the Environment'). The minister in charge of Britain's relations with the outside world is known to everybody as the 'Foreign Secretary'. The one in charge of public safety inside the country is the 'Home Secretary'. Their departments are called 'The Foreign and Commonwealth Office' and 'The Home Office' respectively (the words 'exterior' and 'interior' are not used). The words 'secretary' and 'office' reflect the history of government in Britain, in which government departments were once part of the domestic arrangements of the monarch.

Another important person is the 'Chancellor of the Exchequer', who is the head of the Treasury (in other words, a sort of Minister of Finance).

Once a week, the cabinet meets and takes decisions about new policies, the implementation of existing policies and the running of the various government departments. Because all government members must be seen to agree, exactly who says what at these meetings is a closely guarded secret. The reports of the meetings, which are circulated to government departments, summarize the topics discussed and the decisions taken but they never refer to individuals.

To help run the complexities of a modern government, there is an organization called the cabinet office. It runs a busy communications network, keeping ministers in touch with each other and drawing up the agenda for cabinet meetings. It also does the same things for the many cabinet committees. These committees are appointed by the cabinet to look into various matters in more detail than the cabinet has the time (or knowledge) for. Unlike 'the government' itself, the people on these committees are not necessarily politicians.

The Prime Minister

The position of a British Prime Minister (PM) is in direct contrast to that of the monarch. While the Queen appears to have a lot of power but in reality has very little, the PM appears not to have much power but in reality has a very great deal. As we have seen (in chapter 7), the Queen is, in practice, obliged to give the job of PM to the person who can command a majority in the House of Commons. This normally means the leader of the party with the largest number of MPs.

The traditional phrase describes the position of the PM within the cabinet as *primus inter pares* (Latin for 'first among equals'). But in fact the other ministers are not nearly as powerful. There are several reasons for this. First, the monarch's powers of patronage (the power to appoint people to all kinds of jobs and to confer honours on people) are, by convention, actually the PM's powers of patronage. The fiction is that the Queen appoints people to government jobs 'on the advice of the Prime Minister'. But what actually happens is that the PM simply decides.

The cabinet

The history of the cabinet is a good example of the tendency toward secrecy in British politics. It started in the eighteenth century as an informal grouping of important ministers and officials of the royal household. It had no formal status. Officially, the government was run by the Privy Council, a body of a hundred or more people (including those belonging to 'the cabinet') who reported directly to the monarch (but not to each other). Over the years, the cabinet gradually took over effective power. The Privy Council is now a merely ceremonial body. Among others, it includes all the present ministers and the most important past ministers.

In the last 100 years, the cabinet itself has become more and more 'official' and publicly recognized. It has also grown in size, and so is now often too rigid and formal a body to make the real decisions. In the last 50 years, there have been unofficial 'inner cabinets' (comprising the Prime Minister and a few other important ministers). It is here, and in cabinet committees, that much of the real decision-making takes place.

No. 10 Downing Street

This is the official residence of the Prime Minister. It is an example of the traditional fiction that Prime Ministers are not especially important people. As you can see, it does not have a special name. Nor, from the outside, does it look very special. It is not even a detached house! Inside, though, it is much larger than it looks. The cabinet meets here and the cabinet office works here. The PM lives 'above the shop' on the top floor.

The Chancellor of the Exchequer lives next door at No. 11, and the Government Chief Whip (see chapter 9) at No. 12, so that the whole street is a lot more important than it appears. In the media 'Downing Street' is used to refer to the PM, the cabinet office and other close advisers of the PM. Still, there is something very domestic about this arrangement. When a government loses an election, all three ministers have to wait for the removal vans to turn up, just like anybody else moving house.

The PM also has an official country residence to the west of London called Chequers.

The strength of the PM's power of patronage is apparent from the modern phenomenon known as the 'cabinet reshuffle'. It is the habit of the PM to change his or her cabinet quite frequently (at least once every two years). A few cabinet members are dropped, and a few new members are brought in, but mostly the existing members are shuffled around, like a pack of cards, each getting a new department to look after.

The second reason for a modern PM's dominance over other ministers is the power of the public image. In the age of modern media, politics is a matter of personalities. The details of policies are hard to understand. A single person whose face appears constantly on the television and in the newspapers is much easier to identify with. Everybody in the country can recognize the Prime Minister, while many cannot put a name to the faces of the other ministers. As a result the PM can sometimes go 'over the heads' of the other ministers and appeal directly to the public.

Third, all ministers except the PM are kept busy looking after their government departments. They have little time to think about government policy as a whole. But the PM does. Moreover, the cabinet office is directly under the PM's control and works in the same building. As a result, the PM knows more of what is going on than the other ministers do. Because there is not enough time for the cabinet to discuss everything, a choice has to be made. And it is the PM who makes that choice. Matters that are not discussed can, in effect, be decided by the PM. The convention of collective responsibility then means that the rest of the government has to go along with whatever the PM has decided.

The civil service

Considering how complex modern states are, there are not really very many people in a British 'government' (as defined above). Unlike some other countries (the USA, for example), not even the most senior administrative jobs change hands when a new government comes to power. The day-to-day running of the government and the implementation of its policy continue in the hands of the same people

Prime Ministe

Prime Minister
Winston C (1940–45)
Clement A (1945–51)
Winston Churchill (1951–55)
Anthony Eden (1955–57)
Harold Macmillan (1957–63)
Alec Douglas-Home (1963–64)
Harold Wilson (1964–70)
Edward Heath (1970–74)
Harold Wilson (1974–76)
James Callaghan (1976–79)
Margaret Thatcher (1979–90)
John Major (1990–97)
Tony Blair (1997–2007)
Gordon Brown (2007–2010)
David Cameron (2010–)

Conservative
Labour

The ideal Prime Minister

Here is another extract from *Yes, Prime Minister*, the political satire. It is a section of the private diaries of a senior civil servant. In it, he describes his conversation with another top civil servant, in which they discuss who should become the new Prime Minister.

We take a fairly dim view of them both [the two candidates]. It is a difficult choice, rather like asking which lunatic should run the asylum.

We both agreed that they would present the same problems. They are both interventionists and they would both have foolish notions about running the country themselves if they became Prime Minister. ... It is clearly advisable to look for a compromise candidate.

We agreed that such a candidate must have the following qualities: he must be malleable, flexible, likeable, have no firm opinions, no bright ideas, not be intellectually committed, and be without the strength of purpose to change anything. Above all, he must be someone whom we know can be professionally guided, and who is willing to leave the business of government in the hands of experts.

that were there with the previous government – the top rank of the civil service. Governments come and go, but the civil service remains. It is no accident that the most senior civil servant in a government department has the title of 'Permanent Secretary'.

Unlike politicians, civil servants, even of the highest rank, are unknown to the larger public. Very few people could, if you asked them, give you the names of the present Secretary to the Cabinet (who runs the cabinet office), or the present Head of the Home Civil Service, or any other Permanent Secretary.

For those who belong to it, the British civil service is a career. Its most senior positions are usually filled by people who have been working in it for twenty years or more. These people get a high salary (higher than their ministers), have absolute job security (unlike their ministers) and stand a good chance of being awarded an official honour. By comparison, ministers, even those who have been in the same department for several years, are still new to the job.

For all these reasons, it is often possible for top civil servants to exercise quite a lot of control over their ministers, and it is sometimes said that it is they, and not their ministers, who really govern the country. This is a matter of opinion, but there is evidence that top civil servants do indeed expect to have a degree of influence, if not control. In early 1994, towards the end of a very long period of government by the same party (the Conservatives – see chapter 10), some top civil servants made an official complaint that certain government ministers had 'verbally abused' them and treated them 'with contempt'. It was the first time such a complaint had been made. Then, when in 1997 the governing party finally changed, things got even worse for the civil servants. The new ministers, confident after their huge election victory (see chapter 10), felt they had been installed in their departments with a mandate to wield a new broom and sweep all objections to their actions aside. The civil servants found them arrogant. They even began to organize training courses for their workers on how to deal with ministerial 'bullies'.

It seems, therefore, that career civil servants may be losing some of their former influence. In the second half of the twentieth century, ministers began to appoint experts from outside the civil service to work on various projects, and their own political advisers to work alongside (or, some would say, in competition with) their civil servants. The number of such appointments has steadily increased. These appointees depend for their jobs on their ministers alone, not the civil service career structure.

However, the British civil service has one powerful weapon with which to defend itself from these attacks on its power. This is its (largely) deserved reputation for absolute political impartiality. Many ministers have remarked on the struggle for power between them and their top civil servants, but very few have ever complained of political bias. The main hope for top civil servants to retain some influence on ministers is to continue staying out of 'politics'. This means that they can be trusted in a way which personal advisers cannot.

The origins of the civil service

The British 'cult of the talented amateur' (see chapter 5) is not normally expressed openly. But when, in the middle of the nineteenth century, the structure of the modern civil service was established, it was a consciously stated principle, as described by the contemporary historian Lord Macauley.

We believe that men who have been engaged, up to twenty-one or twenty-two, in studies which have no immediate connection with the business of any profession, and of which the effect is merely to open, to invigorate, and to enrich the mind, will generally be found in the business of every profession superior to men who have, at eighteen or nineteen, devoted themselves to the special studies of their calling.

In other words, it is better to be a non-specialist than a specialist, to have a good brain rather than thorough knowledge. Reforms since then have given greater emphasis to specialist knowledge, but the central belief remains that administration is an art rather an applied science.

Local government

Some countries, such as the USA, Canada, and Germany, are federal. They are made up of a number of states, each of which has its own government with its own powers to make laws and collect taxes. In these countries, the central government has powers only because the states have given it powers. In Britain, it is the other way around. Local government authorities (generally known as 'councils') only have powers because the central government has given them powers. Indeed, they only exist because of the central government. Several times in the last 100 years, British governments have reorganized local government, abolishing some councils and bringing new ones into existence.

The system of local government is essentially the same as it is nationally. There are elected representatives called councillors (the equivalent of MPs), who meet in a council chamber in the Town Hall or County Hall (the equivalent of Parliament), where they make policy which is implemented by local government officers (the equivalent of civil servants).

The relative lack of power of local government in Britain is reflected in the public attitude. Less than half of the electorate normally bothers to vote in local elections and most people are even more ignorant of the names of local politicians than they are of national ones. Nevertheless, the average person in Britain has far more direct dealings with local government than with national government. Local councils traditionally manage nearly all public services. Added together, they employ three times as many people as the national government. In addition, there is no system whereby a national official has responsibility for a particular geographical area. (There is no one like a 'prefect' or 'governor'.) In practice, therefore, local councils have traditionally been fairly free of constant central government interference.

Local councils are allowed to collect one kind of tax. This is known as council tax and is based on the estimated value of a property. (All other kinds are collected by central government.) The money collected from this tax is not nearly enough to provide all the services which the central government has told local councils to provide, especially because governments sometimes impose upper limits on council tax rates and collect the taxes on business properties themselves (and then share the money out between local councils). As a result, more than half of a local council's income is given to it by the central government.

The trend in the last half century has been towards greater control from central government. Perhaps this trend is inevitable because national party politics dominates local politics. Most people vote at local elections according to their national party preferences, so that these elections become a kind of national opinion poll.

The trend is ironic because 'devolution' (the redirecting of power from central government to local communities) is an idea that all political parties say they support. However, recent governments have not given any more powers to local government bodies. Instead, they have

Whitehall

This is the name of the street in London which runs from Trafalgar Square to the Houses of Parliament. Many government departments are located here or in streets running off it. As a result, the term 'Whitehall' is sometimes used as a way of referring to the administrative aspects of government. The phrase 'the opinion in Whitehall ...' refers to the opinions of senior civil servants and other administrators. Thus 'Whitehall' and 'Downing Street' can sometimes be in disagreement.

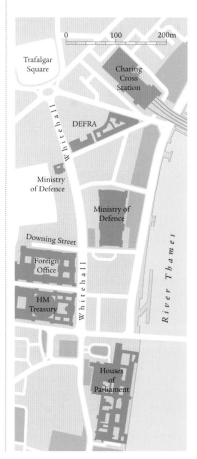

Local government areas in Greater London boroughs

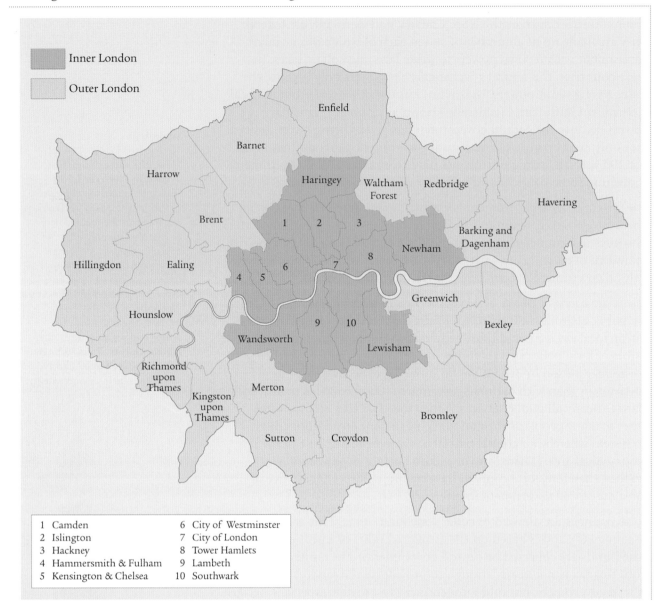

Inner London

Outer London

1 Camden	6 City of Westminster
2 Islington	7 City of London
3 Hackney	8 Tower Hamlets
4 Hammersmith & Fulham	9 Lambeth
5 Kensington & Chelsea	10 Southwark

The structure of local government outside London

Local government in Britain is organized according to its four constituent parts. There are 32 local authorities in Scotland, 22 in Wales, and 26 in Northern Ireland (from 2011, just 11). In England outside London, there are hundreds of local units, more than 120, which answer directly to central government. (Apart from the Greater London Authority, there are no 'regional' government authorities.)

Counties are the oldest divisions of the country in England and Wales. Most of them existed before the Norman conquest (see chapter 2). Many are still used today for local government purposes. Others no longer have any function in government but are still used for other purposes. One of these is Middlesex, which covers the western and some northern parts of Greater London: letters are still addressed to 'Middx' and it is the name

of a top-class cricket team. Many counties have 'shire' in their name (e.g. Hampshire, Leicestershire). 'Shires' is what the counties were originally called.

Parishes were originally villages centred around a local church. They became a unit of local government in the nineteenth century. Today, they are the smallest unit of local government in England and have very few powers. The name 'parish' is still used in the organization of the main Christian churches in England (see chapter 13).

Boroughs were originally towns that had grown large and important enough to be given their own powers, free of county control. These days, the name is used for local government purposes in London and only occasionally elsewhere.

bypassed these bodies and given more autonomy directly to locally provided services such as schools and hospitals. (In theory, the idea is that the 'stakeholders' of these services – the people who use and work in them – participate in decision-making.)

One idea to redress the balance of power is to allow local councils to collect a local income tax. This idea had not attracted much support. But one other attempt to reinvigorate local government in England and Wales has already been implemented. Local authorities can now, if they wish, have a directly elected mayor (along the American model). However, people seem to be suspicious of concentrating too much power in the hands of just one person. At the end of 2008, only around ten per cent of local authorities in Britain had taken a vote on this idea – and even then, most of them had rejected it. The general attitude to the idea, and perhaps to local government generally, is perhaps indicated by the fact that in the town of Hartlepool, the first mayoral election was won by 'H'Angus the monkey', a man in a monkey suit whose only policy was free bananas for schools! The one very notable exception to this failure has been London, whose mayor, disposing of a huge budget for a population larger than the whole of Scotland, has become one of the most powerful people in the country (The story of London's mayor).

Local government services include public hygiene and environmental health inspection, rubbish collection (which is done by 'dustmen'), the cleaning and tidying of all public places (which is done by 'street sweepers') and many others. They also include the provision of public swimming pools and sports centres, which charge admission, and public parks, which do not. The latter are mostly just green, grassy spaces but they often contain children's playgrounds and playing fields for sports such as football and cricket, which can be reserved in advance on payment. Most parks are staffed by employees who do the gardening and keep the place tidy. Public libraries are another well-known service. Anybody can go into one of these to consult the books, newspapers and magazines there (and in many cases recorded material as well) free of charge. If you want to borrow items and take them out of the library, you have to show that you live in the area and get a library card.

QUESTIONS

1 Do you think the theory of collective responsibility is a good one? Does it exist in your country?

2 Look at the extract from *Yes, Prime Minister* on page 86. The fictional diary entry finishes with a mention of 'leave ... government in the hands of the experts'. Who, according to this diarist, are the experts?

3 How does the relation between central and local government in Britain compare with that in your country?

4 Do you think elected mayors are a good idea?

The story of London's mayor

The name of Ken Livingstone is one of the best-known in British politics. Back in the 1980s he was known as 'Red Ken', the leader of the Labour-controlled Greater London Council. At that time, his policies and attitude made Margaret Thatcher, the Conservative Prime Minister, so angry that she simply abolished it. Its powers were given either to one of the 32 London boroughs or to committees controlled by central government. For 14 years, there was no local government authority responsible for London as a whole.

Then, as part of the Labour government's policy of devolution, the Greater London Authority was created and its mayor was to be directly elected. The 'new' Labour party was horrified when Ken insisted on being a candidate – so horrified they expelled him from the party. But Ken just went ahead as an Independent candidate and beat all the other candidates (including the official Labour one) in the 2000 election.

Mayor Livingstone turned out to be not such 'a disaster' as Tony Blair (the Labour Prime Minister) had predicted and the Labour party readmitted him as a member. They could see he was going to win the 2004 election (which he did) and it would not have looked good if he had beaten their official candidate again. And when Ken did embarrassing things like calling the American president 'the greatest threat to life on this planet' and inviting Fidel Castro, the communist president of Cuba, to London, they tried not to hear or see.

The story of London, then, is the single modern example in Britain where local politics has competed with national politics and won.

09 Parliament

The activities of Parliament in Britain are more or less the same as those of the parliament in any western democracy. It makes new laws, gives authority for the government to raise and spend money, keeps a close eye on government activities and discusses these activities.

The British Parliament works in a large building called the Palace of Westminster (popularly known as 'the Houses of Parliament'). This contains offices, committee rooms, restaurants, bars, libraries, and even some places of residence. It also contains two larger rooms. One of these is where the House of Lords holds its meetings. The other is where the House of Commons holds its meetings. The British Parliament is divided into these two 'houses' and its members belong to one or other of them, although only members of the Commons are known as MPs (Members of Parliament). The Commons is by far the more important of the two.

The atmosphere of Parliament

Look at the pictures of the inside of the meeting room of the House of Commons. Its design and layout differ from the interior of the parliament buildings in most other countries. These differences can tell us a lot about what is distinctive about the British Parliament.

The Speaker

Anybody who happened to be watching the live broadcast of Parliament on 22 June 2009 was able to witness an extraordinary spectacle. They saw an MP being physically dragged, apparently against his will, out of his seat on the back benches by fellow MPs and being forced to sit in the large chair in the middle of the House of Commons.

What the House of Commons was actually doing was appointing a new Speaker. The Speaker is the person who chairs and controls discussion in the House, decides which MP is going to speak next and makes sure that the rules of procedure are followed. (If they are not, the Speaker has the power to demand a public apology from an MP or even to ban an MP from the House for a number of days.) It is a very important position. In fact, the Speaker is, officially, the second most important 'commoner' (non-aristocrat) in the kingdom after the Prime Minister.

Why, then, did the man in that scene (John Bercow MP) appear to be resisting? The reason is history. Hundreds of years ago, it was the Speaker's job to communicate the decisions of the Commons to the king (that is where the title 'Speaker' comes from). Because the king was often very displeased with what the Commons had decided, this was not a pleasant task. As a result, nobody wanted the job. They had to be forced to take it.

These days, the position is a much safer one, but the tradition of dragging an unwilling Speaker to the chair has remained.

MPs in the House always address the Speaker as 'Mr Speaker' or 'Madame Speaker'. Once a new Speaker has been appointed, he or she agrees to give up all party politics and normally remains in the job for as long as he or she wants it.

John Bercow MP

First, notice the seating arrangements. There are just two rows of benches facing each other. On the left of the picture are the government benches, where the MPs of the governing party sit. On the right are the opposition benches. There is no opportunity in this layout for a reflection of all the various shades of political opinion (as there is with a semi-circle). According to where they sit, MPs are seen to be either 'for' the government (supporting it) or against it. This physical division is emphasized by the table on the floor of the House between the two rows of benches. The Speaker's Chair, which is raised some way off the floor, is also here. From this commanding position, the Speaker chairs (that is, controls) debate (The Speaker). The arrangement encourages confrontation between government and opposition. It also reinforces psychologically the reality of the British two-party system (see chapter 6). There are no 'cross-benches' for MPs who belong neither to the governing party nor the main opposition party. In practice, these MPs sit on the opposition benches furthest from the Speaker's chair (at the bottom right of the picture).

Second, the Commons has no special place for people to stand when they are speaking. MPs simply stand up and speak from wherever they are sitting. Third, notice that there are no desks for the MPs. The benches where they sit are exactly and only that – benches, just as in a church. This makes it physically easy for them to drift in and drift out of the room – something that they frequently do. Fourth, notice that the room itself is very small. In fact, there isn't enough room for all the MPs. There are about 650 of them, but there is seating for fewer than 400. A candidate at an election is said to have won a 'seat' in the Commons, but this seat

Palace of Westminster floor plan

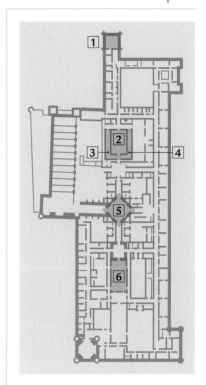

1 clock tower (Big Ben)
2 House of Commons
3 'Aye' Division Lobby
4 'No' Division Lobby
5 central lobby
6 House of Lords

House of Commons

1 Speaker's chair   4 galleries for visitors
2 government benches   5 press gallery
3 opposition benches

is imaginary. MPs do not have their 'own' place to sit. No names are marked on the benches. MPs just sit down wherever (on 'their' side of the House) they can find room.

All these features result in a rather informal atmosphere. Individual MPs, without their own 'territory' (which a personal seat and desk would give them), are encouraged to cooperate. Moreover, the small size of the House, together with the lack of a podium or dais from which to address it, means that MPs do not normally speak in the way that they would at a large public rally. MPs normally speak in a rather conversational tone and, because they have nowhere to place their notes while speaking, they do not normally speak for very long either. It is only on particularly important occasions, when all the MPs are present, that passionate oratory is sometimes used. On these occasions, the fact that some 200 MPs have to stand (because there is no seating room left) makes it clear that it is an important occasion!

It should be noted that the House of Commons was deliberately designed like this. Historically, it was an accident: in medieval times, the Commons first began meeting in a church, and churches of that time often had rows of benches facing each other. But after the House of Commons was badly damaged by bombing in 1941, it was deliberately rebuilt according to the old pattern (with one or two modern comforts such as central heating added). This was because of a belief in the two-way 'for and against' tradition, and also because of a more general belief in continuity.

The ancient habits are preserved today in the many detailed rules and customs of procedure which all new MPs have to learn. The most noticeable of these is the rule that forbids MPs to address one another by name. All remarks and questions must go 'through the chair'. An MP who is speaking refers to or asks a question of 'the honourable member for Winchester' or 'my right honourable friend'. The fellow MP concerned may be sitting directly opposite, but the MP never says 'you'. These ancient rules were originally formulated to take the 'heat' out of debate and decrease the possibility that violence might break out. Today, they lend a touch of formality which balances the informal aspects of the Commons and further increases the feeling of MPs that they belong to a special group of people.

An MP's life

Traditionally, MPs were not supposed to be specialist politicians. They were supposed to be ordinary people who gave some of their time to keeping an eye on the government and representing the people. Ideally, they came from all walks of life, bringing their experience of the everyday world into Parliament with them. This is why MPs were not even paid until the beginning of the twentieth century. Traditionally, they were supposed to be doing the public a service, not making a

Question Time

This is the best attended, and usually the noisiest, part of the parliamentary day. For about an hour, there is no subject for debate. Instead, MPs are allowed to ask questions of government ministers. In this way, they can, in theory at least, force the government to make certain facts public and to make its intentions clear. Opposition MPs in particular have an opportunity to make government ministers look incompetent or perhaps dishonest.

The questions and answers, however, are not spontaneous. Questions to ministers have to be 'tabled' (written down and placed on the table below the Speaker's chair) two days in advance, so that ministers have time to prepare their answers. In this way, the government can usually avoid major embarrassment. The trick, though, is to ask an unexpected 'supplementary' question. After the minister has answered the tabled question, the MP who originally tabled it is allowed to ask a further question relating to the minister's answer. In this way, it is sometimes possible for MPs to catch a minister unprepared.

Question Time has been widely copied around the world. It is also probably the aspect of Parliament best known to the general public. The vast majority of television news excerpts of Parliament are taken from this period of its day. Especially common is for the news to show an excerpt from the 15 minutes each week when it is the Prime Minister's turn to answer questions.

career for themselves. Of course, this tradition meant that only rich people could afford to be MPs so that, although they did indeed come from a wide variety of backgrounds, these were always backgrounds of power and wealth. Even now, British MPs, in comparison with many of their European counterparts, do not get paid very much and, for such a high-status role, their working conditions are somewhat cramped.

This earlier amateur ideal does not, of course, reflect modern reality. Politics in Britain in the last half century has become professional. Most MPs are full-time politicians. If they do another job, it is only part-time. But the amateur tradition is still reflected in the hours of business of the Commons. Until 2003, the House never 'sat' in the mornings. This is when, in the traditional ideal, MPs would be doing their ordinary work or pursuing other interests outside Parliament (When the Commons sits). The House also gives itself quite long holidays, similar to those of schools in Britain (including half-terms).

But this apparently easy life is misleading. In fact, the average modern MP spends more time at work than any other professional in the country. The prepared timetable of sittings sometimes has to be extended and occasionally the House debates all through the night and through the next day without a break. MPs' mornings are taken up with committee work, research, preparing speeches and dealing with the problems of their constituents (the people they represent). At weekends MPs are expected to visit their constituencies (the areas they represent) and listen to the problems of anybody who wants to see them. It is an extremely busy life that leaves little time for pursuing another career. It does not leave MPs much time for their families either. Politicians have a higher rate of divorce than the national average.

Hansard

This is the name given to the daily verbatim reports of everything that has been said in the Commons. They are published within 48 hours of the day they cover.

Frontbenchers and backbenchers

Although MPs do not have their own personal seats in the Commons, there are two seating areas reserved for particular MPs. These areas are the front benches on either side of the House. These benches are where the leading members of the government (i.e. ministers) and, opposite them, the leading members of the opposition sit. These people are thus known as frontbenchers. MPs who do not hold a government post or a post in the shadow cabinet (see chapter 8) are known as backbenchers.

When the Commons sits

The day in the main chamber of the House of Commons normally follows the following order:

1 **Prayers** (one minute).

2 **Question Time** (one hour).

3 **Miscellaneous business**, such as a statement from a minister (up to 45 minutes).

4 **Main business** (up to six and a half hours). On more than half of the days, this is a debate on a proposal for a new law, known as 'a bill'. Most of these bills are introduced by the government but some days in each year are reserved for 'private members' bills'; that is, bills introduced by individual MPs. Not many of these become law, because there is not enough interest among other MPs and not enough time for proper discussion of them.

5 **Adjournment debate** (half an hour). The main business stops and MPs are allowed to bring up a different matter for general discussion.

The parliamentary day used to run from 2.30 p.m. to 10.30 p.m. But in 2003, the hours were changed, with sessions starting in the morning and finishing by early evening. The intention was to allow MPs more time with their families and to present a more normal, sober, nine-to-five image to the public.

The change was also a recognition that, with so many more women MPs than before, some of them with young children, the Commons is no longer a gentleman's club.

But the new hours were very unpopular, and not only with male MPs. Mornings have always been used for committee work, and now these committees had to start working before 9 a.m. Some MPs complained they no longer had time to drop their children off at school. Others, who did not live near London and so could not return to their homes anyway, wandered around in the evening like lost souls. The new system meant MPs had to cram all their other duties into a much shorter period.

At the time of writing a compromise has been reached. The old hours are used for Mondays and Tuesdays and the new ones for Wednesdays and Thursdays, as follows:

Monday 2.30 p.m. – 10.30 p.m.
Tuesday 2.30 p.m. – 10.30 p.m.
Wednesday 11.30 a.m. – 7.30 p.m.
Thursday 10.30 a.m. – 6.30 p.m.
Friday 9.30 a.m. – 3 p.m. (the House does not 'sit' every Friday)

Parliamentary business

The basic procedure by which the Commons conducts its business is by debate on a particular proposal, followed by a resolution which either accepts or rejects the proposal. Sometimes this resolution just expresses a viewpoint, but most often it is a matter of framing a new law or of approving (or not approving) the government's plan to raise taxes or spend money in certain ways. Occasionally, there is no need to take a vote, but there usually is, and at such times there is a 'division'. That is, MPs have to vote for or against a particular proposal. They do this by walking through one of two corridors at the side of the House – one side for the 'Ayes' (those who agree with the proposal) and the other for the 'Noes' (those who disagree).

But the resolutions of the Commons are only part of its activities. There are also the committees. Some committees are appointed to examine particular proposals for laws, but there are also permanent committees whose job is to investigate the activities of government in a particular field. These committees comprise about forty members and are formed to reflect the relative strengths of the parties in the Commons as a whole. They have the power to call certain people, such as civil servants, to come and answer their questions. They are becoming an increasingly important part of the business of the Commons.

The party system in Parliament

Most divisions take place along party lines. MPs know that they owe their position to their party, so they nearly always vote the way that their party tells them to. The people whose job is to make sure that MPs do this are called the Whips. Each of the major parties has several MPs who perform this role. It is their job to inform all MPs in their party how they should vote. By tradition, if the government loses a vote in Parliament on a very important matter, it has to resign. Therefore, when there is a division on such a matter, MPs are expected to go to the House and vote even if they have not been there during the debate.

The Whips act as intermediaries between the backbenchers and the frontbench of a party (Frontbenchers and backbenchers). They keep the party leadership informed about backbench opinion. They are powerful people. Because they 'have the ear' of the party leaders, they can influence which backbenchers get promoted to the front bench. For reasons such as this, 'rebellions' among a group of MPs (in which they vote against their party) are very rare.

Sometimes, the major parties allow a 'free vote', when MPs vote according to their own beliefs and not according to party policy. Some quite important decisions, such as the abolition of the death penalty, allowing TV cameras into the Commons and the banning of foxhunting (see chapter 5) have been made in this way.

How a bill becomes a law

Before a proposal for a new law starts its progress through Parliament, there will have been much discussion. If it is a government proposal, either a Green Paper (which explores the background and ideas behind the proposal) or a White Paper (the same thing but more explicit and committed) or both will probably have been published, explaining the ideas behind the proposal. After this, lawyers draft the proposal into a bill.

Most bills begin in the House of Commons, where they go through a number of stages:

First Reading
This is a formal announcement only, with no debate.

Second Reading
The House debates the general principles of the bill and, in most cases, takes a vote.

Committee Stage
A committee of MPs examines the details of the bill and votes on amendments (changes) to parts of it.

Report Stage
The House considers the amendments.

Third Reading
The amended bill is debated as a whole.

The bill is sent to the House of Lords, where it goes through the same stages. (If the Lords make new amendments, these will be considered by the Commons.)

After both Houses have reached agreement, the bill receives the royal assent and thus becomes an Act of Parliament which can be applied as part of the law.

The House of Lords

Most parliamentary systems have a second chamber. The British one is called the House of Lords. Like some other second chambers, the House of Lords has no real power and only limited influence. Although the Lords can delay a bill, they cannot stop it becoming law in the end, even if they continue to refuse it. Its role, therefore, is a consultative one. In the Lords, bills can be discussed in more detail than the busy Commons has time for – and in this way irregularities or inconsistencies in these proposals can be avoided before they become law. In addition, the Lords act as a forum for discussion, and can sometimes bring to attention matters that the Commons has been ignoring. Most importantly of all, it is argued, the Lords can act as a check on any governments which, through their control of the Commons, are becoming too dictatorial.

But who are the members of the House of Lords and how do they get there? Its name suggests that its members are aristocrats. In fact, only a very small proportion of them are there by hereditary right and even these are unlikely to be there for much longer. It took Britain a long time to reform this undemocratic aspect of its political system. Until 1958, all of the Lords were indeed aristocrats. Then the first step was taken. A law was passed which made it possible to award 'life peerages' through the honours system (see chapter 7). These gave people entitlement to sit in the Lords but not the children of these people. During the second half of the twentieth century, the life peerage system established itself as a means of finding a place in public life for distinguished older politicians who no longer wished to be as busy as an MP in the Commons but still wished to voice their opinions in a public forum. At the time of writing, four of the last six Prime Ministers, as well as hundreds of former ministers and other respected politicians, have accepted the offer of a life peerage. Political parties are, in fact, especially keen to send their older members who once belonged to the leadership of the party to the House of Lords. It is a way of rewarding them with prestige but removing them from the Commons, where their status and reputation might otherwise create trouble for the present party leader and party unity. Informally, this practice has become known as 'being kicked upstairs'.

By the end of the twentieth century, so many life peers had been appointed that it was common for them to form a majority over the hereditary peers at most sitting of the Lords (since many aristocrats are not, of course, interested in politics). The next step was taken in 1999, when the number of aristocrats with the right to sit in the Lords was limited to 92 (about 15% of the total members). At the same time, the numbers of life-peerage appointments was increased.

At the time of writing, it is not clear what the next step will be. The problem is that, while almost everybody agrees that further reform is necessary, nobody can agree on the best way to compose the House of Lords. Many people believe members should be elected. But how?

The Lords Spiritual

As well as life peers (and, at the time of writing, the remaining hereditary peers), there is one other kind of peer in the House of Lords. These are the 26 most senior bishops of the Church of England. (By tradition, the Archbishops of Canterbury and York are also given life peerages on their retirement.) Until 2009, there was also a group of 'Law Lords', who fulfilled the Lords' role as the final court of appeal in the country. But this role is now in the hands of the Supreme Court (see chapter 11).

How the House of Lords lost its power

In 1910, the Liberal government proposed heavy taxes on the rich. The House of Lords rejected the proposal. This rejection went against a long-standing tradition that the House of Commons had control of financial matters.

The government then asked the king for an election and won it. Again, it passed its tax proposals through the Commons, and also a bill limiting the power of the Lords. Again, the Lords rejected both bills, and again the government won another election. It was a constitutional crisis.

What was to happen? Revolution? No. What happened was that the king let it be known that if the Lords rejected the same bills again, he would appoint hundreds of new peers who would vote for the bills – enough for the government to have a majority in the Lords. So, in 1911, rather than have the prestige of their House destroyed in this way, the Lords agreed to both bills, including the one that limited their own powers. From that time, a bill which had been agreed in the Commons for three years in a row could become law without the agreement of the Lords. This was reduced to two years in 1949.

These photographs show two scenes from the annual state opening of Parliament. It is an example of a traditional ceremony which reminds MPs of their special status and of their togetherness. In the first photograph, 'Black Rod', a servant of the Queen, is knocking on the door of the House of Commons and demanding that the MPs let the Queen come in and tell them what 'her' government is going to do in the coming year. However, the Commons refuses her entry. In the seventeenth century, Charles I once burst in and tried to arrest some MPs. Ever since then, the monarch has not been allowed to enter the Commons. Instead, the MPs agree to come through to the House of Lords and listen to the monarch in there. This is what they are doing in the second photograph. By tradition, they always come through in pairs, each pair comprising an MP from two different parties.

And how long should they stay as members? (There would be no point in simply replicating the model of election of MPs in the Commons.) It is widely believed that the value of the Lords lies in the fact that its members do not depend on party politics for their positions. Because they are there for life, they do not have to worry about losing their positions. This means they can take decisions independently, purely on the merits of a case. Indeed, it is noticeable that, since the hereditary element became so small, the Lords has been more assertive, more willing to challenge the decisions of the government-controlled Commons. So others argue that the life-peerage system should remain. This, however, raises the question of who appoints them. At present, they are appointed either on the recommendation of the Prime Minister, political parties or an independent body (set up in 2000) called the House of Lords Appointments Commission.

So the small hereditary element of membership of the House of Lords remains, a fascinating relic of older times. One last thing is worth noting. It is perhaps typically British that there has been no serious discussion about changing the name of the House of Lords. So, whatever happens in the future, the British second chamber will remain as a testament to tradition.

QUESTIONS

1 In what ways do the seating arrangements in the House of Commons differ from those in the parliament of your country? Why are they different? What difference does this make?

2 When the Commons decide to vote, they do not vote immediately. Instead a 'division bell' rings throughout the Palace of Westminster, after which MPs have ten minutes in which to vote. Why?

3 Everybody in Britain agrees that the House of Lords needs further reform. How do you think it should be reformed?

SUGGESTIONS

If you can, watch the late-night, light-hearted political discussion programme *This Week* on the BBC. Another programme worth watching is *Question Time*, which is a public debate and discussion modelled loosely after the real thing in Parliament. But if you want to see the real thing, there is a dedicated TV channel called Parliament Live.

10 Elections

Look at the table below. You can see that the British electoral system doesn't seem to add up. In the 2010 election, the Conservatives received only a little more than one third of all the votes cast but they won nearly half of the seats in the House of Commons. They got only 13% more of the total vote than the Liberal Democratic party but won 38% more seats. Indeed, the Liberal Democrats did very badly out of the system. They got almost a quarter of the votes but less than a tenth of the seats. And even this was luckier than in some previous elections. In 1987, for instance, they got the same proportion of the vote as this time but only 3% of the seats. What's going on?

The system

As is often the case with British institutions, these illogical figures are the result of history. Unlike any other country in the world, the system of political representation that is used in Britain evolved before the coming of democracy. It also evolved before national issues became more important to people than local ones. In theory, the House of Commons is simply a gathering of people who each represent a particular place in the kingdom. Originally, it was not the concern of

Elections

British general election results 2010

Conservative party	Labour party	Liberal Democrat party	All other parties
36% 10.73 million	**29%** 8.61 million	**23%** 6.84 million	**12%** 3.52 million
Number of votes	Number of votes	Number of votes	Number of votes
47% 307 MPs	**40%** 258 MPs	**9%** 57 MPs	**4%** 28 MPs
Number of MPs	Number of MPs	Number of MPs	Number of MPs
34,950	33,350	119,950	125,700
Votes per MP	Votes per MP	Votes per MP	Votes per MP

anybody in government as to how each representative was chosen. That was a matter for each town or county to decide for itself. Not until the nineteenth century were laws passed about how elections were to be conducted (The evolution of the electoral system).

This system was in place before the development of modern political parties (see chapter 6). These days, of course, nearly everybody votes for a candidate because he or she belongs to a particular party. But the tradition remains that an MP is first and foremost a representative of a particular locality. The result of this tradition is that the electoral system is remarkably simple. It goes like this: the country is divided into a number of areas of roughly equal population (about 90,000), known as constituencies. Anybody who wants to be an MP must declare himself or herself as a candidate in one of these constituencies. On polling day (the day of the election), voters go to polling stations and are each given a single piece of paper (the ballot paper) with the names of the candidates for that constituency on it. Each voter then puts a cross next to the name of one candidate. After the polls have closed, the ballot papers are counted. The candidate with the largest number of crosses next to his or her name is the winner and becomes the MP for the constituency.

And that's the end of it. There is no preferential voting (if a voter chooses more than one candidate, that ballot paper is 'spoiled' and is not counted); there is no counting of the proportion of votes for each party (all votes cast for losing candidates are simply ignored); there is no extra allocation of seats in Parliament according to party strengths. At the 2010 election, there were 650 constituencies and 650 MPs were elected. It was called a general election, and of course control of the government depended on it, but in formal terms there were just 650 separate elections going on at the same time.

You can now see the reason for the strange figures in the table on page 99. Here are the results from two constituencies in 2010.

	Conservative	Liberal Democrat	Labour
Results for the constituency of **Chelmsford**	**25,207** Simon Burns	**20,097** Stephen Robinson	**5,980** Peter Dixon
Results for the constituency of **Chesterfield**	**7,214** Carolyn Abbot	**17,342** Paul Holmes	**17,891** Toby Perkins

If we add the votes received by each party in these two constituencies together, we find that the Liberal Democrats got many more votes than Conservative or Labour. And yet these two parties each won a seat while the Liberal Democrats did not. This is because they were not first in either constituency. It is coming first that matters. In fact, the system is known as the 'first-past-the-post' system (an allusion to horse racing).

The evolution of the electoral system

1832

The Great Reform Bill is passed. Very small boroughs, where electors can easily be persuaded who to vote for, are abolished. Seats are given to large new towns such as Birmingham and Manchester, which have until now been unrepresented.

The franchise (the right to vote) is made uniform throughout the country, although differences between rural and urban areas remain. It depends on the value of property owned. About five per cent of the adult population is now enfranchised.

1867

The franchise is extended to include most of the male workers in towns.

1872

Secret Ballot is introduced. (Until now, voting has been by a show of hands.)

1884

The franchise is extended to include male rural labourers.

1918

Women over the age of thirty are given the right to vote.

1928

Women are given the franchise on the same basis as men. All adults over twenty-one now have the right to vote.

1969

The minimum voting age is lowered to eighteen, and candidates are now allowed to enter a 'political description' of themselves next to their name on the ballot paper. Until now, the only information about candidates that has been allowed on the ballot paper was their addresses.

Formal arrangements

In practice, it is the government which decides when to hold an election. The law says that an election has to take place at least every five years. However, the interval between elections is usually a bit shorter than this. A party in power does not normally wait until the last possible moment. In 2001 and 2005, for example, the Labour government called an election after only four years in power. When a party has a very small majority in the House of Commons, or no majority at all, the interval can be much shorter.

After the date of an election has been fixed, people who want to be candidates in a constituency must get their names on the ballot paper for that constituency. To do this, they have to deposit £500 with the Returning Officer (the person responsible for the conduct of the election in each constituency). They get this money back if they get five per cent of the votes or more. Candidates are allowed to indicate their political affiliation after their names on the ballot paper. In most cases, this is the name of the party which they represent. However, it is not necessary to belong to a party to be a candidate. You can write 'Independent' after your name or simply nothing at all. Moreover, it is quite easy to register as a political party and the rules about party names are very relaxed (Crazy parties).

To be eligible to vote, a person must be at least 18 years old and be on the electoral register. This is compiled every year for each constituency separately. Nobody is obliged to vote.

Canvassing

This is the activity that occupies most of the time of local party workers during an election campaign. Canvassers go from door to door, calling on as many houses as possible and asking people how they intend to vote. They rarely make any attempt to change people's minds, but if a voter is identified as 'undecided', the party candidate might later attempt to pay a visit.

The main purpose of canvassing seems to be so that, on election day, transport can be offered to those who claim to be supporters. (This is the only form of material help that parties are allowed to offer voters.) It also allows party workers to estimate how well they are doing on election day. They stand outside polling stations and record whether people who claim to be supporters have voted. If it looks as if these people are not going to bother to vote, party workers might call on them to remind them to do so.

Crazy parties

You don't have to belong to a party to be a candidate at an election. You don't even have to live in the constituency. All you need is £500. In the 2005 election, the voters in the constituency of Sedgefield found themselves staring at 15 names on the ballot paper. They were:

Berony Abraham *Independent*
John Barker *Independent*
Tony Blair *Labour*
Julian Brennan *Independent*
William Brown *UK Independence Party*
Robert Browne *Liberal Democrat*
Jonathan Cockburn *Blair Must Go Party*
Mark Farrell *National Front*
Cherri Gilham *United Kingdom Pathfinders*
Helen John *Independent*
Reg Keys *Independent*
Al Lockwood *Conservative*
Fiona Luckhurst-Matthews *Veritas*
Boney Maroney *Monster Raving Loony Party*
Terry Pattinson *Senior Citizens' Party*

Sedgefield is where the Prime Minister of the time, Tony Blair, was a candidate, so it was a natural choice of constituency for people who knew they had no chance of winning but wanted publicity, either because they felt very strongly about something, or just for fun. Eleven of these candidates did not get their money back!

Until 2001, there was no law which regulated political parties. There was just a law which allowed candidates to give a 'political description' of themselves on the ballot paper. However, this was open to abuse. (For example, one candidate in a previous election had described himself a 'Literal Democrat' and it is thought that some people voted for him in the belief that he was the Liberal Democrat candidate.) So part of the job of the Electoral Commission, which was created in 2001, is to register party names. However, parties can call themselves anything at all as long as it does not cause confusion. Among the 115 parties contesting the 2005 election were: *Vote for Yourself Rainbow Dream Ticket*; *Rock 'N' Roll Loony Party*; *Protest Vote Party*; *Death, Dungeons & Taxes*; *New Millennium Bean Party*; *Glasnost*; *Church of the Militant Elvis Party*; *Personality AND Rational Thinking? Yes! Party*; *Telepathic Partnership*.

The campaign

British elections are comparatively quiet affairs. There is no tradition of large rallies or parades as there is in the USA. However, because of the intense media coverage, it would be very difficult to be in Britain at the time of a campaign and not realize that an election was about to take place.

The campaign reflects the contrast between the formal arrangements and the political reality. Formally, a different campaign takes place in each constituency. The candidates hold meetings, there is local newspaper coverage, party supporters stick up posters in their windows and some wear party rosettes and spend their time canvassing (Canvassing). The amount of money that candidates are allowed to spend on their campaigns is strictly limited and they have to submit detailed accounts for inspection. Any attempt at improperly influencing voters is outlawed. At meetings, for example, it is illegal for candidates to offer a voter even a cup of tea.

But the reality is that all these activities and regulations do not usually make much difference. Nearly everybody votes for a candidate on the basis of the party which he or she represents, not because of his or her individual qualities or political opinions. Few people attend candidates' meetings; most people do not read local newspapers. In any case, the size of constituencies means that candidates cannot meet most voters, however energetically they go from door to door.

It is at a national level that the real campaign takes place. At this level too, party spending is legally controlled. Nevertheless, the big parties spend millions of pounds advertising on hoardings and in newspapers. By agreement, they do not buy time on television as they do in the

The swingometer

This is a device used by television presenters on election night. It indicates the percentage change of support from one party to another since the previous election – the 'swing'. Individual constituencies can be placed at certain points along the swingometer to show how much swing is necessary for them to change the party affiliation of their MPs.

The swingometer was first made popular by Professor Robert McKenzie on the BBC's coverage of the 1964 election. Over the years, it has become more colourful and complicated, especially in the hands of the BBC's Peter Snow, who manipulated it in all elections from 1974 to 2005.

USA. Instead, they are each given a number of strictly timed 'party election broadcasts'. There are also extended editions of the television news every night and each party holds a daily news conference. All of this puts the emphasis on national party personalities rather than on local candidates. Only in the 'marginals' – constituencies where only a small shift in voting behaviour from last time would change the result – might the qualities of an individual candidate affect the outcome.

Polling day and election night

Since 1931, general elections have always taken place on a Thursday. They are not public holidays. People have to work as usual, so polling stations keep long hours (seven in the morning until ten at night) to give everybody the opportunity to vote. The only people who get a holiday are those lucky schoolchildren whose schools are being used as polling stations.

After the polls close, the marked ballot papers are taken in boxes to a central place in the constituency – somewhere with a really big hall – where the boxes are opened and the votes for each candidate are counted. The count is a very public event. Representatives of the candidates are allowed to roam around freely and in many cases members of the public can watch from a distance. TV cameras may be there as well. When all the votes have been counted, the Returning Officer, together with the candidates, gets up onto a stage and announces the votes cast for each candidate and who, therefore, the MP for the constituency is. This declaration is one of the few occasions during the election process when shouting and cheering may be heard.

The period after voting is a TV extravaganza. Both the BBC and ITV start their programmes as soon as voting finishes. With millions watching, they continue right through the night. Certain features of these 'election specials', such as the 'swingometer', have entered popular folklore (The swingometer).

The first excitement of the night is the race to see which constituency can announce their result first (The race to declare). This usually occurs around 11.00 p.m. By midnight, after only a handful of results have been declared, experts (with the help of computers) will be making predictions about the composition of the newly elected House of Commons. Psephology (the study of voting habits) has become very sophisticated in Britain so that, although the experts never get it exactly right, they can get pretty close.

By two in the morning, at least half of the constituencies will have declared their results and, unless the election is a very close one, the experts on the television will now be able to predict with confidence which party will have a majority in the House of Commons, and therefore which party leader is going to be the Prime Minister.

Some constituencies, however, are not able to declare their results until well into Friday afternoon. This is either because they are very rural (mostly in Scotland or Northern Ireland), so that it takes a long

The race to declare

It is a matter of local pride for some constituencies to be the first to announce their result on election night. Doing so will guarantee lots of live TV coverage. To be a realistic candidate for this honour, a constituency must have three characteristics. It must have a comparatively small electorate (so there are not so many votes to count), be densely populated (so the ballot boxes can be gathered together quickly) and be a 'safe' seat for one or other party (so there is no possible chance of a recount). The 'winner' in the last five elections has been Sunderland South (in the north-east of England). In 2001, it set the all-time record by declaring at 10.42 p.m.

time to bring all the ballot papers together, or because the race has been so close that one or more 'recounts' have been necessary. The phenomenon of recounts is a clear demonstration of the ironies of the British system. In most constituencies it would not make any difference to the result if several thousand ballot papers were lost. But in a few, the result depends on a handful of votes. In these cases, candidates are entitled to demand as many recounts as they want until the result is beyond doubt. The record number of recounts is seven (and the record margin of victory is just one vote).

Recent results and the future

Since the middle of the twentieth century, the contest to form the government has effectively been a straight fight between the Labour and Conservative parties. As a general rule, the north of England and most of the inner areas of English cities have returned mostly Labour MPs to Westminster, while the south of England and most areas outside the inner cities have had mostly Conservative MPs. Which of these two parties forms the government depends on which one does better in the suburbs and large towns of England.

Since the 1980s, very few seats in Scotland or Wales have been won by the Conservatives. The majority of MPs from these two countries have been Labour, with the rest being taken by the respective nationalist parties (see chapter 6) or (somewhat more) the Liberal Democrats. The Lib Dems have won a large proportion of the rest of their seats in Parliament in the south west of England, although they have won some all over England. (Northern Ireland has followed a completely different pattern, with always about the same proportion of Protestant Unionist MPs and Catholic Nationalist MPs – slightly more for the former.)

In the fourteen elections from 1945 to 1992, the Conservatives were generally more successful than Labour. Although Labour won a majority of the seats in Parliament five times, on three of these occasions the majority was so small that it was in constant danger of disappearing as a result of by-election defeats (By-elections). In the same period, the Conservatives won a majority eight times, nearly always comfortably. Indeed, when in 1992 they won for the fourth time in a row – the first time this had happened for more than 160 years – it looked as if the swingometer's pendulum had stuck on the right. Sociologists suggested this situation was inevitable because Britain had developed a middle-class majority (as opposed to its former working-class majority). People began to wonder whether Labour could ever win again. Many political observers were worried, as it is considered to be basic to the British system of democracy that power should change hands occasionally.

Then, in 1997, the picture changed dramatically. Labour won the largest majority achieved by any party for 73 years and the Conservative share of the total vote was its lowest for 165 years. What happened? The answer seems to be that voting habits in Britain are no longer based so strongly on class loyalties. There was a time when most working-class people

By-elections

Whenever a sitting MP can no longer fulfil his or her duties, there has to be a special election in the constituency which he or she represents. (There is no system of ready substitutes.) These are called by-elections and can take place at any time. They do not affect who runs the government, but they are watched closely by the media and the parties as indicators of the present level of popularity (or unpopularity) of the government.

A by-election provides the parties with an opportunity to find a seat in Parliament for one of their important people. If a sitting MP dies, the opportunity presents itself. If not, an MP of the same party must be persuaded to resign.

The procedure of resignation offers a fascinating example of the importance attached to tradition. It is considered wrong for an MP simply to resign; MPs represent their constituents and have no right to deprive them of this representation. So what happens is that the MP who wishes to resign applies for a post with the title 'Steward of the Chiltern Hundreds'. This is a job with no duties and no salary. Technically, however, it is 'an office of profit under the Crown' (i.e. a job given by the monarch with rewards attached to it). According to ancient practice, a person cannot be both an MP and hold a post of this nature at the same time because Parliament must be independent of the monarch. (This is why high ranking civil servants and army officers are not allowed to be MPs.) As a result, the holder of this ancient post is automatically disqualified from the House of Commons and the by-election can go ahead.

voted Labour all their lives and nearly all middle-class people voted Conservative all their lives. The winning party at an election was the one which managed to get the support of the small number of 'floating voters'. But since 1997, Labour has shown itself capable of winning as many middle-class votes as the Conservatives (so that the middle-class majority as identified by sociologists does not automatically mean a Conservative majority in Parliament). It won again in 2001 and 2005, both times comfortably. But in the 2010 election, the Conservatives got more votes (though not a majority in Parliament). Meanwhile, support for other parties has grown. The British people in the twenty-first century seem to be much more fluid in their voting habits.

Modern issues

It is important for the health of a democracy that people feel they can take part in the democratic process and that their participation is effective and fair. But the results of recent British elections have caused some people to worry in this respect. For one thing, fewer people, especially younger people, seem to be bothering to vote (Turnout). For another, there has been an increase in support for smaller parties. However, because of the first-past-the-post system, this is not reflected in parliamentary representation (The other votes). The combined result of these two trends is that in 2005 the Labour party was able to form a government even though less than a quarter of the adult population voted for it. It is natural that some people should question whether a party has the right to govern at all in such circumstances.

In response to these concerns, the rules have been changed so that anybody who wants can vote by post. In 2010, about 20% of votes were cast this way. (Previously, there had to be a special reason and only about two per cent of votes were postal ones.) There have even

Size of overall majority in the House of Commons (with the name of the leader of the winning party)

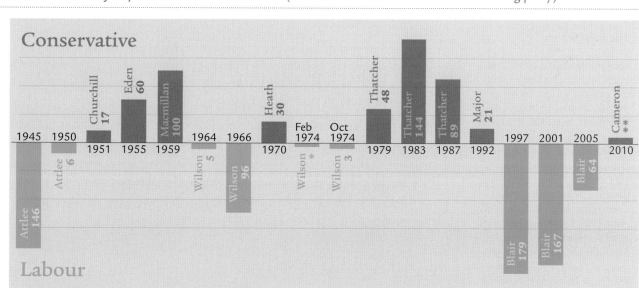

*Labour was the largest party but did not have an overall majority   ** The Conservatives was the largest party but did not have an overall majority

Turnout

Voting is not obligatory in Britain. Throughout the second half of the twentieth century, the turnout (that is, the proportion of people entitled to vote who actually vote) varied from 71% to 84%. But in the three elections this century, it has dropped well below 70%. Moreover, it appears to be the youngest age group who voted the least, causing fears that the trend will continue.

The other votes

Look at the 'votes per MP' row in the table on the first page of this chapter. As you can see, it took fewer than 40,000 votes to elect each Conservative or Labour MP, and on average more than 100,000 to elect each Liberal Democrat or other MP. But the 'All Others' column hides great variation. For example, Plaid Cymru (the Welsh National Party) got 165,000 votes and won three seats at Westminster. On the other hand, the UK Independence Party received nearly a million votes, and the British National Party more than half a million, but neither won any seats at all.

been experiments at local elections with all postal voting and voting by phone and internet. As for the second matter, it is possible that the way in which seats are won at British general elections will change to a more proportional system, as used elsewhere in Europe. This always seemed unlikely because it would not be to the advantage of the big two parties. But in 2010, as part of their 'price' for forming a coalition government with the Conservatives, the Liberal Democrats insisted that a referendum be held on this matter. More proportional systems are already used for elections to the Northern Ireland and Welsh assemblies, the Scottish and European parliaments, and some local government bodies. So perhaps the British people have become more accustomed to such systems and will vote in favour of adopting one of them at national level.

However, both types of change, but especially postal and other forms of 'remote' voting, detract from the system's biggest advantage. Britain has a rightly deserved reputation for freely and fairly conducted elections. A major reason for this is the system's primitive simplicity. Voting, the counting of votes and the declaration of results are all done by human beings in each other's physical presence, without the mediation of anything more technological than pencil and paper. It is notable that the advent of widespread postal voting has led to a dramatic increase in cases of electoral fraud. Similarly, the advantage of the first-past-the-post system is that its simplicity reduces even further the opportunities for cheating during the counting process.

In a poll published just before the 2005 elections, only 22% of people in Britain said they trusted the electoral system 'a lot' and 46% said they used to trust it but no longer did so. Most blamed postal voting for their lack of trust. It may be, therefore, that this attempt to increase participation in the democratic process will only lead to reduced confidence in it.

QUESTIONS

1 In what ways is political campaigning in your country different from that in Britain?

2 Is there a similar level of interest in learning about election results in your country as there is in Britain? Why (not)? Does it seem to reflect the general level of interest in politics which exists at other times – in Britain and in your own country?

3 Britain has 'single-member constituencies'. This means that one MP alone represents one particular group of voters. Is this a good system? Or is it better to have several MPs representing the same area?

4 Do you think Britain should adopt the electoral system used in your country? Or perhaps the other way around? Or are the two different systems the right ones for the two different countries?

SUGGESTIONS

If you can watch or listen to British TV or radio, watch or listen in on the night of the next British general election.

11 The law

The police and the public

There was a time when a supposedly typical British policeman could be found in every tourist brochure for Britain. His strange-looking helmet and the fact that he did not carry a gun made him a unique symbol for tourists. The image of the friendly British 'bobby', with his fatherly manner, was also well-known within the country and was reinforced by popular television serials such as *Dixon of Dock Green*. This positive image was not all myth. The system of policing was based on a single police officer with his own 'beat', a particular neighbourhood which it was his duty to patrol, on foot or by bicycle. The local bobby was a familiar figure on the local streets, a reassuring presence that people felt they could trust absolutely.

But in the 1960s, life became motorized. So did crime. And so did the police. As a result, individual police officers stopped being the familiar faces that they once were. At the same time, the police found themselves increasingly involved in dealing with public demonstrations and with the activities of the 1960s counterculture, whose young representatives started to see the police as the symbol of everything they disliked about society. Police officers were no longer known as 'bobbies' but became the 'fuzz' or the 'cops' or the 'pigs'.

A sign of these changed perceptions was the new television police drama, *Z Cars*, which showed police officers as people with real problems and failings who did not always behave in the conventionally polite and reassuring manner. Police dramas on all British TV channels since then have continued to depict the imperfections of those who represent the law. In 1998, for example, a special 3-part story in the modern series *The Bill*, involved a male officer sexually assaulting a female colleague and then continuing to harass her while turning all their mutual colleagues, who were thereby shown to be stupid and bad-willed, against her. Between 1998 and 2000, *The Cops*, another TV series, featured officers who routinely snorted cocaine, faked evidence, beat up suspects and had sex on the job.

Images of the police: past and present

The organization of the police

There is no national police force for Britain (or for England, Scotland, or Wales). All police employees work for one of the 50 or so separate forces, each with responsibility for a certain geographical area. Originally, these were set up locally. Only later did central government gain some control over them. It inspects them and has influence over senior appointments within them. In return, it provides most of the money to run them. The rest comes from local government.

The exception to this system is the Metropolitan Police, which polices Greater London and over which central government has more direct control. The 'Met' performs certain national police functions such as the registration of all crimes and criminals in England and Wales, and the compilation of the missing persons register. New Scotland Yard is the well-known building which is the headquarters of its Criminal Investigation Department (CID).

Miscarriages of justice

In 1997, three men who had spent 17 years in prison for killing a paper boy were released after their convictions were overturned. They were known as the Bridgewater Four (the fourth man had died in prison). Other well-known miscarriages of justice are known by the same formula. For example, other cases similar to the Bridgewater Four involved the Cardiff Three and the M25 Three.

But the most famous miscarriages of justice occurred in connection with a series of pub bombings by the IRA in the 1970s. The Guildford Four, the Birmingham Six and the Maguire Seven all spent long years in prison before their convictions were overturned (in 1989, 1991, and 1991 respectively) because it had become clear that the police had falsified evidence and/or withheld other evidence and/or extracted confessions using illegal means.

The image of crime

When British people think of crime and criminal behaviour, what usually pops into their heads is young men. And they are right that most crime is committed by young men. But in fact the section of society whose criminal behaviour is increasing the fastest is pensioners! People are living longer but putting aside less money for their old age. At the same time they feel increased pressure to maintain a high standard of living. A survey in 2002 found that a large proportion of pensioners have considered turning to crime and quite a few have actually done so, most of whom have been law-abiding citizens all their lives. The number of prisoners over the age of 65 has more than tripled since 1992. There are now specialist wings in prison to cater for them.

The Cops won several awards! Clearly then, the police lost much of their positive image in the second half of the twentieth century. These days, a child who gets lost is still advised to tell a policeman or policewoman, but the sight of a police officer no longer creates a general feeling of reassurance. In the 1980s and 1990s there were a large number of cases in which it was found that police officers had lied and cheated in order to get people convicted of crimes. As a result, trust in the honesty and incorruptibility of the police declined.

Aware of this problem, police in this century invest much time and energy in public relations. Foot patrols have been re-introduced and other efforts have been made to re-connect with local communities, including attempts to involve them more actively in the fight against lawbreaking (for example, through the registered charity Crimestoppers). In several police forces, officers have to wear name badges in order to make them seem more 'human'. These liaisons with the community can sometimes take a worrying turn when organizations pay the police for special services, leading to murmurings about the 'privatization of policing'.

Generally speaking, however, the relationship between police and public in Britain still compares quite favourably with that in some other European countries. There remains a great deal of public sympathy for the police. Despite the millions of CCTV cameras now in operation, the assumption that they are there to serve the public rather than to be agents of the government persists and it is felt that they are doing a difficult job under increasingly difficult circumstances. Most British police still do not carry guns in the course of normal duty.

Crime and criminal procedure

There is a widespread feeling among the British public that crime is increasing. Figures on this matter are notoriously difficult to evaluate. One reason for this is that the proportion of certain types of crime which is reported can vary over the years. For instance, official figures suggest that instances of rape more than doubled between 1998 and 2007. But these figures may represent an increase in the number of victims willing to report rape rather than a real increase in actual figures.

Consequently, it is impossible to say whether crime overall has increased in the last few decades. But what is certain is that the *fear* of crime has increased. This has gone together with a lack of confidence in the ability of the police to catch criminals. In the last decades of the twentieth century, private security firms were one of the fastest-growing businesses in the country. Another response to the perceived situation has been the growth of Neighbourhood Watch schemes. There are more than 100,000 of these in Britain. They attempt to educate people in crime prevention and to encourage the people of a particular neighbourhood to keep their eyes open for anything suspicious.

There has also been some impatience with the rules of criminal procedure under which the police and courts have to operate. The police are not, of course, above the law. When they arrest somebody, they have to follow certain procedures. For example, unless they obtain special permission, they are not allowed to detain a person for more than 24 hours without formally charging that person with a crime. Even after they have charged somebody, they need permission to remand that person in custody (i.e. to not let him or her go free) until the case is heard in court. In 1994, public concern about criminals 'getting away with it' led the government to make changes in the laws on this matter (Caution!). And in this century, the length of time for which some suspects can be detained without charge has, controversially, increased (The response to terrorism).

The system of justice

The system of justice in England and Wales, in both civil and criminal cases, is (as in North America) an adversarial system. This means that in criminal cases, there is no such thing as an examining magistrate who tries to discover the real truth about what happened. In formal terms, it is not the business of any court to find out 'the truth'. Its job is simply to decide 'yes' or 'no' to a particular proposition (in criminal cases, that a certain person is guilty of a certain crime) after it has heard arguments and evidence from both sides.

The civil justice system has its own courts. All civil cases go through County Courts and High Courts, or other, more specialized tribunals. This section focuses on the criminal justice system. For this there are two kinds of court. More than 90% of all cases are dealt with in magistrates' courts. Every town has one of these. In them, a panel of magistrates (usually three) passes judgement. In cases where they have decided somebody is guilty of a crime, they can also impose a punishment (The sentence of the court is ...).

Magistrates' courts are one example of the importance of amateurism in British public life. Magistrates, who are also known as Justices of the Peace (JPs), are not trained lawyers. They are just ordinary people of good reputation who have been appointed to the job by a local committee. They do not get a salary or a fee for

Caution!

'You do not have to say anything. But it may harm your defence if you do not mention when questioned something which you later rely on in court. Anything you do say may be given in evidence.' These words are those of the official caution which must be read out to anyone being arrested for a crime. An arrest is not legal without it.

Does the arrested person understand it? Is it fair to encourage people to defend themselves immediately against charges about which they do not yet know the details? These are the questions that some people asked when this caution was introduced in 1994. But it was introduced because it was thought that the previous formula ('You do not have to say anything unless you wish to do so, but what you say may be given in evidence'), by emphasizing the absolute 'right to silence', made things too easy for criminals.

The response to terrorism

On 7 July 2005, four British citizens killed themselves and 48 other people by exploding bombs which they were carrying on underground trains and a bus in London. In response to this and other atrocities in the western world (such as in Madrid and New York) and to a perception that there were many potential terrorists living in Britain, a law was passed which allowed the police to detain a terrorist suspect for up to 28 days without charge. This measure provoked opposition at the time because it goes against a fundamental principle of British law – that nobody should be detained by the authorities unless they are charged with a crime, and then brought to trial as quickly as possible.

But it has been argued that terrorist cases are special because they are often very complex, so that it takes a long time to gather enough evidence to bring a charge (and suspects need to be detained to make evidence gathering possible). Indeed, the government originally wanted a 90-day period of detention without charge but it was defeated in Parliament. Even so, the 'compromise' of 28 days was the longest detention-without-charge period in western democracies. In 2008, the government successfully persuaded Parliament to extend this period to 42 days.

Trial by jury

In Britain, it is a centuries old practice that anybody accused of a serious crime has the right to be tried by '12 good men and true', as the saying goes (though of course nowadays women are allowed to be good and true as well!). But modern British governments and some legal experts have sometimes expressed doubts about the jury system. One reason for these may be that juries so often find the defendant 'not guilty'. After remaining stable at around 32% for decades, acquittal rates in the 1990s shot up to 43% (perhaps because juries are less reverential towards police officers, lawyers and judges than they used to be).

But there are more serious reasons for doubts. Modern cases often involve a mass of technical information that an ordinary person cannot be expected to understand. Making this problem worse, it is argued, is the fact that juries are often unrepresentative. It is the duty of every citizen to be available for jury service, but few people want to do it. It means spending weeks, sometimes longer, stuck in a court room listening to frequently boring evidence, instead of getting on with your normal life. And though you get paid expenses, you do not actually earn a fee. So people often try to escape jury service by providing special reasons why they cannot do it. Naturally, it is the more intelligent people who are more successful in these attempts. In 2001, a graffito was found in the toilets of the Central Criminal Court in London (the Old Bailey) which read 'I am being tried by 12 people too stupid to get out of jury service'.

Nevertheless, the jury system remains as a central principle of the law in Britain and, like the absence of identity cards, is widely regarded as a symbol of British freedoms.

their work (though they get paid expenses). Inevitably, they tend to come from the wealthier sections of society and, in times past, their prejudices were very obvious. They were especially harsh, for instance, on people found guilty of poaching (hunting animals on private land), even though these people sometimes had to poach in order to put food on their families' tables. These days efforts are made to recruit JPs from as broad a section of society as possible.

Even serious criminal cases are first heard in a magistrates' court. However, in these cases, the JPs only need to decide that there is a *prima facie* case against the accused (in other words, that it is possible that he or she is guilty). If they do, they then refer the case to a Crown Court, where a professional lawyer acts as the judge. But even in such serious cases, amateurs play a crucial role. Unlike most other countries in the world, the decision regarding guilt or innocence is not taken by the judge or any other legal professional. It is taken by a jury. Juries consist of 12 (in Scotland sometimes 15) people selected at random from the list of voters (Trial by jury). In order to reach a verdict, there must be agreement among at least ten of them. If this does not happen, the judge has to declare a mistrial and the case must start all over again with a different jury. The duty of the judge during a trial is to act as the referee while the prosecution and defence put their cases across and question witnesses, and to decide what evidence can be taken into account by the jury and what cannot. It is also the judge's job to impose a punishment (known as 'pronouncing sentence') on those found guilty. A convicted person may appeal to the Court of Criminal Appeal (generally known just as the Appeal Court) in London either to have the conviction quashed (i.e. the jury's previous verdict is overruled and they are pronounced 'not guilty') or to have the sentence (i.e. punishment) reduced.

The legal profession

As in many other countries, lawyers in Britain are not the most popular of professionals (although in Britain they are probably less unpopular than some journalists and, especially, estate agents). In addition, British lawyers do not often advertise their services directly. So it was with some surprise that in 2004 people in many parts of Britain encountered advertising posters announcing 'My hero – my solicitor'. But there was a reason for this unprecedented public relations campaign. In Britain there are two kinds of lawyers: solicitors and barristers. Typically, the former are the ones who deal with the public; anybody who needs a lawyer goes to see a solicitor. They handle most legal matters for their clients, including the drawing up of documents (such as wills, divorce papers and contracts), communicating with other parties and presenting their client's case in a magistrates' court. But if a case is to be heard in a higher court, the solicitor hires the services of the other kind of lawyer – a barrister. The main function of barristers is to present cases in court. They also offer expert legal opinions when asked.

Until recently, the roles of the two kinds of lawyer were kept rigidly apart. A solicitor could never be 'called to the bar' and so was never allowed to present cases in a higher court; a barrister was not supposed to talk with any of the clients he or she represented in court, or with their witnesses, except in the presence of the solicitor who hired them. Solicitors dealt with the realities of the everyday world and its problems while barristers were farther removed, becoming experts in arcane points of law and acquiring the special skill of eloquence in public speaking.

But in the years around the turn of the century, the rules dividing the roles of these two types of lawyer were relaxed. It became permissible both for members of the public to approach barristers directly, without going through a solicitor first, and also for solicitors to present cases in some higher courts, without hiring the services of a barrister. As a result, the two kinds of lawyer came into competition with each other for the first time. Now, in the popular image, barristers are in some sense 'senior' to solicitors, more highly educated and so, perhaps, 'better'. Unlike solicitors, they are mostly self-employed and have a prestige similar to that of doctors. They belong to one of the four Inns of Court, ancient institutions resembling Oxbridge colleges (see chapter 14). Moreover, there are about seven times as many solicitors as there are barristers, and it is mostly barristers who (after at least ten years in practice) achieve the rank of QC (Queen's Counsel), from whose ranks judges are appointed (until the changes, solicitors were not even allowed to apply for this rank). Because of this popular perception, the country's solicitors felt they needed to defend their territory by boosting their image.

In fact, solicitors and barristers still receive separate training and have to pass different exams, reflecting the different skills they are expected to acquire. After their exams, new solicitors have to secure a two-year training contract with a firm of solicitors to complete their qualification while barristers have to secure a 'pupillage', a one-year period of practical training under the supervision of an experienced barrister. But the changes have gone some way to 'opening up'

The sentence of this court is …

If it is someone's first offence, and the crime is a small one, even a guilty person is often unconditionally discharged and can go free without punishment.

The next step up the ladder is a conditional discharge and/or a suspended sentence. In both cases, this means that the guilty person is set free but if he or she commits another crime within a stated time, the first crime will be taken into account (and any suspended sentence will be imposed). He or she may also be put on probation, which means that regular meetings with a social worker must take place.

A very common form of punishment for minor offences is a fine, which means that the guilty person has to pay a sum of money.

Another possibility is that the convicted person is sentenced to a certain number of hours of community service.

Wherever possible, magistrates and judges try not to imprison people. This costs the state money, the country's prisons are already overcrowded and prisons have a reputation for being 'schools for crime'.

As in the rest of Europe, there is no death penalty in Britain. It was abolished in 1969. For murderers, there is an obligatory life sentence.

A view of the top of The Central Criminal Court, commonly known as the Old Bailey, in central London.

Some terms connected with the legal system in England and Wales

acquitted found not guilty by the court

bail a condition on which a person who has been charged with a crime can go free until the time of the trial. Typically, this is a sum of money guaranteed on behalf of the charged person.

convicted found guilty by the court

claimant (previously known as the 'plaintiff') the party who makes a claim in a civil court case.

defendant the party against whom a claim is brought in a criminal court case (i.e. the person accused of a crime)

on remand in prison awaiting trial

party one of the sides in a court case. Because of the adversarial system, there must always be two parties in any case: one to make a claim and one to deny this claim.

prosecution the party who makes a claim in a criminal court case. This job is done by the Crown Prosecution Service (CPS).

respondent the party against whom a claim is brought in a civil court case

verdict the decision of the court

The final appeal

The highest court of all in Britain used to be the House of Lords (see chapter 9). But this long-established system was considered an anachronism and also a contradiction of the principle of the separation of powers (which states that the people who make the laws and those who decide whether they have been broken should not be the same people). Since 2009, the highest court in the UK has been the Supreme Court. It hears matters on important points of law, mostly civil cases. It also hears some criminal cases of great public importance (except those in Scotland, where the High Court of Justiciary is the highest criminal court).

The law in Scotland

Scotland has its own legal system, separate from the rest of the UK. Although it also uses an adversarial system of legal procedure, the basis of its law is closer to Roman and Dutch law. The names of several officials in Scotland are also different from those in England and Wales (for instance, instead of barristers, there are 'advocates'). A very noticeable feature is that there are three, not just two, possible verdicts. As well as 'guilty' and 'not guilty', a jury may reach a verdict of 'not proven', which means that the accused person cannot be punished but is not completely cleared of guilt either.

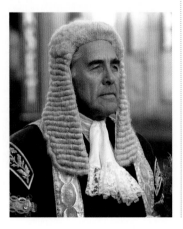

the practice of law and making it seem less old-fashioned and less connected to social class divisions. Previously, barristers were recruited almost entirely from the upper strata of society and those who became judges, although often people of great learning and intelligence, sometimes seemed to have difficulty understanding the problems and circumstances of ordinary people and to be out of step with general public opinion.

At the same time, some traditions remain. Barristers and judges in higher courts still wear the archaic gowns and wigs which, it is supposed, emphasize the impersonal majesty of the law. Similarly, the independence of judges remains. Once they have been appointed, it is almost impossible for them to be dismissed. The only way that this can be done is by a resolution of both Houses of Parliament – something that has never happened. Moreover, their retiring age is later than in most other occupations and they get very high salaries. These things are considered necessary in order to ensure their independence from interference, by the state or any other party.

QUESTIONS

1 How has the public perception of the police changed in the last 50 years in Britain? Why do you think it has changed?

2 Why do you think British people feel that there is more crime than there used to be? What about your own country – do people feel that crime has increased there?

3 What are the main differences between the legal system in your country and that in Britain? Compared with the system in your country, what are the strengths and weaknesses of the British system?

SUGGESTIONS

There are many contemporary British writers who use the theme of crime and detection. One of them is Colin Dexter, whose books feature Inspector Morse and many of which have been adapted for television. P. D. James and Ruth Rendell are two other highly respected writers of crime fiction.

12 International relations

The attitudes of a country's people to the rest of the world and the relationships of its government with other places in the world can tell us a great deal about that country.

British people and the rest of the world

In the days when 'Britannia ruled the waves' (see chapter 2), British people had a rather patronizing attitude towards people in other countries and their ways. Foreigners were often considered amusing, perhaps interesting, even exotic, but not really to be taken seriously. What really mattered – for the whole world – was what Britain and British people did. But this attitude has disappeared with the dismantling of the empire. These days, many foreign ways of doing things are admired (although perhaps a bit resentfully) and there is a greater openness to foreign influences.

The modern British are not really chauvinistic. Open hostility to people from other countries is very rare. If there is any chauvinism at all, it expresses itself through ignorance. Most British people know remarkably little about Europe and who lives there (although not as little as most Americans). This ignorance is not as great as it used to be. But it is indicative that most people have caricatured stereotypes in their minds only for the larger nations of Europe. Ask the average British person what he or she thinks of the Belgians, the Czechs or the Portuguese and the most honest answer would be 'nothing'.

The Commonwealth

The dismantling of the British empire took place comparatively peacefully, so good relations between Britain and the newly independent countries were established. As a result, and with the encouragement of Queen Elizabeth II, an international organization called the Commonwealth, composed of the countries that used to be part of the empire, has continued to hold annual meetings. Some of these countries have even kept the British monarch as head of state.

There are no clear formal economic or political advantages involved in belonging to the Commonwealth, but it has helped to keep cultural contacts alive, and means that every year, the leaders of a sixth of the world's population sit down and talk together. Until quite recently, there were special trading agreements between members. But since Britain became a member of the European Economic Community, most of these agreements have gradually been discontinued.

The remnants of the empire in 2008

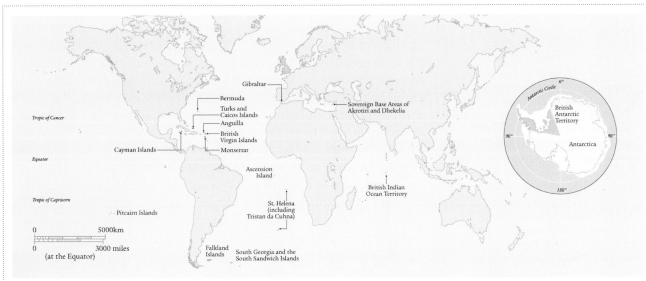

Moreover, the British are very bad about learning other languages. Fluency in any continental European language is generally regarded as exotic. (In fact, the second-most spoken language in Britain is reported to be Punjabi.) As students in Britain do not have to study a foreign language after the age of 14, this situation is unlikely to change. But there is nothing defensive or deliberate about this attitude. The British do not refuse to speak other languages; they are just lazy. The role of English as the world's language makes it too easy for them.

The British state and the rest of the world

Britain lost its empire in the second half of the twentieth century (see chapter 2). However, some small remnants of it remain. Whatever their racial origin, the inhabitants of Bermuda, Gibraltar, the Falklands/Malvinas and several other small islands (The remnants of the empire) have all wished to continue with the imperial arrangement (they are afraid of being swallowed up by their nearest neighbours). For British governments, these wishes are a source of pride on the one hand but embarrassment and irritation on the other: pride, because they suggest how beneficial the British imperial administration must have been; embarrassment, because the possession of colonial territories does not fit with the image of a modern democratic state, and irritation because it costs money.

The old imperial spirit is not quite dead. In 1982, the British government spent hundreds of millions of pounds recapturing the Falklands/Malvinas Islands from the invading Argentinians. We cannot know if it would not have done so if the inhabitants had not been in favour of remaining British and Argentina had not had a military dictatorship at the time. But what we do know is that the government's action received enormous popular support at home. Before the Falklands War, the government of the time was extremely unpopular; afterwards, it suddenly became extremely popular and easily won the general election early in the following year. Here was a rare modern occasion for the British people to be actively patriotic. Many of them felt that here, for once, Britain was doing something right and doing it well.

Opinions about British military interventions since then have been much more lukewarm. In the 1990s, there was majority acceptance of, but little enthusiasm for, Britain's role in the Gulf War and in Balkan peacekeeping efforts. And in 2003, the government's decision to go to war in Iraq provoked heated debate. One public demonstration against it, led by prominent figures which included the Mayor of London and the leader of the Liberal Democrat party, was the largest in British history. The decision has been generally regretted ever since. The British military presence in Afghanistan has also been unpopular. In early 2008, the commander of RAF Wittering, a military barracks near the English town of Peterborough, ordered his personnel not to wear their uniforms in the town for fear of attracting threats and abuse. This precaution was probably unnecessary (Britain's armed forces), but the fact that the order was given shows the strength of feeling that existed at the time against Britain's role in Iraq and Afghanistan.

Britain's armed forces

The loyalty towards the government of the British armed forces has not been in doubt since the Civil War (with the possible exception of a few years at the beginning of the twentieth century – see chapter 2). In addition, the army has only rarely been used to keep order within Great Britain in the last 100 years. These facts probably help to explain why, over the years, opinion polls have shown the armed forces to be one of the few institutions that British people are consistently proud of. Another possible reason is that there is no period of compulsory military service for British citizens. ('National Service', as this was called, was abolished in 1957.)

The British military is divided into three branches: the Royal Navy, the Royal Air Force (RAF) and the army. The navy is the oldest; traditionally, it traces its history right back to King Alfred (see chapter 2) and for this reason is sometimes known as 'the senior service'. But the army is also steeped in tradition. Great upset was caused when, in the 1990s, several famous old regiments were forced to merge with others. At one time, a number of upper-middle class families maintained a tradition down the generations of belonging to a particular regiment. Few such families exist today. However, a career in the armed forces is still highly respectable.

For some time, in fact, there has been uncertainty about the proper level of Britain's role in world affairs. When, at the end of the 1980s, the Cold War between the west and the Soviet Union came to an end and the government began to cut spending on defence, some politicians and many military professionals protested. They said that Britain would not be able to meet its 'commitments' in the world. But there is no general agreement on what these commitments are and on whose behalf they should be undertaken. There is still a feeling in the country that Britain should be able to make significant contributions to international 'peacekeeping'. But should it ever act alone in such efforts or only on behalf of the United Nations or the European Union? Then there is the question of nuclear weapons. Since the 1950s, the Campaign for Nuclear Disarmament (CND) has argued, on both moral and economic grounds, that Britain should cease to be a nuclear power. At certain periods, the CND has had a lot of popular support. However, this support has not been consistent. Britain still has a nuclear force, although it is tiny compared to that of the USA.

Transatlantic relations

British governments are fond of referring to the 'special relationship' between Britain and the USA. There have been occasional low points, such as Suez (see chapter 2) and when the USA invaded the Caribbean island of Grenada (a member of the British Commonwealth). But generally speaking, it has persisted. It survived the Falklands/Malvinas War, when the USA offered Britain important material, but little public support, and regained its strength from 1991 onwards, due to Britain's support for American campaigns in Iraq and Afghanistan.

Public feeling about the relationship is ambivalent. On the one hand, it is reassuring to be so diplomatically close to the most powerful nation in the world, and the shared language gives people some sense of belonging with America. On the other hand, there is some mild bitterness about the power of the USA. There is little distrust, but remarks are often made about Britain being nothing more than the fifty-first state of the USA. Similarly, while some older people remember with gratitude the Americans who came to their aid in the Second World War, others resent the fact that it took them so long to get involved.

In any case, the special relationship has inevitably declined in significance since Britain joined the European Communities. When global trade negotiations take place these days, there is nothing special about Britain's position with regard to America – it is just part of the European trading block. The opening of the channel tunnel in 1994 emphasized that Britain's links are now mainly with Europe. Tourist statistics also point this way. Until the early 1990s, it was always American visitors who arrived in Britain in the greatest numbers. Since then, there have been about the same number of both French visitors and German visitors. The majority of visitors to Britain are now from Europe.

We win fight to save pints

This was the front page headline of *The Sun*, Britain's most popular newspaper, on 11 September 2007, when it was established that British traders could continue to sell goods using imperial measures (see chapter 15). On the same day, the headline of an article in another popular newspaper, *The Daily Mail*, read 'Victory for Britain's metric martyrs as Eurocrats give up the fight'. The article began 'Brussels will today give up the fight to make Britain drop pints, pounds and miles'. In fact, it had never been EU policy to make British people stop buying draught beer in pints or indicating road distances in miles, and it was not Eurocrats who had attempted to abolish pounds and ounces but rather officious local British authorities who had misunderstood the EU regulations.

Even serious, 'quality' British newspapers (see chapter 16) can sometimes get rather upset about the supposed power of Brussels. The day before the headlines mentioned above, *The Daily Telegraph* ran an article headlined 'Queen may be dropped from EU passports', although there had never been any discussion of such a move in any EU bodies. Similarly, *The Times* headline on 13 October 2006 read 'Motorists must switch on lights during day, EU says'. This was a reference to the EU policy that all new cars should be equipped with ecologically-friendly daytime lights, but the policy said nothing about whether people should use them.

European relations

On the morning of 13 December 2007, the prime ministers of the 25 member states of the European Union (EU) gathered to sign the latest European treaty. But one of the prime ministers was missing. Which one? Yes, you guessed it. The British one was too busy to turn up. Gordon Brown had to appear before a (British) parliamentary committee that morning. He went to sign the treaty in the afternoon, all by himself.

This little incident is indicative of the British attitude to its membership of the EU. From the very start, this attitude has been ambivalent. On the one hand, it is seen as an economic necessity and a political advantage (increasing Britain's status as a regional power). The referendum on continued membership in 1975 (the first in British history) produced a two-to-one majority in favour. On the other hand, acceptance has never meant enthusiasm. In fact, the dominant attitude towards the EU among people in Britain is a profound lack of enthusiasm. It tends to be seen as a necessary evil – and there are those who disagree with the 'necessary' part of that description! Talk can still be heard, even in political circles, of leaving the EU. (In the 2004 European elections, the UK Independence Party got 16% of the vote, beating the Liberal Democrats into third place behind the big two parties.)

How can this attitude be explained? The first answer involves the British sense of apartness. British people know that their country is geographically part of Europe and that it is a full member of the European Union. But somehow, they just don't feel it (The British view of world geography). Only about one third of the British electorate bothers to vote in European elections. In their eyes, Britain and 'Europe' are fundamentally two different things.

Is Britain really part of Europe?

It's supposed to be, but sometimes you cannot blame the British for feeling that it isn't. Take the case of car hire, for example. Throughout continental western Europe, you can hire a car and drive it into other countries (including Britain) without special permission or procedures. But if you hire a car in Britain you can only drive it to the continent if you fill in lots of legal documents and pay lots of extra money for insurance!

The British view of world geography

The fact is that the British have a totally private sense of distance. This is most visibly seen in the shared pretence that Britain is a lonely island in the middle of an empty green sea. Oh, yes, I know you are all aware, in an abstract sort of way, that there is a substantial landmass called Europe near by and that from time to time it is necessary to go over there and give old Jerry a drubbing[1] or have a holiday on the Med[2], but it's not near by in any meaningful sense in the way that, say, Disney World is. If your concept of world geography was shaped entirely by what you read in the papers and saw on television, you would have no choice but to conclude that America must be about where Ireland is, that France and Germany lie roughly alongside the Azores, that Australia occupies a hot zone somewhere in the region of the Middle East, and that pretty much all other sovereign states are either mythical or can only be reached by spaceship. [...]

I can remember, after I had been living about a year in Bournemouth and had bought my first car, fiddling with the car radio and being astounded at how many of the stations it picked up were in French, then looking at a map and being even more astounded to realize that I was closer to Cherbourg than I was to London. I mentioned this at work the next day and most of my colleagues refused to believe it. Even when I showed them on a map, they frowned doubtfully and said things like: 'Well, yes, it may be closer in a strict physical sense', as if I were splitting hairs[3] and that really a whole new concept of distance was required once you waded into the English Channel.

You can measure distance objectively, using kilometres or miles. But what really matters in human affairs is subjective distance: how near or far away a certain place *feels*. The extract above is a characterization of British feelings about the distance from Britain of other places in the world. It is written by an American who, having lived in Britain for several years, wrote a humorous book about the country. The book was hugely popular.

Bill Bryson, *Notes from a Small Island*

[1] win a war against Germany. 'Jerry' was a nickname which was used (and sometimes still is) to denote the German people collectively. The 'old' before it suggests an affectionate familiarity.
[2] the Mediterranean
[3] making unnecessary distinctions

As a result, EU laws and regulations are often perceived as interference by a 'foreign' organization. For some politicians and the media, they are a threat to the 'sovereignty' (that is, the autonomy and independence) of the UK; for the average person (who is perhaps not as concerned about matters of sovereignty as the politicians would like them to be), they are a threat to the British 'way of life'.

In fact, it is news about EU regulations pertaining to everyday life and habits that seem to irritate the British more than any other kind. Ask the average British person what comes into their mind if you say 'the EU' and they will tell you about a bunch of interfering, probably French-speaking, busybodies in Brussels who just want to make life difficult for people. One possible reason for this is that the British, like people in Scandinavian countries, tend to take laws and regulations seriously and to interpret them literally. The traditional British attitude is that the law should be applied consistently and precisely; there is little sympathy with the notion that it can be applied selectively or partially to suit the circumstances of each case. As a result, they like to have as few laws and regulations as possible. But what they see coming from Brussels is a steady, never-ending stream of them. Worse still, many of them seem to be about standardization (of products, packaging, and procedures). To many other Europeans, standardization means quality, reliability, and convenience. But to many British people, it means restriction, boring uniformity, and (therefore) inconvenience.

An indication of the British attitude can be found by studying the commercial listings in a telephone directory (known in Britain as 'the Yellow Pages'). In other European countries, you will see that a vast number of companies have chosen to begin their name with the prefix 'Euro'. After all, this is a way of suggesting modern high standards. But if you were to take a look at a British directory, you would see that only a tiny number of companies use the 'Euro' prefix in their names.

Relations inside Great Britain

There is another reason why some politicians at Westminster feel distrust about the idea of greater European integration. It is feared that this may not just be a matter of giving extra power to Brussels. It may also be a matter of giving extra powers to the regions of Britain, especially its different nations.

Before the 1980s, most Scottish people, although they insisted on many differences between themselves and the English, were happy to be part of the UK. But there was always some resentment about the way their country was treated by the central government in London. From the mid 1980s onwards, opinion polls consistently showed that a majority of the Scottish population wanted either internal self-government within the UK or complete independence. (Support for such a move was probably strengthened by the realization that, in the EU, it need not mean international isolation.)

The Battle of the Colours

In late May 2005 near Portsmouth on the south coast of England, a spectacular *son-et-lumière* took place. A dazzling array of pyrotechnics was produced in re-enactment of 'an early nineteenth century sea battle' between 'a Red Fleet and a Blue Fleet'. The event was attended by Queen Elizabeth II and government leaders from 73 countries were invited.

Why would the British authorities have wanted to gather such an impressive collection of dignitaries to witness this spectacle? A new tourism campaign?

The answer is that this was an event to mark the bicentenary of the Battle of Trafalgar, at which the British navy completely destroyed a combined French and Spanish fleet, paving the way for Britannia to rule the waves for the next 100 years.

However, the organizers did not want to embarrass their French and Spanish guests. So the words 'Trafalgar', 'British', and 'French' were absent from the brochure.

A referendum finally decided the issue and in 1999, nearly 300 years after it abolished itself, the Scottish Parliament was reborn. It has considerable powers over internal Scottish affairs. It is only in defence, foreign policy and economic policy that it has few or no powers.

What will the future hold? Support for the Scottish Parliament has grown since that time, and at the time of writing the Scottish National Party (SNP), which wants complete independence from the UK (but with the English monarch as their head of state too), is the largest party in Scottish Parliament. In 2007, an opinion poll produced some interesting results. First, it found a majority in favour of even more powers for the Scottish Parliament. Second, it found that more people identified with the Irish (who already have their own independent state) than with the English. Third, it found that, while only a quarter of Scottish people actively desired complete independence, a majority saw it as inevitable in the long run.

Perhaps they are right. The present arrangement puts pressures on the relationship between Scotland and England (The West Lothian question). These could come to the fore if the policies of any future London government were manifestly against the wishes of a majority of Scottish people (this is more likely under a Conservative government; the Conservative party has very little support in modern Scotland). The political commentator Andrew Marr has spoken of England and Scotland being 'pulled slowly apart, like two pieces of pizza'.

In Wales, the situation is different. The south-eastern and north-eastern parts of this nation are thoroughly anglicized and the country as a whole has been fully incorporated into the English governmental structure for more than 400 years. Nationalism in Wales is felt mostly in the central and western parts of the country, where it tends to express itself not politically, but culturally (see chapter 4). The referendum on a national Welsh Assembly produced only a very narrow majority in favour. The Assembly was duly set up in the same year as the Scottish Parliament. Its powers are much more limited than those of the Scottish body (not much greater than some local government bodies in England). However, in Wales too, there is growing support for greater self-government.

Great Britain and Northern Ireland

On 31 July 2007, a momentous event occurred, although there was no public fanfare and many people did not even notice it. On that day, the last contingent of British soldiers withdrew from Ulster, thus ending 38 years of military occupation. Why had the British soldiers been there?

Politics in this part of the world is dominated by the historic animosity between the two communities there (see chapter 4). The Catholic viewpoint is known as 'nationalist' or 'republican' (in support of the idea of a single Irish nation and its republican government); the Protestant viewpoint is known as 'unionist' or 'loyalist' (loyal to the union with Britain). After the partition of

---

Why are the British so ignorant about the EU?

An additional reason is that views about Britain's position in Europe cut across political party lines – there are people both for and against closer ties with 'Europe' in both the main parties. As a result, it is never promoted as a subject for debate to the electorate. Neither party wishes to raise the subject at election time because to do so would expose divisions within that party (a sure vote-loser).

The West Lothian question

The existence of two parliaments in Great Britain, one for the whole of the UK and one for Scotland alone, has led to a curious situation which is known as the West Lothian question (this being the name of the British parliamentary constituency whose MP first raised it). Westminster MPs cannot vote on matters of health, education, law and order, or welfare in Scotland because Scotland has a separate parliament which decides these matters. They only decide these matters for England and Wales. But they include in their number, of course, MPs from Scotland, who are thus able to vote on matters which have nothing to do with the people they represent! (At the same time, these MPs do not have a vote on matters of great concern to those people because, again, Scotland has a separate parliament for these things!) The situation has caused some resentment in England.

Ireland in 1920, the newly created British province of Northern Ireland was given its own parliament and Prime Minister. The Protestant majority had always had the economic power in the six counties (Ulster). Internal self-government allowed them to take all the political power as well. Matters were arranged so that all positions of power were always filled by Protestants.

In the late 1960s, a Catholic civil rights movement began. There was a violent Protestant reaction and in 1969, British troops were sent in to keep order. At first, they were welcomed by the Catholics. But troops, perhaps inevitably, often act without regard to democratic rights or local sensibilities. The welcome began to cool, violence increased, and the British government reluctantly imposed certain measures not normally acceptable in a modern democracy, such as imprisonment without trial and the outlawing of organizations. The welcome disappeared entirely after 30 January 1972 (known as 'Bloody Sunday') when the troops shot dead 14 unarmed Catholic marchers. Recruitment to extremist organizations from both communities and acts of terrorism increased. One of these groups, the Provisional IRA, started a bombing campaign on the British mainland while Loyalist paramilitaries started committing terrorist attacks in the Republic of Ireland (Extremist groups). In response, the British government imposed direct rule from London. There was a hardening of attitudes in both communities and support for extremist political parties increased.

'The Troubles', as they were known, dragged on into the early years of this century. The first important step towards resolution was the Good Friday Agreement of 1998. (By that time, one in four people in Ulster knew someone who had been killed and one in ten people had had a family member killed.) Significantly, this agreement involved not only all the political parties in the province but also the Irish and British governments. It gave the Republic of Ireland a small degree of power sharing and everybody born in Northern Ireland the right to be a citizen of the Republic. At the same time, it stipulated that the six counties would remain a part of the UK for as long as a majority of its people wanted it that way. It was then ratified by overwhelming majorities in referenda on both sides of the border (which in the Republic's case involved a change to its constitution).

However, sporadic violence and political stalemates continued, and it was only in 2007 that internal self-government, with an elected assembly and a cross-party cabinet, was firmly established. Ironically, the new 'First minister' (a Protestant) and 'Deputy First Minister' (a Catholic) were people who each came from the more extremist wings of their communities. But nothing could be more indicative of the changed climate than the fact that during the ceremony in which they took up their new positions, while these two former mortal enemies sat chatting and joking together over a cup of tea, the only trouble which police encountered was from demonstrators protesting against the Iraq war!

Ulster

This is the name often used for the part of Ireland which belongs to the UK. It is the name of one of the ancient kingdoms of Ireland. (The others are Leinster, Munster, and Connaught). In fact, the British province does not embrace all Ulster's nine counties – three of them are in the republic. Note also that the name 'Northern Ireland' is not used by some nationalists; they think it gives validity to an entity which they do not recognize. One of the alternative names they use is 'the six counties'.

Where is Wales in the flag?

Take another look at the description of the Union Jack in chapter 1. As you may have noticed, there is nothing in it which represents Wales. In 2007, some Welsh MPs asked for a change in the Union Flag. They want the Welsh dragon to appear on it somewhere. The government promised to consider this request. Welsh nationalists, however, are not keen on this idea. They don't like the idea of being fixed into a symbol of the union from which they would like to secede.

Extremist groups

Thousands of people in Ulster were killed during the Troubles. Most of these deaths involved members of one the extremist sectarian groups killing members of the 'other' community.

The most well-known republican group was the IRA (Irish Republican Army). Seventy years ago, this name meant exactly what it says. It was composed of many thousands of people who fought for, and helped to win, independence for most of Ireland. Members of this more recent IRA (also known as 'the Provisionals', because they had split off from the 'official' IRA in the 1960s) were thus using a name that once had great appeal to Irish patriotic sentiments. In fact, it had little support in the modern Irish Republic – and no connection at all with its government.

The most well-known loyalist groups were the UFF (Ulster Freedom Fighters), the UVF (Ulster Volunteer Force), and the UDA (Ulster Defence Association).

(Top) A republican message written during the Troubles. (Bottom) A loyalist mural written during the Troubles.

By this time, however, three other factors had helped to end the violence and soften extremist views. One was the gradual process of righting the economic and social wrongs which led to the Civil Rights movement in the first place. The previous political abuses have now largely disappeared, and Catholics now have the same political rights as Protestants. Another factor, ironically, was the events of 11 September 2001 in the USA. It meant that the republican extremists could no longer expect sympathy, and money, from Irish-Americans with romantic ideas about the 'old country' if they persisted in carrying out terrorist acts. This helped to persuade such groups to disarm, which in turn meant that extremist organizations on the other ('loyalist') side similarly had to refrain from terrorist acts, for fear of a public-relations disaster. But perhaps the most important factor was the transformation of the south of Ireland during the 1990s from a backward and (in Protestant eyes) priest-ridden country to a modern, dynamic economy in which the Catholic church has lost much of its former power. While the Good Friday Agreement calmed Protestant fears that they could be swallowed up in a united Ireland, the transformation of the south has made this prospect seem less terrible to them if, eventually, they are. However, it is unlikely that many Protestants would feel comfortable about a united Ireland in the near future. At the same time, the names 'loyalist' and 'unionist' are somewhat misleading; the Protestants of Ulster are distinct from any other section of society on the British mainland. From their point of view, and also from the point of view of some Catholics, a place for Ulster in a federated Europe is a possible solution.

QUESTIONS

1 What indications can you find in this chapter that British people like to think of their country as an important and independent power in the world?

2 Would you say that British people feel closer to the USA or the EU?

3 Do you think the present boundaries of the UK will stay as they are or should they change? Do you think they will stay as they are?

SUGGESTIONS

This chapter is about the British view of the rest of the world. It might be interesting to set this against some of the rest of the world's view of Britain. Examples of such books are *Over here* by the American Raymond Seitz, *Les Anglais* by Philippe Daudy, which is available in both French and English versions, and *An Italian in Britain* by Beppe Severgnini, available in both English and Italian (as *Inglesi*).

The Last Pink Bits by Harry Ritchie (Sceptre 1998) is an account of a tour around the remnants of the British Empire. (On world maps published in Britain, countries belonging to the empire used to be coloured pink.)

13 Religion

In centuries past, the everyday language of most British people was enriched by their knowledge of the Bible and the *English Book of Common Prayer*. But established kinds of Christianity have an old-fashioned feel about them in modern Britain. It is perhaps indicative that the most familiar English translation of the Bible, known as the *King James Bible*, was written in the early seventeenth century. No later translation has achieved similar status.

In the twenty-first century, the vast majority of people in Britain do not regularly attend religious services. Many do so only a few times in their lives. Surveys suggest more than half the population have no meaningful connection with any recognizable organized religion. Even when they are getting married, two thirds prefer civil ceremonies to religious ones. It also appears that about a half do not even know what the festival of Easter celebrates (and that knowledge of the basic features of other religions is equally poor). This seems strange considering that the law prescribes some collective worship in state schools which (unless they subscribe to another religion) should be 'wholly or mainly of a broadly Christian character'. But most schools, according to the government's chief inspector, fail to meet this requirement. In centuries past, British Christian missionaries energetically spread the word of God around the world. These days, Christian missionaries from Africa and South America are flocking to Britain to save British souls. But they will have a difficult job; according to one survey in 2006, 80% think that religion 'does more harm than good'.

Religion in Britain by numbers

There are many ways to measure the strength of various religions and denominations. The table here shows three different kinds of measurement: (1) shows the results of the 2001 national census question on religion; (2) is from the British Social Attitudes Survey in 2005; (3) gives the results of various surveys and estimates of the numbers of people who actively participated in religious services of worship 2005–2007. (Figures from Churchgoing in the UK 2007. The category 'Independent Christian' denotes the various charismatic and Pentecostalist groups mentioned in the text.)

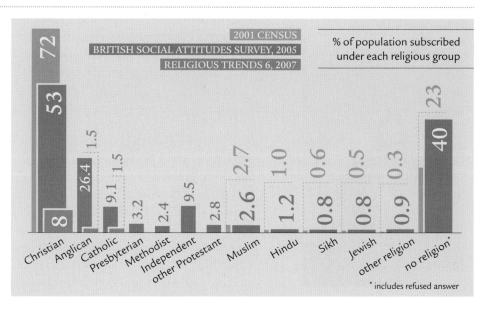

2001 CENSUS
BRITISH SOCIAL ATTITUDES SURVEY, 2005
RELIGIOUS TRENDS 6, 2007

% of population subscribed under each religious group

	Christian	Anglican	Catholic	Presbyterian	Methodist	Independent	other Protestant	Muslim	Hindu	Sikh	Jewish	other religion	no religion*
2001 Census	72												23
BSA 2005	53	26.4	9.1	3.2	2.4		2.8	2.6	1.2	0.8	0.8	0.9	40
Trends	8	1.5	1.5			9.5		2.7	1.0	0.6	0.5	0.3	

* includes refused answer

It is for reasons such as these that Britain is now often described as a secular country. And there is no doubt that most people in Britain cannot strictly be described as religious. However, this does not mean that they have no religious beliefs or inclinations. Between 40% and 60% profess a belief in God (surveys vary widely) and at least three-quarters believe in some sort of general spirit or life force. Moreover, although all the major Christian churches have accepted evolution as the main explanation for the origin of humankind, 'creationism' (that is, the belief that the world and everything in it was created by a divine force) is making a comeback, with some medical teachers predicting that a majority of the next generation of medical practitioners will hold this belief. It is just that, while holding some sort of religious belief, the majority of British people cannot be bothered with organized religion.

Look at the table on page 121 and you will see an apparently paradoxical set of figures. In the 2001 national census, almost three in every four people in Britain described themselves as Christian. But in surveys of attitudes, barely more than half describe themselves as such. And less than ten per cent actually attend Christian services. There are big differences, it seems, between identifying yourself as a Christian in an official context, how you really see yourself in relation to Christianity, and whether you actually practice it.

Perhaps this approach explains why few people object to the fact that the Queen is queen 'by the grace of God', or the fact that she, like all previous British monarchs, was crowned by a religious figure (the Archbishop of Canterbury) in a church (Westminster Abbey) and that the British national anthem (*God Save the Queen*) invokes God's help in protecting her. The overall picture with respect to religion in Britain is rather similar to that towards the monarchy. Just as there is no serious republican movement in the country, so there is no widespread anti-clericalism. And just as there is no royalist movement either, so most people are not active participants in organized religion.

However, the picture painted above does not mean that religion is a dead issue in British public life. There are many ways in which religion and politics impinge on each other, perhaps more than there were half a century ago. The inclusion of a new religion question in the government's 2001 census is perhaps an indication of this renewed public importance.

Politics

Freedom of religious belief and worship is taken for granted in modern Britain. So is the freedom to be a non-believer. Professing disbelief in God or any religion is not regarded as taboo. With the notable exception of Northern Ireland (see chapter 4), a person's religion has almost no political significance. Except, perhaps, for Muslims, there is no recognizable political pressure group in the country which is based on a particular religious ideology. To describe oneself as 'Catholic' or 'Church of England' or 'Methodist' or any other recognized label is to indicate one's personal beliefs but not the way one votes.

The Vicar of Dibley

The Vicar of Dibley was a TV comedy series which revolved around the life of a priest after she arrives at a sleepy Oxfordshire village to be its new vicar. Yes, 'she'! The series was topical in that it began soon after the ordination of the first women priests. As the majority of British people have no connection with organized religion of any kind (and the vast majority do not live in sleepy villages), you might think that this series would have been of only minority interest. But in fact, it was one of the most popular comedy series of the late 1990s and the early years of the twenty-first century. The majority, it seems, had enough familiarity with the religious background and enough goodwill towards it to be able to identify with it.

The religious conflicts of the past and their close relationship with politics (see chapter 2) have left only a few traces in modern times, and the most important of these are institutional rather than political: the fact that the monarch cannot, by law, be a Catholic; the fact that the 26 senior bishops in one particular church (the Church of England) are members of the House of Lords; the fact that the government has the right of veto on the choice of these bishops; the fact that the ultimate authority for this same church is the British Parliament. These facts point to a curious anomaly. Despite the separation of religion and politics, it is in Britain that we find two of the few remaining cases in Europe of 'established' churches – that is, churches which are, by law, the official religion of a country. These cases are the Church of Scotland and the Church of England. The monarch is the official head of both, and the religious leader of the latter, the Archbishop of Canterbury, is appointed by the government.

However, the privileged position of the Church of England (also known as the Anglican Church) is not, in modern times, a political issue. Nobody feels they are discriminated against if they do not belong to it. In any case, the Anglican Church has shown itself to be independent of government in its opinions. Its leaders, and indeed leaders of many other faiths in Britain, are regularly critical of government policies. During the years of Conservative government up to 1997, their opposition was directed at inequitable economic policies which, they argued, were socially divisive and un-Christian in the lack of help extended towards the disadvantaged. This line of criticism has continued into the twenty-first century. But it has been joined by criticism of a different aspect of government policy, which was characterized in 2006 by one Anglican bishop as 'tyranny ... enforced by thought police'. This bishop had in mind a series of police investigations into people – including another bishop and the leader of the Muslim Council of Britain – who had expressed negative opinions about homosexuality. It is in this matter, in fact, that government and most faiths in Britain have come into conflict. In 2008 for instance, some Catholic adoption agencies refused to accept a new law obliging all organizations which offer services to the public not to discriminate on the basis of sexual orientation.

Conflicts of this nature can arise because religious groups are involved in the provision of many social services and often receive state funding to help them carry out these tasks. Another possible source of friction is schooling. Almost a third of state-funded schools in Britain are 'faith schools'. In 2002, it was reported that a state-funded school in the north-east of England had been 'taken over' by fundamentalist Christians who believed in the superiority of the creationist world view. This was possible because, although state schools are obliged to teach evolution, they are not actually banned from teaching any other theory of human origin as well. If more such incidents occur in the future, conflict is likely.

The road to equality

Until 1828, Nonconformists were not allowed to hold any kind of government post or public office or even to go to university. Excluded from public life, many developed interests in trade and commerce as an outlet for their energies and were the leading commercial figures in the industrial revolution. For example, many British chocolate manufacturing companies (most notably, Cadbury's) were started by Quaker families (note also the well-known 'Quaker' brand of cereals).

Catholics were even worse off, having to worship in secret, or, later, at least with discretion. The last restriction on their freedom was lifted in 1924, when bells to announce the celebration of Catholic Mass were allowed to ring for as long as they liked (previously, Mass had to be announced with a single chime of the bell). Catholics were given the right to hold public office in 1829. But signs of the old antagonism remained throughout the twentieth century. When the British government finally re-established diplomatic links with the Vatican (after a break of some 400 years) in 1914, the Foreign Office issued a memo saying that the British representative 'should not be filled with unreasoning awe of the Pope'. The first Catholic British ambassador to the Vatican was appointed in 2005. There is still a law today which forbids Catholic priests to sit in Parliament (though it is doubtful that any would want to!). The prohibition on the monarch being a Catholic also remains. But senior Catholics, many senior Anglicans and politicians and even Prince Charles, the heir to the throne, believe it is time to end this anomaly.

Anglicanism

Although the Anglican Church apparently has much the largest following in England, and large minorities of adherents in the other nations of Britain, appearances can be deceptive. Less than a tenth of those who might describe themselves as Anglicans regularly attend services. Many others are christened, married, and buried in Anglican ceremonies but otherwise hardly ever go to church. Regular attendance for many Anglicans is traditionally as much a social as a religious activity. In times past, it was part of the hierarchical fabric of society, which was one reason for the (now outdated) reputation of the Anglican Church as 'the Conservative party at prayer' (the other reason being a historical hangover – see chapter 2).

The Church of England came into being more for patriotic and political reasons than doctrinal ones (see chapter 2). As a result, it has always been a 'broad church', willing to accommodate a wide variety of beliefs and practices. The nature of its religious services varies quite widely from church to church, depending on the inclinations of the local priest and local tradition.

Three main strands of belief can be identified. One strand is evangelical, or 'low church'. This places great emphasis on the contents of the Bible and is the most consciously opposed to Catholicism. It therefore adheres closely to those elements of Anglicanism that reject Papal doctrines and is suspicious of the hierarchical structure of the Church. It prefers plain services with a minimum of ceremony. In contrast, the beliefs of the 'Anglo-Catholic, or 'high church', strand are virtually identical to those of Catholicism – except that it does not accept the Pope as the ultimate authority. High church services are more colourful and include organ music and elaborate priestly clothing. Both these strands are traditional in their outlook. But there is also a liberal wing, which is willing to question some of the traditional Christian beliefs, is more inclined to view the Bible as merely a historical document, is more tolerant towards homosexuality and was the first to support moves to ordain women priests. It is also more overtly concerned with social justice.

Conflict between the three strands sometimes surfaces. In 2002, the appointment of a member of the liberal wing as the new Archbishop of Canterbury caused fury among some sections of the evangelical wing. The new archbishop received hate mail, some accusing him of not being a 'true Christian'; others, following his opposition to attacking Iraq, of being 'a lily-livered pacifist', and a few even wishing on him 'the fate of the Old Testament prophets' or, more directly, just called for his death.

What holds the strands together and gives Anglicanism its meaning is its 'Englishness'. Without this, many Anglo-Catholics would be Catholic, many low churches and liberals would form their own sects or join existing Nonconformist groups, and others would simply cease to have anything to do with organized religion at all. At present, this national distinctiveness is emphasized by the Anglican Church's position as the

The Christian churches in Britain

The organization of the Anglican and Catholic churches is broadly similar. At the highest level is an archbishop, who presides over a province. There are only two of these in the Church of England: Canterbury and York. The senior Catholic archbishopric is Westminster and its archbishop is the only Cardinal from Britain. At the next level is the diocese, presided over by a bishop. In the Anglican Church, there are other high-ranking positions at the level of the diocese, whose holders can have the title dean, canon or archdeacon. Other Christian churches do not have such a hierarchical organization, though the Methodists have a system of circuits.

At the local level, the terms verger, warden and sexton are variously for lay members of churches (i.e. they are not clergy) who assist in various ways: for example, at services or with the upkeep of the church.

Note also that a priest who caters for the spiritual needs of those in some sort of institution (e.g. a university, a hospital) is called a chaplain.

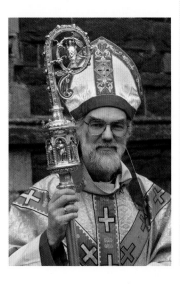

official religion. Some people argue that this tie between church and state should be broken, so that, after losing its extreme members to other churches, the Church could spend less time on internal disagreement and more on the moral and spiritual guidance of its remaining members. But others argue that this would cause the obvious Englishness of the church to disappear and thus for the number of its adherents to drop sharply.

Catholicism

After the establishment of Protestantism in Britain (see chapter 2), Catholicism was for a time an illegal religion and then a barely tolerated one. Only in the last 100 years has it been as open about its activities as any other religion. A large proportion of Catholics in modern Britain are those whose family roots are from Italy, Ireland, Poland or elsewhere in Europe. The Irish connection is evident in the large proportion of priests in England who come from Ireland (they used to be called Ireland's biggest export!).

Catholicism in Britain thus has a historically marginal status. This is one reason why it has a greater cohesiveness and uniformity than the Anglican Church. In modern times, it is possible to detect opposing beliefs within it (there are conservative and radical/liberal wings). However, there is more centralized control over practices of worship. Not having had a public, official role to play in society, it takes doctrine and practice (e.g. weekly attendance at mass) a bit more seriously than Catholicism in countries where it is the majority religion – and a lot more seriously than Anglicanism in general.

This comparative dedication can be seen in two aspects. First, religious instruction is taken more seriously in Catholic schools than it is in Anglican ones, and Catholic schools in Britain usually have a head who is either a monk, a friar or a nun. Second, there is the matter of attendance at church. Many people who hardly ever step inside a church still feel entitled to describe themselves as 'Anglican'. But British people who were brought up as Catholics but who no longer attend mass regularly or receive the sacraments do not normally describe themselves as simply 'Catholic'. They qualify this label with 'brought up as' or 'lapsed'. Despite being a minority religion in most places in the country, as many British Catholics regularly go to church as do Anglicans.

Women priests

On Wednesday 11 November 1992, at five in the afternoon, Dr George Carey, the Archbishop of Canterbury at the time, rose to announce a momentous decision. By just two votes more than the required two-thirds majority, the general Synod of the Anglican Church (its governing body) had voted to allow the ordination of women priests. The debate in the Synod had lasted more than six hours, and had been going on for years before that, both inside and outside the church, all over the country.

About 18 months after that, the first women priests were ordained. Those who supported this development believed that it would help to give the Church of England a greater relevance to the modern world and finally bring it up to date. (Unlike the Catholic Church, it has always allowed its clergy to be married.) Some who were opposed to the change did not accept the Synod's decision, and there were a few local cases of attempts to set up a rebel Church. A few decided to 'go over to Rome' – that is, to join the Catholic Church, which does not have women priests.

Other conventional Christian churches

In many ways, Anglicanism represents a compromise between Protestantism and Catholicism. Its stated doctrine, which rejects the authority of the Pope and other important aspects of Catholic doctrine, is Protestant. But its style, as shown by its hierarchical structure and its forms of worship, is rather Catholic.

When Protestantism first took root in Britain, there were many people who rejected not only Catholic doctrine but also 'Romish' style. These people did not join the newly-established Anglican Church. They regarded both the authority given to its clergy and its continuation of orthodox ritual as obstacles to true worship. Instead, they placed great importance on finding the truth for oneself in the words of the Bible and on living an austere life of hard work and self-sacrifice. They disapproved of the pursuit of pleasure and therefore frowned on public entertainments such as the theatre, on drinking, on gambling and on any celebration of the sexual aspect of life.

This is the origin of the Puritan/Calvinist tradition in Britain. The first church within this tradition was the Presbyterian Church. In Scotland, this form of Protestantism was so strong that it became this nation's established church. The Church of Scotland has a separate organization from the Anglican church. It has no bishops. Its head, the 'Moderator', is elected by its general assembly. It is the biggest religion in Scotland, where it is often known as 'the kirk' (the Scots word for 'church'). There are also many Presbyterians in England and a large number in Northern Ireland.

Episcopalianism

The Anglican Church is the official state religion in England only. There are, however, churches in other countries (such as Scotland, Ireland, the USA, and Australia) which have the same origin and are almost identical to it in their general beliefs and practice. Members of these churches sometimes describe themselves as 'Anglican'. However, the term officially used in Scotland and the USA is 'Episcopalian' (which means that they have bishops), and this is the term which is also often used to denote all of these churches, including the Church of England, as a group.

Every ten years, the bishops of all the Episcopalian churches in the world (about 500 of them) gather together in London for the Lambeth Conference, which is chaired by the Archbishop of Canterbury.

Despite the name 'Canterbury', the official residence of the head of the Church of England is Lambeth Palace in London.

Keeping the Sabbath

In the last two centuries, the influence of the Calvinist tradition has been felt in laws relating to Sundays. Traditionally, many British people regarded it as very strange that in so many continental countries large sporting events and other professional activities took place on a Sunday. The laws relating to (what was called) 'Sunday observance' were relaxed in the 1990s and now shops open as a matter of routine on a Sunday; more so than in most continental countries! However, their hours of opening are still restricted in small ways.

What is it called?

	Anglican	Catholic	Presbyterian and other Nonconformist
Local unit	parish	parish	congregation
Place of worship	church	church	chapel kirk[1] meeting house[2]
Clergy	vicar/rector/parson[3] priests curate[4]	priest	minister pastor
New member of clergy		deacon	novice
Residence of clergy	vicarage rectory		manse[1]

[1] Church of Scotland only
[2] mainly Quaker
[3] one of these is used when referring to an individual, 'priests' is used collectively
[4] a junior member of the clergy

In England, those Protestants who did not accept the authority of the Anglican Church were first known as 'Dissenters' and later, as tolerance grew, as 'Nonconformists'. These days, when refusal to conform to the established church is irrelevant, they are simply called 'members of the free churches'. A great many different free-church groups have come into being over the centuries. In the details of their organization, styles of worship and doctrinal emphasis, they differ considerably. However, they all share, in varying degrees, certain characteristics: they regard simplicity and individual prayer as more important than elaborate ritual and public ceremony; there is comparatively little difference between their clergy (if they have any at all) and their lay members; they praise self-denial. For example, many are teetotal (their members do not drink alcohol).

After Presbyterians, the largest traditional Nonconformist group in Britain is the Methodist Society. Methodists follow the teachings of John Wesley, an eighteenth century preacher who started his career as an Anglican clergyman. He had little doctrinal disagreement with the established church. However, he and his followers considered that it did not care enough about the needs of ordinary people and that its hierarchy was not serious enough about the Christian message. The Salvation Army (see chapter 18) grew out of the Wesleyan movement.

Two other Nonconformist groups with a long history are the Baptists and the Quakers. The former are comparatively strict both in their interpretation of the Bible and in their dislike of worldly pleasures. The latter, also known as the Society of Friends, are a very small group whose notable characteristics are their complete lack of clergy and their pacifism. They refuse to fight in any war, though they will do ambulance and hospital work.

Other religions, churches, and religious movements

Since it is a multicultural country where the pressure to conform is comparatively weak, Britain is home to followers of almost every religion and sect under the sun. Some of these are offshoots, or local combinations, of those already mentioned. For example, the only Church of distinctly Welsh origin calls itself both 'Calvinistic Methodist' and 'Presbyterian Church of Wales'.

The numbers of followers of all the traditional Christian churches have dropped sharply in the last fifty years. Other Christian sects and churches, on the other hand, have been growing. Because of their energetic enthusiasm and desire to attract new followers, they are sometimes characterized by the term 'evangelical'. Most of them are similar to traditional nonconformist groups in that they avoid rigid ritual and put great emphasis on scripture. In the case of some groups, their interpretations are often even more literal: the Mormons, Jehovah's Witnesses and Seventh Day Adventists (all of which originated in the USA) are examples. These groups, and others, also provide a strict code of behaviour for their followers.

Ecumenicalism

This is used to describe the trend which began in the second half of the twentieth century towards greater cooperation, and even unity, among the various Christian churches in Britain. Cynics say that this spirit is the result of the fact that active participation in any form of Christianity has become the pursuit of a rather small minority. However, the churches themselves are quite sincere about it. With political and social divisions far enough behind them, they find that they do indeed have a lot in common.

The only actual union that ecumenicalism has yet produced is the unification of Presbyterians and Congregationalists, who, in 1972, became the United Reformed Church. Anglicans and Methodists came very close (but not quite close enough) to a union in 1968.

The possibility of the Anglican Church rejoining world Catholicism seems to have receded since the introduction of women priests.

Church of Wales?

There is no Welsh equivalent of the Church of England or the Church of Scotland. That is to say, Wales has no officially established Church. It used to be part of the Church of England. But in 1914, the Anglican Church was disestablished in Wales, where it has always had only a tiny following. Wales is predominantly Nonconformist.

The fastest growing type of evangelical Christianity, however, places less emphasis on dogma, sin, or giving people a code of behaviour. Instead, the emphasis is on the spiritual and miraculous, on revelation. Their gatherings often involve joyful singing. Many believe in spiritual healing of the sick. The oldest existing church of this type in Britain is called Pentecostalist, and this term is sometimes used to denote all such groups. Pentecostalism has had a small working-class following for many years. Its recent growth is among the middle class. Many groups began with meetings in people's living rooms, where formality is at a minimum. Another term sometimes used of these groups is 'charismatic' – reflecting both their enthusiasm and their emphasis on the miraculous. The growth of these groups indicates that many British people feel a gap in their lives which neither the material benefits of modern life nor the conventional churches can fill. Large numbers of people in Britain have a belief in the paranormal – in phenomena such as parapsychology, ghosts and clairvoyance. Because the conventional Christian churches have little or nothing to do with these matters, increasing numbers of people are turning to the new charismatic churches instead.

Some people have turned even further afield, beyond the bounds of the Christian tradition. The term 'New Age' is used to cover a very wide range of beliefs which can involve elements of Christianity, eastern religions and ancient pagan beliefs all mixed in together. Interests and beliefs of this kind are not new in Britain. Theosophy, Druidism, Buddhism, Christian Scientism (which believes in the control of the body through the mind) and many other beliefs have all had their followers in this country for a hundred years or more. Until the 1960s, such people came exclusively from a small set of the upper-middle class. Since then, however, just as charismatic Christianity has expanded up the social scale to include sections of the middle class, so New Age beliefs have expanded downwards to include other sections of it. Despite their great variety and lack of exclusiveness, two emphases seem to be common to all New Age beliefs: first, personal development (often seen as spiritual development); second, the importance of respect for the natural environment.

As quiet as a church mouse

Conventional church services in Britain are typically very quiet, except when hymns are being sung. British people attending church services abroad have often been amazed, even shocked, by the noisiness and liveliness of the congregation. They chatter among themselves, they walk in and out.

In Britain, respect and reverence have traditionally been expressed by silence and stillness. Many people find the atmosphere at traditional services rather repressive and unwelcoming. This could help to explain the trend towards evangelical and charismatic Christian churches.

Samye Ling

In February 1993, 35 monks emerged from a four-year retreat. It was a very strict retreat. The monks never left their sleeping quarters. They spent most of their time meditating in wooden boxes – the same boxes in which they slept. They never once listened to the radio, watched TV, or read a newspaper.

If you know something about religion, you will not be surprised to learn that these monks were Tibetan Buddhists and that the name of the monastery in which the retreat took place is Samye Ling.

But what you may be surprised to learn is that Samye Ling is in Eskdalemuir in the south-west of Scotland. It was started in 1967 when a group of Tibetan monks arrived in the area. They soon collected a large number of European followers and set them to work building Europe's largest Buddhist temple. Since then, Samye Ling has continued to attract new followers. It now owns the nearby Holy Island off the west coast, a centre of Celtic Christianity fourteen hundred years ago, where it has opened the Centre for World Peace and Health.

The remaining religious groups with significant numbers of followers in Britain are all associated with ethnic minorities. The most well-established of these is the Jewish faith. Anti-Semitism exists in Britain, but for a long time it has been weaker than it is in most other parts of Europe. The security and confidence of Judaism in Britain can be seen both in the healthy proportion of Jews in Parliament and in the fact that within it there is, quite openly, the same struggle between orthodox and conservative, and liberal and radical viewpoints as there is in the Anglican and Catholic churches.

The numbers of followers of the Christian Orthodox, Sikh, Hindu and Muslim religions are all growing. The last of these is by far the largest (the second largest religion in Britain, in fact). Its continued growth is also for another reason. Relative poverty, racial discrimination and occasional conflicts with the authorities have caused people brought up as Muslims to have a strong sense of social identity – more so than any other religious groups in the country. As a result, young Muslims are less likely to drift away from their religion than the young of other faiths. It was political pressure from Muslims which led to the introduction of Muslim state-schools, on a par with long-established Catholic and Jewish state schools.

Finally, it is necessary to mention what are called 'cults'. The beliefs of these groups vary so widely it is impossible to generalize about them. What they seem to have in common is the style of their belief, involving absolute commitment and unquestioning obedience to the leader round whom they are centred (it is often only in this sense that they can be called religious). Cults have a bad reputation for using mind-control techniques. Their extremist tendencies are offensive to most people and, with a few exceptions, each individual cult is tiny. However, it has been estimated that there are between 500 and 700 of them in the country and that, added together, these have nearly half a million followers.

QUESTIONS

1 How does the relation between religion and politics differ between your country and Britain?

2 Why do religious groups in Britain today sometimes clash with the government?

3 What reasons have been put forward for disestablishing the Anglican Church? What are the arguments for keeping it in its favoured position?

4 In could be argued that the charismatic churches are surprisingly un-British in their approach to religion. In contrast, it could be said that the New Age movement fits quite comfortably into the traditional British approach. Do you agree?

Places of worship in Britain

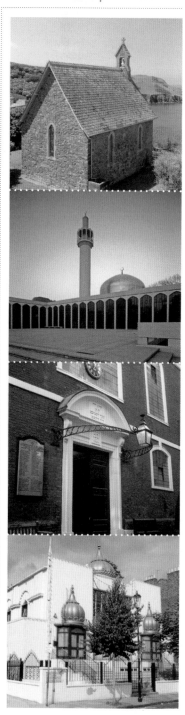

(From top to bottom) A British chapel, a British mosque, a British synagogue, and a British Sikh temple.

14 Education

School children from Harrow school, a public school for boys.

The basic features of the British educational system are the same as they are anywhere else in Europe and North America: full-time education is compulsory up to the middle teenage years; the academic year begins at the end of summer; compulsory education is free of charge, but parents may spend money on educating their child privately if they want to (Public means private!). There are three recognized stages, with children moving from the first stage (primary) to the second stage (secondary) at around the age of eleven or twelve. However, there is quite a lot which distinguishes education in Britain from the way it works in other countries. Much of this is the result of history.

Historical background

British governments attached little importance to education until the end of the nineteenth century. It was one of the last countries in Europe to organize education for everybody. (Britain was leading the world in industry and commerce, so, it was felt, education must somehow be taking care of itself.) Schools and other educational institutions (such as universities) existed in Britain long before the government began to take an interest. When it finally did so, it did not sweep the existing institutions away, nor did it always take them over. In typically British fashion, it sometimes incorporated them into the overall system and sometimes left them alone. Most importantly, the government left alone the small group of schools which were used to educate the sons of the upper and upper-middle classes. At these 'public' schools (The public school system), the emphasis was on 'character building' and the development of 'team spirit' rather than on academic achievement. This involved the use of distinctive customs, attitudes, clothes, and items of vocabulary. They were all 'boarding schools' (that is, the pupils lived there), so they had a deep and lasting influence on their pupils. Their aim was to prepare young men to take up positions in the higher ranks of the army, in business, the legal profession, the civil service, the church, and politics.

When the pupils from these schools finished their education, they formed the ruling elite, retaining the distinctive habits and vocabulary which they had learnt at school. They formed a closed group, to a great extent separate from the rest of society, entry into which was difficult for anybody who had had a different education. When, in the twentieth century, education and its possibilities for social advancement came within everybody's reach, new schools tended to copy the features of the public schools. After all, they were the only model of a successful school that the country had.

Modern times: the education debates

Before the election which brought the Labour party to power in 1997, its leader, Tony Blair, declared that his three main priorities were 'Education, education, education'. This emphasis testified to a general feeling in Britain that there was something very wrong with its system of education. It was not a new feeling. Perhaps because of its rather slow start, the British have long felt a little inadequate about their public educational provision. Education is the area of public life about which British people and governments feel the most uncertain. No other area has been subject to so many changes in the last quarter of a century.

Debates about education in Britain centre around three matters. One of these is quality. For decades, there has been a widespread feeling that British schoolchildren do not get taught properly and do not learn enough, and that they are less literate and less numerate than their European counterparts. Whether or not this is or was ever true is a matter of opinion. But these days it is common for employers and universities to complain that their new recruits do not have the necessary basic knowledge or skills (The three Rs) and there is much talk about 'grade inflation' with respect to exam results (i.e. the standard of a top 'A' grade is lower than it used to be).

Moreover, there is no doubt that Britain suffers from a chronic shortage of teachers (Help from abroad). Although many young people embark on teacher-training courses, only about half of them remain in the profession for longer than three years, so that schools often have an unsettled atmosphere due to rapid turnover of staff and class sizes are large. (In 2003, British primary schools had more children per teacher than any country in Europe except Turkey.)

Why is it so hard for British schools to recruit, and keep, teachers? One reason is probably the tradition of English anti-intellectualism (see chapter 5), which means both that it is often difficult to persuade pupils, especially boys, to be interested in learning (Going back to Poland) and

Help from abroad

What do you do if you're the head of a large school in Britain? Supervise the teaching? Organize the curriculum? Make sure that good order is preserved in the school? Well, yes, that's what you do some of the time. But these days you also spend a lot of your time flying around the world desperately trying to find teachers to come and teach in your school.

Such is the shortage of teachers in Britain that thousands of foreign teachers are recruited every year. The teachers they get are often appalled at the behaviour of pupils in British schools and they find it very hard, but they don't mind too much because it's only temporary and it's good experience. In any case, they are made to feel special – the education authorities that employ them are so grateful they lay on special receptions for them and arrange for visa requirements to be relaxed.

Sometimes, this practice creates bad feeling between the government of Britain and these other countries, who accuse the British of exporting their education crisis.

The public school system

Historically, stereotypical public schools:
- are for boys only, from the age of 13 onwards, most of whom attended a private 'prep' (preparatory) school beforehand
- take fee-paying pupils (and some scholarship pupils who have won a place in a competitive entrance exam and whose parents do not pay)
- are boarding schools (the boys live there during term-time)
- are divided into 'houses', each 'house' being managed by a 'housemaster'
- make some of the senior boys 'prefects', which means that they have authority over the other boys and have their own servants (called 'fags'), who are appointed from amongst the youngest boys
- place great emphasis on team sports
- enforce their rules with the use of physical punishment
- are not at all luxurious or comfortable

However, this traditional image no longer fits the facts. These days, there is not a single public school in the country in which all of the above features apply, and some of them do not apply anywhere. There have been a fairly large number of girls' public schools for the last hundred years, and by now most public schools are mixed sex. Many schools admit day pupils as well as boarders, and some are day schools only; prefects no longer have so much power or have been abolished; fagging has disappeared and so has physical punishment; there is less emphasis on team sport and more on academic achievement; life for the pupils is more physically comfortable than it used to be.

Among the most famous public schools are Eton, Harrow, Rugby, and Winchester.

also that teachers in Britain have, in comparison with other European countries, rather low status. Unfortunately, this status can sometimes become even worse precisely because of the general perception of poor educational standards. People want someone to blame for this, so they blame the teachers. This means teachers have to spend a lot of time being inspected and filling in forms to prove they are doing a proper job, making the job seem even less attractive. The government in this century has tried to alleviate the situation by advertising campaigns and other initiatives (such as national awards for excellence in teaching, known as the teaching 'Oscars').

The other response of British governments to the perceived deficiencies in quality of education has been to revise (sometimes, it seems, almost constantly) the national curriculum. This is the body of documents which specifies what children in state schools are supposed to learn at each stage in their school careers.

But the interesting thing about education debates in Britain is that they are not only or even mainly about quality. Another aspect that is the subject of constant worry is social justice. Perhaps because of the elitist history of schooling in Britain and its social effects (see previous section), or perhaps just because of the importance they attach to fairness, the British are forever worrying about equal opportunities in education. British governments and educational institutions are obsessed with the knowledge that the majority of children who do well in education are from middle-class, comparatively wealthy backgrounds.

It was for this reason that during the 1970s, most areas of the country scrapped the system in which children were separated at the age of 11 into those who went either to a grammar school, where they were taught academic subjects to prepare them for university, the professions or managerial jobs, or to a secondary modern school, where the lessons had a more practical and technical bias. It was noticed that the children who

The three Rs

Basic literacy and numeracy is informally known in Britain as 'the three Rs'. These are Reading, wRiting, and aRithmetic.

The politicians' children

The issue of equal opportunity is often highlighted when the British media report a story about where a prominent government politician is sending his or her children to school. If, as is frequently the case, these children are found to be attending independent schools, there are loud cries of derision and protest. Interestingly, though, the protests rarely focus on the question of inequality. Indeed, they are usually careful to insist that X has the right to send his or her children wherever he or she likes. Instead, they focus on the quality issue and the case is held up as evidence that the government has no faith in its own education system.

Going back to Poland

When Aleksander Kucharski arrived in Britain from Poland, he expected he would get a first-class education. He was accepted at a state school with one of the best academic records in the country.

But after two years he is so disillusioned he has gone home to his old school, saying his British classmates were interested only in shopping and partying. 'The boys were childish,' said 16-year-old Aleksander, 'they didn't read papers and weren't interested in anything. And the girls only talked about shopping and what they were going to do on Friday night.'

In Poland, you have to know the names of all countries, even the rivers. But in England hardly anyone could place Poland or Kenya on the map. The teachers didn't test knowledge, only effort.'

Aleksander said that before he left Poland he was an average student. 'In Poland, I only ever got average marks in Maths, yet in the UK teachers said I was a genius. After a year, I was top of the class in everything, and that includes English.'

A spokesman for the St Thomas More High School in Newcastle said: 'We are disappointed that this pupil has decided to move away. Only two weeks ago the school was recognized by Ofsted[1] as outstanding.'

Here is a newspaper article from 2007 which fuels British people's worries that educational standards in the country are poor. It was headlined 'A sad lesson'.

[1] This is the name of the government organization which inspects schools in Britain.

Source: *The Daily Mail* 26 October 2007

went to grammar schools were almost all from middle-class families; those who went to secondary moderns tended to be seen as 'failures', so the system seemed to reinforce class distinctions. Instead, from this time, most eleven-year-olds have all gone on to the same local school. These schools are known as comprehensive schools.

However, the fact remains that most of the teenagers who get the best exam results, and who therefore progress to university, are those from relatively advantaged backgrounds and vice versa. In recent decades, a university education has become much more important than it used to be. At the same time, the gap between high earners and low earners has become wider than it used to be (see chapter 15). For both these reasons, equality of educational opportunity is more important than it used to be. Various schemes are being tried to correct this imbalance. Most notably, universities are now encouraged to accept students with relatively poor exam results if they come from a disadvantaged background). In some poorer areas, children are even offered, with government approval, cash incentives to pass their exams.

However, it is almost impossible to provide real equality. Inevitably, the children of parents who care about education the most, especially if they have money, tend to get what they want for them. In some cases, this means moving house to make sure they can get their child into a school which gets good exam results (since children must attend a school in the local area). In other cases, if they feel that pupils from good schools are being discriminated against, it even means making sure your child gets into a school with bad exam results – and then hiring private tuition for them!

The only way in which such inequalities could be significantly reduced would be to ban all independent education and introduce lotteries for allocating places in secondary schools. In fact, this second possibility has already been tried (in modified form) in some areas. However, such measures conflict with another principle which is highly valued in Britain, and is the third subject around which there is debate. This is freedom of choice. It is this principle, plus a belief that it would improve the quality of education in schools generally that has led to the publication of 'league tables' of school exam results. This has had the unfortunate effect of making it clear to ambitious parents which are the more desirable schools. (To some extent it has even led to the unofficial re-establishment of the two-tier system which was abandoned in the 1970s. Comprehensive schools are supposed to be all equal, but some are better than others.)

But the belief in freedom of choice involves much more than which school a child goes to. It also implies a limit to what central government can impose generally. The British dislike of uniformity is one reason why Britain's schools got a national curriculum so much later than other European countries. It was not until the end of the nineteenth century that it was fully operative. And since then, complaints that it was too rigid and dictatorial have resulted in modifications which have reduced the number of its compulsory elements (Languages anyone?).

School uniforms

Ever since schools made their appearance in Britain, it has been customary for pupils to wear school uniforms. When few children went to any kind of school, uniforms were a sign of status. It proclaimed the child's attendance and it showed that the parents could afford to buy it. When schooling became universal, most schools took this lead and insisted on their pupils wearing uniform. It was a mark of aspiration.

During the sixties and seventies, more and more schools abandoned uniforms; they were regarded as a burden on the parents' finances and it was believed that they stifled creativity and individualism.

For the last 20 years, however, the pendulum has been swinging the other way. These days, the vast majority of parents are in favour of uniforms. Ironically, this is for the same reason that made them want to get rid of them previously – money. These days, buying a uniform is likely to be less expensive than buying their children the fashionable clothes which they otherwise demand.

There is still a large minority of schools in Britain which do not prescribe a uniform. But they often come under pressure from government advisers, who believe uniforms are symbols of belonging and lead to an improvement in academic performance.

Moreover, it should be noted that the national curriculum has never specified exactly what must be taught on a day-to-day basis or prescribed particular teaching materials. A school can work towards the objectives of the national curriculum in any way it likes. Nor does central government dictate the exact hours of the school day or the exact dates of holidays. It does not manage a school's finances either – it just decides how much money to give it. It does not set or supervise the marking of the exams which older teenagers do (see 'public exams' below). In general, as many details as possible are left up to the individual institution or the Local Education Authority (LEA – a branch of local government). (This was true even of the decision to scrap the pre-1970s system mentioned above. Indeed, a very few areas still have grammar schools.)

One of the reasons for this 'grass-roots' pattern is that the system has been influenced by the public-school tradition that a school is its own community. Most schools develop, to some degree at least, a sense of distinctiveness. Many, for example, have their own uniforms for pupils. Many have associations of former pupils, especially those outside the state system. It is considered desirable (even necessary) for every school to have its own school hall, big enough to accommodate every pupil, for daily assemblies and other occasional ceremonies. Universities, although partly financed by the government, have even more autonomy.

Style

Traditionally, education in Britain gave learning for its own sake, rather than for any particular practical purpose, a comparatively high value. In comparison with most other countries, a relatively high proportion of the emphasis was on the quality of person that education produced (as opposed to the quality of abilities that it produced). Concerns about the practical utility of education have resulted in the virtual disappearance of this attitude in the last 50 years. However, some significant reflexes remain. For example, much

Languages anyone?

For years now, educationalists, economists and official reports have been bemoaning the poor state of language-learning in British schools and the low level of foreign language ability in general among the British population. The British workforce, say these people, is in danger of being left behind in an increasingly internationalized job-market. And yet, when the national curriculum was slimmed down in the early years of this century, 'modern foreign languages' was one of the subjects that was left out. English children are the only pupils in Europe who are allowed to drop foreign languages completely from their studies after the age of 14. Fewer than ten per cent learn a foreign language beyond the age of 16. Rather than trying to educate the many in foreign languages, the present policy is to train a very small section of the population as language specialists.

In Wales, the situation is different. The provision for a 'foreign language' is the same as in England but all pupils study both English and Welsh until the age of 16.

Summerhill and discipline

There may be another reason why it is so hard to find people to teach in Britain's schools. It is a common belief that the pupils are very badly behaved. Again, this is a matter of personal opinion. But the experience of the famous independent school Summerhill is perhaps indicative. When it was founded in 1923 by the educationalist, A. S. Neill, his vision was for a school where children could learn that adults were not people to be frightened of, where they policed themselves and where they learnt because they wanted to, not because they were forced to. Neill once famously said he would

rather turn a child into a happy street-sweeper than a successful but miserable professional. Accordingly, the tradition at Summerhill is that the children themselves set and police the rules and lessons are not compulsory. In the school's heyday in the sixties, it was an icon of the hippy movement, with stories of pupils reciting Shakespeare to cows and going communal nude bathing.

How times change! This noble idea of a libertarian education was all very well when the pupils had already learnt at least the concepts of rules and discipline from their parents and

of co-operation from their brothers and sisters. But now children tend to come from much smaller families, so that these concepts are less necessary. The present head of Summerhill, who is Neill's daughter and in theory just as committed to his ideals, says that they now get children coming along who are so selfish, so badly behaved, such (in her own words) 'spoilt brats', that they have to be taught that living in a community means you cannot always do exactly what you want. Ironically, therefore, Summerhill has found itself in the position of championing a sense of discipline and order.

of the public debate about educational policy still focuses on how schools can help their charges become good members of society. The national curriculum includes provision for the teaching of 'citizenship' and of various other personal matters such as 'sex and relationships education'.

It also prescribes 'physical education'. Indeed, British schools and universities have tended to give a high priority to sport. The idea is that it helps to develop the 'complete' person. The notion of the school as a 'community' can strengthen this emphasis. Sporting success enhances the reputation of an institution. Until the last quarter of the twentieth century, certain sports at some universities (especially Oxford and Cambridge) and medical schools were played to an international standard and people with poor academic records were sometimes accepted as students because of their sporting prowess (although, unlike in the USA, this practice was always unofficial).

Another reflex is that the approach to study tends to give priority to developing understanding and sophistication of approach over the accumulation of factual knowledge. This is why British young people do not appear to have to work so hard as their fellows in other European countries. Primary schoolchildren do not normally have formal homework to do and university students have fewer hours of programmed attendance than students in mainland Europe do, although on the other hand, they receive greater personal guidance with their work.

School life

Britain has been comparatively slow to organize nursery (i.e. pre-primary) education. But at the time of writing all children are guaranteed a free, part-time early education place (up to 12.5 hours per week) for up to two years before reaching compulsory school age, which is the age of 5, and the government has plans for all primary schools to be open from 8 a.m. till 6 p.m., throughout the year, even for children as young as two months. (The idea is not to keep them in the classroom all this time. Rather, it is that schools become the hub of local communities, offering not only conventional education but also breakfast provision, childminding facilities, activity clubs and even health services for parents.)

Even at present, the total number of hours in a year which children spend at school is longer than in other European countries. It is not that the typical school day is especially long. It starts around 9 a.m. and finishes between 3 p.m. and 4 p.m., or a bit later for older children. It includes a lunch break which usually lasts about an hour and a quarter, where nearly half of all children have lunch provided by the school. (Parents pay for this, except for those who are rated poor enough for it to be free. Other children either go home for lunch or bring sandwiches.) On the other hand, it is a full five-day week (there is no half day) and holiday periods are short (The school year).

Learning for its own sake

One effect of the traditional British emphasis on academic learning as opposed to practical training can be seen in the way that people gain qualifications for certain professions. In many cases, this has not traditionally been done within universities. Instead, people go to specialized institutions which are separate from any university. You can study architecture at university, but most architects have learnt their profession at a separate School of Architecture; you can study law at university but this alone does not qualify you to be a lawyer (see chapter 11); you cannot get a teacher's qualification by doing an ordinary university course – most teachers get theirs at a teacher training college. Until recently, schools were not usually involved in helping people to get qualifications for skilled manual jobs such as bricklaying or carpentry or machine-operating.

The trouble with the internet

In the 1980s, universities and post-16 education generally started moving away from timed, sit-down exams as a method of assessment and started awarding some of the total mark for take-home assignments. It was thought that deciding 100% of a mark by sit-down exam put unnecessary stress on many students and unfairly disadvantaged those who were less comfortable working under such conditions. Moreover, take-home pieces of work could be longer and therefore potentially more sophisticated. By the start of this century, in almost all subjects, a large proportion of the mark – and sometimes 100% of it – for a particular qualification was awarded for take-home work.

But the trend is now back towards old-fashioned exams. The problem is that today's students have an opportunity for cheating unavailable to their predecessors – the internet, making it easy for them to download relevant writing and pretend it is their own. In response, educational institutions now require assignments to be submitted electronically, so that any plagiarism can be detected.

But the problem goes further than that. In the years around the turn of the century, thousands of on-line 'essay companies' sprung up. They are not illegal. They say they simply provide information to clients in the requested form but that what the client does with this information is not their business. But of course what the client does is present this work as their own. This 'information' is not available on the web; it is sent to clients in email attachments and so cannot easily be detected. In 2006, it was reported that the largest of these companies had supplied 15,000 people with bespoke essays in the previous three years and that the annual turnover of this new 'service industry' was about £200 million.

Almost all schools are either primary or secondary only, the latter being generally larger. Methods of teaching vary, but there is most commonly a balance between formal lessons with the teacher at the front of the classroom, and activities in which children work in small groups round a table with the teacher supervising. In primary schools, the children are mostly taught by a class teacher who teaches all subjects, often with the help of a teaching assistant. At the ages of seven and eleven, children have to take national tests in English, mathematics and science. In secondary education, pupils get different teachers for different subjects and regular homework.

The older children get, the more likely they are to be separated into groups according to their perceived abilities, sometimes for particular subjects only, sometimes across all subjects. But some schools do not practice such 'streaming' and instead teach all subjects to 'mixed ability' classes. The rights and wrongs of this practice is one of the matters about which there has been heated debate for several decades, as it relates to the social-justice and quality issues.

Public exams

At the end of their compulsory schooling, schoolchildren take exams. Although some of these involve knowledge and skills specified by the national curriculum, they are in principle separate from the school system. They are organized neither by schools nor by the government. That is why they are called 'public'. (There is no unified school-leaving exam or a school-leaving certificate.) There is nothing to stop a 65 year-old doing a few of them for fun. In practice, of course, the vast majority of people who do these exams are school pupils, but formally it is individual people who enter for these exams, not pupils in a particular year of school.

The exams are set and marked by largely independent examining boards. There are several of these. Each board publishes its own separate syllabus for each different subject (History? But which history?). Some boards offer a vast range of subjects. Everywhere except Scotland

The school year

Schools usually divide their year into three 'terms', starting at the beginning of September. In addition, schools have a 'half-term' (half-term holiday) lasting a few days or a week in the middle of each term.

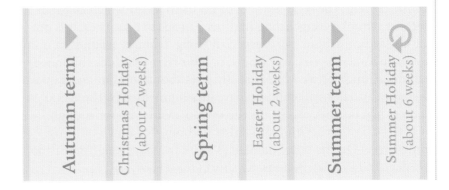

Autumn term ▶ Christmas Holiday (about 2 weeks) ▶ Spring term ▶ Easter Holiday (about 2 weeks) ▶ Summer term ▶ Summer Holiday (about 6 weeks) ↻

(which has its own single board), each school or LEA decides which board's exams its pupils take. Some schools even enter their pupils for the exams of one board in some subjects and another board in other subjects. In practice, nearly all pupils do exams in English language, maths and a science subject. Many take exams in several additional subjects, sometimes as many as seven more.

The assessment of each examinee's performance in each subject is usually a combination of coursework assignments and formal, sit-down exams. Coursework has formed a large component of the total mark in many subjects in the last two decades. But the present trend is towards a return to more conventional exams (The trouble with the internet).

Education beyond sixteen

In the recent past, people were free to leave school at the age of 16. From September 2013, those starting Year 11 or below will need to continue in some form of education or training until the end of the academic year in which they turn 18. Some 16-year-olds take part in training schemes which involve on-the-job training, sometimes combined with part-time college courses. The majority remain in full-time education. About half of them leave their school, either because it does not have a sixth form (The sixth form) or because it does not teach the desired subjects, and go to a sixth-form college, or College of Further Education. An increasing number do vocational training courses for particular jobs and careers. Recent governments have been keen to increase the availability of this type of course and its prestige (which used to be comparatively low). In the era of 'lifelong learning' even older adults participate in such courses. At the time of writing, the proportion of adults over 25 in some kind of education or training is higher than the European average (exceeded only by the Nordic countries).

For those who stay in education and study conventional academic subjects, there is more specialization than there is in most other countries. Typically, a pupil spends a whole two years studying just three or four subjects, usually related ones, in preparation for taking A-level exams, though this is something else which might change in the near future (Academic exams and qualifications).

The independence of Britain's educational institutions is most noticeable in universities. They make their own choices of who to accept for their courses. There is no right of entry to university for anybody. Universities normally select students on the basis of A-level results and a few conduct interviews. Students with better exam grades are more likely to be accepted. But in principle there is nothing to stop a university accepting a student who has no A-levels at all and conversely, a student with top grades in several A-levels is not guaranteed a place. The availability of higher education increased greatly in the last second half of the twentieth century (The growth of higher education), but finding a university place is still not easy. The numbers who can be accepted on each course are limited.

History? But which history?

The exam boards in Britain are not quite as independent as they used to be. There is now a Qualifications and Curriculum Authority (QCA) which oversees them. It was due to pressure from the QCA that the examining boards changed their A-level history syllabuses in 2008. It was decided that these syllabuses needed a larger British component.

This was an interesting development. In the early twentieth century, most history in British schools consisted of learning, in minute detail, about the glories of the British empire. Then, in the second half of the century, a reaction set in, and by the end of the century, Britain was more or less ignored. Instead, the focus was on twentieth century dictatorships such as those of Hitler and Stalin. In one A-level syllabus, it was even possible for students to spend 80% of their time on German history in the first half of the twentieth century. The feeling was that the reaction had gone too far.

And there was another reason for this renewed British emphasis. The reality of multicultural Britain means that a very large number of children cannot rely on learning from their parents about the culture and history of the country in which they were born and are being brought up. It is widely felt that, in order to foster a sense of Britishness, they need to be taught it in school. At the same time, historians and educators have warned against a return to the bad old days of empire glorification.

Because of this limitation, students at university get a relatively high degree of personal supervision. As a result, the vast majority of university students complete their studies – and in a very short time too. In England, Wales, and Northern Ireland, only modern languages and certain vocational studies take more than three years. (In Scotland, four years is the norm for most subjects.) Indeed, it is only in exceptional circumstances that students are allowed to 'retake' years repeatedly. Traditionally, another reason for the low drop-out rate is that students typically live 'on campus', (or, in Oxford and Cambridge 'in college') or in rooms nearby, and are thus surrounded by a university atmosphere.

However, the expansion of higher education during the 1990s caused this characteristic, and other traditional features, to become far less typical. Until this expansion, 'full time' really meant full time. Many students got jobs in the holidays, but were forbidden to take any kind of employment during term-time. But that was in the days when

The sixth form

The word 'form' was the usual word to describe a class of pupils in public schools. It was taken over by some state schools, although many state schools simply used the word 'class'. Since the introduction of the national curriculum and the streamlining of different kinds of educational provision, it has become common to refer simply to 'years'. However, 'form' has been universally retained in the phrase 'sixth form', which refers to those pupils who are studying beyond the age of sixteen.

UCAS

If you want to study full time for a first degree at a British university, you do not apply directly to the university. Instead, you apply through the University Central Admissions Service (UCAS). UCAS does not make any decisions about your application. It just acts as a messenger between you and the universities.

The Open University

This is one development in education in which Britain can claim to have led the world. It was started in 1969. It allows people who do not have the opportunity to be students in the normal way by attending a university to study for a degree through (what has now become known as) distance education. When it started, its courses were taught through television, radio and specially written coursebooks. These days, of course, it uses the internet instead. Students work with tutors, to whom they send their written work and with whom they then discuss it. In the summer, they have to attend short residential courses of about a week.

Academic exams and qualifications

GCSE General Certificate of Secondary Education. The exams taken by most 15 to 16 year olds in England, Wales, and Northern Ireland. Marks are given for each subject separately. The syllabuses and methods of examination of the various examining boards differ. However, there is a uniform system of marks, all being graded from A to G. Grades A, B, and C are regarded as 'good' grades.

SCE Scottish Certificate of Education. The Scottish equivalent of GCSE. These exams are set by the Scottish Examinations Board. Grades are awarded in numbers, 1 being the best.

A Levels Advanced Levels. Higher-level academic exams set by the same examining boards that set GCSE exams. In Year 12 of school or college, students study subjects and take exams at AS (Advanced Subsidiary) level, and then in Year 13 (the final year, when they turn 18) they study and take exams at A2 level. Together AS and A2 level exams form the A-level qualification, which is needed for entrance to universities.

There is a certain amount of dissatisfaction with the A-level system. Many head teachers are now seriously thinking of throwing it out and adopting a foreign model – specifically the baccalaureate. In fact, there are already dozens of schools in Britain which prepare their students for the International Baccalaureate. Many people are now calling for a 'British Bacc'.

SCE 'Advanced Highers' The Scottish equivalent of A-levels.

Degree A qualification from a university. (Other qualifications obtained after secondary education are usually called 'certificate' or 'diploma'.)

Bachelor's Degree The general name for a first degree, most commonly a BA (Bachelor of Arts) or BSc (Bachelor of Science). Students studying for a first degree are called undergraduates. When they have been awarded a degree, they are known as graduates. Most people get honours degrees, awarded in different classes. These are:
Class I (known as 'a first');
Class II.I ('a 2.1' or 'an upper second');
Class II.II ('a 2.2' or 'a lower second');
Class III ('a third')
A student who is below one of these gets a pass degree (i.e. not an honours degree).

Master's Degree The general name for a second (postgraduate) degree, most commonly MA or MSc. At Scottish universities, however, these titles are used for first degrees.

Doctorate The highest academic qualification. This usually (but not everywhere) carries the title PhD (Doctor of Philosophy). The time taken to complete a doctorate varies, but it is generally expected to involve three years of more-or-less full-time study.

Types of university

There are no important official or legal distinctions between the various universities in the country. But it is possible to discern a few broad categories.

Oxbridge

This name denotes the universities of Oxford and Cambridge, both founded in the medieval period. They are federations of semi-independent colleges, each college having its own staff, known as 'fellows'. Most colleges have their own dining hall, library, and chapel and contain enough accommodation for at least half of their students. The fellows teach the college students, either one-to-one or in very small groups (known as 'tutorials' in Oxford and 'supervisions' in Cambridge). Oxbridge has the lowest student/staff ratio in Britain. Lectures and laboratory work are organized at university level. As well as the college libraries, there are the two university libraries, both of which are legally entitled to a free copy of every book published in Britain. Before 1970, all Oxbridge colleges were single-sex (mostly for men). Nearly all now admit both sexes.

The old Scottish universities

By 1600, Scotland boasted four universities. They were Glasgow, Edinburgh, Aberdeen, and St. Andrews. The last of these resembles Oxbridge in many ways, while the other three are more like civic universities (see following column) in that most of the students live at home or find their own rooms in town. At all of them, the pattern of study is closer to the Continental tradition than to the English one – there is less specialization than at Oxbridge.

The early nineteenth-century English universities

Durham University was founded in 1832. Its collegiate living arrangements are similar to Oxbridge, but academic matters are organized at university level. The University of London started in 1836 with just two colleges. Many more have joined since, scattered widely around the city, so that each college (most being non-residential) is almost a separate university. The central organization is responsible for little more than exams and the awarding of degrees.

The older civic ('redbrick') universities

During the nineteenth century, various institutes of higher education, usually with a technical bias, sprang up in the new industrial towns and cities such as Birmingham, Manchester, and Leeds. Their buildings were of local material, often brick, in contrast to the stone of older universities (hence the name, 'redbrick'). They catered only for local people. At first, they prepared students for London University degrees, but later they were given the right to award their own degrees, and so became universities themselves. In the mid twentieth century, they started to accept students from all over the country.

The campus universities

These are purpose-built institutions located in the countryside outside a nearby town. Examples are East Anglia, Lancaster, Sussex, and Warwick. They have accommodation for most of their students on site and from their beginning, mostly in the early 1960s, attracted students from all over the country. (Many were known as centres of student protest in the late 1960s and early 1970s.) They tend to place emphasis on relatively 'new' academic disciplines such as social sciences and to make greater use than other universities of teaching in small groups, often known as 'seminars'.

The newer civic universities

These were originally technical colleges set up by local authorities in the first sixty years of this century. Their upgrading to university status took place in two waves. The first wave occurred in the mid 1960s, when ten of them (e.g. Aston in Birmingham, Salford near Manchester, and Strathclyde in Glasgow) were promoted in this way. Then, in the early 1970s, another thirty became 'polytechnics', which meant that, as well as continuing with their former courses, they were allowed to teach degree courses (the degrees being awarded by a national body). In the early 1990s most of these (and also some other colleges) became universities. Their most notable feature is flexibility with regard to studying arrangements, including 'sandwich' courses (i.e. studies interrupted by periods of time outside education). They are now all financed by central government.

The growth of higher education

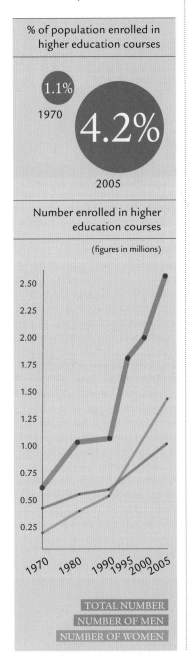

In 1960, there were fewer than 25 universities in the whole of Britain. By 1980, there were more than 40, and by now there are well over 100 institutions which have university status.

% of population enrolled in higher education courses

1.1%
1970

4.2%
2005

Number enrolled in higher education courses

(figures in millions)

2.50
2.25
2.00
1.75
1.50
1.25
1.00
0.75
0.50
0.25

1970   1980   1990 1995 2000 2005

TOTAL NUMBER
NUMBER OF MEN
NUMBER OF WOMEN

students got a grant to cover their term-time expenses. Because of the expansion, the grant has long since disappeared for all but the poorest. And on top of that there are now (unlike before) tuition fees to pay. Despite the existence of a student loan scheme, the result is that universities can no longer insist their students don't take term-time jobs and about half of the country's students do so. Indeed, so important is the income from these jobs that their availability in the area is an important consideration for many prospective students in choosing a university.

There is evidence that students' studies are suffering as a result of this imperative to earn money. There is an irony here. The main thrust of government policy is to open up higher education to the poorer classes. But it is, of course, the students from poorer backgrounds who suffer the most in this way. It is for the same reason – money – that an increasing number of students now live at home.

QUESTIONS

1 Are the main topics of debate around education in Britain the same as they are in your country? If not, how are they different?

2 Is school uniform more or less common in Britain than it is in your country?

3 What would you say are the successes and failures of the British educational system? What things, if any, does it appear to do well and what areas does it seem to neglect or do badly in?

4 From what you have read about British schools, would you like to (have) go(ne) to school in Britain?

SUGGESTIONS

To help you get the flavour of British universities, find a few prospectuses (you can find them on the internet or at a British Council library) and look through them. Remember, though, that they function as advertisements!

Numerous British authors have used university or college settings for their social comedies. Examples (in rough chronological order) are Evelyn Waugh (especially *Brideshead Revisited*), Kinsgley Amis (*Lucky Jim*) David Lodge, Tom Sharpe, Malcolm Bradbury and Howard Jacobson. *Educating Rita* (originally a play by Willy Russell) is a film about a working-class woman from Liverpool whose life is transformed by studying with the Open University.

15 The economy and everyday life

Earning money: working life

The one thing the English will never forgive the Germans for is working too hard.
(George Mikes *How to be Inimitable*)

This statement was written by a Hungarian humourist who immigrated to Britain in 1938. He wrote it in the 1960s, when the German economy was rapidly overtaking Britain's. Living standards in Britain have risen steadily since then. And of course, the statement above is, of course, not literally true. However, it does encapsulate a certain lack of enthusiasm for work in general. At the upper end of the social scale, this attitude to work exists because leisure has always been the main outward sign of aristocracy. And because of Britain's class system, it has had its effects throughout society. If you have to work, then the less it looks like work the better. Traditionally therefore, a major sign of being middle class (as opposed to working class) has been that you do non-manual work. The fact that skilled manual (or 'blue collar') workers have been paid more highly than the lower grades of 'white-collar' (i.e. non-manual) worker for several decades now has only slightly changed this social perception. The effect of the 'anti-work' outlook among the working class has been, traditionally, a relative lack of ambition or enthusiasm, in which pay is more important than job satisfaction.

These attitudes are slowly changing. For example, at least half of the workforce now does non-manual work, and yet a majority describe themselves as working class (see chapter 4). It would therefore seem that the connection between being middle class and doing non-manual work is growing weaker. Nevertheless, remnants of the connection between class distinctions and types of work live on. For example, certain organizations of professional workers, such as the National Union of Teachers (NUT), have never belonged to the Trades Union Congress.

Perhaps the traditional lack of enthusiasm for work is the reason why the working day, in comparison to most European countries, starts rather late (usually at 8 o'clock for manual workers and around 9 o'clock for non-manual workers). However, if measured by the number of hours worked in a week, the British reputation for not working hard enough appears to be false. The normal lunch break is an hour or less, and most people (unless they work part-time) continue working until 5 o'clock or later. Many people often work several hours overtime in a week. In addition, a comparatively large proportion of British people stay in the workforce for a comparatively large part of their lives. The normal retiring age for most people is 65 and this is to be raised in 2024. Finally, annual holidays in Britain are comparatively short.

Labour relations: a glossary

When there is a dispute between employees and management, the matter sometimes goes to arbitration; that is, both sides agree to let an independent investigator settle the dispute for them.

Refusing to work in the normal way is generally referred to as industrial action (even when the work has nothing to do with industry). This can take various forms. One of these is a work-to-rule, in which employees follow the regulations concerning their jobs exactly and refuse to be flexible or cooperative in the normal way. Another is a 'go slow'.

Finally, the employees might go on strike. Strikes can be official, if all the procedures required to make them legal have taken place, or unofficial (when they are sometimes referred to as wildcat strikes). When there is a strike, some strikers act as pickets. They stand at the entrance to the worksite and try to dissuade any fellow-workers who might not want to strike (whom they call blacklegs) from going into work.

There are three main ways in which people look for work in Britain: through newspapers (national ones for posts demanding the highest qualifications; otherwise local ones), through the local job centre (which is run as a government service) and through privately-run employment agencies (which take a commission from employers). Of course, all of these sources are now frequently accessed on the internet. The overall trend in employment over the last 50 years has been basically the same as it is elsewhere in western Europe. The level of unemployment has gradually risen and most new job opportunities are in the service sector (e.g. in communications, health care, and social care).

This trend has led to a period of readjustment with regard to work and the two sexes. The decline of heavy industry has meant fewer jobs in stereotypical 'men's work', while the rise in service occupations has meant an increase in vacancies for stereotypical 'women's work'. In 1970 in Britain, around 65% of all those in work were men. Since the early 1990s, the numbers of men and women in the workforce have been more or less the same. When the law against sex discrimination in employment was passed in 1975, it was intended mainly to protect women. However, in 1994 nearly half of the complaints received by the Equal Opportunities Commission (which helps to enforce the law) came from men. In that year, there were two and a half times as many unemployed men as there were unemployed women. Since then, British men have gradually adjusted to seeking work as, and employers have adjusted to employing them as, nurses, child carers, shop assistants, secretaries, and other kinds of office worker. Nevertheless, unlike nearly all the rest of Europe, in 2004 there were still more unemployed men in Britain than unemployed women. One of the reasons for this may be that employers still seem to pay women less. Although this is illegal if it is the same job, in 2003 the 'gender pay gap' (the difference between the average full-time earnings of men and women) was significantly higher than the European average.

The fight of the working classes

The decline of the unions

In the 1980s, the British government passed several laws to restrict the power of the unions. One of these abolished the 'closed shop' (by which employers had agreed to hire only people who belonged to a union). Another made strikes illegal unless a postal vote of all union members had been conducted. In 1984, there was a long miners' strike. The National Union of Miners refused to follow the new regulations. Its leader, Arthur Scargill, became a symbol (depending on your point of view) of either all the worst lunacies of unionism or the brave fight of the working classes against the rise of Thatcherism. Previous miners' strikes in the twentieth century had been mostly successful. But this one was not (the miners did not achieve their aims); a sign of the decline in union power.

Overall, a little more than a quarter of the British workforce now belongs to a union of any kind (though female membership is actually increasing, slightly).

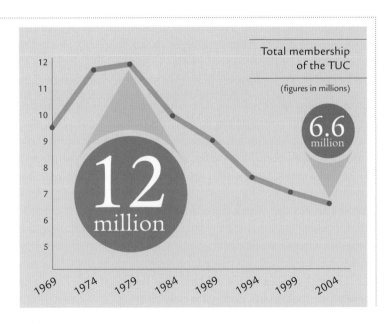

Total membership of the TUC

(figures in millions)

6.6 million

12 million

Work organizations

The organization which represents employers in private industry is called the Confederation of British Industry (CBI). Most employers belong to it and so it is quite influential in the advice which it gives to trade unions and the government. The main organization for groups of employees is the Trades Union Congress (TUC). This is a voluntary association of the country's various trade unions. There are more than a hundred of these, some big, some small, (and some not affiliated to the TUC) representing employees in all kinds of work.

Most British unions are connected with particular occupations. Many belong to the Labour party (see chapter 6) to which their members pay a 'political levy'. That is, they pay a small part of their union membership subscription to the party, although they have the right to 'contract out' if they want to. However, the unions themselves are not usually formed along party lines; that is, there is usually only one union for each group of employees rather than a separate one for each political party within that group.

Unions have local branches, some of which are called 'chapels', reflecting a historical link to Nonconformism (see chapter 13). At the work site, a union is represented by a shop steward, who negotiates with the on-site management. His (very rarely is it 'her') struggles with the foreman, the management-appointed overseer, are part of twentieth century folklore.

Union membership has declined since 1979. Until then, the leader of the TUC (its General Secretary) was one of the most powerful people in the country and was regularly consulted by the Prime Minister and other important government figures. At that time, the members of unions belonging to the TUC made up more than half of all employed people in the country. But a large section of the public became disillusioned with the power of the unions and the government then passed laws to restrict these powers. Perhaps this decline is inevitable in view of the history of British unions as organizations for full-time male industrial workers. To the increasing numbers of female and part-time workers in the workforce, the traditional structure of British unionism has seemed less relevant. In an effort to halt the decline, the TUC declared in 1994 that it was loosening its contacts with the Labour party and was going to forge closer contacts with other parties.

One other work organization needs special mention. This is the National Farmers' Union (NFU). It does not belong to the TUC, being made up mostly of agricultural employers and independent farmers. Considering the small number of people involved in agriculture in Britain (the smallest proportion in the whole of the EU), it has a remarkably large influence. This is perhaps because of the special fascination that 'the land' holds for most British people (see chapter 5), making it relatively easy for the NFU to make its demands heard, and also because many of its members are rich!

Twenty-first century jobs

What are the iconic occupations of early twenty-first century Britain? According to a report in 2006, they include hairdressers and other 'bodily improvers' such as beauticians, personal trainers, manicurists, and even baldness experts. The report notes that the number of British hairdressers trebled in ten years and the numbers of beauticians and 'nail technicians' increased by 10,000 in just four years.

What can be deduced from these figures? Well, it's not just that Britain has become a nation obsessed by physical appearance. Workers with these 'soft skills' also offer emotional support to their clients. And there is another possible reason for the phenomenal growth in this occupational sector. This kind of work – by its nature – can never be outsourced or computerised, so it appears to offer job security.

But it's not all glamour in the twenty-first century workplace. The growth of e-commerce has meant that a large range of products which previously were sold in shops are now stored in warehouses and then distributed direct to the consumer. This new pattern of trade means that two occupations, not mentioned by the report, which are also growing at a very rapid rate are shelf-stackers and van drivers.

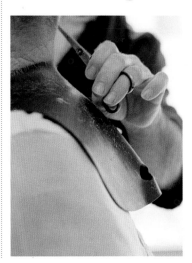

Public and private industry

The 'modernization' of business and industry happened later in Britain than it did in other western European countries. It was not until the 1960s that large corporations started to dominate and that a 'management class', trained at business school, arose. Even after that time, many companies still preferred to recruit their managers from people who had 'worked their way up' through the company ranks and/or who were personally known to the directors. Only in the 1980s did graduate business qualifications become the norm for newly-hired managers.

British industry performed poorly during the decades following the Second World War (some people blamed this on the characteristics previously mentioned). In contrast, British agriculture was very successful. In this field of activity, large scale organization (i.e. big farms) has been more common in Britain than in other European countries for quite a long time.

As in all European countries, the economic system in Britain is a mixture of private and public enterprise. Exactly how much of the country's economy is controlled by the state has fluctuated a great deal in the last fifty years and has been the subject of continual political debate. From 1945 until 1980, the general trend was for the state to have more and more control. Various industries became nationalized (owned by the government), especially those concerned with the production and distribution of energy. So too did the various forms of transport and communication services. By 1980, 'pure' capitalism probably formed a smaller part of the economy than in any other country in western Europe.

From 1980, the trend started going in the other direction. A major part of the philosophy of the Conservative government of the 1980s was to let 'market forces' rule (which meant restricting the freedom of business as little as possible) and to turn state-owned companies into companies owned by individual members of the public instead (who became shareholders). This approach was a major part of the thinking of Thatcherism (Margaret Thatcher was Prime Minister at that time). Between 1980 and 1994, a large number of companies were privatized (or 'de-nationalized'). That is, they were sold off by the government. By 1988, there were more shareholders in the country than there were members of unions. In addition, local government authorities were encouraged to 'contract out' their responsibility for services to commercial organizations. At the time of writing, virtually the only services left in government hands are strictly social ones such as education, social welfare, and health care. 'Pure' capitalism forms a larger part of the economy than in any other country in western Europe.

The British economy has performed rather well in the last two decades and it is possible that this great shift in structure has contributed to this turnaround. (There are, of course, other factors, one of which is Britain's widespread use of temporary labour from other countries.) However, it has also had negative effects.

The widening gap between rich and poor

This graph shows that around 1980, the 20% who earned the most had three times as much money coming in as the 20% who earned the least. By 2005, the income of the top 20% had almost doubled and they were earning four times as much as the bottom 20%, whose earnings had increased by only 40%.

Moreover, it should be noted that this is a graph of earnings. The gap in actual wealth is much greater.

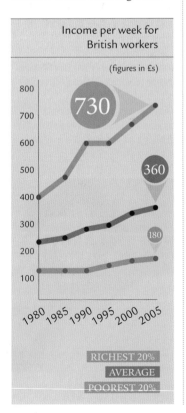

Income per week for British workers

(figures in £s)

RICHEST 20%
AVERAGE
POOREST 20%

Firstly, the privatization of services which western people now regard as essential has necessitated the creation of various public 'watchdog' organizations with regulatory powers over the sector which they monitor. For example, Ofcom monitors the privatized communications industry (including television, radio, and telecommunications) and Ofwat monitors the privatized water companies. But despite the existence of these bodies, consumers often feel cheated by the companies they deal with. Secondly, it has contributed to the widening gap between rich and poor. Letting 'market forces' rule means that there are more opportunities for people to make money, as both shareholders and employees. But it also means there are fewer safety nets and less job security for those who have *not* made money.

The distribution of wealth

In the early 1970s, Britain had one of the most equitable distributions of wealth in western Europe. By the early 1990s, it had one of the least equitable. The rich had got richer but the poor had not. Some surveys suggested that, by this time, the gap between the richest ten per cent of the population and the poorest ten per cent was as great as it had been in the late nineteenth century. The picture has not changed much since then, except that perhaps the difference between rich and poor has become starker. A survey in 2007 indicated that the number of people who were 'average' – that is, neither rich nor poor – was decreasing. Of course, overall British people have become much richer over the last few decades, but the survey also found that an increasing number of households were 'breadline poor'; that is, they had enough money for basic things such as food and heating but none left over to enjoy the opportunities which the rest of society has.

Class and wealth do not run parallel in Britain (see chapter 4), so it is not a country where people are especially keen to flaunt their wealth. Similarly, people are not generally ashamed to be poor. Of course, they don't like being poor, but they do not feel obliged to hide the fact. However, this same characteristic can sometimes lead to an acceptance of relative poverty which is surprising for an 'advanced' country.

Collecting taxes

The government organization which is responsible for collecting taxes in Britain is called the Inland Revenue. For employees, paying their income tax is not something they have to worry about. It is deducted from their pay cheque or pay packet before they receive it. This system is known as PAYE (pay as you earn). The tax added to the price of something you buy is called VAT (value added tax).

Money doesn't buy happiness

This is an old British saying, one that has been less and less believed in the past fifty years. But it turns out to be mostly true! The facts speak for themselves. Life expectancy in Britain has gone up by a whole decade in that time and disposable income – the money left after people have paid for the basic necessities of life – have on average become four times greater. Ten times as many foreign holidays are taken and car ownership has likewise increased tenfold. On the other hand, divorce has more than doubled, reported crimes have increased by a factor of ten and prescriptions for anti-depressant drugs have more than tripled. A 25 year old in Britain today is about four times more likely to be clinically depressed than in the 1950s.

Research in 'happiness studies' has become quite sophisticated. (It sounds crazy, but when serious economists and psychologists from universities like Cambridge and Harvard start publishing papers in it, you have to take notice.) It shows that there is some connection between wealth and happiness; in general the rich are happier than the poor. But it has also shown there is a limit to this correlation. It is only the poor who get happier if they get richer. Once you are in the richest two-thirds of the British population, exactly how rich you are makes no difference at all to your general feeling of well-being.

A study in 2006 put Britain in only twenty-first place in the happiness league table of nations, distinctly less happy than much poorer countries such as Columbia and Ghana.

Although most people believe that the gap between rich and poor is too wide, only a few of them think that steps should be taken (for example through the tax system) to narrow it. Just before the general election of 1997, Tony Blair refused to say, even when invited to do so in a TV interview, that he would try to narrow the gap. And yet his party won the election by a landslide and he became Prime Minister. It seems that people like to grumble about the rich but don't want to do anything about it. And sometimes the lavish spending of the rich even gets advertised as a social service. For example, football fans often grumble about how they are being priced out by rich people who buy leases on all the most luxurious parts of the stadiums. But when this happened in 2006 with the new Wembley stadium, the English Football Association did not try to hide the fact. Instead, it made sure everybody knew. It had decided that the way to counter resentment about 'fat cats' was to promote them as 'angels' paying for the expensive stadium which the rest of us, ordinary mortals, could then enjoy.

One reason for the increasing disparity of wealth in Britain is that rates of income tax have changed. For a short period in the 1960s, the basic rate was 40%. By the early eighties it was 30%. At the time of writing it is 20%. During the same period, the top rate of income tax has fallen from a high of 98% to 40%. Of course, these figures do not mean that this is how much is deducted from a person's earnings. People in different situations are allowed to earn varying amounts before tax is deducted. People earning twice the average have about 25% of their gross incomes deducted. Somebody earning less than half the average pays very little tax. Nevertheless, there is, at the time of writing, a great disparity in different people's 'take-home pay'. Rates of pay for the best-paid jobs continue to increase faster than those for badly-paid jobs. The brutal fact is that most people in Britain today, while not spectacularly rich, are very comfortable economically. This means that the poor are in a minority, so they have little hope of changing their condition through the political process

Using money: finance and investment

Wealth (and poverty) are relative concepts. Britain is still, along with its neighbours in western Europe, one of the wealthiest places in the world. The empire has gone, the great manufacturing industries have gone, but London is still one of the centres of the financial world. The Financial Times Stock Exchange Index (FTSE) of the 100 largest British companies (known popularly as the 'footsie') is one of the main indicators of world stock market prices.

The reason for this is not hard to find. The same features that contributed to the country's decline as a great industrial and political power – the preference for continuity and tradition rather than change, the emphasis on personal contact as opposed to demonstrated ability when deciding who gets the important jobs – are exactly the qualities that attract high finance. When people want to invest a lot of money,

The old lady of Threadneedle Street

This is the nickname of the Bank of England, the institution which controls the supply of money in Britain and which decides on the official interest rate. It is located, of course, in the 'square mile'. Notice how the name suggests both familiarity and age – and also conservative habits. The bank has been described as 'fascinated by its own past'. It is also notable that the people who work there are reported to be proud of the nickname.

what matters to them is an atmosphere of stability and a feeling of personal trust. These are the qualities to be found in 'the City'. This is the phrase used to refer collectively to financial institutions and the people who work in them. As regards stability, many of the city's financial institutions can point to a long and uninterrupted history. Some of them have directors from the same family which started them. Although there have been adaptations to modern conditions, and the stereotyped bowler-hatted 'city gent' is a thing of the past, the sense of continuity is still there. As regards trust, the city has a reputation for habits of secrecy that might be thought undesirable in other aspects of public life but which in financial dealings become an advantage. In this context, 'secrecy' is translated into 'discretion'.

Although more than half of the British population has money invested in the city indirectly (because the insurance companies and pension funds to which they have entrusted their money invest it on the stock market), most people are unaware of what goes on in the world of 'high finance'. To most people, money is just a matter of the cash in their pockets and their account with one of the 'high street' banks. An indication of the importance of banks in people's lives is the strong dislike of them that has developed. People are always grumbling about the charges they impose and sometimes horror stories about charges or other inhumane treatment of customers appear in the national news media. The one clear improvement in high street banks in the last two decades has been their opening times. These used to be from 10 a.m. to 4 p.m., Mondays to Fridays only. Now, they open earlier, stay open later and also open on Saturday mornings.

The high street banks

At the time of writing, the banks which have a branch in almost every town in Britain are Lloyds TSB, HSBC, Barclays Bank, and The Royal Bank of Scotland.

The Royal Bank of Scotland

Currency and cash

The currency of Britain is the pound sterling, whose symbol is '£', always written before the specified amount. Informally, a pound is sometimes called 'a quid', so £20 might be expressed as 'twenty quid'. There are 100 pence (written 'p', pronounced 'pea') in a pound.

In Scotland, banknotes with a different design are issued. These notes are perfectly legal in England, Wales and Northern Ireland, but banks and shops are not obliged to accept them if they don't want to and nobody has the right to demand change in Scottish notes.

Before 1971, Britain used the 'LSD' system. There were 12 pennies in a shilling and 20 shillings in a pound. Amounts were written like this: £3 12s 6d (three pounds, twelve shillings, and sixpence). If you read any novels set in Britain before 1971, you may come across the following:

a farthing a quarter of a penny

a ha'peny (halfpenny) half a penny

a threepenny bit threepence

a tanner an informal name for a sixpenny coin

a bob an informal name for a shilling

a half crown two-and-a-half shillings (or two-and-sixpence)

People were not enthusiastic about the change to what they called 'new money'. For a long time afterwards, the question 'What's that in old money?' was used to imply that what somebody had just said was too complicated to be clear. In fact, money provides frequent opportunities for British conservatism (see chapter 5) to show itself. When the one pound coin was introduced in 1983, it was very unpopular. People said they were sad to see the end of the pound note and that a mere coin didn't seem to be worth as much. Another example is the reaction to the Euro. Since 1991, this has had the same status in Britain as Scottish banknotes in England. But most shops do not accept them.

Spending money: shopping

The British are not very adventurous shoppers. They like reliability and buy brand-name goods wherever possible – preferably with the price clearly marked (they are not keen on haggling about the price either). It is therefore not surprising that a very high proportion of the country's shops are branches of chain stores.

Visitors from northern European countries are sometimes surprised by the shabbiness of shop-window displays, even in prosperous areas. This is not necessarily a sign of economic depression. It is just that the British do not demand art in their shop windows. On the positive side, visitors are also sometimes struck by the variety of types of shop. Most shops are chain stores, but among those that are not, there is much individuality. Independent shop owners feel no need to follow conventional ideas about what a particular shop does and doesn't sell.

In general, the British have been rather slow to take on the idea that shopping might actually be fun. Social commentators sometimes describe it as 'the last great national religion' and in 2007 an advert for a new women's magazine described it as 'the greatest sport'. But a survey in 2004 found that only 16% of British people actually feel this way about it; a clear majority said they aimed to go into a shop, grab what they want and get out again as quickly as they can. This is perhaps why supermarkets and hypermarkets in Britain are flourishing. In these places you can get everything in one place in as short as possible a time. It may also explain the boom in online shopping – you don't have to bother 'going shopping' at all.

All supermarkets now sell alcohol (which previously could only be bought at a special shop called an off-licence) and many other items traditionally found in chemists and newsagents. Many also (the big ones are called hypermarkets) sell clothes, shoes, kitchen utensils and electrical goods. These are, of course, as elsewhere in Europe, located mostly outside town centres. In some cases, the country's chain stores have followed them there, into specially built shopping centres, most of them covered. (Britain has some of the largest covered shopping areas in Europe.) About a third of all shop sales in Britain take place in these locations.

How much do you want?

On tins and packets of food in British shops, the weight of an item is written in the kilos and grams familiar to most people in Europe. However, most British people have little sense of what these mean in reality (see chapter 5). Therefore, many of the packets and tins also record their weight in pounds (written as 'lbs') and ounces (written as 'oz'). Few people ever ask for a kilo of apples or 200 grams of cheese. If those were the amounts you wanted, you would be better asking for 'two pounds or so' of apples and 'half a pound or less' of cheese and you would be about right.

1 lb = 16 oz = 456 g

1 oz = 29.8 g

Shoe and clothing sizes are also measured on different scales. The people who work in shops which sell these things usually know about continental and American sizes too, but most British people don't.

What do British people buy?

One of the jobs of the Office for National Statistics in Britain is to measure increases in the cost of living. It does this by collecting and recording about 120,000 prices each month. But of what? It can't monitor everything that gets sold. A choice has to be made. And this is where the interest lies. The 650 products which constitute its 'basket' of goods get updated each year, thus affording a view of how spending patterns and lifestyles in Britain change. The basket for the year 2006 saw old-fashioned comforts such as slippers and chocolate biscuits thrown out, as well as the old hippy food-staple, muesli and that more recent (but apparently short-lived) fashion trend, the baseball cap. Some of the new items in the basket were consumer electronic items such as MP3 players, flat screen TVs, digital camcorders and legal music downloads. In the furniture category, the dining room table was out and the bedside table was replaced by the home office desk. Some of the replacements in the basket suggested increasing wealth. For example upholstered sofas were replaced by leather ones and typical patio furniture was apparently no longer plastic but wooden. However, many of the other newly-added items suggested that this wealth was achieved at a cost – lack of time. They included chicken nuggets, pre-packed vegetables (no time for food preparation), carpenters' fees (no time for DIY), supermarket home delivery charges (no time to do the shopping), gardeners' fees (no time for that either) and champagne (well, they have to unwind somehow).

The area in town where the local shops are concentrated is known as the high street (the American equivalent is 'Main Street'). British high streets have felt the effects of the move towards out-of-town shopping. In the worst-affected towns, as many as a quarter of the shops are vacant. But high streets have often survived by adapting. In larger towns, shops have tended to become either more specialist or to sell especially cheap goods (for people who are too poor to own a car and drive out of town). Many have become charity shops (selling second-hand items and staffed by volunteers) and discount stores. Many of the central streets are now reserved for pedestrians, so that they are more pleasant to be in.

Even most small high streets still manage to have at least one representative of the various kinds of conventional food shop (e.g. butcher, grocer, fishmonger, greengrocer), which do well by selling more expensive luxury items (although the middle classes use them, supermarkets have never been regarded as 'smart' or fashionable places in which to shop). The survival of the high street has been helped by the fact that department stores have been comparatively slow to move out of town. Almost every large town or suburb has at least one of these. They are usually not chain stores, each company running a maximum of a few branches in the same region. There is one other popular shopping location in Britain. This is a shop by itself in a residential area, normally referred to as 'the corner shop'. These often sell various kinds of food, but they are not always general grocers. Their main business is newspapers, magazines, sweets and tobacco products. It is from them that most 'paper rounds' (see chapter 16) are organized. Thirty years ago, it was thought that, in the motorized age, this kind of shop would die out. But then they were largely taken over by Asians who gave them a new lease of life by staying open very late.

Shop opening hours

The normal time for shops to open is 9 a.m. Large supermarkets stay open all day until about 8 p.m. (and some stay open 24 hours). Most small shops stay open all day and then close at 5.30 p.m. or a bit later. There used to be a tradition of an 'early closing day', when the shops shut at midday and did not open again, but this has now disappeared. In fact, shop opening hours have become more varied then they used to be. Regulations have been relaxed. It is now much easier to find shops open after six. In some areas, the local authorities are encouraging high street shops to stay open very late on some evenings as a way of injecting new life into their 'dead' town centres.

But the most significant change in recent years has been in regard to Sundays. By the early 1990s, many shops, including chain stores, were opening on some Sundays, especially in the period before Christmas. In doing this, they were taking a risk with the law. Sometimes they were taken to court, sometimes they weren't. The rules were so old and confused that nobody really knew what was and what wasn't legal. It was agreed that something had to be done. On one side was the 'Keep Sunday Special' lobby, a group

Brand power

British graffiti artist Banksy comments on modern day consumerism in his piece Tesco generation.

Some well-known names

The best known supermarket chains are Sainsbury's and Tesco, although there are others such as Morrisons, Asda, and Waitrose.

There is only one department store with a large number of branches. This is Marks and Spencer. It is so well-known that it is often referred to as just 'M&S'. M&S clothes are known for their quality and wide range of prices. Unlike most other department stores, some M&S stores have a 'food hall'. It also has a number of outlets that sell only food.

In a category all by itself is Woolworths, which used to have a branch in almost every high street in the country, selling mostly sweets, music, toys, and children's clothes of the cheaper kind.

Most chemists are small, individually-owned shops, but there are two widespread chain stores. These are Boots and Superdrug. Like most chemists, these shops do not deal only in medicines. They also sell toiletries, perfumes and all items connected with photography.

Most newsagents are also small, but not all. W. H. Smith, for example, has branches all over the country. As well as newspapers and a very wide range of magazines, it also sells stationery and books.

Waitrose

Sainsbury's

YOUR M&S

of people from various Christian churches and trade unions. They argued that Sunday should be special; a day of rest, a day for all the family to be together. They also feared that Sunday opening would mean that shop workers would be forced to work too many hours. On the other side were a number of lobbies, especially people from women's and consumer groups. They argued that working women needed more than one day (Saturday) in which to rush around doing the shopping. In any case, they argued, shopping was also something that the whole family could do together. They won the argument. Most shops now open on Sundays. But there are still a few restrictions. At the time of writing, small shops can open on Sundays for as long as they like, but large shops and supermarkets can only open for a maximum of six hours.

QUESTIONS

1 How does the British attitude to work compare with that in your country?

2 Why does London seem to be so important for world banking?

3 Why do you think the gap between rich and poor in Britain is getting bigger?

4 In your country, do shops stay open for more or fewer hours than they do in Britain? Do you think the regulation of shopping hours is a good idea?

16 The media

As in many other European countries, Britain's main newspapers and main TV channels are both in long-term decline; fewer and fewer people are reading the former or watching the latter. In the last quarter of the twentieth century, people became richer, so that they were able to pursue alternative forms of leisure activity. In addition, cheaper means of production and distribution meant that the main papers and the main channels found themselves with more rivals. More recently, there is the internet, which gives people not only a further form of leisure activity but also an alternative source for news. Nevertheless, the main papers and channels remain a central part of everyday national life.

The importance of the national press

Newspaper publication in the country is dominated by the national press – an indication of the comparative weakness of regional identity in the country (see chapter 4). There are more than seventy local and regional daily papers, but the total circulation of all of them together is less than the combined circulation of the handful of national 'dailies'. The only non-national papers with significant circulations

Different approaches, different subjects

Here are some details of the front pages of the national dailies for one date (23 July 2008). For each paper, the first line is the main headline and the figures in brackets are the height of the letters used for it.

BIG BRO LIVE SEX SHOW (4.5 cm)
Topic: events on the *Big Brother* TV programme
Total text on page: 80 words

OUR DESPAIR, OUR FURY, OUR FUTURE (4 cm)
Topic: a couple whose baby is missing
Total text on page: 125 words

PEACHES IN DRUGS OVERDOSE (5 cm)
Topic: the activities of a celebrity
Total text on page: 165 words

Daily Mail
www.dailymail.co.uk

PROSTATE PILL TO SAVE THOUSANDS (3.5 cm)
Topic: progress in medical research
Total text on page: 210 words

DAILY EXPRESS

SUPERMARKET PETROL PRICE BATTLE (4 cm)
Topic: the price of petrol
Total text on page: 270 words

THE **INDEPENDENT**

Captured (4 cm)
Topic: the arrest of Radovan Karadzic (for war crimes)
Total text on page: 210 words

THE **TIMES**

Cancer drug could save the lives of 10,000 a year (1.5 cm)
Topic: progress in medical research
Total text on page: 675 words

Karadzic, Europe's most wanted man, arrested (1.5 cm)
Topic: his arrest (for war crimes)
Total text on page: 1,125 words

The Daily Telegraph

800,000 drinkers a year treated in hospital (1.5 cm)
Topic: alcohol-related illnesses
Total text on page: 1,510 words

are published in the evenings, when they do not compete with the national papers, which always appear in the mornings. The only exception to this pattern is in Scotland, where a number of Scotland-only papers (most notably *The Sunday Post*, *The Sunday Mail* and the *Daily Record*) sell more copies than most of the UK-wide papers in Scotland (which usually produce special Scottish editions anyway).

Most local papers do not appear on Sundays, so on that day the dominance of the national press is absolute. The 'Sunday papers' are so-called because that is the only day on which they appear. Some of them are sisters of a daily (published by the same company) but employ different editors and journalists.

The morning newspaper is a British household institution – such an important one that, until the laws were relaxed in the early 1990s, newsagents were the only shops that were allowed to open on Sundays. People could not be expected to do without their newspapers for even one day, especially a day when there is more free time to read them. The Sunday papers are generally thicker than the dailies and some of them have six or more sections, making up a total of well over 200 pages.

Another indication of the importance of 'the papers' is the morning 'paper round'. Most newsagents organize these, and more than half of the country's readers get their morning paper delivered to their door by a teenager who gets up at around 5.30 a.m. every day in order to earn a bit of pocket money.

How many do they sell?

As you can see, the 'popular' papers sell about four times as many copies as the 'qualities'. The gap, however, is much narrower than in past decades. In 1950, for example, they sold twenty times as many. But their sales have fallen greatly since that time. Overall, newspaper circulation has declined by a third. It has declined especially sharply in the twenty-first century, probably, because of the internet, as well as the increasing number of free newspapers (which get their money from advertising).

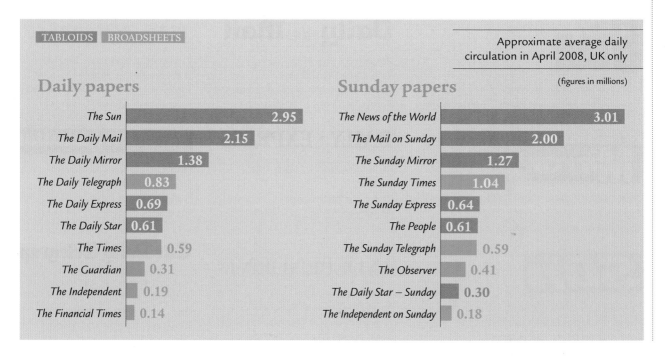

TABLOIDS   BROADSHEETS

Approximate average daily circulation in April 2008, UK only

(figures in millions)

Daily papers

The Sun	2.95
The Daily Mail	2.15
The Daily Mirror	1.38
The Daily Telegraph	0.83
The Daily Express	0.69
The Daily Star	0.61
The Times	0.59
The Guardian	0.31
The Independent	0.19
The Financial Times	0.14

Sunday papers

The News of the World	3.01
The Mail on Sunday	2.00
The Sunday Mirror	1.27
The Sunday Times	1.04
The Sunday Express	0.64
The People	0.61
The Sunday Telegraph	0.59
The Observer	0.41
The Daily Star – Sunday	0.30
The Independent on Sunday	0.18

The two types of national newspaper

Conventionally, the national papers are divided into two distinct types. The quality papers cater for the better educated readers. The popular papers sell to a much larger readership. They contain far less print than the 'qualities' and far more pictures. They use larger headlines and write in a simpler style of English. While the qualities devote much space to politics and other 'serious' news, the popular papers concentrate on 'human interest' stories, which often means sex and scandal.

However, this method of classification has a hint of snobbery about it. It implies that a newspaper can't be both high quality and popular at the same time. Perhaps this is why the two types have also been known by other names: the broadsheets and the tabloids. Not so long ago in Britain, if you saw someone reading a newspaper, you could tell what kind it was without even checking the title. This was because the quality newspapers were all printed on terribly large-sized paper known as broadsheet, so that to be able to read more than one page without looking like you had just taken up origami, you had to have expert page turning skills. The popular papers, on the other hand, were all tabloids; that is, they were printed on much smaller pages (which were therefore much easier to turn). But in 2004, two quality newspapers, *The Times* and *The Independent*, successfully adopted the tabloid format. And then, a year later, another quality, *The Guardian*, broke with tradition even more radically by adopting the Berliner format, which is halfway between broadsheet and tabloid and often used in continental Europe but never before in Britain. Again, the move was a success. And so, the tabloid/broadsheet distinction no longer fits the facts. However, it is still often used, in order to avoid the snobbery of the other method of distinction.

In any case, the differences between the two types can be exaggerated. The 'qualities' do not completely ignore sex and scandal or any other aspect of public life. Both types of paper devote equal amounts of attention to sport. Moreover, some people make a three-way distinction (*The Daily Mail* and *The Express* being in the middle). The differences are in the treatments of the topics covered and in which topics are given the most prominence.

The characteristics of the national press: politics

The way politics is presented in the national newspapers is an example of the fact that British political parties are essentially parliamentary organizations, not countrywide ones (see chapter 6). Although different papers have differing political outlooks, none of the large newspapers is an organ of a political party. Many are often obviously in favour of the policies of this or that party (and even more obviously against the policies of another party) but none of them would ever use 'we' or 'us' to refer to a certain party (Papers and politics).

The rest of the press

If you go into any well-stocked newsagent in Britain, you will not find only newspapers. You will also see rows and rows of magazines catering for almost every imaginable taste and specializing in almost every imaginable pastime. There are around 3,000 consumer magazines published in the country and about four million copies are sold every month. The vast majority of these sales are of 'women's interest' magazines and (even more so) magazines which list all the TV and radio programmes for the coming week. The best known of these is the *Radio Times*, which also contains some fifty pages of articles. (Note the typically British appeal to continuity in the name 'Radio Times'. The magazine was first produced before television existed and has never felt compelled to update its title.)

There are also a few publications dealing with news and current affairs. Partly because the national press is so predictable (and often so trivial), some of these periodicals, such the *New Statesman* and *The Spectator*, are quite widely read. In terms of sales, two of them in particular stand out. One is the *Economist*, which is of the same type as *Time*, *Newsweek*, *Der Spiegel* and *L'Express*. It is fairly obviously right of centre in its views, but the writing is very high quality and that is why it has the reputation of being one of the best weeklies in the world. (In fact, it sells five times as many copies abroad as it does in Britain itself.)

The other is very different. *Private Eye* is a satirical magazine which makes fun of all parties and politicians, and also makes fun of the mainstream press. It also has a serious side, unearthing corruption in public life. Because of this combination of, often rather 'schoolboyish', humour and investigative journalism, it is forever defending itself in legal actions.

What counts for the newspaper publishers is business. All of them want first and foremost to make money. Their primary concern is to sell as many copies as possible and to attract as much advertising as possible. The British press is mostly controlled by a rather small number of extremely large multinational companies. This fact helps to explain two notable features. One of these is its freedom from interference from government influence, which is virtually absolute. The press is so powerful in this respect that it is sometimes referred to as 'the fourth estate' (the other three being the Commons, the Lords and the monarch). This freedom is assisted by a general feeling in the country that 'freedom of speech' is a basic constitutional right.

Papers and politics

None of the big national newspapers 'belongs' to a political party. Moreover, the tabloids devote relatively little space to politics. However, each paper has an idea of what kind of reader it is appealing to, and a fairly predictable political outlook. Each can therefore be seen, rather simplistically, as occupying a certain position on the right-left spectrum.

As you can see, the right seems to be over-represented in the national press. This is not because such a large majority of British people hold right-wing views. It is partly because the press tends to be owned by people with right-wing views. However, the owners normally put selling copies ahead of political viewpoint. *The Sun* for example, supported the Labour party during the 1970s. But just before the 1979 election, it came out in favour of Margaret Thatcher's Conservative party, which won the election. For the next 17 years, it was a strong supporter of the Conservative government. But two months before the 1997 election, when the opinion polls made it clear the Conservatives were not going to win again, it suddenly changed back to Labour!

In any case, a large number of readers are not very interested in the political coverage of a paper. They buy it for the sport, or the human interest stories and scandals, or something else. For these reasons, the descriptions below the chart, although intended as humour, are perhaps more informative of the relation between the nationals dailies and politics. They are taken from the script of the political satire *Yes, Prime Minister*, in which the Prime Minister, Jim Hacker, is trying to reassure his two advisers, Sir Humphrey and Bernard, that he understands the British press.

Left	Centre	Right

Hacker: I know exactly who reads the papers. The Daily Mirror is read by people who think they run the country. The Guardian is read by people who think they ought to run the country. The Times is read by people who actually do run the country. The Daily Mail is read by the wives of the people who run the country. The Financial Times is read by people who own the country. The Morning Star is read by people who think the country ought to be run by another country.[1] The Daily Telegraph is read by people who think it is.
Sir Humphrey: Prime Minister, what about people who read The Sun.
Bernard: Sun readers don't care who runs the country as long as she's got big tits.

[1] *The Morning Star* is a socialist newspaper with a very small circulation (about 20,000). When this satire was written, it often supported the policies of the Soviet Union. That is the 'other country' in the extract.

[2] This newspaper's readers think that other countries have too much influence on British politics.

A striking example occurred during the Second World War. During this time, the country had a coalition government of both Conservative and Labour politicians – so that there was really no opposition in Parliament at all. At one time, the cabinet wanted to use a special wartime regulation to ban, temporarily, *The Daily Mirror*, which had been consistently critical of the government. At once, the Labour party, which until then had been completely loyal to the government, demanded a debate on the matter, and the other national papers, although they disagreed with the opinions of *The Mirror*, all leapt to its defence and opposed the idea. The government was forced to back down and *The Mirror* continued to appear throughout the war.

The characteristics of the national press: sex and scandal

The other feature of the national press which is partially the result of its power and commercial orientation is its shallowness. Few other European countries have a popular press which is so 'low'. Some of the popular papers have almost given up even the pretence of dealing with serious matters. Apart from sport, their pages are full of little except the private lives of famous people. Sometimes, their 'stories' are not articles at all – they are just excuses to show pictures of almost-naked women. During the 1980s, page three of *The Sun* became infamous in this respect. The women who pose for its photographs are now universally known as 'page three girls'.

The desire to attract more readers at all costs has meant that, in the late twentieth century, even the broadsheets in Britain can look rather 'popular' when compared to equivalent 'quality' papers in some other countries. They are still serious newspapers containing high-quality articles whose presentation of factual information is usually reliable. But even they now give a lot of coverage to 'human interest' stories when they have the excuse.

This emphasis on revealing the private details of people's lives has led to discussion about the possible need to restrict the freedom of the press. This is because, in behaving this way, the press has found itself in conflict with another British principle which is as strongly felt as that of freedom of speech – the right to privacy. Many journalists now appear to spend their time trying to dig up the juiciest secrets about well-known personalities, or just ordinary people who, by chance, find themselves connected with some newsworthy situation. There is a widespread feeling that, in doing so, they behave too intrusively.

Complaints regarding invasions of privacy are dealt with by the Press Complaints Commission (PCC). This organization is made up of newspaper editors and journalists. In other words, the press is supposed to regulate itself. Many people are not happy with this arrangement and various governments have tried to formulate laws on the matter. However, at the time of writing, no such law has been passed. Against the right to privacy, the press has successfully been able to oppose the concept of the public's 'right to know'.

Of course, Britain is not the only country where the press is controlled by large companies with the same single aim of making profits. So why is the British press more frivolous? The answer may lie in the function of the British press for its readers. British adults never read comics. These publications, which consist entirely of picture stories, are read only by children. It would be embarrassing for an adult to be seen reading one. Adults who want to read something very simple, with plenty of pictures to help them, have nowhere to go but the national press. Most people don't use newspapers for 'serious' news. For this, they turn to another source – broadcasting.

The BBC

Just as the British Parliament has the reputation for being 'the mother of parliaments', so the BBC might be said to be 'the mother of information services'. Its reputation for impartiality and objectivity in news reporting is, at least when compared to news broadcasting in many other countries, largely justified. Whenever it is accused of bias by one political side, it can always point out that the other side has complained of the same thing at some other time – so the complaints are evenly balanced. In fact, the BBC is rather proud of the fact that it gets complaints from both sides of the political divide, because this testifies not only to its impartiality but also to its independence.

Interestingly, though, this independence is as much the result of habit and common agreement as it is the result of its legal status. It is true that it depends neither on advertising nor (directly) on the government for its income. It gets this from the licence fee which everybody who uses a television set has to pay. However, the government decides how much this fee is going to be, appoints its

Broadcasting House

Situated in central London Broadcasting House is the headquarters of the BBC.

High ideals and independence

Below is an inscription to be found in the entrance to Broadcasting House (the BBC's first purpose-built headquarters). The reference to one man in the inscription is appropriate. British politicians were slow to appreciate the social significance of 'the wireless' (this is what the radio was generally known as until the 1960s). Moreover, being British, they did not like the idea of having to debate culture in Parliament. They were only too happy to leave the matter to a suitable organization and its Director General, John (later Lord) Reith. Reith was a man with a mission. He saw in the radio an opportunity for education and initiation into high culture for the masses. He included light entertainment in the programming, but only as a way of capturing an audience for the more 'important' programmes of classical music and drama, and discussions of various topics by famous academics and authors who Reith had persuaded to take part.

> THIS TEMPLE TO THE ARTS AND MUSES IS DEDICATED
> TO ALMIGHTY GOD
> BY THE FIRST GOVERNORS
> IN THE YEAR OF OUR LORD 1931
> JOHN REITH BEING DIRECTOR GENERAL
> AND THEY PRAY THAT THE GOOD SEED SOWN
> MAY BRING FORTH GOOD HARVESTS
> THAT ALL THINGS FOUL OR HOSTILE TO PEACE
> MAY BE BANISHED HENCE
> AND THAT THE PEOPLE INCLINING THEIR EAR
> TO WHATSOEVER THINGS ARE LOVELY AND HONEST
> WHATSOEVER THINGS ARE OF GOOD REPORT
> MAY TREAD THE PATH OF VIRTUE
> AND OF WISDOM

board of governors and its director-general, has the right to veto any BBC programme before it has been transmitted and even has the right to take away the BBC's licence to broadcast. In theory, therefore, it would be easy for a government to influence what the BBC does.

Nevertheless, partly by historical accident (High ideals and independence), the BBC began, right from the start, to establish its effective independence and its reputation for impartiality. This first occurred through the medium of radio broadcasts to people in Britain. Then, in 1932 The BBC World Service was set up, with a licence to broadcast first to the empire and then to other parts of the world. During the Second World War, it became identified with the principles of democracy and free speech. In this way the BBC's fame became international. Today, the World Service still broadcasts around the globe, in English and several other languages. The BBC also runs ten national radio stations inside Britain and several local ones (BBC Radio).

Television: organization

TV channels in general are also independent of government interference. This again is largely a matter of tacit agreement. There have been occasions when the government has successfully persuaded the BBC not to show something. But there have also been many occasions when the BBC has refused to bow to government pressure. Similarly, when the government or some other public body criticizes the BBC for its behaviour, the BBC sometimes accepts the criticism and apologizes (and one or more of its top people resign), and sometimes successfully argues its case and refuses to apologize.

There is no advertising on the BBC. But Independent Television (ITV), which started in 1954, gets its money from advertisements. ITV is a network of commercial companies, each of which is responsible for programming in different parts of the country on the single channel given to it. In practice, these companies cannot afford to make all their own programmes, and so they generally share those they make. As a result, it is common for exactly the same programme to be showing on the ITV channel throughout the country (just like on the BBC).

When commercial television began, it was feared that advertisers would have too much control over programming and that the new channel would exhibit all the worst features of tabloid journalism. Over the years, however, these fears have proved to be unfounded. Although commercial TV has recently adopted the habit of allowing programmes to be 'sponsored' by other commercial companies, as a form of advertising for them, these advertisers do not have the influence over programming that they have often had in the USA. Most importantly for the structure of commercial television, ITV news is not made by the individual companies. Independent Television News (ITN) is a separate company. For this and other reasons, it has always been protected from commercial influence. There is no significant difference between the style and content of ITN news and BBC news.

BBC radio

Radio 1 began in 1967. Devoted almost entirely to pop music, its birth was a signal that popular youth culture could no longer be ignored by the country's established institutions.

Radio 2 also broadcasts popular music but less contemporary than that on Radio 1. At the time of writing it is Britain's most popular radio station.

Radio 3 is devoted to classical music.

Radio 4 broadcasts a variety of programmes, from plays and comedy shows to consumer advice programmes and in-depth news coverage. It has a small but dedicated following.

Radio 5 is largely given over to sports coverage and news. Because of all the sport, it is sometimes referred to as 'Radio Bloke'. ('Bloke' is an informal word for a man which emphasizes male interests.)

Two particular radio programmes should be mentioned. Soap operas are normally associated with television (see below), but *The Archers* is actually the longest-running soap in the world. It describes itself as 'an everyday story of country folk'. Its audience, which is mainly middle-class with a large proportion of elderly people, cannot compare in size with the television soaps, but it has become so famous that everybody in Britain knows about it and tourist attractions have been designed to capitalize on its fame.

Another radio 'institution' is the live commentary of cricket test matches in the summer (see chapter 21).

The same fears that had been expressed about the quality of television when ITV started are now heard with regard to satellite and cable television. To some extent, these fears may be more justified, as the companies that run channels in this way are in exactly the same position as those which own the major newspapers (and in some cases actually are the same companies). In any case, new technology has meant that, instead of just the few channels they had been used to (The traditional TV channels), British households now have access to a vast number of channels, so they just have to become more discriminating themselves.

Television: style

Although the advent of ITV did not affect television coverage of news and current affairs, it did cause a change in the style and content of other programmes shown on television. The amount of money that a television company can charge an advertiser depends on the expected number of viewers at the time when the advertisement is to be shown. Therefore, there was pressure on ITV from the start to make its programmes popular. In its early years, ITV captured nearly three-quarters of the BBC's audience. The BBC then responded by making its own programming equally accessible to a mass audience.

Ever since then, there has been little significant difference in the programming of the BBC and the main commercial television channels. All show a wide variety of programmes, including news, documentaries, drama, films, light entertainment, comedies, and sports. They are in constant competition with each other to get the largest audience (this is known as the ratings war). But this competition does not mean that they each try to show a more popular type of programme than the other. Rather it means that each tries to do the same type of programme 'better'.

Of particular importance in the ratings war are the performances of the channels' various soap operas. These are also of interest because of what they can show about British attitudes and taste. The two most popular and long-running of these, which are shown at least twice a week, are not glamorous American productions showing rich and powerful people. They are ITV's *Coronation Street*, which is set in a working-class area near Manchester, and BBC1's *EastEnders*, which is set in a working-class area of London. They and other British-made soaps certainly do not paint an idealized picture of life. They depict relatively ordinary lives in relatively ordinary circumstances. The same is largely true of British situation comedies (known as 'sitcoms'). These are usually about people less fortunate and/or less able and/or less popular than the average. These people often have plans to be especially successful and popular, but the plans always fail.

It became obvious in the 1960s that the popularity of soap operas and light entertainment shows meant that there was less room for programmes which lived up to the original educational aims of television.

This was the main impetus for the founding of two other big channels (BBC2 and Channel 4), which acted as the main promoters of learning and 'culture'. To some extent they still do this. But the vast choice of channels now available means that this 'public service' is less essential.

The ratings: a typical week

Ten million viewers may look like a lot. But in fact it is far fewer than the number which the most popular soaps used to get. In 1994, *Coronation Street* used to get 18 million viewers per week. In the 1970s, the most popular programmes used to get more than 20 million viewers. But now people have so much more choice. Some people are sad about this because it means that they do not have as much shared experience as they used to have.

The chart below shows the 30 most watched programmes on the main channels in the second week of April 2008 (the top 18 from BBC1 and ITV1 and the top 12 from BBC2 and Channel 4). The ratings are dominated by three broad types of programme.

Soaps All of these are set in England (*Coronation Street, EastEnders,* and *Emmerdale*).

Soap-style dramas Three of these are set in a hospital (*Casualty, Holby City,* and *House*). The others are *The Bill* and *Crime Scene Investigation,* which are about the police, *Shameless,* which is about a family on welfare, and *Desperate Housewives,* set in an American suburb. The last two of these incorporate comedy into the drama.

Reality TV shows There are two types of these. In *Britain's Got Talent, The Apprentice, All Star Mr and Mrs, I'd Do Anything,* and *Come Dine With Me,* people compete against each other for some sort of prize. In *Grand Designs, Property Ladder,* and *How To Look Good Naked,* people are assisted by experts to improve some aspects of their lives.

There are three comedy programmes in the list. *My Family* and *Benidorm* are situation comedies, while *Headcases* is a satirical sketch show. *Pushing Daises* is a comedy drama.

The list includes one documentary programme (*Bodyshock: I am the Elephant Man*). *Doctor Who* is a science-fiction drama. *Foyle's War* is a period drama. There is one sports broadcast (*UEFA Champions League*) and one quiz programme (*University Challenge*).

The One Show is a general interest, 'soft news' magazine programme. *Delia* is a conventional cookery programme.

Only four of the programmes in the list are American (*Desperate Housewives, Crime Scene Investigation, House,* and *Pushing Daisies*).

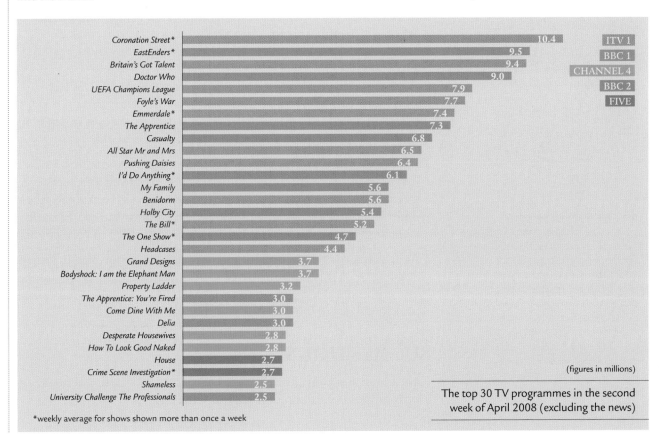

Programme	Viewers
Coronation Street*	10.4
EastEnders*	9.5
Britain's Got Talent	9.4
Doctor Who	9.0
UEFA Champions League	7.9
Foyle's War	7.7
Emmerdale*	7.4
The Apprentice	7.3
Casualty	6.8
All Star Mr and Mrs	6.5
Pushing Daisies	6.4
I'd Do Anything*	6.1
My Family	5.6
Benidorm	5.6
Holby City	5.4
The Bill*	5.2
The One Show*	4.7
Headcases	4.4
Grand Designs	3.7
Bodyshock: I am the Elephant Man	3.7
Property Ladder	3.2
The Apprentice: You're Fired	3.0
Come Dine With Me	3.0
Delia	3.0
Desperate Housewives	2.8
How To Look Good Naked	2.8
House	2.7
Crime Scene Investigation*	2.7
Shameless	2.5
University Challenge The Professionals	2.5

Channels: ITV 1, BBC 1, CHANNEL 4, BBC 2, FIVE

(figures in millions)

The top 30 TV programmes in the second week of April 2008 (excluding the news)

*weekly average for shows shown more than once a week

What do the British really like to watch?

All TV producers want their programme to make it to the top of the ratings. The fact that more people are watching your show than others is supposedly an indication of its popularity. But are all those people really watching your show? Many households, after all, just happen to have the TV switched on at certain times of day. And even if they are actually watching, does that mean they enjoy it? Some interesting results of a BBC survey were released in 2006 and the answers to these questions seems to be 'no'.

The Appreciation Index (AI) is a score from 0 to 100 given to each programme which is based on the weekly diaries kept by thousands of viewers around Britain. In 2004, the set of programmes which topped the AI figures were completely different from those which typically topped the ratings. They included a New Year's Day concert, several nature documentaries, coverage of the sixtieth anniversary commemoration of D-Day and a documentary about a brain operation. The soap *EastEnders* topped the ratings that year, but it wasn't even in the top ten of the AI.

Mass television programming is now more than half a century old. This means that TV channels have large and ever-expanding larger archives at their disposal. As a result, they can show (cheaply) numerous programmes based on lists: the top 100 comedy shows, the 20 favourite soaps, the 100 best ever music videos, and so on. Many people find these programmes either tedious or irritating (because not enough time is given to each item in the list). But the programme *The 50 Greatest Documentaries*, shown in 2005, was a reminder that, despite all the soaps and all the programmes which go by the misleading name of 'reality TV', Britain has made, and can still make, really good television. Among the top ten were the natural history series, *Life on Earth*, and the art history series *Civilization*, both from the 1970s, and the heart-rending story of a man with a rare fatal disease (*The Boy Whose Skin Fell Off*) from 2004. But the winner was a series of films almost as old as TV itself. Intended as a 'one-off' to show the divisions in social class which existed in 1950s Britain, *Seven Up* showed the lives of 20 seven-year-olds from different backgrounds. It captured the public imagination, so seven years later, the same children were revisited for a second programme. This too was rated a success and in 2005, the seventh programme in the series (*49 Up*) was shown.

In any case, perhaps worries about the 'dumbing down' of British television are unfounded. In 2002, for instance, the highest paid performer on British TV was not an actor or actress, not a sports presenter or game-show host, not even a newsreader. It was a history professor called David Starkey! (In that year, Channel 4 arranged to pay him £2 million for a series of 25 programmes on British monarchs.)

QUESTIONS

1 The dominant force in British Broadcasting is the BBC. What enabled it to achieve its position, and how does it maintain this? Can you describe some of the characteristics which give the BBC its special position in Britain and in the rest of the world?

2 It is often felt that newspapers' invasion of privacy goes too far. Legislation to control it has sometimes been drafted, but has never become law. What problems are there in Britain with getting legislation like this approved? What arguments can be put forward in favour of keeping the status quo? How is the press controlled in your country?

3 What does the television ratings chart tell you about British viewing habits? Does this tell you anything about the British? What are the most popular television programmes in your country? What does this reveal, if anything, about your nation?

SUGGESTIONS

Have a look at a couple of examples of each type of national newspaper. Try to get hold of examples from the same day.

If you don't already do so, listen to the BBC World Service if you can.

17 Transport

The British are enthusiastic about mobility. They regard the ability to travel far and frequently as a right. Some commuters can spend up to two or three hours each day getting to work in London or some other big city and back home to their suburban or country homes in the evening. Most people do not spend quite so long each day travelling, but it is taken for granted that they will not live near enough to their work or secondary school to get there on foot. Around 800 billion passenger kilometres are travelled inside Britain each year. That works out as more than 1,000 kilometres each month for every man, woman and child in the country!

The vast majority (more than 80%) of these journeys are made by private road transport, leading to the attendant problems of traffic congestion and pollution familiar in so much of the world. Congestion is especially high in Britain, not only because it is densely populated and because a very high proportion of goods are transported by road, but also because of the British phenomenon of 'Nimbyism'. NIMBY stands for 'Not In My Back Yard'. While the British want the freedom to move around easily, they do not like living near big roads or railways. Any proposed new road or rail project leads to 'housing blight'; that is, the value of houses along or near the proposed route goes down. Every such project is attended by an energetic campaign to stop construction. Partly for this reason, Britain has, in proportion to its population, fewer kilometres of main road and railway than any other country in northern Europe.

There are signs that the British love affair with the motor car is now over. In the 1980s, when Prime Minister Margaret Thatcher hailed Britain as 'the great car-owning democracy', road building was given priority and the activists who tried to stop the construction of new roads (and also airport expansions) were seen as nothing but mad extremists. But the public attitude changed during the 1990s, and the same people began to be hailed as public folk heroes and were referred to as 'eco-warriors'. British governments now talk about introducing taxes on pollution, about discriminating against larger cars, about 'road pricing', and about organizing things so that buses in cities go faster than cars. At the time of writing, central government has not done much more than talk. But local authorities have been taking the lead in this matter. In Edinburgh, for instance, buses and cyclists now have absolute priority on all routes into the city. The 'congestion charge' in London and some other cities, by which car drivers have to pay to enter the central area of the city, has been a great success in persuading people to leave their cars at home and use public transport.

Trainspotting, truck spotting – and plane spotting!

Perhaps because they were the first means of mass transportation, perhaps because they go through the heart of the countryside, there is an aura of romance attached to trains in Britain. Many thousands of people are enthusiastic 'trainspotters' who spend an astonishing amount of time at stations and along the sides of railway lines trying to 'spot' as many different engines as possible. Steam trains, symbolizing the country's lost industrial power, have the greatest romance of all. Many enthusiasts spend their free time keeping them in operation and finance this by offering rides to tourists.

This hobby is peculiarly British. When the film *Trainspotting* (which is not really about trainspotting at all) was shown in France and Germany, the original English title was, unusually, retained – neither French nor German has a word for it!

This kind of hobby doesn't end with trains. There are also many enthusiastic plane spotters. Again, this activity is seen as strange in other countries – so strange that in 2001, when a party of British plane spotters were seen hanging around a military airport in Greece with binoculars and handbooks, they were arrested and charged with spying!

It is now generally accepted that transport policy should attempt more than merely accommodating the number of cars on the road and should consider wider issues.

On the road

Three-quarters of households in Britain have regular use of a car and a third have more than one car. Part of the widespread enthusiasm for cars is, as elsewhere, a result of people using them to project an image of themselves. Another, more British, possible reason is the opportunity which cars provide to indulge the national passion for privacy. Being in a car is like taking your 'castle' with you wherever you go (see chapter 19). Perhaps this is why the occasional appeals to people to 'car pool' (to share the use of a car to and from work) have met with little success. The majority of cars on the road at any one time have just the driver inside them.

The privacy motive may also be the reason why British drivers are less 'communicative' than the drivers of many other countries. They use their horns very little, are not in the habit of signalling their displeasure at the behaviour of other road users with their hands and are a little more tolerant of both other drivers and pedestrians. They are also a little more safety conscious. Britain has almost the best road safety record in Europe. The speed limit on motorways is a little lower than in most other countries (70 mph = 112 kph). Another indication of the perception of the car as a private space is the fact that Britain was one of the last countries in western Europe to introduce the compulsory wearing of seat belts.

The British are not very keen on mopeds or motorcycles. They exist, of course, but they are not private enough for British tastes. Millions of bicycles are used, especially by younger people, but except for certain university towns such as Cambridge, they are not as common as they are in other parts of north-western Europe and the cycle-lane network is comparatively undeveloped. On the other hand, the comparative safety of the roads means that parents are not too worried about their children cycling on the road along with cars and lorries.

Public transport in towns and cities

Public transport services in urban areas, as elsewhere in Europe, suffer from the fact that there is so much private traffic on the roads, so that they are not as cheap, as frequent or as fast as they otherwise could be and stop running inconveniently early at night. However, cities and towns all over the country now have dedicated bus lanes which have helped to speed up journey times. An interesting modern development is that trams, which disappeared from the country's towns during the 1950s and 1960s, are now making a comeback. Research has shown that people seem to have more confidence in the reliability of a service which runs on tracks, and are therefore readier to use a tram than they would be to use an ordinary bus.

The lollipop lady

In 1953, most schoolchildren walked to school. For this reason, school crossing patrols were introduced. This 'patrol' consists of an adult wearing a bright waterproof coat and carrying a black and white stick with a circle at the top which reads 'STOP'. Armed with this 'lollipop', the adult walks out into the middle of the road, stops the traffic and allows children to cross. 'Lollipop ladies' and men (80% of them are women) are a familiar part of the British landscape. During the 1980s, they became a species in decline because more and more children were being driven to school by car. But in the twenty-first century, this trend has stopped. About half of primary schoolchildren still walk to school. At the same time, the amount of traffic on the roads continues to increase, so that lollipop ladies and men are needed more than ever.

Anoraks

The British sometimes refer to people who indulge in compulsive, fact-collecting hobbies such as trainspotting as 'anoraks', a reference to the outdoor jackets which they typically wear.

Even the roads are not free of anoraks. Some people are truck spotters! Thousands of them, for instance, belong to the Eddie Stobart fan club and try to spot the distinctive lorries of the haulage company of that name.

Britain is one of the few countries in Europe where double-decker buses (i.e. with two floors) are a common sight. Although single-deckers have also been in use since the 1960s, London still has more than 3,000 double-deckers in operation. The famous London Underground, known as the tube, is feeling the effects of its age (it was first opened in 1863). It is now one of the dirtiest and least efficient of all such systems in European cities. However, it is still heavily used because it provides excellent connections with the main line train stations and with the suburbs surrounding the city. (In fact almost as many journeys are taken on the tube as are taken on the whole of the country's rail network.)

Another symbol of London is the distinctive black taxi (in fact, they are not all black these days, nor are they confined to London). According to the traditional stereotype, the owner-drivers of London taxis, known as cabbies, are friendly Cockneys (see chapter 4) who never stop talking. While it may not be true that they are all like this, they all have to demonstrate, in a difficult examination, detailed familiarity with London's streets and buildings before they are given their taxi licence. (This familiarity is known simply as 'the knowledge'.) Normally, these traditional taxis cannot be hired by phone. You simply have to find one on the street. But there are also many taxi companies who get most of their business over the phone. These taxis are known as 'minicabs'. Taxis and minicabs are expensive and most British people rarely use them, except, perhaps, when going home late at night after public transport has stopped running, especially if they have been drinking alcohol.

Public transport between towns and cities

It is possible to travel between any two towns or cities by either road or rail. Coach services are generally slower than trains but also much cheaper. In some parts of the country, particularly the south-east of England, there is a dense suburban rail network, but the most commercially successful trains are inter-city services that run between London and the thirty or so largest cities in the country. Inter-City trains are quite fast, but by modern European standards they cannot be called 'high speed'. (The only train that qualifies for this description is the international Eurostar train from London which goes through the channel tunnel.) Pressure for a genuinely high-speed train network is growing, partly for environmental reasons (fast enough service would persuade more people to travel from London to the far north of England and Scotland by train rather than plane) and partly because trains are getting more and more overcrowded. But at the time of writing, no definite plans are in place

Britain's railway network was privatized in the early 1990s. This means that, unlike in most other countries, Britain's trains are not run by the state. Instead, they are run by a number of different companies, each of which has the contract to run trains on certain routes. The idea of privatization was to make trains pay for themselves (i.e. not to rely on

The end of the Routemaster

At 2.00 p.m. on 9 December 2005, double-decker bus No. 159 left Marble Arch in central London. It was unusually crowded. About an hour later, it crawled slowly – very slowly – into Brixton bus garage in south London. It was working perfectly well, but it had to go slowly because it was surrounded by crowds of well-wishers who were saying goodbye to an old friend.

This ended the career of the Routemaster. At one time, almost every London bus was a Routemaster. Originally intended to work for a mere 17 years, they proved so durable, convenient and popular that they lasted half a century. They were convenient because they were 'hop-on hop-off' buses. That is, they had no doors which open and close, just an open-sided platform instead, so you didn't have to wait for the next bus stop – you could 'hop off' any time you wanted. (In off-peak hours you could hop on anywhere too. But in rush hours this was classed as queue-jumping and was not tolerated). But this feature was also their downfall. It meant they did not conform to modern expectations regarding pram and wheelchair access.

The other distinctive feature of Routemasters was that they had not only a driver but also a conductor, who walked around collecting fares while the bus was moving.

government money) and make them more efficient and user-friendly (because the companies would want to encourage as many people as possible to use them). But there is a widespread feeling in the country that this has not worked. Calling travellers 'customers' instead of 'passengers' has not disguised the fact that fares, reliability, convenience, comfort and safety are no better, and in some cases worse, than they were before privatization. Naturally, each company wants to be able to boast about an excellent record for punctuality. The result is that it refuses to delay the departure of one of its trains when an incoming train of another company is late – so travellers miss their connections! Moreover, because the companies have to make a profit, fares are expensive (and also bewildering in their complexity).

In 2004, the annual conference of the governing Labour party voted to re-nationalize the railways. The government minister responsible promptly rejected the vote, but in the same year even the boss of one major rail company said he believed trains would be better off under central control and that steps will eventually be taken to bring this about. In fact, a small step has already been taken. Since 2002, the company that runs the rail infrastructure (the tracks, the stations, the bridges, etc.), although officially still not a government organization, is not allowed to make a profit, has its debts guaranteed by government and is heavily controlled by government.

The channel tunnel

On Friday 6 May 1994, Queen Elizabeth II of Britain and President Mitterrand of France travelled ceremonially under the sea that separates their two countries and officially opened the channel tunnel (for a while it was known as 'the chunnel') between Calais and

Queueing

Whether the British passion for queueing really signifies civilized patience is debatable (see chapter 5). But queueing is certainly taken seriously. When buses serving several different numbered routes stop at the same bus stop, instructions on it sometimes tell people to queue on one side for some of the buses and on the other side for others. And yes, people do get offended if anybody tries to 'jump the queue'.

What the British motorist hates most

Traffic wardens are not police, but they have the force of law behind them as they walk around leaving parking tickets on the windscreens of cars that are illegally parked. By convention, they are widely feared and disliked by British motorists. Although it is only thanks to traffic wardens that Britain's cities and towns do not come to a complete halt, the dislike sometimes turns to hate. In June 2000 many police forces issued body armour to traffic wardens after a spate of attacks from angry drivers. Officially, they have a variety of names, such as 'parking attendants', 'parking enforcement officers' or even 'civil enforcement officers', depending on the extent of their powers. But everyone still calls them traffic wardens.

Speed cameras have become so sophisticated these days that it is almost impossible for a driver to escape detection if caught speeding by one of these. Motorists feel that, speed cameras, like traffic wardens, are not really there to make traffic safe but rather to raise money for local authorities.

Traffic cones are orange and white, about a metre tall and made of plastic. Their appearance signals that some part of the road is being repaired and that therefore there is probably going to be a long delay. Workers placing them in position have had eggs thrown at them; lorry drivers have been accused by police of holding competitions to run them down; one local radio station once started a campaign for people to adopt them 'for charity' (i.e. steal them).

Folkestone. For the first time in about 8,000 years, people were able to travel between Britain and mainland Europe without taking their feet off solid ground.

The channel tunnel was by far the biggest building project in which Britain was involved in the twentieth century. The history of this project, however, was not a happy one. Several workers were killed during construction, the price of construction turned out to be more than double that first estimated and the start of regular services was repeatedly postponed, the last time even after tickets had gone on sale. Moreover, at first the public did not show much enthusiasm for the tunnel, perhaps because it was only available to those travelling by private transport. For them, the small saving in time did not compensate for the discomfort of a train with no windows and no facilities other than toilets, especially as the competing ferry companies had made their ships more attractive. In addition, some people felt it was unnatural and frightening to travel under all that water.

These negative attitudes have only partially disappeared. Passenger numbers on this service are still much lower than originally expected. However, the passenger train service, Eurostar, has been a great success. This success has increased since, finally (see chapter 4) the British side of the high speed rail track was completed in 2007. It means that passengers not only reach London from Paris in two hours and from Brussels in less than two hours; now that the Eurostar terminates at St. Pancras station in London, they do not have to travel through London to access the inter-city network of trains to other parts of Britain.

Air and water

A small but increasing minority, of mostly business people, travel within Britain by air. International air travel, however, is very economically important to Britain. As measured by numbers of international passengers, it has four airports in the world's top 30. They are Gatwick Airport (to the south of London), Stansted Airport (to the north of London), Manchester and, pre-eminently, Heathrow (on the western edge of London), which is the world's busiest passenger airport. However, Heathrow may not hold on to this crown much longer. Although, the opening of a fifth terminal in 2008 increased capacity on the ground, it has only two runways and these are operating at maximum capacity. There are plans for a third runway, but this will take a long time to build – or may not be built at all. While some British people are proud of Heathrow's status, others are not. First, people living close to the airport are worried about the destruction of their communities. Second, Londoners in general are worried about the noise (which British people tend to regard as an invasion of their privacy). Finally, green campaigners are against the idea on principle. They failed to stop the building of terminal 5 (despite holding a month long protest in 2007), but as time goes on public opinion is becoming more sympathetic to green views.

The AA and the RAC

These are the initials for the Automobile Association and the Royal Automobile Club. Drivers who are members of one of them (by paying a subscription fee) can get emergency help when their car breaks down. The fact that both organizations are very well-known is an indication of the importance of the car in modern British life.

The road to hell

The M25 is the motorway which circles London. Its history exemplifies the transport crisis in Britain. When, in the 1960s, it was first opened, it was seen as the answer to the area's traffic problems. But by the early 1990s the congestion on it was so bad that traffic jams had become an everyday occurrence. A rock song of the time called it 'the road to hell'. In an effort to relieve the congestion, the government announced plans to widen some parts of it to 14 lanes – and thus to import from America what would be Europe's first 'super highway'. This plan provoked widespread opposition and has not been implemented.

The dominance of London

The country's transport network illustrates the dominance of London. London is at the centre of the network, with a 'web' of roads and railways emanating from it. Britain's road numbering system, (M for motorways, then A, B, and C class roads) is based on the direction out of London that roads take.

It is notable that the names of the main London railway stations are known to almost everybody in the country, whereas the names of stations in other cities are only known to those who use them regularly or live nearby. The names of the London stations are: Charing Cross, Euston, King's Cross, London Bridge, Liverpool Street, Paddington, St. Pancras, Victoria and Waterloo. Each runs trains only in a certain direction out of London. If your journey takes you through London, you have to use the Underground to get from one of these stations to another.

Modern Britain makes surprisingly little use of its many inland waterways. In previous centuries, large rivers such as the Thames were busy thoroughfares, and the profession of 'watermen', the river equivalent of London cabbies, was well-known. In the last 100 years, transport by land has almost completely taken over. A few barges still go up and down the Thames through London, but are used mostly by tourists. Several attempts have been made to set up a regular service for commuters, but none have been a success so far. There is no obvious practical reason for this failure. It just seems that British people have lost the habit of travelling this way.

The story of goods transport by water is the same. In the nineteenth century, the network of canals used for this purpose was vital to the country's economy and as extensive as the modern motorway network. By now, the vast majority of these canals are no longer used in this way. Recently, the leisure industry has found a use for the country's waterways as boating holidays become increasingly popular.

QUESTIONS

1 The car is the preferred means of transport for most people in Britain. The same is perhaps true in your country. What effects has this had, in Britain and in your country?

2 Although freedom of movement (usually by car) is dear to the hearts of most British people, there is something even more dear to their hearts which makes the building of new roads a slow and difficult process. What is this? Does the objection to new roads, rail links and even airport terminals surprise you?

3 British individualism shows itself in many ways in the area of transport. Can you find examples in this chapter?

4 When people in Britain want to sell their car, they sometimes write 'one careful owner' in the advertisement as a way of indicating that the car is in good condition. On a hill outside the town of Folkstone, there is an enormous drill with a sign on it which reads 'For sale: one careful owner'. Who do you think the owner is? What was the drill used for?

The tube map

When London Transport first published the London Underground map (designed by Harry Beck) in 1931, they thought the public would probably reject it. At that time it was a revolutionary concept to make so free with the realities of geography. But the public loved it.

It somehow suggested that the underground was an exotic, exciting place where normal spatial laws did not apply. The design now appears on official merchandise all over the place, from mugs to tea-towels, making it as widely reproduced as certain works of modern art, and the concept has been copied by route map makers in the rest of Britain and the world.

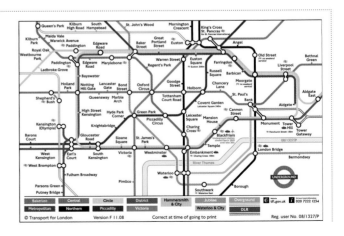

18 Welfare

Britain can claim to have been the first large country in the world to set up what is generally known as a 'welfare state', whereby it is part of the job of the government to help any citizen in need.

The benefits system

The most straightforward way in which people are helped is by direct payments of government money. Any adult who cannot find paid work, or any family whose total income is not sufficient for its needs, is entitled to one or more of various kinds of financial help. All retired people are entitled to the standard old-age pension, provided they have paid their national insurance contributions every week for most of their working lives. After a certain age, even people who are still earning can receive their pension (though at a slightly reduced rate). Pensions account for the greatest proportion of the money which the government spends on benefits.

The government pension, however, is not very high. Many people therefore make arrangements during their working lives to have some additional form of income after they retire. There are two ways of doing this. One is to contribute to a pension fund (also called a 'superannuation scheme'). These are usually organized by employers and both employer and employee make regular contributions to them. The other way is to take out a life insurance policy, which is used as a form of saving. A lump sum is paid out by the insurance company at around the age of retirement.

Some people are entitled to neither pension nor money for being unemployed (because they have not previously worked for long enough or because they have been unemployed for a long time). These people can apply for income support and if they have no significant savings, they will receive it. Income support is also sometimes paid to those with paid work but who need extra money, for instance because they have a particularly large family or because their earnings are especially low.

A wide range of other benefits exist. For example, child benefit is a small payment for each child, usually paid directly to mothers, regardless of their circumstances. Other examples are sickness benefit, maternity benefit and death grants (to cover funeral expenses). The system, of course, has its imperfections. On the one hand, there are people who are entitled to various benefits but who do not receive them, sometimes because they do not understand the complicated system and do not know what they are entitled to, sometimes because they do not want their privacy invaded. (Some benefits, most notably

The origins of the welfare state in Britain

Before the twentieth century, welfare was considered to be the responsibility of local communities. The 'care' provided was often very poor. An especially hated institution in the nineteenth century was the workhouse, where the old, the sick, the mentally handicapped and orphans were sent. People were often treated very harshly in workhouses, or given as virtual slaves to equally harsh employers.

During the first half of the twentieth century, a number of measures were introduced. These were a small old-age pension scheme (1908), partial sickness and unemployment insurance (1912) and unemployment benefits conditional on regular contributions and a means test (1934). The real impetus for the welfare state came in 1942 from a government commission, headed by William Beveridge, and its report on 'social insurance and allied services'. In 1948, the National Health Act turned the report's recommendations into law and the National Health Service was set up.

The mass rush for free treatment caused the government health bill to swell enormously. In response to this, the first payment within the NHS (a small fixed charge for medicines) was introduced in 1951. Other charges (such as that for dental treatment in 1952) followed.

income support, are only granted after a 'means test'. This is an official investigation into a person's financial circumstances.) On the other hand, some people can 'play the system' so well that they can get more money (through claiming various benefits) when not working than they can when being employed.

The whole social security system is coming under increasing pressure because of the rising numbers of pensioners in society. It is believed that if everybody actually claimed the benefits to which they are entitled, the system would reach breaking point. It has long been a principle of the system that some benefits are available to everybody who qualifies for them. You don't have to be poor in order to receive your pension or your child benefit. It is argued by some people that this blanket distribution of benefits should be modified and that only those people who really need them should get them. However, this brings up the possibility of constant means tests for millions of households, which is a very unpopular idea (and would in itself be very expensive to administer).

Social services and charities

As well as giving financial help, the government also takes a more active role in looking after people's welfare. These services are either run directly or indirectly (through 'contracting out' to private companies) by local government. Examples are the building and staffing of old people's homes and the provision of 'home helps' for people who are disabled in some way.

Professional social workers have the task of identifying and helping members of the community in need. These include the old, the mentally handicapped and children suffering from neglect or from maltreatment. Social workers do a great deal of valuable work. But their task is often a thankless one. For example, they are often blamed for not moving in and protecting children from violent parents. But they are also sometimes blamed for exactly the opposite – for taking children away from their families unnecessarily. The problem is perhaps that there is a conflict of values in modern Britain. On the one hand, there is the traditional respect for privacy and the preaching of successive governments about 'family values'; on the other hand, there is the modern expectation that agencies will intervene in people's private lives and their legal ability to do so.

Before the welfare state was established and the concept of 'social services' came into being, the poor and needy in Britain turned to the many charitable organizations for help. These organizations were, and still are, staffed mostly by unpaid volunteers, especially women, and relied, and still do rely, on voluntary contributions from the public. There are more than 150,000 registered charities in the country today. Most of them are charities only in the legal sense that they are non-profit making and so do not pay income tax and have never had any relevance to the poor and needy. However, there are still today a large number which offer help to large sections of the public in various ways (Some well-known charities).

The language of unemployment

Over the last 50 years, the average level of unemployment in Britain has risen. In addition, jobs are not as secure as they used to be, so that many people find themselves out of work for a short time. As a result, some terms connected with unemployment have become well known in society at large.

If you find yourself without paid work, you go to the local Job Centre and 'sign on'. This means that you declare yourself to be unemployed and that you are applying for a 'jobseeker's allowance' (as it is officially called). To get this money, you have to keep a record of your search for work and present it regularly at the Job Centre. Colloquially, this situation is known as being 'on the dole' and the jobseeker's allowance is often referred to as 'dole money'. It is usually paid fortnightly into a bank account.

Some social services are run by state authorities but with the help of volunteers. An example is the 'meals-on-wheels' system, whereby food is cooked and distributed to the homes of people who cannot cook for themselves. Another is the Citizen's Advice Bureau (CAB), which has a network of offices throughout the country offering free information and advice.

The National Health Service

The NHS (it is most commonly referred to by this abbreviation) is generally regarded as the jewel in the crown of the welfare state. Interestingly, it was set up in a rather 'un-British' manner. It did not, as was done in so many other areas of British public life, accommodate itself to what had already come into existence. Instead of entering into a partnership with the hundreds of existing hospitals run by charities, it simply took most of them over. Most of system is organized centrally and there is little interaction with the private sector. For instance, there is no working together with health insurance companies and so no choice for the public regarding which one they join. Medical insurance is organized by the government and is compulsory ('national insurance contributions' are deducted from people's salaries).

However, in another respect the NHS is very typically British. For patients, the system is beautifully simple. For medical professionals it is different (Bureaucracy in the NHS). There are no forms to fill in and no payments to be made which are later refunded. All that anybody has to do to be assured the full benefits of the system is to register with a local NHS doctor. Most doctors in the country are General Practitioners (GPs) and they are at the heart of the system. A visit to the GP is the first step towards getting any kind of treatment. The GP then arranges for whatever tests, surgery, specialist consultation or medicine are considered necessary. Only if it is an emergency or if the patient is away from home can treatment be obtained in some other way. As in most other European countries, the exceptions to free medical care are the teeth and eyes of adults. In fact, dental treatment on the NHS for adults has become virtually non-existent.

Some well-known charities

The Samaritans organization offers free counselling by phone, with anonymity guaranteed, to anybody who is in despair.

Barnardo's, also founded in the nineteenth century, used to provide homes for orphaned children and still helps children in need.

The Salvation Army is organized on military lines and grew out of Christian missionary work in the slums of London in the nineteenth century. It offers various kinds of help to the most desperate and needy, for example, overnight accommodation in hostels for the homeless.

MENCAP and **MIND** are two charities which help the mentally handicapped and campaign on their behalf.

Bureaucracy in the NHS

Doctors earn a lot of money in Britain – more than anywhere else in Europe. So why are there never enough of them? Why does Britain always need to rely on doctors imported from abroad? The answer might lie in the capitation system. This means patients often turn up for consultations when they don't really need to. Moreover, because they are part of the NHS system, GPs often find themselves buried under a mountain of paperwork, especially these days when various 'targets' for 'performance' are a political matter (see chapter 8). To many of them, it seems that the high earnings do not make up for these stresses.

Bureaucracy is a problem in the NHS more generally. In 2002, it was revealed that there were more administrative staff in the NHS than there were hospital beds. These staff go by a wide variety of names: information analysts, service planners, access managers, programme facilitators, and even 'patient pathway managers'. But not a single one of them is directly engaged in healing or caring for the sick. Ironically, this absurd situation is partly the result of the drive for efficiency, part of which is the setting of hundreds of targets. But how can people know whether the targets have been met? Easy! Hire more administrative staff! In 2002, 12,000 new staff were appointed whose jobs were simply to monitor progress towards them.

Getting medicine on the NHS

When medicine is needed, the doctor writes out a prescription which the patient then takes to a chemist's (that is, a pharmacy, but this latter word is used only by medical professionals). There is a charge for each item prescribed, which is always the same regardless of its real cost. Charges have increased considerably in the last quarter of the twentieth century. However, so many categories of people (e.g. pensioners, expectant and nursing mothers, those on income support) are exempt that only around half of all the people who are prescribed medicine actually pay for it.

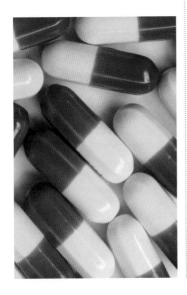

The main problem faced by the NHS in the twenty-first century is the same as that faced by equivalent systems in other countries. The potential of medical treatment of conditions which are otherwise fatal has increased dramatically. As a result, so have people's expectations about what medical science can do for them. But the treatments are so expensive that, if they were to be made freely available to everybody who could benefit from them, taxation would have to double. (The NHS already employs well over a million people, making it the largest single employer in the country.) Medical practitioners frequently have to decide which patients will get the limited resources available and which will not. For the latter, it is sometimes a case of whether they have the money to buy their survival by getting the treatment privately. This is one reason why an increasing number of people in recent decades have turned to private medical insurance, even though they are still obliged to pay state medical insurance as well if they have a job (Going private ...).

In Britain, this main problem is made worse by one simple fact. The amount of money that British people are prepared to pay for health care, either through taxation or personal expenditure, has not kept pace with their increased expectations of it. The country as a whole spends relatively little money per person on health care. This may have something to do with the British 'stiff upper lip'. In general, people do not like to make a big drama out of being ill. If the doctor tells them that there is nothing to worry about, they are likely to accept this diagnosis. Partly as a result of this, British GPs prescribe significantly less medicine for their patients than doctors in other countries in Europe do.

Another possible reason is that the way GPs are paid helps to keep costs down. It is not that they don't get paid well. In fact they earn more than anywhere else in Europe. It is that their pay does not depend on the number of consultations they perform. Instead, it depends on the number of registered patients they have – they get a 'capitation' allowance for each one. Therefore, they have no incentive to arrange more consultations than are necessary. It is in their interest that their patients remain as healthy as possible and come to see them

Going private ...

There are a number of private medical schemes in the country. The biggest is BUPA. Private treatment, especially for surgery, is becoming increasingly popular. This is not because people believe that it is any better than NHS treatment from a purely medical point of view. But it is widely recognized as more convenient and psychologically comfortable. NHS patients who need a non-urgent operation often have to wait more than a year, and those who need a relatively urgent operation sometimes

have to wait more than a month. Under private schemes, people can choose to have their operation whenever, and as soon as, they want.

Private patients sometimes go to 'pay beds' in NHS hospitals, which are usually in a separate room (NHS patients are usually accommodated in wards containing several beds). There are also some hospitals and clinics which are completely private. These are sometimes called 'nursing homes'.

... and going abroad

The long waiting lists in the NHS and the high cost of private surgery in Britain have led to the phenomenon known as health tourism whereby British people go to other countries to get the treatment they need more quickly and/or more cheaply than they could get it at home. Indeed, the NHS itself sometimes sends its own patients to other countries. This way, it reduces the length of its waiting lists.

as little as possible, so that they can have more patients on their books. It is also possible that government reforms in the last two decades, which have given hospitals and GPs more control over their budgets, have made the system more cost-efficient.

However, whether the reforms really have increased efficiency is debatable. In any case, there is a limit to what such apparent cost-efficiency can provide. Hospitals sometimes simply run out of money and have to suspend all non-urgent treatment. Moreover, Britain has one of the lowest ratios of doctors per person in Europe. As a result, patients have to wait a long time for treatment. The 'waiting lists' on which they find themselves are a frequent political issue and they are the other reason why more people are 'going private' if they can afford it. In addition, and despite the fact that Britain has one of the highest ratios of nurses in Europe, it has a rather bad record for hospital hygiene (so that people catch diseases while they are in hospital) and this is another frequently discussed public issue. But despite all these failings, the NHS can still claim to be largely successful in fulfilling the aim for which it was originally intended – to take the financial hardship out of sickness and offer people medical insurance 'from the womb to the tomb'.

The medical profession

Doctors generally have the same very high status in Britain that they have throughout the world. Specialist doctors have greater prestige than ordinary GPs, with hospital consultants at the top. These specialists are allowed to work part-time for the NHS and spend the rest of their time earning big fees from private patients. Some have a surgery in Harley Street in London, conventionally the sign that a doctor is of the very highest quality. However, the difference in status between specialists and ordinary GPs is not as marked as it is in most other countries. At medical school, it is not automatically assumed that a brilliant student will become a specialist. GPs are not in any way regarded as second-class. The idea of the family doctor with personal knowledge of the circumstances of his or her patients was established in the days when only rich people could afford to pay for the services of a doctor. But the NHS capitation system has encouraged this idea to spread to the population as a whole.

Most GPs work in a 'group practice'. That is, they work in the same building as several other GPs. This allows them to share facilities such as waiting rooms and receptionists. Each patient is registered with just one doctor in the practice, but this system means that, when his or her doctor is unavailable, the patient can be seen by one of the doctor's colleagues.

The status of nurses in Britain may be traced to their origins in the nineteenth century. The Victorian reformer Florence Nightingale became a national heroine for her organization of nursing and hospital facilities during the Crimean War in the 1850s. Because of

Alternative medicine

An additional reason why the British are, per person, prescribed the fewest drugs in Europe is possibly the common feeling that such drugs are dangerous and should only be taken when absolutely necessary. An increasing number of people regard them as actually bad for you. These people, and others, are turning instead to some of the forms of treatment which generally go under the name of 'alternative medicine'. There are a great variety of these in the country (reflecting, perhaps, British individualism). However, the medical 'establishment' (as represented, for example, by the British Medical Association) has been slow to consider the possible advantages of such treatments and the majority of the population still tends to regard them with suspicion. Homeopathic medicine, for example, is not as widely available in chemists as it is in other countries in north-western Europe. One of the few alternative treatments to have originated in Britain is Bach flower remedies.

The emergency services

From any phone anywhere in Britain, public or private, a person who needs emergency help can call '999' free of charge. The operator then asks 'Which service do you require?' and the caller says 'fire', 'ambulance', or 'police'.

her, nurses have an almost saintly image in the minds of the British public, being widely admired for their caring work. However, this image suggests that they are doing their work out of the goodness of their hearts rather than to earn a living wage. (Florence Nightingale herself was firmly middle-class and had no need to worry about money.) As a result, the nursing profession has always been rather badly paid and there is a very high turnover of nursing staff. Most nurses, the vast majority of whom are still women, give up their jobs after only a few years. The style of the British nursing profession can also be traced back to its origins. Born at a time of war, it is distinctively military in its uniforms, its clear-cut separation of ranks, its insistence on rigid procedural rules, and its tendency to place a high value on group loyalty.

QUESTIONS

1 Would you say that the balance in Britain between welfare provided by the state and welfare offered by charities is different from that in your country?

2 From your reading of this chapter do you think that the British welfare state is successful in giving help to everybody who needs it? How many and what kinds of people do you think 'slip through the net' of care?

3 What, according to this chapter, are the main problems of the welfare state in modern Britain? Are similar problems encountered in your country?

4 How does the general status and public image of nurses in Britain compare with that of nurses in your country?

Modern medicine and ethics

Another, rather frightening, way in which the cost of the NHS can be reduced is by making treatment conditional on patients' behaviour. For example, hospitals sometimes refuse to perform heart surgery on patients because they smoke. Doctors say that smokers stay in hospital longer than non-smokers and have only half the chance of making a full recovery; that they deprive healthier patients of much-needed treatment and will die prematurely anyway. Other surgeons in Britain are horrified by this new trend. They say it is unethical and immoral. And, as some have pointed out, the very high taxes on cigarettes help to train heart surgeons and pay their salaries!

Issues of this kind are likely to become more frequent in the future and the ethics committee of the British Medical Association (the BMA – the organization which represents the country's doctors) will be kept busy.

19 Housing

Most people in Britain dream of living in a detached house; that is, a house which is a separate building. The saying, 'An Englishman's home is his castle', is well known. It illustrates the desire for privacy and the importance attached to ownership which seems to be at the heart of the British attitude to housing.

Houses, not flats

A large, detached house not only ensures privacy, it is also a status symbol. At the extreme end of the scale there is the aristocratic 'stately home' set in acres of garden. Of course, such a house is an unrealistic dream for most people. But even a modest detached house, surrounded by garden, gives the required suggestion of rural life which is dear to the hearts of many British people. Most people would be happy to live in a cottage, and if this is a thatched cottage, reminiscent of a pre-industrial age, so much the better.

Most people try to avoid living in blocks of flats (what the Americans call 'apartment blocks'). Flats, they feel, provide the least amount of privacy. With a few exceptions, mostly in certain locations in central London, flats are the cheapest kind of home. The people who live in them are those who cannot afford to live anywhere else.

The dislike of living in flats is very strong. In the 1950s, millions of poorer people lived in old, cold, uncomfortable nineteenth-century houses, often with only an outside toilet and no bathroom. During the next twenty years, many of them were given smart new 'high rise' blocks of flats to live in which, with central heating and bathrooms, were much more comfortable and were surrounded by grassy open spaces. But people hated their new homes (which became known as 'tower blocks'). They said they felt cut off from the world all those floors up. They missed the neighbourliness. They couldn't keep a watchful eye on their children playing down there in those lovely green spaces. The new high-rise blocks quickly deteriorated. The lifts broke down. The lights in the corridors didn't work. Windows got broken and were not repaired. There was graffiti all over the walls.

It seems that living in flats does not suit British attitudes. As the writer and broadcaster Jeremy Paxman rhetorically asks (in his book *The English*): 'Where else in Europe would you find it seriously argued that living in flats causes riots?'

The thatched cottage

Private property and public property

The image of a home as a castle implies a clear demarcation between private property and the public domain. This is very clear in the case of a detached house. Flats, on the other hand, involve uncertainties. You share the corridor outside your front door, but who with? The other residents on the same floor, or all the residents in the building? What about the foyer downstairs? Is this only for the use of the people who live in the block, or for the public in general? These uncertainties perhaps explain why the 'communal' living expected of flat-dwellers has been unsuccessful in most of Britain.

Law and custom seem to support a clear separation between public and private. For example, people have no general right to reserve the road directly outside their house for their own cars. The castle puts limits on the domain of its owner as well as keeping out others. It also limits responsibility. It is comparatively rare, for example, for people to attempt to keep the bit of pavement outside their house clean and tidy. That is not their job. It is outside their domain.

To emphasize this clear division, people prefer to live in houses a little bit set back from the road. This way, they can have a front garden or yard as a kind of buffer between them and the world. These areas are not normally very big, but they allow residents to have little low fences, walls or hedges around them. Usually, these barriers do not physically prevent even a two-year old child from entering, but they have psychological force. They announce to the world exactly where the private property begins. Even in the depths of the countryside, where there may be no road immediately outside, the same phenomenon can be seen.

There's no place like home

The most desirable home: a detached house
Notice:

- the 'traditional' building materials of brick (the walls) and slate (the roof);

- the irregular, 'non-classical', shape, with all those little corners, making the house feel 'cosy' (see main text);

- the suggestion of a large front garden with a tree and bushes, evoking not only the countryside but also giving greater privacy;

- that the garage (on the left) is hidden discreetly away, so that it is not too obvious and doesn't spoil the rural feeling;

- that the front door is not even in the picture. This is the privacy criterion at work again.

Second best: a semi detached

Detached houses are too expensive for most people. So this is what a very large proportion of people live in: one building with two separate households. Each house is the mirror of the other, inside and out. These houses can be found, street after street, in the suburbs of cities and the outskirts of towns all over Britain. Notice the separate front garden for each house. At the sides, there is access to the back, where there will also be two gardens. The most common building material is brick. The typical semi-detached house has two floors and three bedrooms.

The least desirable: a flat

Not having a separate entrance to the outside world does not suit British tastes. Although it is densely populated, Britain has the second lowest proportion of flat-dwellers in the EU (the lowest of all is Ireland). Less than 20% of the country's households live in flats of any kind.

A thatched cottage: an idealized country retreat

How desirable? A terraced house

This kind of house has no way through to the back except through the house itself. Each house in the row is joined to the next one. (Houses at the end of the row are a bit more desirable – they are the most like a semi-detached). The stereotypical terraced house has two floors, with two bedrooms upstairs.

Before the 1960s, Britain had millions of such houses, most with no inside toilet or bathroom. These were regarded as definitely undesirable and many were then knocked down. Most of those that survive, although they now have modern conveniences, remain relatively undesirable. But in some areas, they have been 'gentrified' and have become quite desirable – after modern conveniences have been installed.

In fact, there has always been great variety in the design and use of terraced houses. Some, to be found in 'good' areas in the centre of cities and known as 'town houses', have always been thought highly desirable. They often have three or more floors, perhaps including a basement or semi-basement. Many have been broken up into flats or rooms for rent. Sometimes, these are 'self-contained' flats (they have washing and cooking facilities and it is not necessary to walk through anybody else's flat to get to your own); sometimes, they are 'bedsits' (bed-sitting rooms; residents have one room to themselves and share washing and cooking facilities with other residents).

In recent decades, many new terraced houses have been built which are somewhere between the two extremes above.

The stately home

Among the British, there is one exception to the rule that 'homes' are more important than 'houses'. This is the aristocracy. Many of these families own fine old country houses, often with a great deal of land attached, in which they have lived for hundreds of years. They have a very great emotional investment in their houses – and are prepared to try very hard to stay in them. This can be very difficult in modern times, partly because of death duties (very high taxes which the inheritor of a large property has to pay). So, in order to stay there, many aristocrats live lives which are less physically comfortable than those of most people (they may not, for example, have central heating). Many have also turned their houses and land into tourist attractions. These are popular not only with foreign tourists: British visitors are also happy to be able to walk around in the rural surroundings as they inspect a part of their country's history.

The importance of 'home'

Despite the reverence they tend to feel for 'home', British people have little deep-rooted attachment to their house as an object, or to the land on which it stands. It is the abstract idea of 'home' which is important, not the building. This will be sold when the time and price is right and its previous occupiers will move into some other house which they will then turn into 'home' – a home which they will love just as much as they did the previous one.

But the houses themselves are just investments. An illustration of this lack of attachment to mere houses (as opposed to homes) is that two-thirds of all inherited houses are immediately sold by the people who inherit them, even if these people have lived there themselves at some time in their lives. Another is the fact that it is extremely rare for people to commission the building of their own houses. (Most houses are commissioned by private companies known as 'property developers' who sell them on the open market.)

This notion of houses principally as investments leads to a strange approach towards house prices. Whenever these fall, it is generally regarded as a 'bad thing'. You might think that it would be a good thing, because people can then find somewhere to live more cheaply. But for homeowners, falling prices means that most people cannot afford to sell their house. They have borrowed a lot of money to buy it and they are stuck! To British homeowners, such immobility is a terrible misfortune.

Individuality and conformity

Flats are not unpopular just because they do not give enough privacy. It is also that they do not allow enough scope for the expression of individuality. People like to choose the colour of their own front door and window frames, and also to choose what they are going to do with a little bit of outside territory, however small that may be.

The opportunity which it affords for individual self-expression is another advantage of the front garden. In any one street, some are paved, some are full of flowerbeds with paths in between, others are just

A place in the country. But for whom?

Until recently, for most people the dream of rural life was just that – a dream. People could not actually go ahead and move to the country because there were no jobs there and they couldn't afford the time and money to commute long distances to work every day. But two features of modern life have changed this situation. One is the telecommunications revolution, which makes it possible for more and more people to work from home, so they can live wherever they choose. The other is that more city dwellers have become rich enough to buy a second home in the country, which they use for weekends and holidays.

The result of these changes is that house prices in these highly-prized rustic paradises have shot up, with catastrophic consequences for real country people, the ones who have always lived there. They can't afford to buy homes in their own areas, so they have to move to towns. This results in severe labour shortages in farming. If it were not for cheap migrant labour from eastern Europe, many crops would remain unharvested. In 2003, a government adviser suggested a radical solution to this problem; a law requiring that all homes in country areas be sold only to people who have lived in the area for at least three years.

patches of grass, others are a mixture of these. Some are demarcated by walls, others by fences, others by privet hedges and some with no barrier at all. The possibilities for variety are almost endless!

However, not everything about housing in Britain displays individuality. Because most houses are built by organizations, not individuals, they are not usually built one at a time. Instead, whole streets, even neighbourhoods (often called 'estates'), are built at the same time. For reasons of economy, all the houses on an estate are usually built to the same design. Viewed from the air, adjacent streets in British towns often seem to be full of houses that are identical (Similar, but not the same). Indeed, they are so similar that when a building company advertises a new estate, it often invites people to its 'show house'. This is just one of the houses, but by looking around it, people can get a fairly accurate impression of any house on the estate.

However, if, later, you walked down the same streets that you saw from the air, every single house would seem different. The residents will have made sure of that! In an attempt to achieve extra individuality, some people even give their house a name (although others regard this as pretentious). In suburbs and towns, there is a constant battle going on between the individualistic desires of the householder and the necessity for some element of regimentation in a densely populated area. This contest is illustrated by the fact that anybody who wants to build an extension to their house, or even a garden shed, must (if it is over a certain size) first get 'planning permission' from the local authorities.

Interiors: the importance of cosiness

British houses have a reputation for being the coldest in Europe. Moreover, to many people from other countries, British people seem to be ridiculously keen on 'fresh air'. This reputation is exaggerated. It is partly the result of the fact that houses in Britain are, on average, older than they are in other countries and are not so well insulated. In fact, almost all houses now have central heating. However, there is a grain of truth in it. Windows, for example, are designed so that they can be conveniently opened to a great variety of degrees – instead of, as in many other countries, the choice between completely shut and fully open. This way, air can be let into the house in winter without freezing its inhabitants.

Just as the British idea of home is as much psychological as physical, so is their idea of domestic comfort. The important thing is to feel cosy – that is, to create an atmosphere which seems warm. This desire usually has priority over aesthetic concerns, which is why the British also have a reputation for bad taste. Most people would rather buy several items of cheap, mass-produced furniture, with chairs and sofas covered in synthetic material, than one more beautiful and more physically comfortable item. The same is true with regard to ornaments – if you want to be cosy, you have to fill the room up.

Similar, but not the same

A typical suburban district. You might think that living in one of these streets would be much the same as living in the one next to it, but the attempt at individuality is found here too. In Britain, there are an enormous number of words which are used in place of the word 'street' (avenue, close, crescent, drive, lane and park are common examples). It is quite common to find three streets next to each other named, for example, 'Pownall Close', 'Pownall Gardens' and 'Pownall Crescent'. The idea here is that one street is different from a neighbouring street not just because it has a different name – it is a different kind of place!

Rooms: uses and names

It is difficult to generalize about how British people use the various rooms in their houses. They may like the idea of tradition, but they are too individualistic to follow the same traditional habits. The only safe generalization is that, in a house with two floors, the rooms upstairs are the ones used as bedrooms. The bathroom and toilet (if there is only one) are also usually upstairs. The living room(s) and kitchen are downstairs. The latter is usually small, but those who can afford the space often like to have a 'farmhouse kitchen', big enough for the family to eat in.

Social class divisions are sometimes involved in the names used for rooms. With living rooms, for example, the terms 'sitting room' and 'drawing room' are regarded as upper-middle class, while 'lounge' is regarded as lower class. 'Front room' and 'back room' are also sometimes looked down on.

In any case, not everybody in Britain sees the comforts of modernity as automatically good. To many, part of cosiness is the feeling of tradition, which can be suggested by being surrounded by old, but not necessarily comfortable or beautiful, items of furniture. And if you cannot have items which are actually old, you can always have things that suggest age. The open fire is an example. In Britain, it is regarded as very desirable to have a 'real fire' (as it is often known), not just for the warmth but also because it suggests age (because that is what most people used in the past). These days, most houses in towns and suburbs are not allowed to use open fires (they cause too much pollution). And yet, so strong is the attraction of the 'real fire' idea that many houses have an imitation open fire, complete with plastic coal which glows red when it is switched on. Bad taste? So what!

Privacy is an element of cosiness. Most older houses, even small ones, have not one but two general living rooms (which estate agents call 'reception rooms'). This arrangement allows the front room to be kept for comparatively formal visits, while family members and close friends can spend their time, safely hidden from public view, in the back room. Most modern smaller houses are built with just one living room (and in some older houses the two reception rooms have been converted into one). However, privacy must be preserved so these houses normally have a 'hall' onto which the front door opens. It is rare for it to open straight onto the living room. Some houses also have a tiny 'porch',

Trouble over the garden wall

For many people in Britain, their back garden is a vital part of their life. You can potter around doing a bit of gardening there, sit out there on sunny days and have tea, drinking in all the nature around you, maybe even do a bit of sunbathing. Mostly, though, it's nice just to look at. But people's garden habits are changing. Many British back gardens have been turned into 'outdoor rooms'. They are being used as kitchens and dining rooms (about a third of British homes have barbecues), as offices for the self-employed and as general entertainment areas complete with built-in sound systems, hot tubs, skateboard ramps and trampolines. But that's where the trouble starts. Those hot tubs have whirring motors, those skateboards clatter, those sound systems can be heard half a mile away and those trampolines allow children to peek over the garden fence. And that means the tranquillity and the privacy for the people next door has gone. Every summer, complaints about noisy and otherwise intrusive neighbours increase.

So do the number of 'anti-social behaviour orders' (known as 'ASBOS') and 'noise abatement orders' issued by local authorities. These are legally binding strictures which would be regarded as ridiculous in many other countries. The British have some decisions to make. What are their gardens for? And what constitutes an invasion of privacy?

And when does your privacy become someone else's nightmare? In the 1990s, many suburban dwellers enthusiastically planted a coniferous hedge called leylandii in their gardens. The attraction of these plants was that, as they grow up to a metre in height every year, it only took a few years before their garden was entirely protected from prying eyes. And their neighbour's house was shrouded in darkness even in the summer! Leylandii quickly became the biggest single cause of bad feeling and official complaints in the suburbs. In the end, the problem was solved by laws empowering councils to order a hedge to be cut down to two metres in height.

with its own door, through which people pass before getting to the hall – an extra line of defence! The same concern can be seen in the existence of both a front door and a back door – even if both can be reached from the street. The back door is for family and close friends only.

Owning and renting

Most British people do not 'belong' to a particular place (see chapter 4), nor are they brought up in a long-established family house which will always be 'there' for them. Perhaps this is why they are not usually content to rent their accommodation. Wherever they are, they like to put down roots.

The desire to own the place where you live is almost universal in Britain. However, house prices are high. This dilemma is overcome by the mortgage system. About 70% of all houses are occupied by their owners and almost all of these were bought with a mortgage. At any one time, half of these are 'owned' by people who have borrowed 80% (or even more) of their price and are now paying this money back month by month. The normal arrangement is for the borrower to pay back the money over a period of 20–25 years. The financial institutions known as 'building societies' were originally set up to organize mortgages, but these days all the high street banks offer mortgages as well.

People are happy to take out mortgages because house prices normally increase a bit faster than the increase in the general cost of living. Therefore, they can make a profit when they sell a house. So strong is this expectation that phrases such as 'first-time buyer' and 'second-time buyer' are well-known. The former can only afford a house up to a certain price. But around ten years later, when some of their mortgage has been paid off, they can sell their house at a profit and move up (what is called) the 'property ladder' into a more expensive house.

However, this general attitude has led to a situation in which house prices are generally very expensive. When prices are rising fast, some people 'buy to let'; that is, they buy a house and then pay the mortgage on it by renting it out, which drives up prices even more (and, it is claimed, ruins neighbourhoods). All this means that more and more of the people who don't already own a house simply can't get their feet on even the lowest rung of the ladder. In the south-east of England, where prices are highest, young teachers, nurses and other essential public servants have no chance of buying without special government help.

Although nearly everybody wants to own their house, it is only in the last quarter of the twentieth century that a majority of people have done so. Before that time, most working-class people lived in rented accommodation. At one time, most of them rented from private landlords, some of whom exploited them badly. Then in the 1950s and 1960s, millions of homes were built by local government authorities. By 1977, two-thirds of all tenants lived in these 'council houses' (or, in some cases, flats).

Owning and renting: modern developments

This graph shows how home ownership has increased in the last 40 years. Britain now has a percentage of owner-occupied households which is slightly above the European average.

In general, the poorer housing conditions are found in the rented sector. The poorest neighbourhoods with the worst conditions and their attendant social problems are known as 'sink estates'.

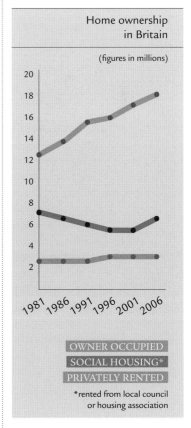

Home ownership in Britain

(figures in millions)

1981 1986 1991 1996 2001 2006

OWNER OCCUPIED
SOCIAL HOUSING*
PRIVATELY RENTED

*rented from local council or housing association

Source: Social Trends 38

Owning and renting: class

In the middle years of the twentieth century, whether you owned or rented your house was a marker of class. If you owned your house, you were middle class; if you lived in a council house, you were working class. However, this is no longer true. A clear majority of almost all groups are owner-occupiers. But only a small proportion of people (of any category other than 'retired') own their house 'outright' (i.e. they have finished paying off the mortgage).

In the last quarter of the twentieth century, the proportion of 'owner-occupiers' increased significantly. Owning was made easier by government policies which offered people various kinds of financial assistance to help them do so. In particular, council tenants were allowed, and encouraged, to buy their council house. Meanwhile, the number of people living in council houses dropped even more sharply, as councils sold many of their properties to housing associations. These are organizations which run their properties like a business but are obliged to run them for social benefit. Each local council keeps a waiting list of households who want to move into a rented council or housing association property. The order of preference is worked out by a complicated set of priorities.

Homelessness

Estimates of the numbers of people who have nowhere to live in Britain vary, but at the present time they probably stand at something between a quarter and a half a million. Even the lower figure is a lot! Why are so many people homeless?

There are various reasons why a person or family cannot find anywhere to live. But they all amount to the simple fact that there isn't enough affordable accommodation for them. This situation is the result of several factors. One of them is that private landlords often find it more convenient to keep their properties empty; they still make money because the value of their properties increases, while tenants are

Who owns? Who rents?

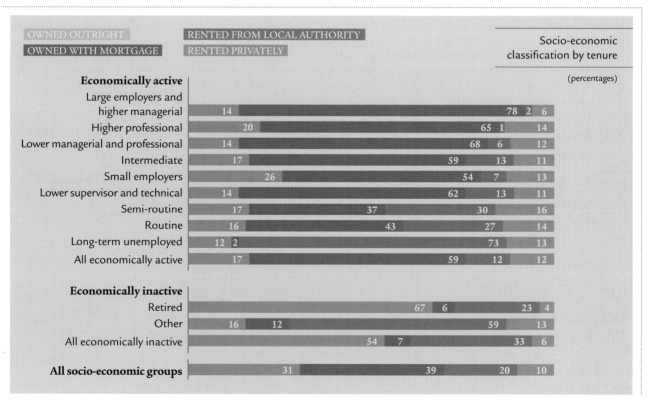

Socio-economic classification by tenure

OWNED OUTRIGHT
OWNED WITH MORTGAGE
RENTED FROM LOCAL AUTHORITY
RENTED PRIVATELY

(percentages)

	Owned outright	Owned with mortgage	Rented from local authority	Rented privately
Economically active				
Large employers and higher managerial	14	78	2	6
Higher professional	20	65	1	14
Lower managerial and professional	14	68	6	12
Intermediate	17	59	13	11
Small employers	26	54	7	13
Lower supervisor and technical	14	62	13	11
Semi-routine	17	37	30	16
Routine	16	43	27	14
Long-term unemployed	12	2	73	13
All economically active	17	59	12	12
Economically inactive				
Retired	67	6	23	4
Other	16	12	59	13
All economically inactive	54	7	33	6
All socio-economic groups	31	39	20	10

protected by law, so that it is not so easy to evict them. Another is that some older properties are no longer inhabitable. And on top of that, the decrease in the size of the average household means that more places to live are needed.

Most homeless families find temporary accommodation in boarding houses (small privately run guest houses), which is paid for by their local council. Some families, and many single people, find even more temporary shelter in hostels for the homeless which are run by charitable organizations. Some just live on the streets, where they 'sleep rough'. In the 1990s, there were thousands of rough sleepers. This situation helped the public to become more aware of homelessness (The Big Issue) – but only briefly. Once action had been taken by the authorities to reduce the numbers of rough sleepers drastically, it slipped out of public consciousness again. As a result, it is not a priority for any political party (in spite of the efforts of charities such as Shelter and Crisis, who give advice to the homeless and campaign on their behalf).

In many cases, the homeless are those with personal problems which make it difficult for them to settle down. In some cases, they are people who simply don't want to settle down. There are, for example, tens of thousands of 'travellers' in the country, both traditional Roma (who are known as gypsies) and more recent converts to this lifestyle (often known as 'New Age Travellers' – see chapter 13). Their only home is the vehicle which they use to move from place to place, often persecuted by unsympathetic authorities. For these people, the problem is not that they are 'homeless' but in the official attitudes towards their way of life.

The future

In Britain today, there are not enough homes to go round. Although the population has risen only slowly in the last 40 years, more and more people want to live on their own or in small families. As a result, it has been estimated that millions of new homes will need to be built in the next decade or so. But where can they be built? The problem is not just that Britain is a densely populated country; it is also the traditional attitudes to housing described in the first few sections of this chapter. The dislike of flats, the desire for gardens, and for clearly marked demarcation between domestic territory and the public domain all mean that housing takes up an awful lot of space and eats up too much countryside.

The British government is taking a keen interest in the layout and style of all planned new settlements. A 'green points' system has been drawn up, whereby developers can obtain planning permission only if they achieve a certain score. Points are awarded for measures such as planting trees, covering walls with climbing plants, providing roof gardens, providing energy from renewable resources and, most significantly, building for high-density occupation.

The Big Issue

The magazine of this name is one of the great success stories in the tradition of self-help in modern Britain. It concentrates on matters concerned with housing and homelessness and boasts a reasonably high standard of journalism. It is sold on streets all over Britain by people who are themselves homeless. They retain most of the takings from sales, giving them both an income and self-respect (because it is not simply begging) and has allowed a large number of people to find their feet again.

The Big Issue has also helped to raise awareness about homelessness among the general public.

Finding somewhere to live

If you want to buy a house, it is very rare to deal directly with the person selling. Instead, you go to an estate agent. These companies exist to act as the go-betweens for people buying and selling houses. They advertise their current properties in local newspapers and on the internet. They help with all the various legal procedures – and take a large commission! If you are interested in one of the houses 'on their books', they will arrange a 'viewing'. You can also spot houses for sale by the 'for sale' signs which are put up on wooden posts outside the houses concerned.

If you want to rent privately, you can also go to an estate agent. But to avoid the fees they charge, you can look in the local newspaper or on the internet and try to contact the owner directly. Houses for rent have a 'to let' sign outside them.

Another possible but unusual way of finding somewhere to live is to 'squat'. Squatters are people who occupy empty houses and do not pay. If you do not cause any damage when moving in to an empty house, you have not broken the law. If the owner wants to get you out, he or she has to get an order from the courts to have you evicted.

It is this last point which is potentially the most revolutionary and which the British will find the most challenging. The government wants house-builders to design three story buildings with large family apartments, gardens reduced to small backyards and 'play streets' where children can play in safety. In this century, almost half of the new homes built have been flats. The question is whether enough people in Britain will accept this more communal, less private, lifestyle.

QUESTIONS

1 British people living in flats in other parts of Europe have sometimes been absolutely horrified when they realize that they are supposed to have the same colour flowers on their balconies as all the other flats in the block. Why are they so horrified?

2 How do you explain the popularity of the different types of dwelling in Britain? Are the same types popular in your country?

3 Even in a small town in Britain, several offices and shops will be occupied by companies called 'estate agents', whose only role is to help people buy and sell their houses. In the same town, however, there may be no house building companies at all to which people could go. Why do you think this is? Is the same true in your country?

4 In modern Britain there is no widespread feeling of resentment against aristocrats who live in large, beautiful country houses. Why not?

SUGGESTIONS

You might like to look up a few estate agents (you can do this on the internet) and study their descriptions of dwellings.

20 Food and drink

On the Continent people have good food; in England people have good table manners.

(George Mikes, humourist and Hungarian émigré to Britain)

You can't trust people who cook as badly as that.

(Jacques Chirac, President of France 1995 – 2007)

As the two quotes above exemplify, Britain and good food are two things which are not commonly associated. Visitors to Britain often have varying opinions about all sorts of aspects of the country, but most seem to agree that the food is terrible. Why? The answer cannot be that British tastes are different from everybody else's. The most common complaint is not that British food has a strange, unpleasant taste, but rather that it has very little taste at all. The vegetables, for example, are overcooked. It is all too bland.

Another possible explanation is that most visitors to Britain do not get the opportunity to sample home cooking. They either eat the food cooked in an institution, such as a university canteen, or in rather cheap restaurants and cafés. These places are definitely not where to find good British food. Typical British cooking involves a lot of roasting (roast beef with roast potatoes and vegetables is supposed to be the English national dish), which does not suit the larger scale production or the quick preparation which is required in such places. For one thing, food should, according to British people, be eaten hot, which is difficult to arrange when feeding large numbers of people.

Eating habits and attitudes

The explanations above can only serve as a partial excuse for the unfortunate reputation of British cuisine. Even in fast food restaurants and everyday cafés, the quality seems to be lower than it is in equivalent places in other countries. Life and habits in Britain are simply not oriented to food very much. The country has neither a widespread 'restaurant culture' nor 'café society'. In the middle of the day, people just want to eat up quickly (the lunch break is an hour at most). The coffee is often horrible not because British people prefer it that way but because they just don't care very much. When they go to a café, they go there for relaxation, conversation, and caffeine; the quality of the coffee itself is of comparatively minor importance. Expectations are low.

Even at home, food and drink are given relatively little attention. The coffee is often just as bad as it is in the cafés. British supermarkets sell far more instant coffee than (what the few people who drink it often

The Fat Duck

People say horrible things about British food. So it was something of a shock when, in 2005, an international panel of more than 600 chefs, food critics and restaurateurs named no less than fourteen British restaurants in the world's top 50.

Number one on the list was The Fat Duck in Berkshire (between London and Oxford). This is the restaurant which introduced the world to such delicacies as sardine-on-toast sorbet, bacon and egg ice cream, snail porridge and orange and beetroot jelly. With a menu like this, British food does not look so boring after all!

However, not too much can be read into this British culinary victory. The panel of experts did not consider price as a criterion. Their top 50 were all restaurants far beyond the pockets of most people and thus had nothing to do with their everyday experience of food.

call) 'real' coffee. Instant coffee is less trouble. Meals tend to be eaten quickly and the table cleared. Parties and celebrations are not normally centred around the food.

When the British do pay attention to food, it is most frequently not to appreciate it but to consider its health implications. There are quite large numbers of vegetarians in Britain and an even larger number who are aware of food from the point of view of health. Health food shops are as abundant in the country's high streets as delicatessens. When in 2005 the TV chef Jamie Oliver showed how the food in a city school could be improved, and also what rubbish the kids were getting, there was a public outcry and Jamie soon found himself presenting a petition signed by 270,000 parents to Downing Street demanding more money for school dinners. As it had recently also been revealed that France spent three times more per child than Britain on its school meals, the government was quick to oblige. But changing habits is hard work. In 2006, after one school had decided to stop its pupils from going out to the local fast food eateries at lunchtime, a group of parents, enraged by this imposition, started handing their children their favourite hamburgers and frozen pizzas through the school railings!

Ultimately, the explanation for these poor standards, low expectations and lack of general interest in food and drink is historical. Until the second half of the twentieth century, the ruling classes in Britain – and thus the opinion leaders – had been educated at boarding schools (see chapter 14) where they were, deliberately, given rather plain food to eat.

Going for an Indian

British food can sometimes taste bland because it does not make use of many spices. Perhaps this is one reason why Indian restaurants are so popular in Britain. It is a cliché of British life that, after a heavy drinking session in the pub, a group of British people often decide to 'go for an Indian'. There, some of the men in the group will display their macho credentials by ordering 'the hottest thing on the menu' (that is, the dish with the hottest spices).

The British Asian comedy *Goodness Gracious Me* (see chapter 4) once used this cliché for one of its most famous sketches, in which a drunken group of Asians 'go for an English' (meaning 'go to an English restaurant') and one of them displays his macho credentials by ordering 'the blandest thing on the menu'.

What British people eat

Because Britain is full of individualists and people from different cultures, generalizations are dangerous. However, the following distinctive features may be noted:

A 'fry up' is a phrase used informally to denote several items fried together. The most common items are eggs, bacon, sausages, tomatoes, mushrooms, and even (fried) bread. It is not generally accompanied by 'chips' (the normal British word for French fried potatoes). The British eat rather a lot of fried food.

Although it is sometimes poetically referred to as 'the staff of life', bread is not an accompaniment to every meal. It is most commonly eaten, with butter and almost anything else, for a snack, either as a sandwich or as toast (a British household regards toasting facilities as a basic necessity). This may explain why sliced bread is the most popular type. On the other hand, the British use a lot of flour for making pastry dishes, both savoury and sweet, called pies, and for making cakes.

Eggs are a basic part of most people's diet. If they are not fried, they are either soft-boiled and eaten directly out of their shells with a spoon, or hard-boiled (so that they can be eaten with the fingers or put into sandwiches).

Cold meats are not very popular. In a small supermarket, you can find a large variety of cheeses, but perhaps only one kind of ham and no salami at all. To many British people, preserved meats are typically 'continental'.

It is common in most households for a family meal to finish with a prepared sweet dish. This is called either 'pudding', 'sweet', or 'dessert' (class distinctions are involved here). There is a great variety of well-known dishes for this purpose, many of which are hot (often a pie of some sort). In fact, the British love 'sweets' (plural) generally, by which they mean both all kinds of chocolate and also what the Americans call 'candy'.

They also love crisps (what the Americans call 'chips'). A market research report in 2005 found that they eat more than all the rest of Western Europe put together.

They were encouraged to be hard and pure, not soft and sensual. Too much enthusiasm for food was seen as decadent (and, indeed, 'foreign'). In addition, British people have been mostly urban, with little contact with 'the land', for longer than the people of other countries. They are therefore rather ignorant of the origins of what arrives on the dinner table or in their lunch boxes. In 2004, a poll of children aged eight to eleven found that half of them thought that margarine came from cows, a third thought that ham came from chickens and a quarter reckoned bread was made from potatoes or rice. Perhaps this is why the range of plants and animals which British people eat is rather narrow. There are plenty of enthusiastic British meat eaters who feel quite sick at the thought of eating horsemeat. To most people, the idea of going out to pick wild plants for the table is exotic. It is perhaps significant that when the British want to refer to the people of another country insultingly, they often allude to their eating habits. Because of the strange things they do with cabbage, for example, the Germans are 'krauts'. Because of their outrageous taste for frog's legs, the French are 'frogs'.

However, this conservatism is not nearly as extreme as it used to be. In the 1960s, it was reported that the first British package tourists in Spain not only insisted on eating (traditionally British) fish and chips but also on having them, as was traditional, wrapped up in specially imported British newspaper! A lot has changed since that time. Items which 50 years ago were thought exotic and viewed with suspicion, such as peppers, garlic, and olive oil, are now to be found in every shop selling food. The country's supermarket shelves are full of the ingredients needed for cooking dishes from all over the world (the increasing multicultural mix has helped in this respect). In fact, the package holidaymakers seem to have 'imported' some European dishes. For example, as well as various traditional British dishes, an extraordinary number of pubs now offer dishes such as moussaka and lasagna. The latter dish is reported to be the country's most popular 'ready meal'. This claim is also sometimes made for chicken tikka masala, which can perhaps claim to be the modern British national dish because it was invented in Britain by a Bangladeshi chef who adapted chicken tikka to British tastes.

British people are also showing increasing interest in the pure enjoyment aspect of food. There are numerous cookery and food programmes on TV, all of them watched with close enthusiasm. It is possible, then, that the negative reputation of British food will eventually become a historical hangover. Attitudes have changed, but the quality of food in everyday life is still poor because these changes have not had enough time to change habits and expectations. One final example: In 2005, the buffet bar of the Eurostar train had a special offer. If you bought a sandwich, you could buy a soft drink and something sweet at an especially low price. There was a poster in the bar advertising the offer. It showed a Coca-Cola and a chocolate bar, with a slogan written in Dutch,

When people eat what: meals

Again, generalizations are dangerous. Below is described what everybody knows about – but this is not necessarily what everybody does!

Breakfast is usually a packeted 'cereal' (e.g. cornflakes) and/or toast and marmalade. People do not usually eat a 'traditional' British breakfast (see chapter 5).

Elevenses is, conventionally, a cup of tea and biscuits at around 11 a.m. In fact, people have tea or coffee and biscuits whenever they feel like it. This is usually quite often. (There is a vast range of biscuits on offer in even a small supermarket, far more than other countries.)

Lunch is typically at 1 p.m. but it is often a bit earlier for schoolchildren and those who start work at 8 a.m. Traditionally, Sunday lunch is an important meal when the family sits down together. But in fact only ten per cent of the British population now does this.

Tea for the urban working class (and a wider section of the population in Scotland and Ireland) is the evening meal, eaten as soon as people get home from work (at around 6 p.m.). For other classes, it means a cup of tea and a snack at around 4 p.m.

Supper is a word for the evening meal used by some of the people who do not call it 'tea'.

Dinner is the other word for the evening meal. It suggests a later time than 'tea'. The word is also used in connection with a special meal, as when friends are invited for a 'dinner party'. Many people talk about 'Christmas dinner', even if they have it in the middle of the day. The same word is also sometimes used to refer to the midday meal in schools, which is served by 'dinner ladies'.

The modern story of tea in Britain

Tea made its first appearance in Britain some 350 years ago and by the end of the seventeenth century tea-drinking was well established. However, during the eighteenth century, its growing popularity was halted by the breweries who, concerned by this competition, successfully lobbied for a series of tax rises on all tea imports. It was only in nineteenth-century Britain that polite society's ritual of afternoon tea was born.

For most of the twentieth century, tea reigned supreme in Britain. To this day, 'standard' (black) tea, served strong and with milk, remains an indispensable aspect of most British households. However, it is in slow decline. This started in the 1970s, when it first saw serious competition from fizzy soft drinks. It continued in the 1990s, when bottled water became popular, and continues today with the increasing popularity of green tea and herbal teas. And through all this time, coffee has been gradually on the rise. In town centres, the number of 'tea rooms' has fallen while the number of cafés specializing in coffee has risen.

These days, sales of coffee are larger than those of standard tea. However, the British tea industry can proudly point to the fact that tea still accounts for a third of all liquid refreshment taken in Britain – far more than any other drink. In fact, there is a sense in which the industry's problem is a result of standard black tea's absolutely central place in British habits. It is regarded as a basic staple, so that British consumers expect to be able to buy it in supermarkets very cheaply.

French and English. The Dutch and French versions of the slogan translated into English as 'A little something extra'. But the English version was 'Make it a meal'. Only in English could a can of fizzy drink and an industrially produced chocolate bar, when combined with a sandwich, be described as a 'meal'.

Eating out

Not so long ago, going to a restaurant was a rare event for most British people. Regular eating out was confined to the richest section of society. By now, a far larger number of people do it. But because of this history, there remains an element of snobbery attached to it. Merely being in an expensive restaurant sometimes seems to be more important to people than the food eaten in it. And in such restaurants, and even some less expensive ones, in a country where few public notices appear in any language other than English, you find a unique phenomenon – many of the dishes have non-English names, most commonly French (reflecting the general high regard for French cuisine). The only exception to this rule is the puddings, which is the one course of a meal that the British have always been confident about.

There is another reason for this lack of English nomenclature. Very few restaurants in Britain could be described as British; that is, they do not serve distinctively British food, so the names of the dishes are not in English. History may also help to explain this fact. Because they did it so rarely, people wanted something different when they went out to eat. By now, people have got used to several kinds of 'ethnic' cuisine and Britain's towns and cities are almost totally dominated by restaurants offering them. A survey in 2006 found that fully a quarter of all restaurants in Glasgow were Italian, that in London there were no less than 87 kebab outlets per square mile (2.6 km²) and that in Nottingham (population 270,000) you could visit a different Italian restaurant every week for half a year and a different Indian one every week for nine months. Even the smallest towns have at least one Indian restaurant, one Italian, and probably a Chinese one as well. Thai restaurants have also become numerous in recent decades. Larger towns and cities have restaurants representing cuisine from all over the world.

Apart from pubs, only three types of distinctively British eating places exist. One offers mostly fried food of the 'English breakfast' type (see chapter 5) and for this reason it is sometimes known as a 'greasy spoon'. Traditionally, it is used principally by manual workers, and is therefore also sometimes called a 'workman's café' (pronounced 'caff'). But these days (when there are fewer manual workers) it is also used by anybody who wants a filling meal and likes the informal atmosphere. Many of them are 'transport cafés' at the sides of main roads. Second, there is the fish and chip shop, used mainly for takeaway meals. Again, the fish is fried. Finally, there are establishments in the centre of towns which are commonly referred to as 'tea rooms'. They are open only during the day and cater for a different kind of clientele with waitress service. They serve scones and other light snacks (and, of course, tea).

Fast food outlets are probably more common in Britain than they are in most other countries. Cynics might claim this is because the British have no taste. However, their popularity is probably better explained sociologically. Except for greasy spoons, other types of restaurant still retain echoes of social pretension, so that some people feel uncomfortable in them. A fast food place does not have these associations. And they are cheap!

Alcohol

The British attitude to alcohol in Britain is ambivalent. On the one hand, it is accepted and liked as an integral, deeply-rooted part of the national culture. And the prevalent attitude to getting drunk is that, provided this does not lead to violence, there is no shame attached. On the other hand, the puritan tradition has led to the widespread assumption that drinking is something dangerous which should therefore be restricted, with regard to both who can do it and also where it can be done. Most people, including regular drinkers, consider that it would be wrong to give a child even half a glass of beer. Quite frequently, horror stories appear in the media about the shocking amount of alcohol drunk by teenagers. By law, people cannot be served or drink any kind of alcohol in pubs until the age of eighteen. In fact, both teenage drinking and alcohol consumption generally are often regarded these days as major social 'problems', even though the British actually consume less alcohol per head of population than many other countries in Europe. Perhaps this is because for many people, drinking is confined to pubs. Most cafés are not allowed to serve beer or wine and these drinks are not as much a part of home life as they are in some other European countries.

For most of the twentieth century, pubs operated under strict laws which limited their opening hours. These have now been relaxed. Moreover, many more types of shop now sell alcohol than previously. However, this lessening of the negative attitude to alcohol has been balanced by increasing concerns about its impact on health and safety. Government-sponsored guidelines state the maximum amount of alcohol which it is advisable for people to drink in a week without endangering their health. Although millions of people pay little attention to these, the general feeling that alcohol can be bad for you has increased.

Nevertheless, alcohol, especially beer, remains an important part of the lives of many people. The occasional trip across the channel solely for the purpose of buying cheaper beer and wine in France or Belgium is such a regular part of many people's calendar that it has led to a well-known colloquial coinage – the 'booze cruise'.

At the time of writing, there is continuing debate about licensing laws. When further relaxing of the laws was planned in 2005, it caused a major political row. The medical profession, residents' groups, and most (but not all) of the police were against the plan. One national

What people drink

As well as large amounts of hot drinks such as tea, coffee and hot chocolate, British people – especially children – drink squash (a sweetened fruit concentrate that has to be diluted with water) and brand-name 'soft' (non-alcoholic) drinks. They also expect to be able to drink water straight from the tap.

Before the 1960s, wine was drunk only by the higher social classes and was associated in most people's minds with expensive restaurants. Since that time, it has increased enormously in popularity.

Beer is still the most popular alcoholic drink. The most popular kind of pub beer is usually known as 'bitter', which is draught (from the barrel). A sweeter, darker version of bitter is 'mild'. Conventionally, these beers (which are often known as 'ales') should be drunk at room temperature, although many pubs now serve them chilled. They have a comparatively low alcoholic content. This is one reason why people are able to drink so much of them! In most pubs, several kinds of bottled beer are also available.

Beer which is closer to continental European varieties is known as 'lager'. During the 1980s, strong lager became popular among some young people who, because they were used to weaker traditional beer, sometimes drank too much of it and became aggressive. They became known as 'lager louts'.

In some pubs, cider is available on draught, and in some parts of Britain, most typically in the English west country, it is this, and not beer, which is the most common pub drink.

Shandy is half beer and half fizzy lemonade. It has the reputation of being very good for quenching thirst.

The meanings of the word 'bar' in British English

1 The area in a hotel or other public place where alcoholic drinks are sold and drunk.

2 The counter in a pub where you go to get your drinks.

3 A place in the centre of a town or city similar to a pub in general purpose, but which serves a greater choice of wines than the typical pub (some are even known as 'wine bars') and usually looks unashamedly modern. Indeed, these bars are a relatively recent phenomenon.

4 The different rooms in a pub. This is an outdated meaning which you may find used in books about life in Britain before the 1980s, when pubs had two distinct kinds of room. The 'public bar' had hard seats, bare floorboards, a dart board and other pub games and was typically used by the working class. The 'saloon bar', on the other hand, was typically used by the middle classes. Here there was a carpet on the floor, softer seats and the drinks were a little more expensive. Some pubs also had a 'private bar', which was even more exclusive.

A typical pub sign.

newspaper organized a campaign to stop it. Much of the debate revolves around the issue of 'binge drinking'. There has always been something of a problem of public drunkenness in Britain and the perception these days is that among young people it is an 'epidemic'. Those who want fewer regulations argue that this would reduce drunkenness, which, they say, is largely the result of having to drink too fast. (And indeed, there is no doubt that the average British drinker finishes a drink more quickly than the average drinker of other European countries. This is a habit born of generations subject to limited drinking time.) They have a vision of introducing to Britain the more civilized drinking habits of mainland Europe.

Pubs

The British pub is unique. This is not just because it is different in character from bars or cafés in other countries. It is also because it is different from any other public place in Britain itself. Without pubs, Britain would be a less sociable country. The pub is the only indoor place where the average person can comfortably meet others, even strangers, and get into prolonged conversation with them. In cafés and fast food places, people are expected to eat, drink, and get out. The atmosphere in other eating places makes some people feel uncomfortable. But pubs are classless. A pub with forty customers in it is nearly always much noisier than a café or restaurant with the same number of people in it.

The local pub plays an important role in almost every neighbourhood – and pubs, it should be noted, are predominantly for the drinking of beer and spirits. Indicative of this role is the fact that it is commonly referred to as 'the local' and people who go there are often known as 'regulars'. The action in all of the country's most popular soaps (see chapter 16) revolves around a pub.

As with other aspects of British life, pubs have become a bit less distinctive in the last thirty years. They used to serve almost nothing but beer and spirits and only things to eat you could get were 'bar snacks' such peanuts and crisps. These days, you can get wine, coffee, and hot food at most of them as well. This has helped to widen their appeal.

Nevertheless, pubs have retained their special character. One of their notable aspects is that there is no waiter service. If you want something, you have to go and ask for it at the bar. This may not seem very welcoming and a strange way of making people feel comfortable and relaxed. But to British people it is precisely this. To be served at a table is discomforting for many people. It makes them feel they have to be on their best behaviour. But because in pubs you have to go and fetch your drinks yourself, it is more informal. You can get up and walk around whenever you want – like being in your own house. This 'home from home' aspect of the pub is encouraged by the relationship between customers and those who work there. The latter are expected to know the regulars personally, to know what their usual drink is and to chat with them when they are not serving someone. It is also encouraged by the availability of pub games (most typically darts) and, frequently, a television.

A notable aspect of British pubs is their frequent appeal to the idea of tradition. For example, each has its own name, proclaimed on a sign hanging outside, always with old-fashioned associations. Many are called by the name of some aristocrat (e.g. 'The Duke of Cambridge') or after a monarch; others take their names from some traditional occupation (e.g. 'The Bricklayer's Arms'); they often have rural associations (e.g. 'The Sheep Shearers', 'The Bull'). To call a pub 'The Computer Programmers' or 'The Ford Focus' or something like that would be to make a very definite statement! For the same reason, the person who runs a pub is referred to as the 'landlord' – even though he or she is, in reality, a tenant. Nearly all pubs are owned by commercial companies. The 'landlord' is simply employed by the company as its manager. But the word is used because it evokes earlier times when all pubs were privately owned 'inns' where travellers could find a bed for the night.

QUESTIONS

1 How would you say British food is different from food in your country?

2 Why do British people prefer to eat food from other countries when they go out?

3 What are the differences (if any) between laws relating to alcohol in Britain and those in your country? What possible reasons are there for these differences?

4 In what ways are British pubs different from typical bars and cafés in your country?

SUGGESTIONS

The most consistently popular and well-known cookery writer and broadcaster in Britain is probably Delia Smith. Any of her books will give you a good idea of the kind of food British people cook (or would like to cook) at home.

The pub

This photograph of a pub shows several typical features. First, notice that it looks old. Most pubs are like this. It is part of their appeal to tradition. Even a newly built pub is often designed to look, inside and out, as if it were several hundred years old. Second, notice the windows. They are small because, unlike the large plate-glass windows of cafés, they help to make the pub feel homely. But notice also that it is difficult to see inside the pub from the outside. The Victorians felt that it was somehow not proper for people to be seen drinking. Indeed, many pubs did not use to have chairs and tables outside, though a garden at the back was and is highly prized. Outside areas have become more important for pubs since 2007, when smoking inside them was banned.

21 Sport and competition

Think of your favourite sport. Whatever it is, there is a good chance that it was first played in Britain, and an even better chance that its modern rules were first codified in Britain. The public schools (see chapter 14) of the Victorian era believed that organized competitive games carried many psychological benefits. These games appealed to, and developed, the British sense of 'fair play'. This concept went far beyond abiding by the written rules of a game. It also meant observing its unwritten rules regarding behaviour before and after the game. You had to be a good loser. To be a cheat was a genuine shame, but to lose was just 'part of the game'. Team games were best – they developed team spirit.

Modern sport in Britain is very different now. 'Winning isn't everything' and 'it's only a game' are still well-known sayings which spring from the amateur approach of the past. But to modern professional players, who value a professional attitude and talk about doing their job well, it is clearly not just a game (The end of the amateur ethos). Nevertheless, the public school attitude to sport and its enthusiasm for simply taking part has had a lasting influence on the nature and role of sport in Britain today.

A national passion

Sport probably plays a more important part in people's lives in Britain than it does in most other countries. British schools still devote more time to organized sport than schools in most other European countries. For a very large number, especially men, it is their main form of entertainment. Millions take part in some kind of sport at least once a week. Many millions more are habitual spectators and followers of one or more sports. Every newspaper, national or local, quality or popular, devotes several pages entirely to sport.

Other sections in this chapter examine the sports which are the most publicized and have the largest followings in Britain. But it should be noted that hundreds of other sports are played, each with its own small but enthusiastic following. Some of these may not be seen as a sport at all by most people. For them, games such as indoor bowling, darts, or snooker are just enjoyable social pastimes. But to a few, they are deadly serious competitions. Even board games, the kind you buy in a toy shop, have their national champions. Think of any pastime, however trivial, which involves some element of competition and, somewhere in Britain, there is probably a 'national association' for it which organizes contests.

In the 1980s and 1990s British educational experts decided that activities which set children 'against' each other and involved winning and losing were psychologically and socially harmful. Competitive activities in schools were either avoided or their competitive elements were weakened. (For example, some children's football leagues allowed teams losing heavily to introduce more players so that the contest would become more even.) But in Britain, you can't make the thirst for competition just go away. It is surely significant that since the mid 1990s, almost every light entertainment programme on TV has been framed as some kind of competition. The British people, it seems, need their daily dose of competition – and if they did not get enough of it at school, they have to get it elsewhere.

The British are so fond of competition that they introduce it into their other enthusiasms. Gardening is one example. Many people indulge in an informal rivalry with their neighbours as to who can grow the better flowers or vegetables. But the rivalry is sometimes formalized. Throughout the country, there are competitions at which gardeners enter their cabbages, leeks, onions, carrots, flowers, or more general floral displays in the hope that they will be judged 'the best'. The most famous annual event of this kind, the Chelsea Flower Show, gets nationwide publicity. The same occurs with people's animals. There are hundreds of dog shows throughout the country (the most famous of which is Crufts) at which owners hope that their pet will win a prize.

The social importance of sport

The importance of participation in sport has legal recognition in Britain. Every local authority has a duty to provide and maintain playing fields and other facilities, which are usually very cheap and sometimes even free. Spectator sport is also a matter of official public concern. For example, there is a law which prevents the television rights of the most famous annual sporting occasions being sold to channels which are not freely available. In these cases, it seems to be the event itself, rather than the particular sport, which is important. Every year, events such as the Cup Final, the Oxford and Cambridge boat race, and the Grand National (The sporting calendar) are watched on television by millions of people who have no great interest in football, rowing, or horse racing.

Sometimes, the traditions which accompany an event can seem as important as the actual sporting contest. Wimbledon, for example, is not just a tennis tournament. It means summer fashions, strawberries and cream, garden parties, and long, warm English summer evenings. At Royal Ascot, a horse racing meeting held every summer, most of the media attention is focused on the hats worn by women! The football Cup Final at Wembley is preceded by hours of traditional events including 'community singing'.

The long history of these events has meant that many of them, and their venues, have become world-famous. Therefore, it is not only the

Sabotage at the flower show

The desire to win is deadly serious. Here is a newspaper article reporting dark deeds around the annual Britain in Bloom flower competition.

Something nasty was lurking in Dorothy Mill's shrubbery – and it was armed with wire clippers.

Days before judges arrived to examine Mrs Mills's award-winning floral display, her hanging baskets were snipped off and stolen.

On the same night, two tubs from her front garden and a number of potted geraniums also went missing.

For the past two years Mrs Mills has won an award in the Best Small Town Garden section of the In-Bloom competition – and someone didn't want her to make it a hat-trick.

Soon after the theft on Thursday last week, she received a phone call. The female voice on the other end of the line said: 'You will not win for a third time.' Then they hung up.

This is not the first time entrants of the competition have fallen victim to jealous rivals. Last year, Peter Dungworth thought the thousands of daffodils he had planted on grass verges around his home would help his village (Harthill-with-Woodall) win the competition's small village section for the first time.

But on the eve of the judging he discovered every single flower had been beheaded by a saboteur.

Locals in the nearby village of Thorpe Salvin, which has won the competition's small village section three times, denied any wrongdoing.

The Daily Mail 28 July 2007

British who tune in to watch. The Grand National, for example, gets a television audience of 600 million. This worldwide enthusiasm has little to do with the standard of British sport. The cup finals of other countries often have better quality and more entertaining football on view – but more Europeans watch the English Cup Final than any other. The standard of British tennis is not especially high, and Wimbledon is only one of the world's major tournaments. But ask any top tennis player, Wimbledon is the one they really want to win. Every footballer in the world dreams of playing at Wembley; every cricketer in the world of playing at Lord's. Wimbledon, Wembley, and Lord's (Famous sporting venues) are the 'spiritual homes' of their respective sports. Sport is a British export!

Cricket

Judging by the numbers of people who play it and watch it, cricket is definitely not the national sport of Britain. In Scotland, Wales, and Northern Ireland, interest in it is largely confined to the middle classes. Only in England and a small part of Wales is it played at top level. And even in England, where its enthusiasts come from all classes, the majority of the population do not understand its rules. Moreover, it is rare for the English national team to be the best in the world.

When people refer to cricket as the English national game, they are not thinking so much of its level of popularity or of the standard of English players but more of the very English associations that it carries with it. Cricket is much more than just a sport; it symbolizes a way of life – a slow and peaceful, rural way of life. The images of a sunny summer afternoon, the smell of newly-mown grass and the sound of leather (the ball) connecting with willow (the wood from which cricket bats are made) are what makes it important. Cricket is special because it combines competition with the British dream of rural life. Cricket is what the village green is for! As if to emphasize this, 'first class' cricket teams in England, unlike those in other sports, do not bear the names of towns but of counties (e.g. Essex, Yorkshire, Somerset).

Notes on cricket

Rules A game played on grass by two teams of eleven players. Players score points called runs, by hitting a ball with a wooden bat and running between two sets of vertical wooden sticks, called stumps.

Players per team 11

Playing time It varies a lot. Amateur club matches typically last about five hours. But in the conventional form of the sport at top level, matches last for several days of six hours each and Test matches between national teams can last up to five days.

One day matches at top level were introduced in the 1960s and in this century an even shorter form of the game (lasting about four hours) has been introduced.

Countries that play at top level Australia, New Zealand, Bangladesh, India, Pakistan, Sri Lanka, South Africa, England, West Indies (the Anglophone Caribbean), Zimbabwe.

The most popular sport In the Indian subcontinent (Bangladesh, India, Pakistan, Sri Lanka), and some parts of the West Indies.

Cricket is, therefore, the national English game in a symbolic sense. Moreover, the comparatively low attendance at top class matches does not give a true picture of the level of interest in the country. Cricket can take a terribly long time (Notes on cricket), which a lot of people simply don't have. But in fact there are millions of people in the country who don't just enjoy cricket – they are passionate about it. These people spend thirty or more days each summer tuned to the live radio commentary of 'Test' (international) Matches. When they get the chance, they will watch a bit of the live television coverage. Some people even do both at the same time (they turn the sound down on the television and listen to the radio). To these people, the commentators become well-loved figures. When, in 1994, one famous commentator died, the Prime Minister at the time (John Major) publicly lamented that 'summers will never be the same again'.

Football

The full official name of 'soccer' (as it is called in America and sometimes in Britain) is 'Association Football'. This distinguishes it from other kinds such as rugby football, Gaelic football, Australian football, and American football. However, most people in Britain call it simply 'football'. This is indicative of its dominant role. Everywhere in the country (except south Wales), it is easily the most popular spectator sport, the most-played sport in the country's state schools and one of the most popular participatory sports for adults. In terms of numbers, football, not cricket, is the national sport, just as it is everywhere else in Europe.

Traditionally, British football drew its main following from the working class. In general, the intelligentsia ignored it. But in the last two decades of the twentieth century, it started to attract wider interest. The appearance of fanzines and then internet blogs allowed intelligent and witty discussion about football and matters surrounding it among the fans of various clubs. One or two books of literary merit appeared which focused not only on players, teams and tactics but also on the wider social aspects of the game. Light-hearted football programmes appeared on television which similarly included attention to 'off-the-field' matters. At the same time football stars have taken on the more general appeal of film stars and pop idols.

This much wider appeal has had good and bad effects. On the good side, it seems to have reduced the problem of hooliganism. Football support in Britain has tended to be a men only, 'tribal' affair. In America, the whole family goes to watch the baseball. Similarly, the whole family goes along to cheer the Irish national football team. But in Britain, only a handful of children or women used to go to football matches. Perhaps this is why active support for the local team had a tendency to become violent. During the 1970s and 1980s this phenomenon was a major problem in England. But in the 1990s, it declined and English fans in Europe are now no worse than the fans of many other countries.

The Ashes

Quite often, sporting contests involving British teams have a traditional prize attached to them which gives them a special significance, even when they are not the most important contest in the sport as a whole. Examples in rugby are The Calcutta Cup match between England and Scotland and the Triple Crown, which is won by one of the four nations (see chapter 1) if they beat all the other three in the same year.

But the most famous example of this kind in Britain involves England and Australia. Every two years, cricket teams from these two countries play each other in a series of matches where they are said to be competing for the Ashes. In 1882, after a heavy defeat by Australia, the 'ashes' of English cricket (actually a burnt piece of cricketing equipment) were placed inside an urn as a symbol of the 'death' of English cricket. In fact, the urn never leaves Lord's cricket ground in London, but the idea of the Ashes is so well-known that it is often applied to contests between these two nations in any sport.

The Ashes urn is made of terracotta and stands only 15 cm tall.

Until the mid 1990s, attendance at British club matches had been falling for several decades. Many stadiums were old, uncomfortable and sometimes dangerous. There were several disasters at football matches in the last few years of the twentieth century. The official response to these was to oblige all grounds in the country to become 'all-seater' stadiums. As a result, the habit of fans to stand, jump, shout, and sway on the cheap 'terraces' behind the goals disappeared (causing emotional farewells at many grounds to a traditional 'way of life'). It was argued that being seated would make fans more well-behaved and safer, as would more family-friendly facilities. Attendance started rising again in the new century and the proportion of women spectators has doubled since the 1980s, but they are still very much a minority (20% or less).

It remains to be seen whether football matches will become events for the whole family. It is possible they will not because it is simply too expensive. And this is the bad side of recent developments. Going to watch a premier league match has become a fashionable status symbol. Businesses take their clients there. Ticket prices have rocketed, putting them beyond the reach of many genuine fans.

Rugby

There are two, separately organized, versions of this fast and aggressive ball game. They are so similar that somebody who is good at one of them can quickly learn to become good at the other. The difference between them is a matter of social history. Rugby union is the older of the two.

Sporting language

The central place of sport in British consciousness is indicated by the very large number of sporting expressions and metaphors which have entered the everyday language. Here are some of them.

From cricket
on a sticky wicket in a difficult situation
on an easy wicket in a comfortable situation
stumped at a loss for an answer or solution to a problem
hit something for six dismiss something emphatically
play with a straight bat do something in an orthodox and careful manner
it's not cricket it is not the proper or fair way of doing something (cricket is supposed to be the perfect example of the concept of 'fair play')
have a good innings have a large or adequate amount of time in a certain post; have a long life
all off one's own bat without help or influence from anyone else
a big hitter an important person in an organization whose actions have a significant effect

From boxing
saved by the bell saved from a bad or dangerous situation by a sudden event
on the ropes in a weak position; close to defeat or failure
floored defeated or confused in an argument or discussion
throw in the towel admit defeat

From horse racing and riding
first past the post the winner
to have the bit between the teeth to be determined
to be given free rein to be allowed to do exactly what one wants, without restrictions
in the saddle in control (nowadays, the expression 'in the driving seat' is often used instead)

From other sports or sport in general
team player somebody who is good at cooperating with other people in groups
run with the pack (from hunting) have no individual opinions but just blindly follow the majority
win hands down (from gambling) win easily
go to the dogs start to lead an aimless and self-destructive life
on the final straight/on the last lap in the last stage of some process
a safe pair of hands reliable
a level playing field a situation where neither side in a contest starts with an advantage over the other

It should be noted that these expressions are not only used in informal conversation. On the TV news, you will hear politicians described as (for example) playing with a straight bat, a big hitter or a safe pair of hands.

In the nineteenth century, it was enthusiastically taken up by most of Britain's public schools. Rugby league split off from rugby union at the end of that century. Although it has now spread to many of the same places in the world where rugby union is played (Notes on rugby), its traditional home is among the working class of the north of England, where it was a way for miners and factory workers to make a little bit of money from their sporting talents. Rugby union, on the other hand, remained resolutely amateur for most of the twentieth century.

Because of these social origins, rugby league in Britain was seen as a working class sport, while rugby union was for the middle classes. (The exception is in south Wales, where it has always been a sport for all classes, and more popular than football. In Cardiff, the phrase 'international day' means only one thing – that the national rugby team are playing.) But rugby union has had some success in recent years in selling itself to a wider audience. As a result, just as football has become less exclusively working class in character, rugby union has become less exclusively middle class. In the process, it has become far more popular worldwide than rugby league. Now that rugby union is professional too, the old class antagonisms between followers of the two codes have faded. It is not impossible that in the future they will become the same sport, or at least be governed by the same organization.

They already have much in common, not only on the field, but off it. One of these is the behaviour of their supporters. There have hardly ever been reports of 'crowd trouble' at rugby matches and no effort is made to segregate fans, as is the case with football. Perhaps the violence which is an integral part of the sport itself means there is no need for violence on the part of its followers.

Giant killers

The British love of 'the underdog' is seen very clearly in sport. Each football season, the English FA Cup in England generates enthusiasm at the prospect of giant-killing. It does happen, quite often. In 2008, for example, all of the favourites were knocked out. The final that year was contested between just one (mid-table) premier league team and one (also mid-table) team from the next league down.

But it was the Scottish FA Cup which, in 2006, produced the biggest giant-killing story of all time when a team of semi-professionals in the third tier of Scottish football got through to the final. And so the team from Gretna, which has a population of 3,000, found themselves taking the field at the 52,000-seater Hampden Park in Glasgow. (And they only lost the final on penalties.)

Notes on rugby

Rules Similar to football in that the aim is to get the ball into a particular place. But the ball is egg-shaped, and instead of propelling it into the opposing team's goal, you have to place it down over the opposing team's goal line with your hands. It is mainly a ball-handling game. You can try to stop (tackle) an opposing player who is carrying the ball any way you like except with a punch or kick.

Players per team union 15, league 13

Playing time 80 minutes

Countries that play at top level England, Ireland, Scotland, Wales, France, Italy, Argentina, South Africa, Australia, New Zealand, Fiji, Samoa, Tonga.

The most popular sport In the Pacific islands (New Zealand, Fiji, Samoa, Tonga), south Wales and among white South Africans.

Animals in sport

Traditionally, the favourite sports of the British upper class are 'huntin', shootin' and fishin". Despite its becoming illegal (see chapter 5), the most widespread form of hunting is foxhunting – indeed, that is what the word 'hunting' usually means in Britain. Killing birds with guns is known as 'shooting'. It is a minority pastime confined largely to the higher social classes; there are more than three times as many licensed guns for this purpose in France as there are in Britain. The birds which people try to shoot (such as grouse) may only be shot during certain specified times of the year. The upper classes often organize 'shooting parties' during the 'season'. The one kind of 'hunting' which is popular among all social classes is fishing. When fishing is done competitively, it is called 'angling'.

Animals are involved in sport in Britain in other ways too. Horse-racing is so well-established that it is often refererred to simply as 'racing'. Both 'flat-racing' and 'national hunt' racing (where there are jumps for the horses), sometimes know as 'steeplechasing', are very popular. The former became known as 'the sport of kings' in the seventeenth century, and modern British royalty has close connections with sport involving horses. Some members of the royal family own racehorses and attend certain annual race meetings (Ascot, for instance); some are also active participants in the sports of polo, showjumping, and eventing (all of which involve riding a horse).

The chief attraction of horse racing for most people is the opportunity it provides for gambling. Greyhound racing, although declining, is still popular for the same reason. In this sport, the dogs chase a mechanical hare around a racetrack. It is easier to organize than horse racing and 'the dogs' has a reputation for being the 'poor man's racing'.

Other sports

Almost every sport which exists is played in Britain. As well as the sports already mentioned, hockey (mostly on a field but also on ice), basketball (for men), netball (for women), and the ancient game of rounders are all quite popular.

In general, British spectators and TV viewers have more interest in team games than individual sports. Athletics, cycling, golf, gymnastics, and swimming, although taken part in by many, have comparatively small followings. Large numbers of people become interested in them only when British competitors do well in international events. The more popular individual sports are those in which socializing is an important aspect (e.g. tennis, golf, sailing, and snooker). It is notable in this context that, apart from international competition, the only athletics events which generate a lot of enthusiasm are those such as the annual London Marathon and Great North Run, most of whose tens of thousands of participants are 'fun runners' who are merely trying to complete it, sometimes in outrageous costumes, and so collect money for charity.

There seem to be two main exceptions to this tendency. One is boxing, where some of the attraction lies in the opportunity for gambling. While boxing is declining in popularity, the other exception, motor sport, is becoming more popular.

Gambling

Even if they are not taking part or watching, British people like to be involved in sport. They can do this by placing bets on future results. Gambling is very widespread throughout all social classes. It is so basic to sport that the word 'sportsman' used to be a synonym for 'gambler'. When, in 1993, the starting procedure for the Grand National did not work properly, so that the race could not take place, it was widely regarded as a national disaster. £70 million had been gambled on the result (that's more than a pound for each man, woman, and child in the country). All that money had to be given back.

Every year, billions of pounds are bet on horse races. So well known is this activity that everybody in the country, even those with no interest in horse racing, would understand the meaning of a question such as 'Who won the 2.30 at Chester?' ('Which horse won the race that was scheduled to take place at half past two today at the Chester racecourse?' The questioner probably wants to know because he or she has gambled some money on the result.) The central role of horse racing in gambling is also shown by one of the names used to denote companies and individuals whose business is to take bets. Although these are generally known as 'bookmakers', they sometimes announce themselves as 'turf accountants' on shop fronts ('turf' is a word for the ground where grass grows).

Rounders

This sport is rather similar to baseball, but it is played with a soft ball. It has a long history in England as something that people (young and old, male and female) can do together at village fetes. It is often seen as not a 'real' sport.

However, despite this image, it is one of the most popular sports for state schools in Britain because it is easier to organize than more traditional sports such as cricket and rugby. It is especially attractive for state schools because it does not require much special equipment or money and boys and girls can play it together.

The cheese chasers of Brockworth

'Extreme sports' such as bungy jumping and paragliding are supposed to be a modern phenomenon. But some activities which are just as extreme have been held in Britain for hundreds of years. One example is the annual cheese rolling at Cooper's Hill near Brockworth in Gloucestershire. Every year, thousands of people come to watch the proceedings. A hundred or so are actually foolhardy enough to take an active part. This is what happens. A 3.6 kg cheese is ceremoniously rolled off the top of the very steep hill – and then competitors chase it. The winner – that is, the person who runs, rolls, slithers, bounces, or somersaults down the 200-metre slope the fastest – gets to keep the cheese.

It's not a pastime for the faint-hearted. Everybody gets cuts and bruises, many get sprained ankles and some suffer dislocations or fractures. 2006 was a 'good year'. The wet conditions that year meant that people tended to slide rather than tumble down the hill, which meant there were fewer injuries. Only 25 people needed treatment (twelve of whom were spectators!) and only two had to be taken to hospital.

The sporting calendar

This chart shows the seasons for Britain's most popular spectator sports and some of the most important sporting events which take place every year. There are other, less regular, events which can be very important, and other annual events in particular sports which are more important for followers of those sports. But these are the ones that are better known to the general public.

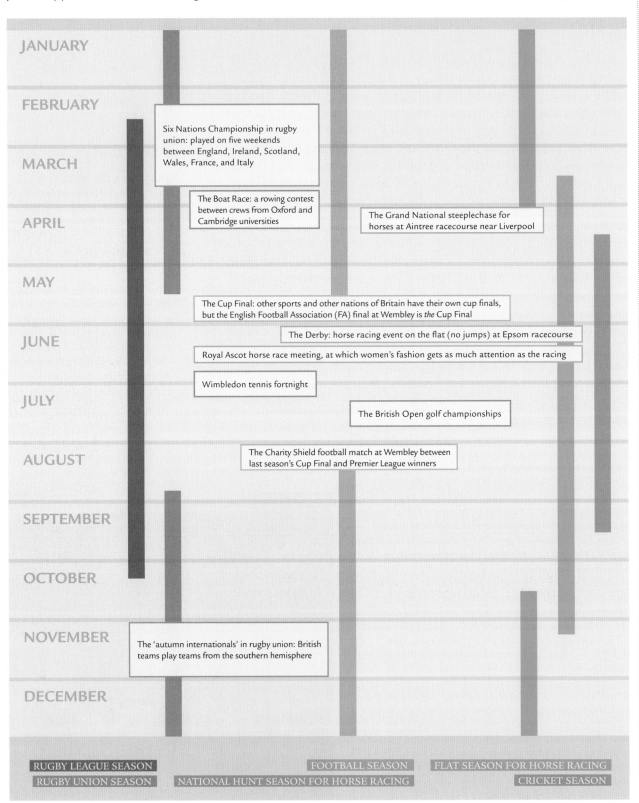

JANUARY

FEBRUARY

MARCH

APRIL

MAY

JUNE

JULY

AUGUST

SEPTEMBER

OCTOBER

NOVEMBER

DECEMBER

Six Nations Championship in rugby union: played on five weekends between England, Ireland, Scotland, Wales, France, and Italy

The Boat Race: a rowing contest between crews from Oxford and Cambridge universities

The Grand National steeplechase for horses at Aintree racecourse near Liverpool

The Cup Final: other sports and other nations of Britain have their own cup finals, but the English Football Association (FA) final at Wembley is *the* Cup Final

The Derby: horse racing event on the flat (no jumps) at Epsom racecourse

Royal Ascot horse race meeting, at which women's fashion gets as much attention as the racing

Wimbledon tennis fortnight

The British Open golf championships

The Charity Shield football match at Wembley between last season's Cup Final and Premier League winners

The 'autumn internationals' in rugby union: British teams play teams from the southern hemisphere

RUGBY LEAGUE SEASON

RUGBY UNION SEASON

FOOTBALL SEASON

FLAT SEASON FOR HORSE RACING

NATIONAL HUNT SEASON FOR HORSE RACING

CRICKET SEASON

The most popular mode of gambling of any kind is the national lottery, which is participated in by more than half the adult population. Another popular type of gambling, stereotypically for middle-aged working class women, is bingo. For bingo enthusiasts, the social aspect is just as important as the prospect of a small win.

Some sections of British society frown upon gambling (most notably, it is part of the tradition of Nonconformist religious groups – see chapter 13) and their disapproval has always had some influence. For example, in 2005, the government announced plans to allow a number of Las Vegas style 'super-casinos' in Britain. But there was so much opposition, the plans were abandoned two years later. Perhaps these misgivings about gambling explain why Britain did not have a national lottery until 1995. But if people want to gamble, then they will. For instance, before the national lottery started, the British gambled £250,000 on which company would be given the licence to run it! The country's big bookmakers are willing to offer odds on almost anything at all if asked. Weather is a popular theme. Will it rain during the Wimbledon tennis tournament? Will it snow on Christmas Day? Anything can be used for 'a flutter'. In 1997, one man even bet £100 he would live to be 100. He won the bet! The odds were 250-1, so in 2007 he collected £25,000.

QUESTIONS

1 In general, and especially to watch, sports such as football, rugby, and cricket are more popular than sports such as athletics, cycling, golf, or tennis in Britain. Why do you think this is?

2 The manager of Liverpool football club in the 1970s once said, 'Football is not a matter of life and death to me – it's more important than that'. What do you think he meant? Is his comment typical of the British attitude to sport?

3 A big problem for cricket is that it cannot be played during or immediately after rain because the grass is too wet. To solve this problem, it was once suggested that cricket should be played on plastic surfaces, so that play could begin again as soon as the rain stopped. English cricket enthusiasts were horrified at this idea. One member of the MCC (Marylebone Cricket Club, the organization which partly controls the game in England) commented 'The man must have been drunk when he thought of it'. How do you explain this extreme reaction?

SUGGESTIONS

If you get the opportunity, watch the beginning of TV programmes which cover some of the sporting events listed in the British sporting calendar. This will give you an idea of their social importance.

If you would like to know more about cricket, look up MCC or Lord's on the internet.

A nation of gamblers

In 2006, around £25 billion was wagered – that's around £500 for every adult in the country. By far the most popular form of gambling was the national lottery, in which 57% of adults took part. The chart below shows the percentage of people who gambled in other different ways.

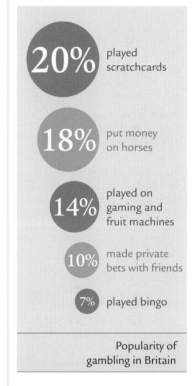

20% played scratchcards

18% put money on horses

14% played on gaming and fruit machines

10% made private bets with friends

7% played bingo

Popularity of gambling in Britain

22 The arts

The arts in society

Interest in the arts in Britain used to be largely confined to a small elite. Far more people read books, visit art galleries, and go to the theatre and concerts today than fifty years ago. Nevertheless, the fact remains that most British people prefer sport, television, chatting with friends and family, and other free-time activities to anything 'cultural' (What is 'culture'?).

The position of the arts in Britain may be described as a mixture of public apathy and private enthusiasm. Publicly, the arts are accepted and tolerated but not actively encouraged. As a proportion of its total expenditure, government financial support for the arts is comparatively low. There has always been a widespread suspicion in Britain that such funding is undemocratic because it merely subsidizes the tastes of the wealthy. The counter argument – that this funding is democratic because it makes the arts cheap enough for the ordinary person to have access to them – is not one that usually carries much weight in Britain. Many forms of the arts in Britain rely heavily on private sponsorship (which amounts to almost half the total contributions of public authorities). Most arts organizations say they would not be able to do what they do without private backing. They are fortunate in that British private sponsors are usually more generous than those of other European countries.

It is notable that the biggest beneficiaries of private support are organizations which do not all pertain to the arts exclusively. As well as art galleries, they are museums and heritage organizations such as the National Trust (see chapter 5). And indeed, it is museums and galleries that provide the one exception to the prevailing belief that the arts should not be subsidized. Britain is almost unique in Europe in that admission to its museums and art galleries is normally free. (It is charged only when special exhibitions are being held.) There was a brief period in the 1980s and 1990s when charges were imposed, but there was such a public outcry that a great tradition of 'free education' was being lost that they were soon abolished. Perhaps this is a key to understanding the British attitude to the arts. The arts seem to be valued most when they involve general knowledge and national heritage rather than for their purely aesthetic aspects.

In general, the arts have a low profile in Britain. In schools, subjects such as art and music, though always available, tend to be pushed to the sidelines and pupils are allowed to drop them completely at the age of 14. Television programmes on 'cultural' subjects are usually shown late at night. Each summer, tens of high-quality arts festivals take place

What is 'culture'?

The word **culture** also has two meanings. In this book, it is used in its anthropological sense to mean 'way of life'. But many people also use it as a synonym for 'the arts'. When it is used this way in this chapter, it has inverted commas around it.

What are 'the arts'?

The arts is an umbrella term for literature, music, painting, sculpture, crafts, theatre, opera, ballet, film, etc. It usually implies seriousness, so that particular examples of these activities which are regarded as too 'light' may not be included. These may be referred to simply as 'entertainment' instead.

Art, or **fine arts**, is often used to refer to those arts which use space, but not time, for their appreciation (e.g. painting or sculpture). This, for example, is what is covered by the subject 'art' in schools.

The word **artist** can sometimes refer only to a person working in the fine arts, and sometimes to a person working in any field of the arts. In this chapter, it is used in this latter sense.

around the country (Some well-known annual arts festivals), but the vast majority of people do not even know of their existence. London has some of the finest collections of painting and sculpture in the world, but tourist brochures give little space to this aspect of the city.

As with the arts, so with artists themselves. Except for the most famous of them, they have comparatively little public recognition. Some British artists have international reputations, and yet most people in Britain don't even know their names. It is very rare, for example, for any British artist to use his or her fame in the arts as a springboard onto the political stage. If you were to ask the average person to name some famous painters, composers, opera singers, and ballet dancers, you would probably be given very few British names – or even none at all.

It is almost as if the British are keen to present themselves as a nation of philistines. And yet, hundreds of thousands of people are enthusiastically involved in one or other of the arts, but (in typically British fashion) with a more-or-less amateur or part-time status. For example, most towns in the country have at least one 'amateur dramatics' society, which regularly gives performances and charges no more than enough to cover its costs. All over the country, thousands of people learn handicrafts (such as pottery) in their free time, and sometimes sell their work in local craft shops. Similarly, there are thousands of musicians of every kind, performing around the country for very little money and making their own recordings under very difficult circumstances. Some amateur British choirs such as the Philharmonia Chorus are well known throughout the world.

The characteristics of British arts and letters

If there is one characteristic of British work in the arts that seems to stand out, it is its lack of identification with wider intellectual trends. It is not usually ideologically committed, nor associated with particular political movements. Playwrights and directors, for instance, can be left-wing in their political outlook, but the plays which they produce rarely convey a straightforward political message. The same is largely true of British novelists and poets. Their writing is typically naturalistic and unconnected with particular intellectual movements. They tend to be individualistic, exploring emotions rather than ideas, the personal rather than the political. Whatever critics read into them, it is quite common for British playwrights and novelists to claim that they just write down 'what they see' and that they do not consciously intend any social or

Some well-known annual arts festivals

Aldeburgh
June, East Anglia. Classical music. Relatively informal atmosphere.

Edinburgh International Festival
August, Edinburgh. All the performing arts, including avant-garde. More than ten different performances every day around the city. World famous.

The Proms
July–September, London. Classical music. 'Proms' is short for 'promenades', so-called because most of the seats are taken out of the Albert Hall, and the audience stands or (if there is room) walks around instead.

Glyndebourne
All summer, Sussex. In the grounds of a large country house. Opera.

Royal National Eisteddfod
July, Wales. Music, choirs and dance from many different countries. Mostly in the form of competitions, with special categories for Welsh performing arts.

Glastonbury
Midsummer, south-western England. By far the best known of the rock music festivals. The Reading and Leeds festivals in August are also well known.

Womad
July, southern England. Folk music and other performing arts from around the world.

Architectural disasters

There is an old cliché often used in Britain which is supposed to represent uneducated attitudes towards art. It goes: 'I don't know much about art, but I know what I like'. But in the case of architecture, what British people seem to know is what they don't like.

Architecture has a generally low profile in Britain, but in 2005, when Channel 4 (see chapter 16) asked people to name the building which they would most like to see demolished, there was an enthusiastic response. More than 1,000 different buildings were nominated.

The 'winner' of this dubious distinction was the shopping centre in the new town of Cumbernauld in Scotland. Like so many of the top ten most hated buildings, it was built in the 1960s. According to the producer of the TV programme which followed the poll, 'The depth of passionate opposition to [it] was quite incredible'.

symbolic message. The work of British artists is also individualistic within its own field. That is, British artists do not usually consider themselves to belong to this or that 'movement'. In any field of the arts, even those in which many British artists have strong international reputations, it is difficult to identify a 'British school'.

The style of the arts also tends to be conventional. The avant-garde exists, of course, but, with the possible exception of painting and sculpture, it is not through such work that British artists become famous. In the 1980s, Peter Brook was a highly successful theatre director. But when he occasionally directed avant-garde productions, he staged them in Paris!

In these features of the work of British artists (lonely individualism expressing itself within conventional formats), it is perhaps possible to find an explanation for the apparent contradiction between, on the one hand, the low level of public support for the arts, and on the other hand, the rather high level of enthusiasm on the part of individual people. There appears to be a general assumption in Britain that artistic creation is a personal affair, not a social one, and that therefore the flowering of artistic talent cannot be engineered. Either it happens, or it doesn't. It is not something for which society should feel responsible.

Theatre and cinema

The theatre has always been very strong in Britain. Its centre is, of course, London, where successful plays can sometimes run without a break for years and years (The record breakers). But every large town in the country has its theatres. Even small towns often have 'repertory' theatres, where the same group of professional actors stages a different play every week.

It seems that the conventional format of the theatrical play gives the undemonstrative British people a safe opportunity to look behind the mask of accepted social behaviour. The country's most successful and respected playwrights are usually those who explore the darker side of the personality and of personal relationships (albeit often through comedy).

British theatre has such a fine acting tradition that Hollywood is forever raiding its talent for people to star in films. British television does the same thing. Moreover, Broadway, when looking for its next blockbuster musical, pays close attention to London productions. In short, British theatre is much admired. As a consequence, it is something that British actors are proud of. Many of the most well-known television actors, though they might make most of their money in this latter medium, continue to see themselves first and foremost as theatre actors. (This reputation means that, conversely, Hollywood actors are often keen to appear on the London stage. It enhances their credibility as 'real' actors, not just stars.)

In contrast, cinema in Britain is generally regarded as not quite part of 'the arts' at all – it is simply entertainment. (For example, in the official publication Social Trends, cinema attendance is discussed under 'Leisure and entertainment', separate from 'Cultural activities'.)

The record breakers

The longest-running theatrical comedy in London was the farce *No Sex Please, We're British*, which ran continuously from 1971 to 1987. But by far the longest-running theatrical production anywhere in the world is *The Mousetrap*, a 'whodunnit' from the book by Agatha Christie. It opened in London in 1952. And, more than 23,000 performances later, it's still going!

British films

Here are some of the most successful and respected British films since 1981.

Chariots of Fire (1981)
Gregory's Girl (1981)
Ghandi (1982)
A Letter to Brezhnev (1985)
My Beautiful Launderette (1985)
A Room with a View (1985)
A Fish Called Wanda (1988)
Shirley Valentine (1989)
The Crying Game (1992)
Howard's End (1992)
Much Ado About Nothing (1993)
The Madness of King George (1994)
Four Weddings and a Funeral (1994)
Trainspotting (1996)
The Full Monty (1997)
Shakespeare in Love (1998)
Notting Hill (1999)
Chicken Run (2000)
Billy Elliot (2000)
Bridget Jones's Diary (2001)
Love Actually (2003)
Vera Drake (2004)
The Queen (2006)
The Last King of Scotland (2006)

Partly for this reason, Britain gives much less financial help to its film industry than other European countries do. Therefore, although cinemagoing is a regular habit for a much larger number of people than is theatregoing, Britain produces very few films. This is not because expertise in film making does not exist. It does. American productions often use studios and technical facilities in Britain and British film directors often find work in Hollywood. Moreover, some of the few films that Britain does manage to make become highly respected around the world (British films). Nevertheless, films shown at cinemas in Britain are overwhelmingly American films.

Music

Listening to music is a very common leisure time activity in Britain. But for the vast majority of people in the country, it is not classical music that they listen to. Few classical musicians, whether British or foreign, become famous to the general public. When they do, it is usually because of circumstances which have nothing to do with their music. For example, the Italian tenor Pavarotti became famous in the country when an aria sung by him was used by the BBC to introduce its 1990 football World Cup coverage. Despite this low profile, thousands of British people are dedicated musicians and many public libraries have a well-stocked music section. Several British orchestras, soloists, singers, choirs, opera companies, and ballet companies, and also certain annual musical events, have international reputations.

In the 1960s, British artists had a great influence on the development of music in the modern, or 'pop' idiom. The Beatles (from Liverpool) and other British groups were responsible for several innovations which were then adopted by America and the rest of the pop world. These included the writing of words and music by the performers themselves, and more active audience participation. The words of their songs also helped to liberate the pop idiom from its former limitation to the topics of love and teenage affection. Other British bands such as Pink Floyd and Cream took a major part in making the musical structure of pop music similarly more sophisticated.

Since that time, popular music in Britain has been an enormous and profitable industry. The Beatles were awarded MBEs for their services to British exports. Although America continues to dominate popular music in a number of ways (for example, very few British singers do not sing in

Some well-known venues for the performing arts

The Shakespeare Memorial Theatre in Stratford is the home of the Royal Shakespeare Company (RSC). Most other well-known venues are in London.

Theatres include the Old Vic (the home of the National Theatre Company), the Mermaid, the Royal Court, and the Barbican (where the RSC also perform).

For opera and ballet, there is the Royal Opera House at Covent Garden and the English National Opera (formerly the Sadler's Wells Company), which performs at the Coliseum.

The South Bank area has many concert halls (notably the Royal Festival Hall), and the National Film Theatre.

Mountains of books!

For the really scholarly reader, there is the British Library, which receives a copy of every publication produced in Britain and Ireland. Its collection includes more than 13 million books, 300,000 of them in manuscript form. It possesses more than 6,000 different editions of Shakespeare's plays and more than 100 different editions of most novels by Charles Dickens. It also has nearly a million journal and newspaper titles and four million maps, three million sound recordings and eight million stamps. The collection needs more than 600 km of shelves and in 2007 it was expanding at the rate of one kilometre every month.

The arts and broadcasting

Although they have been increasing since the mid 1990s, visits to the cinema in Britain are still only a fraction of what they were in the late 1940s. The big drop took place during the 1950s and 1960s as people acquired televisions. In fact, broadcasters have taken an important supporting role in the arts. The making of some high-quality British films has only been possible because of the financial help of Channel 4. The BBC regularly commissions new works of music for the proms. Television drama and comedy help to keep hundreds of actors in work.

Moreover, television can actually help to promote other art forms. When a book is dramatized on television, its sales often rocket. This happened, for example, with the BBC's production of the novel *Pride and Prejudice* by Jane Austen in the mid 1990s. The most spectacular example occurred in the late 1960s. *The Forsythe Saga* was a Victorian novel by John Galsworthy which had been out of print for several decades. After an adaptation of it was shown on the BBC, half a million copies were sold.

A child could do that!

British people often complain about modern abstract painting by saying, 'It doesn't look very special to me. A child of four could do that'. Well, in 2007 in England, a child of two did that.

One of the artists exhibiting in that year at Saatchi Online, a virtual art gallery, was Freddie Linsky. His work attracted rave reviews from art experts. One of his paintings was bought for £20 by a Manchester collector. Then Freddie got an email from a gallery in Berlin asking whether he would be willing to exhibit his paintings there. Unfortunately, he didn't read the email. That's because he couldn't read. He was only two years old. The paintings were submitted by Freddie's mother as a joke.

The news of this discovery was greatly enjoyed by people in Britain. Everybody loves it when experts are made to look like fools – especially when they are experts about something that most people don't understand (and secretly believe that there is actually nothing to understand anyway). It did not occur to many people to think that perhaps a child genius had been discovered.

---

their own version of an American accent!), many trends with worldwide influence have come out of Britain (notably 'punk' in the 1970s). British artists in this idiom have also been active in attempting to cross the boundaries between popular music, folk music, and classical music.

Words

Although the British are comparatively uninterested in formal education, and although they watch a lot of television, they are still enthusiastic readers. Reading is only slightly less popular as a free-time activity than listening to music. Over 60 per cent of the population has a library card, and borrowing a book from the library is one of the country's most popular pastimes; much more popular, for example, than going to watch a professional football game.

In fact, the written word is the one form of the arts with which the British are generally comfortable. It has been said that Britain is primarily a verbal culture, not a visual one. While many people would struggle to name a handful of British painters, sculptors, architects, film directors or classical musicians, few would have difficulty with a list of famous British writers. In recent years, the BBC has conducted polls to find the country's most popular paintings and books, in which people were invited to phone up and nominate their favourite. The book poll attracted seven times as many votes as the painting poll (The nation's favourite books).

Literature written in English is, of course, not the preserve of British writers. While only two such writers (William Golding and Harold Pinter) have won the Nobel Prize for literature in the last 50 years, many, many other recipients of this prize have written in English. It is the same story with the Man Booker Prize – the most important annual prize in Britain for a work of fiction. Since 1981, about half its winners have been writers from former British colonies (e.g. Canada, India, Ireland, Nigeria).

The literary canon

	Poetry	Drama	Prose
14th century	Geoffrey Chaucer		
16th century	William Shakespeare		
17th century	John Donne John Milton		
18th century	Alexander Pope		
19th century	William Wordsworth		Jane Austen Charles Dickens George Eliot
20th century	W. B. Yeats* T. S. Eliot Seamus Heaney*	Samuel Beckett* Harold Pinter	James Joyce D. H. Lawrence William Golding

Artistic merit is ultimately a matter of opinion. But below is a list of some of the writers of past centuries who are widely regarded as the 'cream' of serious British literature. (Those marked with an asterisk (*) are/were actually Irish. But by convention, they are usually seen as part of the same literary 'world'.)

Many, more modern, writers are famous at this time, but it is too early to know whether their reputations will last.

One other author should be mentioned. In the eighteenth century, Samuel Johnson produced his famous dictionary. His highly individual definitions, together with other comments he made during his life, have made him the second most quoted writer in the English language after Shakespeare.

Although many of the best 'serious' British writers manage to be popular as well as profound, the vast majority of the books that are read in Britain are not 'serious' literature. Britain is the home of what might be called 'middlebrow' literature. (That is, mid-way between serious, or 'highbrow' literature and popular, or 'pulp' fiction.) For example, the distinctly British genre of detective fiction (e.g. Agatha Christie, Ruth Rendell) is regarded as entertainment rather then literature – but it is intelligent entertainment. As well as this, there are many British authors, mostly female, who write novels about the lives of fictional people and their relationships, usually in a historical setting, (e.g. Norah Lofts, Mary Stewart). These are sometimes classified as 'romances' but are actually more serious and sensitive than that term often implies. They are neither popular 'blockbusters' nor the sort of books which are reviewed in the serious literary press. And yet they continue to be read, year after year, by hundreds of thousands of people. From 1997 to 2004, three writers of this kind of book – Catherine Cookson, Josephine Cox and Danielle Steel – were all always among the top five most borrowed authors from Britain's public libraries.

It is more than 200 years since poetry stopped being the normal mode of literary self-expression. And yet, poetry in the first decade of the twenty-first century is surprisingly popular in Britain. Books of poetry sell in comparatively large numbers – not nearly as large as prose, but large enough so that a few small publishers (often, though, with a small amount of funding) can survive entirely on poetry. Many poets find themselves in demand to do readings of their work on radio and at arts festivals. Many of these poets are not academics and their writing is accessible to non-specialists. Perhaps the 'pop' idiom and easy availability of sound recording have made more people comfortable with spoken verse than they were fifty years ago.

The fine arts

Painting is not as widely popular as music in Britain. There is a general feeling that you have to be a specialist to appreciate it, especially if it is contemporary. Small art galleries, where people might look at paintings with a view to buying them, are rare. Nevertheless, London is one of the main centres of the rich art collector's world. The two major auction houses of Sotheby's and Christie's are world-famous.

The same general lack of appreciation applies to small-scale sculpture. It only makes the news when the annual Turner prize is awarded for a piece of *avant-garde* artwork that most of the media ridicules. Sculpture on a grand scale, however, is a different story. 'Public art', as it is sometimes called, seems to have general public approval. The two most notable examples are both near the city of Newcastle in the north-east of England. One is the 20-metre high figure of the Angel of the North, whose 54-metre wing span makes it difficult to miss. A little further to the north is an even larger earthwork that mimics the ancient British tradition of sculpting in or with the land. The Goddess of the North

The nation's favourite books

In 2003, the BBC staged The Big Read, a competition to find 'the nation's favourite book' – or, more precisely, which book the most people were prepared to spend time and money phoning up to vote for. The winner, despite the reputation of the English for anti-intellectualism, was the work of an otherwise obscure university professor. It was *Lord of the Rings* by J.R.R. Tolkien. Notably, only one of the top five books was set in the real world – and even in this case (Jane Austen's *Pride and Prejudice*) it was the real world of two centuries ago. The other four were all works of fantasy.

The Big Read project was a great success. Libraries all over Britain had to buy multiple copies of the top books to satisfy demand. Sales also went up.

However, this apparent love of books should be put into perspective. In total, about 900,000 votes were cast, over a period of six months, for The Big Read. On the same night as the 'final' was shown on TV, on another channel, the semi-final of *Pop Idol* attracted no less than three million votes!

The Top Ten books were:

1 *Lord of the Rings* (J. R. R. Tolkien)
2 *Pride and Prejudice* (Jane Austen)
3 *His Dark Materials* (Philip Pullman)
4 *The Hitchhiker's Guide to the Galaxy* (Douglas Adams)
5 *Harry Potter and the Goblet of Fire* (J. K. Rowling)
6 *To Kill a Mockingbird* (Harper Lee)
7 *Winnie the Pooh* (A. A. Milne)
8 *Nineteen Eighty-Four* (George Orwell)
9 *The Lion, the Witch and the Wardrobe* (C. S. Lewis)
10 *Jane Eyre* (Charlotte Brontë)

is a huge reclining figure with breasts which are 30 metres high which stretches for more than half a kilometre between the main road and the east coast railway line to Scotland. She is made out of the earth and other waste materials that have been taken out of the ground there for mining.

QUESTIONS

1 How do British governments justify their policy of low spending on the arts? Does the government in your country subsidize the arts more or less than in Britain?

2 Which areas of the arts seem to be particularly appreciated and valued in Britain and which seem to be ignored or under-valued? In what ways does the appreciation of the different aspects of the arts vary in your country?

3 The British are generally very conscious of the distinction between high art of 'culture' and light 'entertainment'. In which area of the arts have they succeeded in establishing a widely accepted and approved compromise which appeals to a broad range of people from different social backgrounds and with varying levels of education?

SUGGESTIONS

Find some of the top ten books listed in the Big Read ... and read them!

Most of the major museums publish guides to their collections, pointing out their most highly-prized exhibits. Look them up online, or visit them if you get the chance.

Any biography of any of the major British theatrical figures would reveal a lot about the history of the theatre in Britain and about British theatre in general.

Museums and art galleries

The major museums in London are the British Museum (the national collection of antiquities), the Victoria and Albert Museum (which houses the world's largest display of the decorative arts), the enormous National History Museum, and the Science Museum. There are numerous other small, specialist museums in London and throughout the rest of the country, usually with an emphasis on history and British 'heritage'. Many of these now attract visitors by adding appropriate sounds and even smells.

Art galleries in London which house permanent collections include the National gallery, the adjoining National Portrait Gallery, the Tate Britain, which is the nation's gallery of art from 1500 until modern times, and the Tate Modern. These galleries also hold special temporary exhibitions. The Hayward Gallery and the Royal Academy put on a series of shows, some of which are very popular.

Outside London there is the Burrell collection near Glasgow, and the Tate galleries in Liverpool and St. Ives. Most major towns and cities have their own museums, galleries and 'cultural' centres. A recently built example is the Lowry centre in Salford (near Manchester), which houses all 300 works of the town's most famous son, L. S. Lowry.

The Tate Modern, Britain's national museum of international modern art.

23 Holidays and special occasions

Britain is a country governed by routine. It has fewer public holidays than most other countries in Europe. Even New Year's Day was not an official public holiday (except in Scotland) until 1974, but so many people gave themselves a holiday anyway that it was thought it might as well become official! There are almost no semi-official holidays either. Most official holidays occur either just before or just after a weekend, so that the practice of making a 'bridge' between the holiday and the weekend is almost unknown. Moreover, there are no traditional extra holidays in particular localities. Although the origin of the word 'holiday' is 'holy day', not all public holidays during the year (usually known as 'bank holidays') are connected with religious celebrations.

The British also seem to do comparatively badly with regard to annual holidays. These are not as long as they are in many other countries. Although the average employee gets about four weeks' paid holiday a year, in no town or city in the country would a visitor ever get the impression that the place had 'shut down' for the summer break.

Traditional holiday resorts in England

A national holiday?

The idea of a national holiday (which Britain does not have at the moment – see chapter 4) is in the air these days. If Britain were to get an extra holiday, what day would it be? In 2006, the BBC conducted a poll of 5,000 people to see which day they would prefer. Perhaps surprisingly, the day which got the most votes was not a military victory like the Battle of Trafalgar (which came fifth) or Waterloo (seventh) or even VE Day, the end of the Second World War in Europe in 1945 (second). By a clear margin, the winner was 15 June, the day on which the Magna Carta was signed by King John in 1215 (see chapter 2).

Historians and social commentators were not only astonished by this result – they had assumed that the Magna Carta had been lost to popular memory in the mists of time. They were also delighted that the winner was not an event celebrating military prowess but rather one which celebrates political freedoms and constitutionalism.

Traditional seaside holidays

The British upper class started the fashion for seaside holidays in the late eighteenth century. The middle classes soon followed them and when, around the beginning of the twentieth century, they were given the opportunity, so did the working classes. It soon became normal for families to spend a week or two every year at one of the seaside resort towns which sprang up to cater for this new mass market. The most well known of these are near to the bigger towns and cities (Traditional holiday resorts in England).

These resorts quickly developed certain characteristics that are now regarded as typical of the 'traditional' English holiday. They have some hotels where richer people stay, but most families stay at boarding houses. These are small family businesses, offering either 'bed and breakfast' or, more rarely, 'full board' (all meals). Some streets in seaside resorts are full of nothing but boarding houses. The food in these, and in local restaurants, is cheap and conventional with an emphasis on traditional British food.

Stereotypically, daytime entertainment in sunny weather centres around the beach, where the children can sometimes go for donkey rides, make sandcastles, buy ice-creams, and swim in the sea. Older adults often do not bother to go swimming. They are happy just to sit in their deck chairs and occasionally go for a paddle with their skirts or trouser-legs hitched up. The water is always cold, and despite efforts to clean it up, sometimes very dirty. But for adults who swim, some resorts still have wooden huts on or near the beach, known as 'beach huts', 'bathing huts', or 'beach cabins', in which people can change into swimming costumes (The perfect summer house). Swimming and sunbathing without any clothing is rare. All resorts have various other kinds of attraction, including more-or-less permanent funfairs.

For the evenings, and when it is raining, there are amusement arcades, bingo halls, discos, theatres, bowling alleys, and so on, many of these situated on the pier. This distinctively British architectural structure

The perfect summer house

Typically, beach huts measure less than four square metres and have no electricity or water supply. All that they provide, therefore, is a degree of privacy on the beach and a place on it which you can call 'your own'. But that is enough to make then highly prized, so highly prized, in fact, that one retired couple were happy to see in the New Year of 2006 sitting in sub-zero temperatures in their car. For four days and nights they queued there (taking turns to go and warm up in a nearby shop), just to make sure they had first choice of two newly-available huts on Avon Beach in Dorset. For £700, they bought exclusive use of this desirable property between the hours of sunrise and sunset from Easter to late September of the coming year.

is a platform extending out into the sea. The large resorts have lighted decorations which are switched on at night. The 'Blackpool illuminations', for example, are famous.

Another type of holiday that was very popular in the 1950s and 1960s is the holiday camp, where visitors stayed in chalets in self-contained villages with all their food and entertainment organized for them. Butlin's and Pontin's, the companies which owned most of these, are well-known names in Britain. The enforced good humour, strict meal times and events such as 'knobbly knees' competitions and beauty contests that were characteristic of these camps have now been replaced by a more relaxed atmosphere.

Modern holidays

Both of these traditional types of holiday have become less popular in the last quarter of the twentieth century. The increase in car ownership has encouraged many people to take caravan holidays. But the greatest cause in the decline of the traditional holiday is foreign tourism. Before the 1960s, only rich people took holidays abroad. By 1972, the British were taking seven million foreign holidays per year and by 1987, 20 million. In 2006, the figure was 45 million.

Most foreign holidays are package holidays, in which flights and accommodation are booked and paid for through a travel agent. These holidays are often booked a long time in advance. In midwinter, the television companies run programmes which give information about the packages being offered. People need cheering up at this time of the year! In many British homes, it has become traditional to get the brochures out and start talking about where to go in the summer on Boxing Day. Spain is by far the most popular destination for this kind of holiday. In fact, more than a quarter of all kinds of holiday taken abroad by British people in 2006 were to Spain. Hundreds of thousands of British people now own (or part-own) villas in Spain and, because flights are so cheap, they go there more than once a year. In fact, the availability of cheap flights has allowed some people to go to distant European cities just for long weekends. The possible effects that this is having on the climate, however, mean that this habit may not last much longer. The next most popular destination for British tourists is France, where they can travel by taking their cars across the channel.

Half of all the holidays taken within Britain are now for three days or less. Every bank holiday weekend, the television carries news of long traffic jams along the routes to the most popular holiday areas. The traditional seaside resorts have survived by adjusting themselves to this trend. (Only the rich have second houses or cottages in the countryside to which they can escape at weekends.) But there are also many other types of holiday. Hiking in the country and sleeping at youth hostels has long been popular (see chapter 5). There are also a wide range of 'activity' holidays

Seaside postcards

Humorous postcards like the one below can still be seen at seaside resorts in Britain. They often involve sexual innuendo. The traditional seaside holiday represented a relaxing of Victorian restrictions on overt reference to sex. These days, of course, no such restrictions exist anywhere, so these postcards are mainly enjoyed in a spirit of nostalgia.

Rock

There is one kind of sweet associated with holiday resorts. It is called 'rock', a hard thick stick of sugar. Each resort has the letters of its name appearing throughout the stick, so that one hears of 'Brighton Rock', 'Blackpool Rock', and so on.

offered, giving full expression to British individualism. You can, for example, take part in a 'murder mystery weekend', and find yourself living out the plot of a detective story.

Some people go on 'working' holidays, during which they help to repair an ancient stone wall or take part in an archaeological dig. This is an echo of another traditional type of holiday – fruit picking. It used to be the habit of poor people from the east end of London, for example, to go down to Kent and help with the hop harvest (hops are used for making beer).

Christmas

Christmas is the one occasion in modern Britain when a large number of customs are enthusiastically observed by most ordinary people at family level. The slow decrease in participation in organized religion (see chapter 13), and the fact that Christmas in modern times is as much a secular celebration as a religious one, has had little effect on these traditions. Even people who consider themselves to be anti-religious quite happily wish each other a 'Happy Christmas' or a 'Merry Christmas'. They do not (as in some other countries) self-consciously wish each other a 'Happy New Year' instead.

Indeed, the 'commercialization' of Christmas has itself become part of tradition. Every November in Oxford Street (one of the main shopping streets in the centre of London), a famous personality ceremoniously switches on the 'Christmas lights' (decorations), thus 'officially'

The Christmas party

In thousands of companies throughout Britain, the last working afternoon before Christmas is the time of the annual office party. A lot of alcohol is often consumed on these occasions and feelings hidden throughout the year come into to the open. This is a problem for company bosses. By law, an employer is responsible for any sexual harassment that occurs at his or her workplace and may have to pay as much as £10,000 in compensation. The peak time for complaints of sexual harassment is in January – just after the annual office party. Many employers now insure themselves against claims for compensation at this time.

Christmas cards

Many people send cards depicting some aspect of the birth of Christ. Most people, however, do not. Christmas is an opportunity for the British to indulge their dreams about a vanished rural past. You can see this on the typical Christmas cards. They usually show scenes from either the nineteenth or eighteenth centuries or are set in the countryside, very frequently with snow. (In fact, snow at Christmas is rare in most parts of Britain.)

marking the start of the period of frantic Christmas shopping. And it certainly is frantic. Between that time and the middle of January, most shops do nearly half of their total business for the year. (As soon as the Christmas rush finishes, on Boxing Day, the shops begin their winter sales.) Most people buy presents for the other members of their household and also for other relatives, especially children. Some people also buy presents for their close friends. And to a wider circle of friends and relatives, and sometimes also to working associates and neighbours, they send Christmas cards (Christmas cards). Some even send such greetings to people who they have not seen for many years, often using the excuse of this tradition to include a letter passing on the year's news.

People also buy Christmas trees (a tradition imported from Germany in the late nineteenth century). Most households have a tree and decorate it themselves (in many cases, with coloured lights). Most people also put up other decorations around the house. Exactly what these are varies a great deal, but certain symbols of Christmas, such as bits of the holly and mistletoe plants, are very common, and the Christmas cards which the household has received are usually displayed. A few people go even further and put up decorations outside their house. These most commonly consist of lights arranged in the shape of seasonal motifs. A few households also have a 'crib', a model depicting the birth of Christ.

Another feature of December is the singing of carols (usually, but not always, with a religious theme). These are sung in churches and schools, often at special concerts, and also, though less often than in the past, by groups of people who go from house to house raising money for charitable causes.

An indication of the importance attached to Christmas in British people's minds is that many people who do not go to church during the rest of the year do so at this time, and churches find attendance swelling by three times its normal amount. A 2005 poll found that 43% of the adult population expected to attend a church service over the Christmas period.

Customs concerning the role of Father Christmas (Santa Claus) in the giving of gifts vary from family to family. Most households continue the traditional child's concept that Father Christmas comes down the chimney on the night of Christmas Eve, even though most houses no longer have a working chimney! Many children lay out a Christmas

Panto

The Christmas and New Year holiday seasons bring with them a popular theatrical tradition. This is pantomime (often abbreviated to 'panto'), staged in hundreds of theatres and specifically designed to appeal to young children. It usually involves the acting out of a well-known folk tale with plenty of opportunity for audience participation.

There are certain established conventions of panto. For example, the cast includes a 'principle boy' (the young hero) who is always played by a woman, and a 'dame' (an older female character), who is always played by a man.

The continuing popularity of panto is assisted by the fact that these leading roles are frequently taken by well-known personalities from the worlds of television or sport.

stocking at the foot of their beds, which they expect to see filled when they wake up on Christmas morning. Most families lay out presents, wrapped, around or on the Christmas tree, and these are opened at some time on Christmas Day.

Other activities in which many families engage on Christmas Day are the eating of Christmas dinner (Christmas dinner) and listening to the Queen's Christmas message. This ten minute television broadcast is normally the only time in the year when the monarch speaks directly to 'her' people on television. (But if people don't like this idea, there is an 'alternative', sometimes controversial Christmas message on Channel 4, delivered by a different person each year.)

There is a general feeling that Christmas is a time for families. Many of the gatherings in houses on Christmas Day and Boxing Day consist of extended families (more than just parents and children). In many families, Christmas is the only time that such gatherings occur.

New Year

All that celebrating is very tiring and many employers now give their employees the whole of the time between Christmas and New Year off. In contrast to the family emphasis on Christmas, parties at New Year's Eve are regarded more as a time for friends. Most people attend a gathering at this time and 'see in' the new year together, often drinking a large amount of alcohol as they do so. Some people in the London region go to the traditional celebrations at Trafalgar Square (where there is an enormous Christmas tree – an annual gift from the people of Norway).

In Scotland, where Calvinist tradition was not happy about parties and celebrations connected with religious occasions (such as Christmas), New Year, called Hogmanay, is given particular importance – so much importance that, in Scotland only, 2 January (as well as New Year's Day) is also a public holiday, so people have two days to recover from their New Year's Eve parties instead of just one! The crowd at the Hogmanay street party in Edinburgh is actually much larger than that in Trafalgar Square. Some British New Year customs, such as the singing of the song *Auld Lang Syne*, originated in Scotland. Another, less common, one is the custom of 'first footing', in which the first person to visit a house in the new year is supposed to arrive with tokens of certain important items for survival (such as a lump of coal for the fire).

As a well-known Christmas carol reminds people, there are twelve days of Christmas. In fact, most people go back to work and school soon after New Year. Nobody pays much attention to the feast of the epiphany on 6 January (the twelfth day of Christmas), except that this is traditionally the day on which Christmas decorations are taken down. Some people say it is bad luck to keep them up after this date.

Christmas dinner

The traditional menu consists of stuffed roast turkey with roast potatoes and other vegetables (including Brussels sprouts). But not everybody likes turkey. A popular alternative is goose. Other foods associated with Christmas are Christmas pudding, an extremely heavy sweet dish made of dried fruits – over which it is traditional to pour brandy then set it alight – and Christmas cake, an equally heavy fruit cake, covered with a layer of marzipan and then a layer of hard white icing.

Calendar of special occasions

New Year's Day* (1 January)
In Scotland, **2 January** is also a public holiday.

St. Valentine's Day (14 February)

Shrove Tuesday (47 days before Easter)

St. Patrick's Day (17 March)
This is a public holiday in Northern Ireland.

Mother's Day (the fourth Sunday in Lent)
Millions of bouquets of flowers are bought for this day. Cards are also sent.

April Fools' Day (1 April)
On this day, it is traditional for people to play tricks on each other. Children are the most enthusiastic about this custom, but even the BBC and serious newspapers sometimes have 'joke' (i.e. not genuine) features on this day.

Good Friday*
The strange name in English for the day commemorating Christ's crucifixion.

Easter Sunday

Easter Monday* The day after Easter Sunday.

May Day* (the first Monday in May)
In Britain, this day is associated more with ancient folklore than with the workers. In some villages, the custom of dancing round a maypole is acted out.

Spring Bank Holiday* (the last Monday in May)
There used to be a holiday on 'Whit Monday' celebrating the Christian feast of Pentecost. Because this is seven weeks after Easter, the date varied. This fixed holiday has replaced it.

The Queen's Official Birthday (the second or third Saturday in June)
This is not her real birthday (which is on 21 April). Her official birthday is when she celebrates her birthday in public and certain public ceremonies are performed.

Father's Day (the third Sunday in June)
The fathers' equivalent of Mother's Day above.

Orangemen's Day (12 July)
This is a public holiday in Northern Ireland. It is associated with the Protestant part of the community and balances with St. Patrick's Day, which is associated with the Catholics.

Summer Bank Holiday* (the last Monday in August)

Halloween (31 October)

Guy Fawkes Night (5 November)

Remembrance Sunday (the second Sunday in November)
This day originated from Armistice Day (11 November) which marked the end of the First World War. It is used to commemorate the dead of both World Wars and of more recent conflicts. On and before this day, money is collected in the street on behalf of charities for ex-servicemen. The people who donate money are given paper poppies to pin to their clothes. No politician would be seen on this day without a poppy!

St. Andrew's Day (30 November)
This is a public holiday in Scotland.

Christmas Eve (24 December)

Christmas Day* (25 December)

Boxing Day* (26 December)
Explanations for the origin of this name vary. One is that it was the day on which landowners and householders would present their tenants and servants with gifts (in boxes). Another is that it was the day in which the collecting boxes in churches were opened and contents distributed to the poor.

New Year's Eve (31 December)

(* = public holiday)

Other notable annual occasions

Easter is far less important than Christmas in Britain. Although it involves a four-day weekend, there are very few customs and habits associated generally with it, other than the mountains of chocolate Easter eggs which children consume. Some people preserve the tradition of eating hot cross buns on Good Friday (Calendar of special occasions). Quite a lot of people go away on holiday.

None of the other days of the year to which traditional customs are attached is a holiday, and not everybody takes part in these customs. In fact, many people in Britain live through occasions such as Shrove Tuesday and April Fools' Day without even knowing they have happened.

There are two other days which, although many people do not do anything special on them, are very difficult to ignore. One of these is Halloween, the day before All Saints' Day in the Christian calendar. It has long been associated with the supernatural (witches, ghosts, etc.). Some people hold Halloween parties, which are fancy-dress. Traditionally, this day was observed much more energetically in America than in Britain. But recently, the American custom of 'trick or treat' (in which groups of children call at houses and challenge the person who answers the door to give them something nice to eat or be prepared to have a trick played on them) has been imported.

The other day is only five days later. This is the day which celebrates a famous event in British history – the gunpowder plot. It is called Guy Fawkes Day – or, more commonly, Guy Fawkes Night. At the beginning of the seventeenth century, a group of Catholics planned to blow up the Houses of Parliament while the king was in there. Before they could achieve this, one of them, Guy Fawkes, was caught in the cellars under Parliament with the gunpowder. He and his fellow conspirators were all brought to trial and then killed. At the time, the failure of the gunpowder plot was celebrated as a victory for British Protestantism over rebel Catholicism. In modern times, it has lost its religious and patriotic connotations. In most parts of Britain, Catholic children celebrate it just as enthusiastically as Protestant children – or, for that matter, children brought up in any other religious faith (as with Christmas, most of the customs associated with this day are mainly for the benefit of children). Some children make a 'Guy' out of old clothes stuffed with newspaper several weeks beforehand. They then place this somewhere on the street and ask passers-by for 'a penny for the Guy'. What they are actually asking for is money to buy fireworks.

On Guy Fawkes Night itself, there are bonfire parties throughout the country, at which the 'Guy' is burnt. Some people cook food in the embers of the bonfire, especially chestnuts or potatoes. So many fireworks are set off that, by the end of the evening, the air in all British cities smells strongly of sulphur. Every year, accidents with the fireworks injure or even kill several people. In an effort to make things safer, some local authorities arrange public firework displays and bonfires.

Shrove Tuesday

This day is also known as Pancake Day. In past centuries, lent was a time of fasting. Both meat and eggs were forbidden throughout the six weeks. The tradition was to eat up all your meat on the Monday before it started, and all your eggs on the Tuesday – in pancakes. Nowadays, the fasting has gone and only the eating remains.

Two events are associated with Shrove Tuesday. One of them is the pancake tossing contest (to see how many pancakes you can throw into the air, rotate and catch within a certain time). The other is the pancake race. These are still held in many places all over Britain. You have to run while continuously tossing a pancake – if you drop it when it comes down, you're out.

Finally, one other day should be mentioned. This is a different day for everybody – their birthday. Once again, it is most important for children, all of whom receive presents on this day from their parents, and often from other relatives as well. Adults may or may not receive presents, depending on the customs of their family and their circle of friends. Many will simply be wished 'Happy Birthday' (not 'Congratulations' unless it is a special birthday, such as a twenty-first). Some children and adults have a party on their birthdays, but not all. Moreover, nobody, including adults, is automatically expected to extend hospitality to other people on their birthday, and it is not expected that people should bring along cakes or anything to share with their colleagues at work (although some people do).

QUESTIONS

1 Why have traditional British holidays become less popular in the last 50 years? Is the modern pattern of British holidaymaking the same as it is for people in your country?

2 What aspects of Christmas in Britain, and the customs associated with it, are different from those in your country?

3 In Britain, you are generally considered to be unfortunate if your birthday is in the second half of December. Why?

4 There is a science fiction story in which beings from outer space fly over Britain one night and conclude that planet earth is full of barbaric, cruel people. Which night was it?

SUGGESTIONS

A Christmas Carol by Charles Dickens (which features the famous miserly character of Scrooge) paints a picture of the Victorian idea of Christmas, which remains very influential.

St. Valentine's Day and Gretna Green

Despite the unromantic reputation of the British, on or just before this day every year millions of pounds worth of flowers are delivered, tens of millions of chocolates are sold and greetings-card manufacturers get very rich.

Every St. Valentine's Day, thousands of people travel to a tiny village on Scotland's border with England. Many of them go to get married, and many more couples go through mock wedding ceremonies. The village is Gretna Green. Its romantic reputation began in 1754. In England in that year, marriage for people under the age of 21 without permission from parents was banned. In Scotland, however, this permission was not required, and Gretna Green was the first stop across the border. The laws that brought fame to Gretna Green no longer apply. But its reputation is secure. In this small place, more than ten people get married, on average, every day of the year. On St. Valentine's Day, the number is around 40.

Index